English Grammar in Use

A reference and practice book for intermediate students of English

THIRD EDITION

Raym

CAMBRIDGE
UNIVERSITY PRESS

PUBLISHED BY THE PRESS SYNDICATE OF THE UNIVERSITY OF CAMBRIDGE
The Pitt Building, Trumpington Street, Cambridge, United Kingdom

CAMBRIDGE UNIVERSITY PRESS
The Edinburgh Building, Cambridge CB2 2RU, UK
40 West 20th Street, New York, NY 10011–4211, USA
477 Williamstown Road, Port Melbourne, VIC 3207, Australia
Ruiz de Alarcón 13, 28014 Madrid, Spain
Dock House, The Waterfront, Cape Town 8001, South Africa

http://www.cambridge.org

First published 2004

Printed in Italy by Eurografica (part of the LEGO group)

Typeface Sabon 10/13pt *System* QuarkXPress® [KAMAE]

A catalogue record for this book is available from the British Library

ISBN 0 521 53289 2   English Grammar in Use with answers
ISBN 0 521 53290 6   English Grammar in Use
ISBN 0 521 53762 2   English Grammar in Use with CD Rom
ISBN 0 521 84311 1   English Grammar in Use hardback edition with CD Rom
ISBN 3 125 34086 1   English Grammar in Use with CD Rom Klett paperback edition
ISBN 3 125 34084 5   English Grammar in Use Klett paperback edition

Contents

Thanks

I wrote the original edition of English Grammar in Use when I was a teacher at the Swan School of English, Oxford. I would like to repeat my thanks to my colleagues and students at the school for their help, encouragement and interest at that time.

More recently I would like to thank all the teachers and students I met and who offered their thoughts on the previous edition. It was fun to meet you all and extremely helpful for me.

Regarding the production of this third edition, I am grateful to Alison Sharpe, Liz Driscoll, Jane Mairs and Kamae Design. I would also like to thank Cambridge University Press for permission to access the Cambridge International Corpus.

Thank you also to the following illustrators: Paul Fellows, Gillian Martin, Roger Penwill, Lisa Smith and Simon Williams.

To the teacher

English Grammar in Use is a book for intermediate students of English who need to study and practise using the grammar of the language. All the important points of English grammar are explained and there are exercises on each point. The book is written for self-study, but teachers may also find it useful as additional course material in cases where further work on grammar is necessary.

Level

The book is intended mainly for *intermediate* students (students who have already studied the basic grammar of English). It concentrates on those structures which intermediate students want to use, but which often cause difficulty. The explanations are addressed to the intermediate student, and the language used is as simple as possible.

The book will probably be most useful at middle- and upper-intermediate levels (where all or nearly all of the material will be relevant), and can serve both as a basis for revision and as a means for practising new structures. It will also be useful for some more advanced students who have problems with grammar and need a book for reference and practice.

The book is not intended to be used by elementary learners.

How the book is organised

The book consists of 145 units, each of which concentrates on a particular point of grammar. Some areas (for example, the present perfect or the use of articles) are covered in more than one unit. For a list of units, see the *Contents* at the beginning of the book.

Each unit consists of two facing pages. On the left there are explanations and examples; on the right there are exercises.

The units are organised in grammatical categories (*Present and past*, *Articles and nouns*, *Prepositions* etc.). They are not ordered according to level of difficulty, so the book should not be worked through from beginning to end. It should be used selectively and flexibly in accordance with the grammar syllabus being used and the difficulties students are having.

There are also seven *Appendices* at the back of the book (pages 292–301). These include irregular verbs, summaries of verb forms, spelling and American English. It might be useful for the teacher to draw students' attention to these.

Finally, there is a detailed *Index* at the back of the book for easy reference (page 326).

How to use the book

The book can be used for immediate consolidation, or for later revision or remedial work. It might be used by the whole class or by individual students needing extra help.

The left-hand pages (explanations and examples) are written for the student to use individually, but they may of course be used by the teacher as a source of ideas and information on which to base a lesson. The student then has the left-hand page as a record of what has been taught and can refer to it in the future. The exercises can be done individually, in class or as homework.

Alternatively (and additionally), individual students can be directed to study certain units of the book by themselves if they have particular difficulties not shared by other students in their class.

An edition of *English Grammar in Use* with answers is available for students working on their own.

Additional exercises

At the back of the book (pages 302–325) there is a set of *Additional exercises* which provide 'mixed' practice bringing together grammar points from a number of different units. For example, Exercise 16 covers grammar points from Units 26–36. These exercises can be used for extra practice after students have studied and practised the grammar in the units concerned.

English Grammar in Use *Third Edition*

This is a new edition of *English Grammar in Use*. The differences between this edition and the second edition are:

☐ There are eight new units on phrasal verbs (Units 138–145). There is also a new unit on *wish* (Unit 41). Units 42–81 and 83–137 all have different numbers from the second edition.

☐ Some of the material has been revised or reorganised, and in most units there are minor changes in the examples, explanations and exercises.

☐ The *Additional exercises* have been extended. The new exercises are 14–16, 25, 30–31, and 37–41.

☐ The book has been redesigned with new colour illustrations.

English Grammar in Use

Present continuous (I am doing)

A Study this example situation:

> Sarah is in her car. She is on her way to work.
> She **is driving** to work.
>
> This means: she is driving *now*, at the time of speaking.
> The action is not finished.
>
> **Am/is/are + -ing** is the *present continuous:*
>
> | | | | |
> |---|---|---|---|
> | I | **am** | (= I'm) | driving |
> | he/she/it | **is** | (= he's etc.) | working |
> | we/you/they | **are** | (= we're etc.) | doing etc. |

B **I am doing** something = I'm in the middle of doing it; I've started doing it and I haven't finished yet:

- ☐ Please don't make so much noise. **I'm trying** to work. (*not* I try)
- ☐ 'Where's Mark?' 'He's **having** a shower.' (*not* He has a shower)
- ☐ Let's go out now. It **isn't raining** any more. (*not* It doesn't rain)
- ☐ *(at a party)* Hello, Jane. **Are** you **enjoying** the party? (*not* Do you enjoy)
- ☐ What's all that noise? What's **going** on? (= What's happening?)

The action is not necessarily happening at the time of speaking. For example:

> Steve is talking to a friend on the phone. He says:
>
>
>
> > I'm reading a really good book at the moment.
> > It's about a man who ...
>
> Steve is not reading the book at the time of speaking.
> He means that he has started it, but has not finished it yet.
> He is in the middle of reading it.

Some more examples:

- ☐ Kate wants to work in Italy, so she's **learning** Italian. (but perhaps she isn't learning Italian at the time of speaking)
- ☐ Some friends of mine **are building** their own house. They hope to finish it next summer.

C You can use the present continuous with **today / this week / this year** etc. (periods around now):

- ☐ A: You're **working** hard **today**. (*not* You work hard today)
  B: Yes, I have a lot to do.
- ☐ The company I work for **isn't doing** so well **this year**.

D We use the present continuous when we talk about changes happening around now, especially with these verbs:

get	change	become	increase	rise	fall	grow	improve	begin	start

- ☐ **Is** your English **getting** better? (*not* Does your English get better)
- ☐ The population of the world **is increasing** very fast. (*not* increases)
- ☐ At first I didn't like my job, but **I'm beginning** to enjoy it now. (*not* I begin)

Present continuous and present simple → Units 3–4   Present tenses for the future → Unit 19

Exercises

1.1 Complete the sentences with the following verbs in the correct form:

get   happen   look   lose   make   start   stay   try   ~~work~~

1 'You _'re working_ hard today.' 'Yes, I have a lot to do.'
2 I _am_ .... for Christine. Do you know where she is?
3 It .... dark. Shall I turn on the light?
4 They don't have anywhere to live at the moment. They .... with friends until they find somewhere.
5 Things are not so good at work. The company .... money.
6 Have you got an umbrella? It .... to rain.
7 You .... a lot of noise. Can you be quieter? I _am trying_ .... to concentrate.
8 Why are all these people here? What .... ?

1.2 Put the verb into the correct form. Sometimes you need the negative (**I'm not doing** etc.).

1 Please don't make so much noise. I _'m trying_ (try) to work.
2 Let's go out now. It _isn't raining_ (rain) any more.
3 You can turn off the radio. I .... (listen) to it.
4 Kate phoned me last night. She's on holiday in France. She .... (have) a great time and doesn't want to come back.
5 I want to lose weight, so this week I .... (eat) lunch.
6 Andrew has just started evening classes. He .... (learn) German.
7 Paul and Sally have had an argument. They .... (speak) to each other.
8 I .... (get) tired. I need a rest.
9 Tim .... (work) this week. He's on holiday.

1.3 Complete the conversations.

1 A: I saw Brian a few days ago.
   B: Oh, did you? _What's he doing_ these days? (what / he / do)
   A: He's at university.
   B: .... ? (what / he / study)
   A: Psychology.
   B: .... it? (he / enjoy)
   A: Yes, he says it's a very good course.

2 A: Hi, Liz. How .... in your new job? (you / get on)
   B: Not bad. It wasn't so good at first, but .... better now. (things / get)
   A: What about Jonathan? Is he OK?
   B: Yes, but .... his work at the moment. (he / not / enjoy) He's been in the same job for a long time and .... to get bored with it. (he / begin)

1.4 Complete the sentences using the following verbs:

begin   change   get   ~~increase~~   rise

1 The population of the world _is increasing_ very fast.
2 The world .... Things never stay the same.
3 The situation is already bad and it .... worse.
4 The cost of living .... Every year things are more expensive.
5 The weather .... to improve. The rain has stopped, and the wind isn't as strong.

A Study this example situation:

Alex is a bus driver, but now he is in bed asleep.
He is not driving a bus. (He is asleep.)

but He **drives** a bus. (He is a bus driver.)

Drive(s)/work(s)/do(es) etc. is the *present simple*:

I/we/you/they **drive/work/do** etc.
he/she/it **drives/works/does** etc.

B We use the present simple to talk about things in general. We use it to say that something happens all the time or repeatedly, or that something is true in general:

- □ Nurses **look** after patients in hospitals.
- □ I usually **go** away at weekends.
- □ The earth **goes** round the sun.
- □ The café **opens** at 7.30 in the morning.

Remember:

I work ...   *but*   **He works** ...   **They teach** ...   *but*   My sister **teaches** ...

For spelling (-s or -es), see Appendix 6.

C We use **do/does** to make questions and negative sentences:

do does	I/we/you/they he/she/it	work? drive? do?

I/we/you/they he/she/it	don't doesn't	work drive do

- □ I come from Canada. Where **do** you **come** from?
- □ I **don't go** away very often.
- □ What **does** this word **mean**? (*not* What means this word?)
- □ Rice **doesn't grow** in cold climates.

In the following examples, **do** is also the main verb (do you **do** / doesn't **do** etc.):

- □ 'What **do** you **do**?' 'I work in a shop.'
- □ He's always so lazy. He **doesn't do** anything to help.

D We use the present simple to say how often we do things:

- □ I **get** up at 8 o'clock **every morning**.
- □ **How often** do you **go** to the dentist?
- □ Julie **doesn't drink** tea **very often**.
- □ Robert usually **goes** away **two or three times a year**.

E **I promise / I apologise** etc.

Sometimes we do things by saying something. For example, when you *promise* to do something, you can say '**I promise** ...'; when you *suggest* something, you can say '**I suggest** ...':

- □ I **promise** I won't be late. (*not* I'm promising)
- □ 'What do you **suggest** I do?' 'I **suggest** that you ...'

In the same way we say: I **apologise** ... / I **advise** ... / I **insist** ... / I **agree** ... / I **refuse** ... etc.

Exercises

2.1 Complete the sentences using the following verbs:

    cause(s)   **connect**(s)   **drink**(s)   **live**(s)   **open**(s)   ~~**speak**(s)~~   **take**(s)

1 Tanya ......*speaks*...... German very well.
2 I don't often .... coffee.
3 The swimming pool .... at 7.30 every morning.
4 Bad driving .... many accidents.
5 My parents .... in a very small flat.
6 The Olympic Games .... place every four years.
7 The Panama Canal .... the Atlantic and Pacific oceans.

2.2 Put the verb into the correct form.

1 Julie ......*doesn't drink*...... (not / drink) tea very often.
2 What time .... (the banks / close) here?
3 I've got a computer, but I .... (not / use) it much.
4 'Where .... (Martin / come) from?' 'He's Scottish.'
5 'What .... (you / do)?' 'I'm an electrician.'
6 It .... (take) me an hour to get to work. How long .... (it / take) you?
7 Look at this sentence. What .... (this word / mean)?
8 David isn't very fit. He .... (not / do) any sport.

2.3 Use the following verbs to complete the sentences. Sometimes you need the negative:

    believe   **eat**   **flow**   ~~**go**~~   ~~**grow**~~   **make**   **rise**   **tell**   **translate**

1 The earth ......*goes*...... round the sun.
2 Rice ......*doesn't grow*...... in Britain.
3 The sun .... in the east.
4 Bees .... honey.
5 Vegetarians .... meat.
6 An atheist .... in God.
7 An interpreter .... from one language into another.
8 Liars are people who .... the truth.
9 The River Amazon .... into the Atlantic Ocean.

2.4 You ask Liz questions about herself and her family. Write the questions.

1 You know that Liz plays tennis. You want to know how often. Ask her.
How often ......*do you play tennis*.. ?
2 Perhaps Liz's sister plays tennis too. You want to know. Ask Liz.
.... your sister .... ?
3 You know that Liz reads a newspaper every day. You want to know which one. Ask her.
.... ?
4 You know that Liz's brother works. You want to know what he does. Ask Liz.
.... ?
5 You know that Liz goes to the cinema a lot. You want to know how often. Ask her.
.... ?
6 You don't know where Liz's grandparents live. You want to know. Ask Liz.
.... ?

2.5 Complete using the following:

    I apologise   **I insist**   **I promise**   **I recommend**   ~~**I suggest**~~

1 It's a nice day. ......*I suggest*...... we go out for a walk.
2 I won't tell anybody what you said. ....
3 *(in a restaurant)* You must let me pay for the meal. ....
4 .... for what I did. It won't happen again.
5 The new restaurant in Hill Street is very good. .... it.

Present continuous and present simple 1 (I am doing and I do)

A

Compare:

Present continuous (I am doing)

We use the continuous for things happening at or around the time of speaking. The action is not complete.

I am doing

past — *now* — *future*

- ☐ The water **is boiling**. Can you turn it off?
- ☐ Listen to those people. What language **are** they **speaking**?
- ☐ Let's go out. It **isn't raining** now.
- ☐ 'I'm busy.' 'What **are you doing**?'
- ☐ **I'm getting** hungry. Let's go and eat.
- ☐ Kate wants to work in Italy, so she**'s learning** Italian.
- ☐ The population of the world **is increasing** very fast.

We use the continuous for *temporary* situations:

- ☐ **I'm living** with some friends until I find a place of my own.
- ☐ A: You**'re working** hard today.
    B: Yes, I have a lot to do.

See Unit 1 for more information.

Present simple (I do)

We use the simple for things in general or things that happen repeatedly.

←——— I do ———→

past — *now* — *future*

- ☐ Water **boils** at 100 degrees Celsius.
- ☐ Excuse me, **do** you **speak** English?

- ☐ It **doesn't rain** very much in summer.
- ☐ What **do** you usually **do** at weekends?
- ☐ I always **get** hungry in the afternoon.
- ☐ Most people **learn** to swim when they are children.
- ☐ Every day the population of the world **increases** by about 200,000 people.

We use the simple for *permanent* situations:

- ☐ My parents **live** in London. They have lived there all their lives.
- ☐ John isn't lazy. He **works** hard most of the time.

See Unit 2 for more information.

B

I always do and **I'm always doing**

I **always do** (something) = I do it every time:
- ☐ I **always go** to work by car. (*not* I'm always going)

'I**'m always doing** something' has a different meaning. For example:

I've lost my pen again. I**'m always losing** things.

I**'m always losing** things = I lose things very often, perhaps too often, or more often than normal.

Two more examples:
- ☐ You**'re always watching** television. You should do something more active.
    (= You watch television too often)
- ☐ Tim is never satisfied. He**'s always complaining**. (= He complains too much)

Exercises

3.1 Are the <u>underlined</u> verbs right or wrong? Correct them where necessary.

1 Water <u>boils</u> at 100 degrees Celsius. — _OK_
2 The water <u>boils</u>. Can you turn it off? — _is boiling_
3 Look! That man <u>tries</u> to open the door of your car. — _trying_
4 Can you hear those people? What <u>do</u> they <u>talk</u> about? — _are talking_
5 The moon <u>goes</u> round the earth in about 27 days. — _OK_
6 I must go now. It <u>gets</u> late. — _is getting_
7 I usually <u>go</u> to work by car. — _OK_
8 'Hurry up! It's time to leave.' 'OK, I <u>come</u>.' — _I m coming_
9 I hear you've got a new job. How <u>do</u> you <u>get</u> on? — _OK_
10 Paul is never late. He<u>'s</u> always <u>getting</u> to work on time. — _OK_
11 They don't get on well. They<u>'re</u> always <u>arguing</u>. — _OK_

3.2 Put the verb into the correct form, present continuous or present simple.

1 Let's go out. It _isn't raining_ (not / rain) now.
2 Julia is very good at languages. She _speaks_ (speak) four languages very well.
3 Hurry up! Everybody _is waiting_ (wait) for you.
4 '_Do you listening_ (you / listen) to the radio?' 'No, you can turn it off.'
5 '_Do you usually_ (you / listen) to the radio every day?' 'No, just occasionally.'
6 The River Nile _flowing_ (flow) into the Mediterranean.
7 The river _flows_ (flow) very fast today – much faster than usual.
8 We usually _grows_ (grow) vegetables in our garden, but this year we _didn't grow_ (not / grow) any.
9 A: How's your English?
   B: Not bad. I think it _s improving_ (improve) slowly.
10 Rachel is in London at the moment. She _is staying_ (stay) at the Park Hotel.
   She always _stays_ (stay) there when she's in London.
11 Can we stop walking soon? I _start_ (start) to feel tired.
12 A: Can you drive?
   B: I _m learning_ (learn). My father _is teaching_ (teach) me.
13 Normally I _finish_ (finish) work at five, but this week I _m working_ (work) until six to earn a little more money.
14 My parents _lives_ (live) in Manchester. They were born there and have never lived anywhere else. Where _is your parents lives_ (your parents / live)?
15 Sonia _is looking_ (look) for a place to live. She _is staying_ (stay) with her sister until she finds somewhere.
16 A: What _is your brother do_ (your brother / do)?
   B: He's an architect, but he _is not working_ (not / work) at the moment.
17 (at a party) I usually _enjoy_ (enjoy) parties, but I _didn't enjoy_ (not / enjoy) this one very much.

3.3 Finish B's sentences. Use **always -ing**.

1 A: I've lost my pen again.
   B: Not again! _You're always losing your pen_ .
2 A: The car has broken down again.
   B: That car is useless. It _s always breaking down_ .
3 A: Look! You've made the same mistake again.
   B: Oh no, not again! I _always do same mistake_ .
4 A: Oh, I've forgotten my glasses again.
   B: Typical! _I always forgot my glasses_ .

Present continuous and present simple 2 (I am doing and I do)

A

We use continuous forms for actions and happenings that have started but not finished (they **are eating** / it **is raining** etc.). Some verbs (for example, **know** and **like**) are not normally used in this way. We don't say 'I am knowing' or 'they are liking'; we say '**I know**', 'they **like**'.

The following verbs are not normally used in the present continuous:

like   love   hate   want   need   prefer
know   realise   suppose   mean   understand   believe   remember
belong   fit   contain   consist   seem

- ☐ I'm hungry. **I want** something to eat. (*not* I'm wanting)
- ☐ **Do** you **understand** what I **mean**?
- ☐ Ann **doesn't seem** very happy at the moment.

B   Think

When **think** means 'believe' or 'have an opinion', we do not use the continuous:
- ☐ **I think** Mary is Canadian, but I'm not sure. (*not* I'm thinking)
- ☐ What **do** you **think** about my plan? (= What is your opinion?)

When **think** means 'consider', the continuous is possible:
- ☐ **I'm thinking** about what happened. I often **think** about it.
- ☐ Nicky **is thinking** of giving up her job. (= she is considering it)

C   He is selfish and He is being selfish

He's being = He's behaving / He's acting. Compare:
- ☐ I can't understand why he**'s being** so selfish. He isn't usually like that.
  (**being** selfish = behaving selfishly at the moment)
- ☐ He never thinks about other people. He **is** very selfish. (*not* He is being)
  (= He is selfish generally, not only at the moment)

We use **am/is/are being** to say how somebody is *behaving*. It is not usually possible in other sentences:
- ☐ It's hot today. (*not* It is being hot)
- ☐ Sarah **is** very tired. (*not* is being tired)

D   See   hear   smell   taste

We normally use the present simple (not continuous) with these verbs:
- ☐ **Do** you **see** that man over there? (*not* Are you seeing)
- ☐ This room **smells**. Let's open a window.

We often use **can** + see/hear/smell/taste:
- ☐ I **can hear** a strange noise. **Can** you **hear** it?

E   Look   feel

You can use the present simple or continuous to say how somebody looks or feels now:
- ☐ You **look** well today. *or* You**'re looking** well today.
- ☐ How **do** you **feel** now? *or* How **are** you **feeling** now?

but
- ☐ I usually **feel** tired in the morning. (*not* I'm usually feeling)

Present continuous and simple 1 → Unit 3   **Have** → Unit 17   **Present tenses for the future** → Unit 19

Exercises

4.1 Are the <u>underlined</u> verbs right or wrong? Correct them where necessary.

1 Nicky <u>is thinking</u> of giving up her job. — *OK*
2 <u>Are</u> you <u>believing</u> in God? — *Do you believe in God?*
3 <u>I'm feeling</u> hungry. Is there anything to eat? — *OK*
4 This sauce is great. It<u>'s tasting</u> really good. — *It taste really good*
5 <u>I'm thinking</u> this is your key. Am I right? — *I think this is your key*

4.2 Use the words in brackets to make sentences. (You should also study Unit 3 before you do this exercise.)

1 (you / not / seem / very happy today)
You don't seem very happy today.

2 (what / you / do?)
What are you doing
Be quiet! (I / think)
I'm thinking

3 (who / this umbrella / belong to?)
Who is this umbrella belong to
I have no idea.

4 (the dinner / smell / good)
The dinner is smelling good

5 Excuse me. (anybody / sit / there?)
Is anybody sitting there?
No, it's free.

6 (these gloves / not / fit / me)
Thees gloves is not fitting me
They're too small.

4.3 Put the verb into the correct form, present continuous or present simple.

1 Are you hungry? __Do you want__ (you / want) something to eat?
2 Don't put the dictionary away. I __m going to use__ (use) it.
3 Don't put the dictionary away. I __need__ (need) it.
4 Who is that man? What __he want__ (he / want)?
5 Who is that man? Why __he is looking__ (he / look) at us?
6 Alan says he's 80 years old, but nobody __believe__ (believe) him.
7 She told me her name, but I __don't remember__ (not / remember) it now.
8 I __m thinking__ (think) of selling my car. Would you be interested in buying it?
9 I __think__ (think) you should sell your car. You __dont use__ (not / use) it very often.
10 Air __consists__ (consist) mainly of nitrogen and oxygen.

4.4 Complete the sentences using the most suitable form of **be**. Sometimes you must use the simple (**am/is/are**) and sometimes the continuous is more suitable (**am/is/are being**).

1 I can't understand why __he's being__ so selfish. He isn't usually like that.
2 Sarah __is being__ very nice to me at the moment. I wonder why.
3 You'll like Debbie when you meet her. She __is__ very nice.
4 You're usually very patient, so why __are you__ so unreasonable about waiting ten more minutes?
5 Why isn't Steve at work today? __Is he__ ill?

Past simple (I did)

Study this example:

> Wolfgang Amadeus Mozart was an Austrian musician and composer. He **lived** from 1756 to 1791. He **started** composing at the age of five and **wrote** more than 600 pieces of music. He **was** only 35 years old when he **died**.

> Lived/started/wrote/was/died are all *past simple.*

Very often the past simple ends in **-ed** (*regular* verbs):
- ☐ I work in a travel agency now. Before that I **worked** in a department store.
- ☐ We **invited** them to our party, but they **decided** not to come.
- ☐ The police **stopped** me on my way home last night.
- ☐ Laura **passed** her examination because she **studied** very hard.

For spelling (stopped, studied etc.), see Appendix 6.

But many verbs are *irregular*. The past simple does *not* end in **-ed**. For example:

write	→ **wrote**	☐ Mozart **wrote** more than 600 pieces of music.
see	→ **saw**	☐ We **saw** Rose in town a few days ago.
go	→ **went**	☐ I **went** to the cinema three times last week.
shut	→ **shut**	☐ It **was** cold, so I **shut** the window.

For a list of irregular verbs, see Appendix 1.

In questions and negatives we use **did/didn't** + *infinitive* (**enjoy/see/go** etc.):

I	enjoyed
she	saw
they	went

	you	enjoy?
did	she	see?
	they	go?

I		enjoy
she	**didn't**	see
they		go

- ☐ A: **Did** you **go** out last night?
  B: Yes, I **went** to the cinema, but I **didn't enjoy** the film much.
- ☐ 'When **did** Mr Thomas **die**?' 'About ten years ago.'
- ☐ They **didn't invite** her to the party, so she **didn't go**.
- ☐ '**Did** you **have** time to write the letter?' 'No, I **didn't**.'

In the following examples, **do** is the main verb in the sentence (**did … do / didn't do**):
- ☐ What **did** you **do** at the weekend? (*not* What did you at the weekend?)
- ☐ I **didn't do** anything. (*not* I didn't anything)

The past of **be** (**am/is/are**) is **was/were**:

I/he/she/it	was/wasn't
we/you/they	were/weren't

was	I/he/she/it?
were	we/you/they?

Note that we do not use **did** in negatives and questions with **was/were**:
- ☐ I **was** angry because they **were** late.
- ☐ **Was** the weather good when you **were** on holiday?
- ☐ They **weren't** able to come because they **were** so busy.
- ☐ Did you go out last night or **were** you too tired?

Exercises

5.1 Read what Laura says about a typical working day:

I usually get up at 7 o'clock and have a big breakfast. I walk to work, which takes me about half an hour. I start work at 8.45. I never have lunch. I finish work at 5 o'clock. I'm always tired when I get home. I usually cook a meal in the evening. I don't usually go out. I go to bed at about 11 o'clock, and I always sleep well.

Laura

Yesterday was a typical working day for Laura. Write what she did or didn't do yesterday.

1 _She got up at 7 o'clock._
2 She ____ *had* ____ a big breakfast.
3 She ___ *started work at 8.45* ___ .
4 It ___ *time to* ___ to get to work.
5 _____ at 8.45.
6 _____ lunch.
7 _She finished her work_ at 5 o'clock.
8 _____ tired when _____ home.
9 _____ a meal yesterday evening.
10 _____ out yesterday evening.
11 _____ at 11 o'clock.
12 _____ well last night.

5.2 Complete the sentences using the following verbs in the correct form:

buy   ~~catch~~   cost   ~~fall~~   ~~hurt~~   ~~sell~~   ~~spend~~   teach   ~~throw~~   ~~write~~

1 Mozart __*wrote*__ more than 600 pieces of music.
2 'How did you learn to drive?' 'My father ___ *taught* ___ me.'
3 We couldn't afford to keep our car, so we ___ *sold* ___ it.
4 Dave ___ *fell* ___ down the stairs this morning and ___ *hurt* ___ his leg.
5 Jim ___ *catched* ___ the ball to Sue, who ___ *threw* ___ it.
6 Ann ___ *spent* ___ a lot of money yesterday. She ___ *bough* ___ a dress which ___ *costed* ___ £100.

5.3 You ask James about his holiday. Write your questions.

Hi. How are things?

  Fine, thanks. I've just had a great holiday.

1 Where ___ *did you go* ___ ?

  To the U.S. We went on a trip from San Francisco to Denver.

2 How _____ ? By car?

  Yes, we hired a car in San Francisco.

3 It's a long way to drive. How long _____ ?

  Two weeks.

4 Where _____ ? In hotels?

  Yes, small hotels or motels.

5 _____ ?

  Yes, but it was very hot – sometimes too hot.

6 _____ the Grand Canyon?

  Of course. It was wonderful.

5.4 Complete the sentences. Put the verb into the correct form, positive or negative.

1 It was warm, so I __*took*__ off my coat. (take)
2 The film wasn't very good. I __*didn't enjoy*__ it very much. (enjoy)
3 I knew Sarah was very busy, so I _____ her. (disturb)
4 I was very tired, so I _____ the party early. (leave)
5 The bed was very uncomfortable. I _____ very well. (sleep)
6 The window was open and a bird _____ into the room. (fly)
7 The hotel wasn't very expensive. It _____ very much. (cost)
8 I was in a hurry, so I _____ time to phone you. (have)
9 It was hard carrying the bags. They _____ very heavy. (be)

Past continuous (I was doing)

A Study this example situation:

Yesterday Karen and Jim played tennis. They began at 10 o'clock and finished at 11.30.
So, at 10.30 they **were playing** tennis.

They **were playing** = they were in the middle of playing. They had not finished playing.

Was/were -ing is the *past continuous*:

I/he/she/it	**was**	play**ing**
we/you/they	**were**	doing
		work**ing** etc.

B I **was doing** something = I was in the middle of doing something at a certain time. The action or situation had already started before this time, but had not finished:

I started doing   I was doing   I finished doing

past   *past*   *now*

- ☐ This time last year I **was living** in Brazil.
- ☐ What **were** you **doing** at 10 o'clock last night?
- ☐ I waved to Helen, but she **wasn't looking**.

C Compare the *past continuous* (I **was doing**) and *past simple* (I **did**):

Past continuous (in the middle of an action)	*Past simple* (complete action)
☐ I **was walking** home when I met Dave. (in the middle of an action)	☐ I **walked** home after the party last night. (= all the way, completely)
☐ Kate **was watching** television when we arrived.	☐ Kate **watched** television a lot when she was ill last year.

D We often use the past simple and the past continuous together to say that something happened in the middle of something else:

- ☐ Matt **phoned** while we **were having** dinner.
- ☐ It **was raining** when I **got** up.
- ☐ I **saw** you in the park yesterday. You **were sitting** on the grass and **reading** a book.
- ☐ I **hurt** my back while I **was working** in the garden.

But we use the past simple to say that one thing happened after another:

- ☐ I **was walking** along the road when I **saw** Dave. So I **stopped**, and we **had** a chat.

Compare:

☐ When Karen arrived, we **were having** dinner. (= we had already started before she arrived)	☐ When Karen arrived, we **had** dinner. (= Karen arrived, and then we had dinner)

E Some verbs (for example, **know** and **want**) are not normally used in the continuous (see Unit 4A):

- ☐ We were good friends. We **knew** each other well. (*not* We were knowing)
- ☐ I was enjoying the party, but Chris **wanted** to go home. (*not* was wanting)

Exercises

6.1 What were you doing at these times? Write sentences as in the examples. The past continuous is not always necessary (see the second example).

1 (at 8 o'clock yesterday evening)   _I was having dinner._
2 (at 5 o'clock last Monday)   _I was on a bus on my way home._
3 (at 10.15 yesterday morning) ....
4 (at 4.30 this morning) ....
5 (at 7.45 yesterday evening) ....
6 (half an hour ago) ....

6.2 Use your own ideas to complete the sentences. Use the past continuous.

1 Matt phoned while we _were having dinner_ ....
2 The doorbell rang while I ....
3 We saw an accident while we ....
4 Ann fell asleep while she ....
5 The television was on, but nobody ....

6.3 Put the verb into the correct form, past continuous or past simple.

1	2 ◁GATES 1-10	3
SUE	PARIS ROME	
I ..._saw_.. (see) Sue in town yesterday, but she .... (not / see) me. She .... (look) the other way.	I .... (meet) Tom and Jane at the airport a few weeks ago. They .... (go) to Paris and I .... (go) to Rome. We .... (have) a chat while we .... (wait) for our flights.	I .... (cycle) home yesterday when a man .... (step) out into the road in front of me. I .... (go) quite fast, but luckily I .... (manage) to stop in time and .... (not / hit) him.

6.4 Put the verb into the correct form, past continuous or past simple.

1 Jenny _was waiting_ (wait) for me when I _arrived_ (arrive).
2 'What .... (you / do) at this time yesterday?'   'I was asleep.'
3 '.. (you / go) out last night?'   'No, I was too tired.'
4 How fast .... (you / drive) when the accident .... (happen)?
5 Sam .... (take) a photograph of me while I .... (not / look).
6 We were in a very difficult position. We .... (not / know) what to do.
7 I haven't seen Alan for ages. When I last .... (see) him, he .... (try) to find a job.
8 I .... (walk) along the street when suddenly I .... (hear) footsteps behind me. Somebody .... (follow) me. I was scared and I .... (start) to run.
9 When I was young, I .... (want) to be a pilot.
10 Last night I .... (drop) a plate when I .... (do) the washing up. Fortunately it .... (not / break).

→ Additional exercise 1 (page 302)

Present perfect 1 (I have done)

Study this example situation:

Tom is looking for his key. He can't find it.
He **has lost** his key.

He **has lost** his key = He lost it recently, and he still doesn't have it.

Have/has lost is the *present perfect simple*:

			finished
I/we/they/you	**have**	(= I've etc.)	lost
he/she/it	**has**	(= he's etc.)	done
			been etc.

The present perfect simple is **have/has** + *past participle*. The past participle often ends in **-ed** (finished/decided etc.), but many important verbs are *irregular* (**lost/done/written** etc.).

For a list of irregular verbs, see Appendix 1.

When we say that 'something **has happened**', this is usually new information:
- □ Ow! **I've cut** my finger.
- □ The road is closed. There**'s been** (there **has** been) an accident.
- □ (*from the news*) Police **have arrested** two men in connection with the robbery.

When we use the present perfect, there is a connection with *now*. The action in the past has a result *now*:
- □ 'Where's your key?' 'I don't know. **I've lost** it.' (= I don't have it *now*)
- □ He told me his name, but **I've forgotten** it. (= I can't remember it *now*)
- □ 'Is Sally here?' 'No, she**'s gone** out.' (= she is out *now*)
- □ I can't find my bag. **Have** you **seen** it? (= Do you know where it is *now*?)

You can use the present perfect with **just**, **already** and **yet**.

Just = a short time ago:
- □ 'Are you hungry?' 'No, I**'ve just had** lunch.'
- □ Hello. **Have** you **just arrived**?

We use **already** to say that something happened sooner than expected:
- □ 'Don't forget to send the letter.' '**I've already sent** it.'
- □ 'What time is Mark leaving?' 'He**'s already gone**.'

Yet = until now. **Yet** shows that the speaker is expecting something to happen. Use **yet** only in questions and negative sentences:
- □ **Has** it **stopped** raining **yet**?
- □ I've written the letter, but I **haven't sent** it **yet**.

Note the difference between **gone** (**to**) and **been** (**to**):
- □ Jim is on holiday. He **has gone to** Italy. (= he is there now or on his way there)
- □ Jane is back home now. She **has been** to Italy. (= she has now come back)

Present perfect → Units 8, 11   **Been to** → Units 8A, 126B   Present perfect continuous → Units 9–10
Present perfect and past → Units 12–14   Yet and already → Unit 111   American English → Appendix 7

14

Exercises

7.1 Read the situations and write sentences. Use the following verbs:

arrive	break	fall	go up	grow	improve	~~lose~~

1 Tom is looking for his key. He can't find it.   _He has lost his key._
2 Margaret can't walk and her leg is in plaster.   She ....
3 Last week the bus fare was 80 pence. Now it is 90.   The bus fare ....
4 Maria's English wasn't very good. Now it is better.   Her English ....
5 Dan didn't have a beard before. Now he has a beard.   He ....
6 This morning I was expecting a letter. Now I have it.   The letter ....
7 The temperature was 20 degrees. Now it is only 12.   The ....

7.2 Complete B's sentences. Use the verb in brackets + **just/already/yet**.

A	B
1 Would you like something to eat?	No, thanks. _I've just had lunch._ (I / just / have / lunch)
2 Do you know where Julia is?	Yes, ... (I / just / see / her)
3 What time is David leaving?	.... (he / already / leave)
4 What's in the newspaper today?	I don't know. .... (I / not / read / it yet)
5 Is Sue coming to the cinema with us?	No, ... (she / already / see / the film)
6 Are your friends here yet?	Yes, ... (they / just / arrive)
7 What does Tim think about your plan?	.... (we / not / tell / him yet)

7.3 Read the situations and write sentences with **just**, **already** or **yet**.

1 After lunch you go to see a friend at her house. She says, 'Would you like something to eat?'
   You say: No thank you. _I've just had lunch_ . (have lunch)
2 Joe goes out. Five minutes later, the phone rings and the caller says, 'Can I speak to Joe?'
   You say: I'm afraid .... (go out)
3 You are eating in a restaurant. The waiter thinks you have finished and starts to take your
   plate away. You say: Wait a minute! .... (not / finish)
4 You are going to a restaurant tonight. You phone to reserve a table. Later your friend says,
   'Shall I phone to reserve a table.' You say: No, ... (do it)
5 You know that a friend of yours is looking for a place to live. Perhaps she has been successful.
   Ask her. You say: .... ? (find)
6 You are still thinking about where to go for your holiday. A friend asks, 'Where are you going
   for your holiday?' You say: .... (not /decide)
7 Linda went to the bank, but a few minutes ago she returned. Somebody asks, 'Is Linda still at
   the bank?' You say: No, ... (come back)

7.4 Put in **been** or **gone**.

1 Jim is on holiday. He's ...._gone_.... to Italy.
2 Hello! I've just .... to the shops. I've bought lots of things.
3 Alice isn't here at the moment. She's .... to the shop to get a newspaper.
4 Tom has .... out. He'll be back in about an hour.
5 'Are you going to the bank?' 'No, I've already .... to the bank.'

Present perfect 2 (I have done)

Study this example conversation:

DAVE: **Have** you **travelled** a lot, Jane?

JANE: Yes, **I've been** to lots of places.

DAVE: Really? **Have** you ever **been** to China?

JANE: Yes, **I've been** to China twice.

DAVE: What about India?

JANE: No, **I haven't been** to India.

Jane's life
(a period until now)

past   *now*

When we talk about a period of time that continues from the past until now, we use the *present perfect* (**have been / have travelled** etc.). Here, Dave and Jane are talking about the places Jane has visited in her life (which is a period that continues until now).

Some more examples:

□ **Have** you ever **eaten** caviar? (in your life)

□ **We've** never **had** a car.

□ '**Have** you **read** *Hamlet*?' 'No, I **haven't read** any of Shakespeare's plays.'

□ Susan really loves that film. **She's seen** it eight times!

□ What a boring film! It's the most boring film **I've ever seen**.

Been (**to**) = visited:

□ I've never **been** to China. Have you **been** there?

In the following examples too, the speakers are talking about a period that continues until now (**recently / in the last few days / so far / since breakfast** etc.):

□ **Have** you **heard** from Brian **recently**?

□ **I've met** a lot of people **in the last few days**.

□ Everything is going well. We **haven't had** any problems **so far**.

□ I'm hungry. I **haven't eaten** anything **since breakfast**. (= from breakfast until now)

□ It's good to see you again. We **haven't seen** each other **for a long time**.

————recently————→

——in the last few days——→

———since breakfast———→

past   *now*

We use the present perfect with **today / this evening / this year** etc. when these periods are not finished at the time of speaking (see also Unit 14B):

□ **I've drunk** four cups of coffee **today**.

□ **Have** you **had** a holiday **this year** (yet)?

□ I **haven't seen** Tom **this morning**. Have you?

□ Rob **hasn't studied** very hard **this term**.

————today————→

past   *now*

We say: It's the (first) time something **has happened**. For example:

□ Don is having a driving lesson. It's his first one.
It's the first time he **has driven** a car. (*not* drives)

or   He **has never driven** a car **before**.

This is the first time
I've **driven** a car.

DRIVING SCHOOL

□ Sarah has lost her passport again. This is the second time this **has happened**. (*not* happens)

□ Bill is phoning his girlfriend again. That's the third time **he's phoned** her **this evening**.

Present perfect 1 → Unit 7   Present perfect + **for/since** → Units 11–12
Present perfect and past → Units 12–14

Exercises

8.1 You are asking people questions about things they have done. Make questions with **ever** using the words in brackets.

1 (ride / horse?) _Have you ever ridden a horse?_
2 (be / California?) Have ....
3 (run / marathon?) ....
4 (speak / famous person?) ....
5 (most beautiful place / visit?) What's ....

8.2 Complete B's answers. Some sentences are positive and some negative. Use the following verbs:

be   be   eat   happen   have   ~~meet~~   play   read   see   see   try

A

1 What's Mark's sister like?
2 How is Diane these days?
3 Are you hungry?
4 Can you play chess?
5 Are you enjoying your holiday?
6 What's that book like?
7 Is Brussels an interesting place?
8 Mike was late for work again today.
9 Do you like caviar?
10 I hear your car broke down again yesterday.
11 Who's that woman by the door?

B

1 I've no idea. _I've never met_ her.
2 I don't know. I .... her recently.
3 Yes. I .... much today.
4 Yes, but .... for ages.
5 Yes, it's the best holiday .... for a long time.
6 I don't know. .... it.
7 I've no idea. .... there.
8 Again? He .... late every day this week.
9 I don't know. .... it.
10 Yes, it's the second time .... this week.
11 I don't know. .... her before.

8.3 Complete the sentences using **today / this year / this term** etc.

1 I saw Tom yesterday, but _I haven't seen him today_ .
3 I read a newspaper yesterday, but I .... today.
4 Last year the company made a profit, but this year ....
4 Tracy worked hard at school last term, but ....
5 It snowed a lot last winter, but ....
6 Our football team won a lot of games last season, but we ....

8.4 Read the situations and write sentences as shown in the example.

1 Jack is driving a car, but he's very nervous and not sure what to do.
You ask: _Have you driven a car before?_
He says: _No, this is the first time I've driven a car._
2 Ben is playing tennis. He's not good at it and he doesn't know the rules.
You ask: Have ....
He says: No, this is the first ....
3 Sue is riding a horse. She doesn't look very confident or comfortable.
You ask: ....
She says: ....
4 Maria is in London. She has just arrived and it's very new for her.
You ask: ....
She says: ....

A — It has been raining

Study this example situation:

Is it raining?
No, but the ground is wet.
It has been raining.

Have/has been -ing is the *present perfect continuous*:

I/we/they/you **have** (= I've etc.) he/she/it **has** (= he's etc.)	**been**	doing waiting playing etc.

We use the present perfect continuous for an activity that has recently stopped or just stopped. There is a connection with *now*:

- ☐ You're out of breath. **Have** you **been running?** (= you're out of breath *now*)
- ☐ Paul is very tired. He's **been working** very hard. (= he's tired *now*)
- ☐ Why are your clothes so dirty? What **have** you **been doing?**
- ☐ I've **been talking** to Amanda about the problem and she agrees with me.
- ☐ Where have you been? I've **been looking** for you everywhere.

B — It has been raining for two hours.

Study this example situation:

It began raining two hours ago and it is still raining.

How long has it **been raining?**
It **has been raining** for two hours.

We use the present perfect continuous in this way with **how long, for** … and **since** … . The activity is still happening (as in this example) or has just stopped.

- ☐ **How long have** you **been learning** English? (= you're still learning English)
- ☐ Tim is still watching television. He's **been watching** television **all day.**
- ☐ Where have you been? I've **been looking** for you **for the last half hour.**
- ☐ Chris **hasn't been feeling** well **recently.**

You can use the present perfect continuous for actions repeated over a period of time:

- ☐ Debbie is a very good tennis player. She's **been playing since** she was eight.
- ☐ Every morning they meet in the same café. They've **been going** there **for years.**

C

Compare **I am doing** (see Unit 1) and **I have been doing:**

I am doing *present continuous*	**I have been doing** *present perfect continuous*
now	*now*
☐ Don't disturb me now. **I'm working.**	☐ I've **been working** hard. Now I'm going to have a break.
☐ We need an umbrella. It's **raining.**	☐ The ground is wet. It's **been raining.**
☐ Hurry up! We're **waiting.**	☐ We've **been waiting** for an hour.

Present perfect continuous and simple → Units 10–11   Present perfect + for/since → Units 11–12

Exercises

9.1 What have these people been doing or what has been happening?

1 *earlier* *now*	2 *earlier* *now*
They 've been shopping	She
3 *earlier* *now*	4 *earlier* *now*
They	He

9.2 Write a question for each situation.

1 You meet Paul as he is leaving the swimming pool.
  You ask: (you / swim?)   Have you been swimming?

2 You have just arrived to meet a friend who is waiting for you.
  You ask: (you / wait / long?)

3 You meet a friend in the street. His face and hands are very dirty.
  You ask: (what / you / do?)

4 A friend of yours is now working in a shop. You want to know how long.
  You ask: (how long / you / work / there?)

5 A friend tells you about his job – he sells computers. You want to know how long.
  You ask: (how long / you / sell / computers?)

9.3 Read the situations and complete the sentences.

1 It's raining. The rain started two hours ago.
  It 's been raining for two hours.

2 We are waiting for the bus. We started waiting 20 minutes ago.
  We   for 20 minutes.

3 I'm learning Spanish. I started classes in December.
  I   since December.

4 Mary is working in London. She started working there on 18 January.
                                        since 18 January.

5 Our friends always spend their holidays in Italy. They started going there years ago.
                                        for years.

9.4 Put the verb into the present continuous (**I am –ing**) or present perfect continuous
(**I have been –ing**).

1 Maria has been learning (Maria / learn) English for two years.
2 Hello, Tom.   (I / look) for you. Where have you been?
3 Why   (you / look) at me like that? Stop it!
4 Linda is a teacher.   (she / teach) for ten years.
5   (I / think) about what you said and I've decided to take your
  advice.
6 'Is Paul on holiday this week?' 'No,   (he / work).'
7 Sarah is very tired.   (she / work) very hard recently.

Present perfect continuous and simple (I have been doing and I have done)

A Study this example situation:

Kate's clothes are covered in paint.
She **has been painting** the ceiling.

Has been painting is the *present perfect continuous*.

We are interested in the activity. It does not matter whether something has been finished or not. In this example, the activity (painting the ceiling) has not been finished.

The ceiling was white. Now it is red.
She **has painted** the ceiling.

Has painted is the *present perfect simple*.

Here, the important thing is that something has been finished. **Has painted** is a completed action. We are interested in the result of the activity (the painted ceiling), not the activity itself.

Compare these examples:

- ☐ My hands are very dirty. **I've been repairing** the car.
- ☐ Joe **has been eating** too much recently. He should eat less.
- ☐ It's nice to see you again. What **have** you **been doing** since we last met?
- ☐ Where have you been? **Have** you **been playing** tennis?

- ☐ The car is OK again now. **I've repaired** it.
- ☐ Somebody **has eaten** all my chocolates. The box is empty.
- ☐ Where's the book I gave you? What **have** you **done** with it?
- ☐ **Have** you ever **played** tennis?

B We use the continuous to say *how long* (for an activity that is still happening):

- ☐ How long **have** you **been reading** that book?
- ☐ Lisa is still writing letters. She'**s been writing** letters **all day**.
- ☐ They'**ve been playing** tennis **since 2 o'clock**.
- ☐ I'm learning Spanish, but I **haven't been learning** it very long.

We use the simple to say *how much, how many* or *how many times* (for completed actions):

- ☐ How much of that book **have** you **read**?
- ☐ Lisa **has written** ten letters today.
- ☐ They'**ve played** tennis three times this week.
- ☐ I'm learning Spanish, but I **haven't learnt** very much yet.

C Some verbs (for example, **know/like/believe**) are not normally used in the continuous:
- ☐ **I've known** about it for a long time. (*not* I've been knowing)

For a list of these verbs, see Unit 4A. But note that you *can* use **want** and **mean** in the present perfect continuous:
- ☐ **I've been meaning** to phone Jane, but I keep forgetting.

Present perfect simple → Units 7–8   Present perfect continuous → Unit 9
Present perfect + for/since → Units 11–12

Exercises

10.1 For each situation, write two sentences using the words in brackets.

1 Tom started reading a book two hours ago. He is still reading it and now he is on page 53.
(read / for two hours) *He has been reading for two hours.*
(read / 53 pages so far) *He has read 53 pages so far.*

2 Rachel is from Australia. She is travelling round Europe at the moment. She began her trip three months ago.
(travel / for three months) She ....
(visit / six countries so far) ....

3 Patrick is a tennis player. He began playing tennis when he was ten years old. This year he is national champion again – for the fourth time.
(win / the national championships / four times) ....
(play / tennis since he was ten) ....

4 When they left college, Lisa and Sue started making films together. They still make films.
(make / five films since they left college) They ....
(make / films since they left college) ....

10.2 For each situation, ask a question using the words in brackets.

1 You have a friend who is learning Arabic. You ask:
(how long / learn / Arabic?) *How long have you been learning Arabic?*

2 You have just arrived to meet a friend. She is waiting for you. You ask:
(wait / long?) Have ....

3 You see somebody fishing by the river. You ask:
(catch / any fish?) ....

4 Some friends of yours are having a party next week. You ask:
(how many people / invite?) ....

5 A friend of yours is a teacher. You ask:
(how long / teach?) ....

6 You meet somebody who is a writer. You ask:
(how many books / write?) ....
(how long / write / books?) ....

7 A friend of yours is saving money to go on holiday. You ask:
(how long / save?) ....
(how much money / save?) ....

10.3 Put the verb into the more suitable form, present perfect simple (**I have done**) or continuous (**I have been doing**).

1 Where have you been? *Have you been playing* (you / play) tennis?
2 Look! .... (somebody / break) that window.
3 You look tired. .... (you / work) hard?
4 '.. (you / ever / work) in a factory?' 'No, never.'
5 'Liz is away on holiday.' 'Is she? Where .... (she / go)?
6 My brother is an actor. .... (he / appear) in several films.
7 'Sorry I'm late.' 'That's all right. .... (I / not / wait) long.'
8 'Is it still raining?' 'No, ... (it / stop).'
9 .... (I / lose) my address book. ....
(you / see) it?
10 .... (I / read) the book you lent me, but ....
.... (I / not / finish) it yet. It's very interesting.
11 .... (I / read) the book you lent me, so you can have it back now.

A Study this example situation:

Dan and Jenny are married. They got married exactly 20 years ago, so today is their 20th wedding anniversary.

They **have been** married **for 20 years**.

We say: They **are** married. *(present)*

but **How long have** they **been** married? *(present perfect)*
(*not* How long are they married?)
They **have been** married **for 20 years**.
(*not* They are married for 20 years)

We use the *present perfect* to talk about something that began in the past and still continues now. Compare the *present* and the *present perfect*:

☐ Bill **is** in hospital.
but He **has been** in hospital **since Monday**.
(*not* Bill is in hospital since Monday)

☐ **Do** you **know** each other well?
but **Have** you **known** each other **for a long time**?
(*not* Do you know)

☐ She's **waiting** for somebody.
but She's **been waiting** all morning.

☐ **Do** they **have** a car?
but **How long have** they **had** their car?

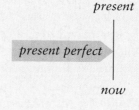

present

present perfect

now

B **I have known/had/lived** etc. is the *present perfect simple*.
I have been learning / been waiting / been doing etc. is the *present perfect continuous*.

When we ask or say 'how long', the continuous is more usual (see Unit 10):
☐ I've **been learning** English **for six months**.
☐ It's **been raining** since lunchtime.
☐ Richard **has been doing** the same job **for 20 years**.
☐ '**How long have** you **been driving**?' 'Since I was 17.'

Some verbs (for example, **know/like/believe**) are not normally used in the continuous:
☐ How long **have** you **known** Jane? (*not* have you been knowing)
☐ I've **had** a pain in my stomach all day. (*not* I've been having)
See also Units 4A and 10C. For **have**, see Unit 17.

C You can use either the present perfect continuous or simple with **live** and **work**:
☐ Julia **has been living** / **has lived** in Paris for a long time.
☐ How long **have** you **been working** / **have** you **worked** here?

But we use the simple (**I've lived** / **I've done** etc.) with **always**:
☐ I've **always lived** in the country. (*not* always been living)

D We say '**I haven't done** something **since/for** ...' (*present perfect simple*):
☐ I **haven't seen** Tom since Monday. (= Monday was the last time I saw him)
☐ Sue **hasn't phoned** for ages. (= the last time she phoned was ages ago)

I haven't ... since/for → Unit 8A **Present perfect continuous** → Units 9–10 **For and since** → Unit 12A

Exercises

11.1 Are the <u>underlined</u> verbs right or wrong? Correct them where necessary.

1 Bob is a friend of mine. <u>I know him</u> very well.   _OK_
2 Bob is a friend of mine. <u>I know him</u> for a long time.   _I've known him_
3 Sue and Alan <u>are married</u> since July.
4 The weather is awful. <u>It's raining</u> again.
5 The weather is awful. <u>It's raining</u> all day.
6 I like your house. How long <u>are you living</u> there?
7 Gary <u>is working</u> in a shop for the last few months.
8 <u>I don't know</u> Tim well. We've only met a few times.
9 I gave up drinking coffee. I <u>don't drink</u> it for a year.
10 That's a very old bike. How long <u>do you have</u> it?

11.2 Read the situations and write questions from the words in brackets.

1 John tells you that his mother is in hospital. You ask him:
(how long / be / in hospital?) _How long has your mother been in hospital?_
2 You meet a woman who tells you that she teaches English. You ask her:
(how long / teach / English?)
3 You know that Jane is a good friend of Caroline's. You ask Jane:
(how long / know / Caroline?)
4 Your friend's brother went to Australia some time ago and he's still there. You ask your friend:
(how long / be / in Australia?)
5 Tim always wears the same jacket. It's a very old jacket. You ask him:
(how long / have / that jacket?)
6 You are talking to a friend about Joe. Joe now works at the airport. You ask your friend:
(how long / work / at the airport?)
7 A friend of yours is learning to drive. You ask him:
(how long / learn / to drive?)
8 You meet somebody on a plane. She says that she lives in Chicago. You ask her:
(always / live / in Chicago?)

11.3 Complete B's answers to A's questions.

	A	B
1	Bill is in hospital, isn't he?	Yes, he _has been_ in hospital since Monday.
2	Do you see Ann very often?	No, I _haven't seen_ her for three months.
3	Is Margaret married?	Yes, she .... married for ten years.
4	Are you waiting for me?	Yes, I .... for the last half hour.
5	You know Linda, don't you?	Yes, we .... each other a long time.
6	Do you still play tennis?	No, I .... tennis for years.
7	Is Jim watching TV?	Yes, he .... TV all evening.
8	Do you watch TV a lot?	No, I .... TV for ages.
9	Have you got a headache?	Yes, I .... a headache all morning.
10	George is never ill, is he?	No, he .... ill since I've known him.
11	Are you feeling ill?	Yes, I .... ill all day.
12	Sue lives in London, doesn't she?	Yes, she .... in London for the last few years.
13	Do you go to the cinema a lot?	No, I .... to the cinema for ages.
14	Would you like to go to New York one day?	Yes, I .... to go to New York. (_use_ **always / want**)

A

We use **for** and **since** to say how long something has been happening.

We use **for** + a period of time (**two hours, six weeks** etc.):	We use **since** + the start of a period (**8 o'clock, Monday, 1999** etc.):
□ I've been waiting **for two hours**.	□ I've been waiting **since 8 o'clock**.

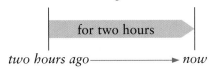

two hours ago ──────→ *now*

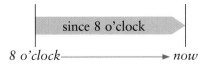

8 o'clock ──────→ *now*

for		
two hours	a long time	a week
20 minutes	six months	ages
five days	50 years	years

since		
8 o'clock	April	lunchtime
Monday	1985	we arrived
12 May	Christmas	I got up

□ Sally has been working here **for six months**. (*not* since six months)
□ I haven't seen Tom **for three days**. (*not* since three days)

□ Sally has been working here **since April**. (= from April until now)
□ I haven't seen Tom **since Monday**. (= from Monday until now)

It is possible to leave out **for** (but not usually in negative sentences):
  □ They've been married (for) **ten years**. (with or without **for**)
  □ They **haven't had** a holiday **for** ten years. (you must use **for**)

We do *not* use for + all ... (all day / all my life etc.):
  □ I've lived here **all my life**. (*not* for all my life)

B

Compare **when** ... ? (+ *past simple*) and **how long** ... ? (+ *present perfect*):

A: **When** did it start raining?
B: It started raining   **an hour ago / at 1 o'clock**.

A: **How long** has it been raining?
B: It's been raining   **for an hour / since 1 o'clock**.

A: **When** did Joe and Carol first meet?
B: They first met { **a long time ago.**
                   { **when they were at school.**

A: **How long** have they known each other?
B: They've known each other { **for a long time.**
                             { **since they were at school.**

C

We say 'It's (a long time / two years etc.) **since** something happened':
  □ It's **two years since** I last saw Joe. (= I **haven't seen** Joe for two years)
  □ It's **ages since** we went to the cinema. (= We **haven't been** to the cinema for ages)

You can ask 'How long is it since ... ?':
  □ **How long is it since** you last saw Joe? (= When did you last see Joe?)
  □ **How long is it since** Mrs Hill died? (= When did Mrs Hill die?)

You can also say 'It's been (= It has been) ... since ... ':
  □ **It's been** two years since I last saw Joe.

How long have you (been) ... ? → Unit 11

12.1 Write **for** or **since**.

1 It's been raining ....*since*.... lunchtime.
2 Sarah has lived in Paris .... 1995.
3 Paul has lived in London .... ten years.
4 I'm tired of waiting. We've been sitting here .... an hour.
5 Kevin has been looking for a job .... he left school.
6 I haven't been to a party .... ages.
7 I wonder where Joe is. I haven't seen him .... last week.
8 Jane is away. She's been away .... Friday.
9 The weather is dry. It hasn't rained .... a few weeks.

12.2 Write questions with **how long** and **when**.

1 It's raining.
   (how long?) ....*How long has it been raining?*....
   (when?) ....*When did it start raining?*....
2 Kate is learning Japanese.
   (how long / learn?) ....
   (when / start?) ....
3 I know Simon.
   (how long / you / know?) ....
   (when / you / first / meet?) ....
4 Rebecca and David are married.
   (how long?) ....
   (when?) ....

12.3 Read the situations and complete the sentences.

1 It's raining. It's been raining since lunchtime.   It ....*started raining*.... at lunchtime.
2 Ann and Sue are friends. They first met years ago.   They've ....*known each other for*.... years.
3 Joe is ill. He became ill on Sunday.   He has .... Sunday.
4 Joe is ill. He became ill a few days ago.   He has .... a few days.
5 Liz is married. She's been married for a year.   She got ....
6 You have a headache. It started when you woke up.
   I've .... I woke up.
7 Sue has been in Italy for the last three weeks.
   She went ....
8 You're working in a hotel. You started six months ago.
   I've ....

12.4 Write B's sentences using the words in brackets.

1 A: Do you often go on holiday?
   B: (no / five years) ....*No, I haven't had a holiday for five years.*....
2 A: Do you often see Sarah?
   B: (no / about a month) No, ...
3 A: Do you often go to the cinema?
   B: (no / a long time) ....
4 A: Do you often eat in restaurants?
   B: (no / ages) No, I ....

Now write B's answers again. This time use **It's ... since ...** .

5 (1) ....*No, it's five years since I had a holiday.*....
6 (2) No, ...
7 (3) ....
8 (4) No, it's ....

A Study this example situation:

Tom is looking for his key. He can't find it.

He **has lost** his key. (*present perfect*)

This means that he doesn't have his key *now*.

Ten minutes later:

Now Tom **has found** his key. He has it now.

Has he **lost** his key?   No, he **has found** it.

Did he **lose** his key?   Yes, he **did**.

He **lost** his key (*past simple*)

but now he **has found** it. (*present perfect*)

The present perfect (something **has happened**) is a *present* tense. It always tells us about the situation *now*. 'Tom **has lost** his key' = he doesn't have his key *now* (see Unit 7).

The past simple (something **happened**) tells us only about the *past*. If somebody says 'Tom **lost** his key', this doesn't tell us whether he has the key now or not. It tells us only that he lost his key at some time in the past.

Do *not* use the present perfect if the situation now is different. Compare:
- They've **gone** away. They'll be back on Friday. (they are away *now*)
  They **went** away, but I think they're back at home now. (*not* They've gone)

- It **has stopped** raining now, so we don't need the umbrella. (it isn't raining *now*)
  It **stopped** raining for a while, but now it's raining again. (*not* It has stopped)

B You can use the present perfect for new or recent happenings:
- 'I've **repaired** the TV. It's working OK now.' 'Oh, that's good.'
- Have you heard the news? Sally **has won** the lottery!

Use the past simple (*not* the present perfect) for things that are not recent or new:
- Mozart **was** a composer. He **wrote** more than 600 pieces of music.
  (*not* has been ... has written)
- My mother **grew** up in Scotland. (*not* has grown)

Compare:
- Did you know that somebody **has invented** a new type of washing machine?
- Who **invented** the telephone? (*not* has invented)

C We use the present perfect to give new information (see Unit 7). But if we continue to talk about it, we normally use the past simple:
- A: Ow! I've **burnt** myself.
  B: How **did** you **do** that? (*not* have you done)
  A: I **picked** up a hot dish. (*not* have picked)

- A: Look! Somebody **has spilt** something on the sofa.
  B: Well, it **wasn't** me. I **didn't do** it. (*not* hasn't been ... haven't done)

Exercises

13.1 Complete the sentences using the verbs in brackets. Use the present perfect where possible. Otherwise use the past simple.

1
I can't get in.
I __'ve lost__ (lose) my key.

2
The office is empty now.
Everybody .... (go) home.

3
I meant to call you last night, but I .... (forget).

4
Mary .... (go) to Egypt for a holiday, but she's back home in England now.

MARY

5
Are you OK?
Yes, I .... (have) a headache, but I feel fine now.

6
Can you help us? Our car .... (break) down.

13.2 Put the verb into the correct form, present perfect or past simple.

1 It ___stopped___ raining for a while, but now it's raining again. (stop)
2 The town is very different now. It ___has changed___ a lot. (change)
3 I did German at school, but I .... most of it now. (forget)
4 The police .... three people, but later they let them go. (arrest)
5 What do you think of my English? Do you think it .... ? (improve)
6 A: Are you still reading the paper?
  B: No, I .... with it. You can have it. (finish)
7 I .... for a job as a tourist guide, but I wasn't successful. (apply)
8 Where's my bike? It .... outside the house, but it's not there now. (be)
9 Look! There's an ambulance over there. There .... an accident. (be)
10 A: Have you heard about Ben? He .... his arm. (break)
   B: Really? How .... that .... ? (happen)
   A: He .... off a ladder. (fall)

13.3 Are the underlined parts of these sentences right or wrong? Correct them where necessary.

1 Do you know about Sue? She's given up her job.   ___OK___
2 My mother has grown up in Scotland.   ___grew___
3 How many plays has Shakespeare written?   ....
4 Ow! I've cut my finger. It's bleeding.   ....
5 Drugs have become a big problem everywhere.   ....
6 The Chinese have invented paper.   ....
7 Where have you been born?   ....
8 Mary isn't at home. She's gone shopping.   ....
9 Albert Einstein has been the scientist who has developed the theory of relativity.   ....

Present perfect and past 2 (I have done and I did)

A

Do not use the present perfect (**I have done**) when you talk about a *finished* time (for example, **yesterday / ten minutes ago / in 1999 / when I was a child**). Use a past tense:

- It **was** very cold **yesterday**. (*not* has been)
- Paul and Lucy **arrived ten minutes ago**. (*not* have arrived)
- **Did** you **eat** a lot of sweets **when you were a child**? (*not* have you eaten)
- I **got** home late **last night**. I **was** very tired and **went** straight to bed.

Use the past to ask **When … ?** or **What time … ?**:

- **When did** your friends **arrive**? (*not* have … arrived)
- **What time did** you **finish** work?

Compare:

Present perfect	Past simple
- Tom **has lost** his key. He can't get into the house. - Is Carla here or **has** she **left**?	- Tom **lost** his key **yesterday**. He couldn't get into the house. - **When did** Carla **leave**?

B

Compare:

Present perfect (**have done**)	Past simple (**did**)
- I've **done** a lot of work **today**.	- I **did** a lot of work **yesterday**.
We use the present perfect for a period of time that continues *until now*. For example: **today / this week / since 1985**.	We use the past simple for a *finished* time in the past. For example: **yesterday / last week / from 1995 to 2001**.

┌─*unfinished*─┐ **today** *past* — **now**	┌─*finished*─┐ **yesterday** *past* — *now*

- It **hasn't rained** this week.	- It **didn't rain** last week.
- **Have** you **seen** Anna **this morning**? (it is still morning)	- **Did** you **see** Anna **this morning**? (it is now afternoon or evening)
- **Have** you **seen** Tim **recently**?	- **Did** you **see** Tim **on Sunday**?
- I don't know where Lisa is. I **haven't seen** her. (= I haven't seen her recently)	- A: **Was** Lisa at the party **on Sunday**? B: I don't think so. I **didn't see** her.
- We've **been waiting** for an hour. (we are still waiting now)	- We **waited** (*or* **were waiting**) for an hour. (we are no longer waiting)
- Ian lives in London. He **has lived** there for seven years.	- Ian **lived** in Scotland for ten years. Now he lives in London.
- I **have never played** golf. (in my life)	- I **didn't play** golf **last summer**.
- *It's the last day of your holiday. You say:* It's **been** a really good holiday. I've really **enjoyed** it.	- *After you come back from holiday you say:* It **was** a really good holiday. I really **enjoyed** it.

Past simple → Unit 5   Present perfect → Units 7–8   Present perfect and past 1 → Unit 13

Exercises

Unit 14

14.1 Are the <u>underlined</u> parts of these sentences right or wrong? Correct them where necessary.

1 <u>I've lost</u> my key. I can't find it anywhere.   *OK*
2 <u>Have you eaten</u> a lot of sweets when you were a child?   *Did you eat*
3 <u>I've bought</u> a new car. You must come and see it.   ....
4 <u>I've bought</u> a new car last week.   ....
5 Where <u>have you been</u> yesterday evening?   ....
6 Lucy <u>has left</u> school in 1999.   ....
7 I'm looking for Mike. <u>Have you seen</u> him?   ....
8 '<u>Have you been</u> to Paris?' 'Yes, many times.'   ....
9 I'm very hungry. <u>I haven't eaten</u> much today.   ....
10 When <u>has this book been</u> published?   ....

14.2 Make sentences from the words in brackets. Use the present perfect or past simple.

1 (it / not / rain / this week)   *It hasn't rained this week.*
2 (the weather / be / cold / recently) The weather ....
3 (it / cold / last week) It ....
4 (I / not / read / a newspaper yesterday) I ....
5 (I / not / read / a newspaper today) ....
6 (Emily / earn / a lot of money / this year) ....
7 (she / not / earn / so much / last year) ....
8 (you / have / a holiday recently?) ....

14.3 Put the verb into the correct form, present perfect or past simple.

1 I don't know where Lisa is.   *Have you seen* (you / see) her?
2 When I .... (get) home last night, I .... (be) very
  tired and I .... (go) straight to bed.
3 A: .... (you / finish) painting the bedroom?
  B: Not yet. I'll finish it tomorrow.
4 George .... (not / be) very well last week.
5 Mr Clark .... (work) in a bank for 15 years. Then he gave it up.
6 Molly lives in Dublin. She .... (live) there all her life.
7 A: .... (you / go) to the cinema last night?
  B: Yes, but it .... (be) a mistake. The film .... (be) awful.
8 My grandfather .... (die) before I was born. I
  .... (never / meet) him.
9 I don't know Carol's husband. I .... (never / meet) him.
10 A: Is Martin here?   B: No, he .... (go) out.
   A: When exactly .... (he / go) out?   B: About ten minutes ago.
11 A: Where do you live?   B: In Boston.
   A: How long .... (you / live) there?   B: Five years.
   A: Where .... (you / live) before that?   B: In Chicago.
   A: And how long .... (you / live) in Chicago?   B: Two years.

14.4 Write sentences about yourself using the ideas in brackets.

1 (something you haven't done today)   *I haven't eaten any fruit today.*
2 (something you haven't done today) ....
3 (something you didn't do yesterday) ....
4 (something you did yesterday evening) ....
5 (something you haven't done recently) ....
6 (something you've done a lot recently) ....

→ Additional exercises 2–4 (pages 303–04), 14–15 (pages 310–11)

A

Study this example situation:

at 10.30 Bye!

at 11.00 Hello!

PAUL   SARAH

Sarah went to a party last week. Paul went to the party too, but they didn't see each other. Paul left the party at 10.30 and Sarah arrived at 11 o'clock. So:

When Sarah arrived at the party, Paul wasn't there.
He **had gone** home.

Had gone is the *past perfect (simple)*:

I/we/they/you he/she/it	had	(= I'd etc.) (= he'd etc.)	gone seen finished etc.

The past perfect simple is **had** + *past participle* (**gone/seen/finished** etc).

Sometimes we talk about something that happened in the past:
  ☐ Sarah **arrived** at the party.
This is the starting point of the story. Then, if we want to talk about things that happened *before* this time, we use the past perfect (**had ...**):
  ☐ When Sarah arrived at the party, Paul **had** already **gone** home.

Some more examples:
  ☐ When we got home last night, we found that somebody **had broken** into the flat.
  ☐ Karen didn't want to go to the cinema with us because she'**d** already **seen** the film.
  ☐ At first I thought I'**d done** the right thing, but I soon realised that I'**d made** a big mistake.
  ☐ The man sitting next to me on the plane was very nervous. He **hadn't flown** before.
    or ... He **had** never **flown** before.

B

Compare the *present perfect* (**have seen** etc.) and the *past perfect* (**had seen** etc.):

Present perfect

have seen ▷

past   *now*

Past perfect

had seen ▷

past   *now*

  ☐ Who is that woman? I'**ve** never **seen** her before.
  ☐ We aren't hungry. We'**ve** just **had** lunch.
  ☐ The house is dirty. They **haven't cleaned** it for weeks.

  ☐ I didn't know who she was. I'**d** never **seen** her before. (= before that time)
  ☐ We weren't hungry. We'**d** just **had** lunch.
  ☐ The house was dirty. They **hadn't cleaned** it for weeks.

C

Compare the *past simple* (**left, was** etc.) and the *past perfect* (**had left, had been** etc.):

  ☐ A: Was Tom there when you arrived?
    B: Yes, but he **left** soon afterwards.

  ☐ Kate **wasn't** at home when I phoned. She **was** at her mother's house.

  ☐ A: Was Tom there when you arrived?
    B: No, he **had** already **left**.

  ☐ Kate **had** just **got** home when I phoned. She **had been** at her mother's house.

Past perfect continuous → Unit 16   Irregular verbs (gone/seen etc.) → Appendix 1

15.1 Read the situations and write sentences from the words in brackets.

1 You went to Sue's house, but she wasn't there.
(she / go / out) ___She had gone out.___

2 You went back to your home town after many years. It wasn't the same as before.
(it / change / a lot) ___

3 I invited Rachel to the party, but she couldn't come.
(she / arrange / to do something else) ___

4 You went to the cinema last night. You got to the cinema late.
(the film / already / begin) ___

5 It was nice to see Dan again after such a long time.
(I / not / see / him for five years) ___

6 I offered Sue something to eat, but she wasn't hungry.
(she / just / have / breakfast) ___

15.2 For each situation, write a sentence ending with **never ... before**. Use the verb in brackets.

1 The man sitting next to you on the plane was very nervous. It was his first flight.
(fly) ___He'd never flown before.___

2 A woman walked into the room. She was a complete stranger to me.
(see) I ___ before.

3 Sam played tennis yesterday. He wasn't very good at it because it was his first game.
(play) He ___

4 Last year we went to Denmark. It was our first time there.
(be there) We ___

15.3 Use the sentences on the left to complete the paragraphs on the right. These sentences are in the order in which they happened – so (1) happened before (2), (2) before (3) etc. But your paragraph begins with the underlined sentence, so sometimes you need the past perfect.

1 (1) Somebody broke into the office during the night.
(2) We arrived at work in the morning.
(3) We called the police.

We arrived at work in the morning and found that somebody ___had broken___ into the office during the night. So we ___ .

2 (1) Laura went out this morning.
(2) I tried to phone her.
(3) There was no answer.

I tried to phone Laura this morning, but ___ no answer.
She ___ out.

3 (1) Jim came back from holiday a few days ago.
(2) I met him the same day.
(3) He looked very well.

I met Jim a few days ago. ___
just ___ holiday.
___ very well.

4 (1) Kevin sent Sally lots of emails.
(2) She never replied to them.
(3) Yesterday he got a phone call from her.
(4) He was very surprised.

Yesterday Kevin ___ from Sally. He ___ very surprised.
He ___ lots of emails, but she ___ .

15.4 Put the verb into the correct form, past perfect (**I had done**) or past simple (**I did**).

1 'Was Paul at the party when you arrived?' 'No, he ___had gone___ (go) home.'

2 I felt very tired when I got home, so I ___ (go) straight to bed.

3 The house was very quiet when I got home. Everybody ___ (go) to bed.

4 Sorry I'm late. The car ___ (break) down on my way here.

5 We were driving along the road when we ___ (see) a car which ___ (break) down, so we ___ (stop) to help.

→ Additional exercises 5–8 (pages 304–07)

Past perfect continuous (I had been doing)

A Study this example situation:

yesterday morning

Yesterday morning I got up and looked out of the window. The sun was shining, but the ground was very wet.

It **had been raining**.

It was *not* raining when I looked out of the window; the sun was shining. But it **had been** raining before.

Had been -ing is the *past perfect continuous*:

I/we/you/they he/she/it	had	(= I'd etc.) (= he'd etc.)	been	doing working playing etc.

Some more examples:

- □ When the boys came into the house, their clothes were dirty, their hair was untidy and one of them had a black eye. They**'d been fighting**.
- □ I was very tired when I got home. I**'d been working** hard all day.
- □ When I went to Madrid a few years ago, I stayed with a friend of mine. She**'d been living** there only a short time but knew the city very well.

B You can say that something **had been happening** for a period of time before something else happened:

- □ We**'d been playing** tennis for about half an hour when it started to rain heavily.
- □ George went to the doctor last Friday. He **hadn't been feeling** well for some time.

C Compare **have been -ing** (*present perfect continuous*) and **had been -ing** (*past perfect continuous*):

Present perfect continuous

I have been -ing

past   now

- □ I hope the bus comes soon. I**'ve been waiting** for 20 minutes. *(before now)*
- □ James is out of breath. He **has been running**.

Past perfect continuous

I had been -ing

past   now

- □ At last the bus came. I**'d been waiting** for 20 minutes. *(before the bus came)*
- □ James was out of breath. He **had been running**.

D Compare **was -ing** (*past continuous*) and **had been -ing**:

- □ It **wasn't raining** when we went out. The sun **was shining**. But it **had been raining**, so the ground was wet.
- □ Cathy **was sitting** in an armchair resting. She was tired because she**'d been working** very hard.

E Some verbs (for example, **know** and **like**) are not normally used in the continuous:

- □ We were good friends. We **had known** each other for years. (*not* had been knowing)

For a list of these verbs, see Unit 4A.

Exercises

16.1 Read the situations and make sentences from the words in brackets.

1 I was very tired when I arrived home.
   (I / work / hard all day) __I'd been working hard all day.__

2 The two boys came into the house. They had a football and they were both very tired.
   (they / play / football) _____

3 I was disappointed when I had to cancel my holiday.
   (I / look / forward to it) _____

4 Ann woke up in the middle of the night. She was frightened and didn't know where she was.
   (she / dream) _____

5 When I got home, Tom was sitting in front of the TV. He had just turned it off.
   (he / watch / a film) _____

16.2 Read the situations and complete the sentences.

1 We played tennis yesterday. Half an hour after we began playing, it started to rain.
   We __had been playing for half an hour__ when __it started to rain__ .

2 I had arranged to meet Tom in a restaurant. I arrived and waited for him. After 20 minutes
   I suddenly realised that I was in the wrong restaurant.
   I _____ for 20 minutes when I _____
   _____ the wrong restaurant.

3 Sarah got a job in factory. Five years later the factory closed down.
   At the time the factory _____ , Sarah _____
   _____ there for five years.

4 I went to a concert last week. The orchestra began playing. After about ten minutes a man in
   the audience suddenly started shouting.
   The orchestra _____ when
   _____

This time make your own sentence:

5 I began walking along the road. I _____
   when _____

16.3 Put the verb into the most suitable form, past continuous (**I was doing**), past perfect
(**I had done**) or past perfect continuous (**I had been doing**).

1 It was very noisy next door. Our neighbours __were having__ (have) a party.

2 We were good friends. We __had known__ (know) each other for years.

3 John and I went for a walk. I had difficulty keeping up with him because he
   _____ (walk) so fast.

4 Sue was sitting on the ground. She was out of breath. She _____ (run).

5 When I arrived, everybody was sitting round the table with their mouths full. They
   _____ (eat).

6 When I arrived, everybody was sitting round the table and talking. Their mouths were empty,
   but their stomachs were full. They _____ (eat).

7 Jim was on his hands and knees on the floor. He _____ (look) for his
   contact lens.

8 When I arrived, Kate _____ (wait) for me. She was annoyed with me
   because I was late and she _____ (wait) for a long time.

9 I was sad when I sold my car. I _____ (have) it for a very long time.

10 We were extremely tired at the end of the journey. We _____ (travel) for
   more than 24 hours.

Have got and have

Have got and **have** (= for possession, relationships, illnesses etc.)

You can use **have got** or **have** (without **got**). There is no difference in meaning:
- □ They**'ve got** a new car.   *or*   They **have** a new car.
- □ Lisa**'s got** two brothers.   *or*   Lisa **has** two brothers.
- □ I**'ve got** a headache.   *or*   I **have** a headache.
- □ Our house **has got** a small garden.   *or*   Our house **has** a small garden.
- □ He**'s got** a few problems.   *or*   He **has** a few problems.

With these meanings (possession etc.), you cannot use continuous forms (**am having** etc.):
- □ We're enjoying our holiday. We**'ve got** / We **have** a nice room in the hotel. (*not* We're having)

For the past we use **had** (without **got**):
- □ Lisa **had** long hair when she was a child. (*not* Lisa had got)

In questions and negative sentences there are three possible forms:

Have you got any questions? **Do you have** any questions? **Have you** any questions? *(less usual)*	I **haven't got** any questions. I **don't have** any questions. I **haven't** any questions. *(less usual)*
Has she got a car? **Does she have** a car? **Has she** a car? *(less usual)*	She **hasn't got** a car. She **doesn't have** a car. She **hasn't** a car. *(less usual)*

In past questions and negative sentences, we use **did/didn't**:
- □ **Did** you **have** a car when you were living in London?
- □ I **didn't have** a watch, so I didn't know the time.
- □ Lisa **had** long hair, **didn't** she?

Have breakfast / have a bath / have a good time etc.

We also use **have** (*but not* have got) for many actions and experiences. For example:

have	breakfast / dinner / a cup of coffee / something to eat etc. a bath / a shower / a swim / a break / a rest / a party / a holiday an accident / an experience / a dream a look (at something) a chat / a conversation / a discussion (with somebody) difficulty / trouble / fun / a good time etc. a baby (= give birth to a baby)

Have got is *not* possible in the expressions in the box. Compare:
- □ Sometimes I **have** (= eat) a sandwich for my lunch. (*not* I've got)

but   I**'ve got** / I **have** some sandwiches. Would you like one?

You can use continuous forms (**am having** etc.) with the expressions in the box:
- □ We're enjoying our holiday. We**'re having** a great time. (*not* We have)
- □ Mike **is having** a shower at the moment. He has a shower every day.

In questions and negative sentences we use **do/does/did**:
- □ I **don't** usually **have** a big breakfast. (*not* I usually haven't)
- □ What time **does** Jenny **have** lunch? (*not* has Jenny lunch)
- □ **Did** you **have** difficulty finding a place to live?

Have (got) to ... → Unit 31   American English → Appendix 7

Exercises

17.1 Write negative sentences with **have**. Some are present (**can't**) and some are past (**couldn't**).

1 I can't get into the house. (a key) _I haven't got a key._
2 I couldn't read the letter. (my glasses) _I didn't have my glasses._
3 I can't get onto the roof. (a ladder) I ....
4 We couldn't visit the museum. (enough time) We ....
5 He couldn't find his way to our house. (a map) ....
6 She can't pay her bills. (any money) ....
7 I can't go swimming today. (enough energy) ....
8 They couldn't take any photographs. (a camera) ....

17.2 Complete the questions with **have**. Some are present and some are past.

1 Excuse me, _have you got_ a pen I could borrow?
2 Why are you holding your face like that? .... a toothache?
3 .... a lot of toys when you were a child?
4 A: .... the time, please?
  B: Yes, it's ten past seven.
5 I need a stamp for this letter. .... one?
6 When you worked in your last job, ... your own office?
7 A: It started to rain very heavily while I was out.
  B: .... an umbrella?

17.3 Write sentences about yourself. Have you got these things now? Did you have them ten years ago?
Write two sentences each time using **I've got / I haven't got** and **I had / I didn't have**.
(You can also write about your family: **We've got ... / We had ...** etc.).

	now	*ten years ago*
1 (a car)	_I've got a car._	_I didn't have a car._
2 (a bike)	I	I ....
3 (a mobile phone)	....	....
4 (a dog)	....	....
5 (a guitar)	....	....
6 (long hair)	....	....
7 (a driving licence)	....	....

17.4 Complete the sentences. Use an expression from the list and put the verb into the correct form where necessary.

have a baby	have a break	have a chat	have difficulty	have a good flight
have a look	~~have lunch~~	have a party	have a nice time	have a shower

1 I don't eat much during the day. I never _have lunch_ .
2 David starts work at 8 o'clock and .... at 10.30.
3 We .... last week. It was great – we invited lots of people.
4 Excuse me, can I .... at your newspaper, please?
5 Jim is away on holiday at the moment. I hope he ....
6 I met Ann in the supermarket yesterday. We stopped and ....
7 A: .... finding the book you wanted?
  B: No, I found it OK.
8 Suzanne .... a few weeks ago. It's her second child.
9 A: Why didn't you answer the phone?
  B: I ....
10 *You meet your friend Sally at the airport. She has just arrived. You say:*
  Hi, Sally. How are you? .... ?

Unit 18 Used to (do)

A

Study this example situation:

a few years ago

these days

Diane doesn't travel much these days.
She prefers to stay at home.

But she **used to travel** a lot.
She **used to go** away two or three times a year.

She **used to travel** a lot = she travelled a lot regularly in the past, but she doesn't do this any more.

she used to travel	she doesn't travel
past	*now*

B

Something **used to** happen = it happened regularly in the past, but no longer happens:

- □ I **used to play** tennis a lot, but I don't play very often now.
- □ David **used to spend** a lot of money on clothes. These days he can't afford it.
- □ 'Do you go to the cinema much?' 'Not now, but I **used to**.' (= I used to go)

We also use **used to** ... for things that were true, but are not true any more:

- □ This building is now a furniture shop. It **used to be** a cinema.
- □ I **used to think** Mark was unfriendly, but now I realise he's a very nice person.
- □ I've started drinking tea recently. I never **used to like** it before.
- □ Nicole **used to have** very long hair when she was a child.

C

'I **used to** do something' is past. There is no present form. You cannot say 'I use to do'.
To talk about the present, use the present simple (I **do**).

Compare:

past	he **used to play**	we **used to live**	there **used to be**
present	he **plays**	we **live**	there **is**

- □ We **used to live** in a small village, but now we **live** in London.
- □ There **used to be** four cinemas in the town. Now there **is** only one.

D

The normal question form is **did** (you) **use to** ... ?:

- □ **Did** you **use to eat** a lot of sweets when you were a child?

The negative form is **didn't use to** ... (**used not to** ... is also possible):

- □ I **didn't use to** like him. (*or* I **used not to** like him.)

E

Compare I **used to do** and I **was doing**:

- □ I **used to watch** TV a lot. (= I watched TV regularly in the past, but I no longer do this)
- □ I **was watching** TV when Mike called. (= I was in the middle of watching TV)

F

Do not confuse I **used to do** and I **am used to doing** (see Unit 61). The structures and meanings are different:

- □ I **used to live** alone. (= I lived alone in the past, but I no longer live alone.)
- □ I **am used** to **living** alone. (= I live alone, and I don't find it strange or difficult because I've been living alone for some time.)

Past continuous (I was doing) → Unit 6   Would (= used to) → Unit 36
Be/get used to (doing) something → Unit 61

18.1   Complete the sentences with **use(d) to** + a suitable verb.

1   Diane doesn't travel much now. She ......*used to travel*...... a lot, but she prefers to stay at home these days.
2   Liz .... a motorbike, but last year she sold it and bought a car.
3   We came to live in London a few years ago. We .... in Leeds.
4   I rarely eat ice-cream now, but I .... it when I was a child.
5   Jim .... my best friend, but we aren't good friends any longer.
6   It only takes me about 40 minutes to get to work now that the new road is open. It .... more than an hour.
7   There .... a hotel near the airport, but it closed a long time ago.
8   When you lived in New York, ... to the theatre very often?

18.2   Matt changed his life style. He stopped doing some things and started doing other things:

He stopped ⎰ studying hard
         ⎨ going to bed early
         ⎱ running three miles every morning

He started ⎰ sleeping late
         ⎨ going out in the evening
         ⎱ spending a lot of money

Write sentences about Matt with **used to** and **didn't use to.**

1   *He used to study hard.*
2   *He didn't use to sleep late.*
3   ....
4   ....
5   ....
6   ....

18.3   Compare what Karen said five years ago and what she says today:

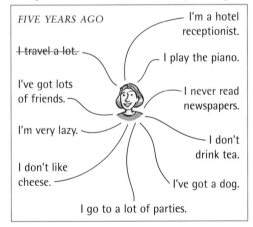

FIVE YEARS AGO
I'm a hotel receptionist.
~~I travel a lot.~~
I play the piano.
I've got lots of friends.
I never read newspapers.
I'm very lazy.
I don't drink tea.
I don't like cheese.
I've got a dog.
I go to a lot of parties.

TODAY
My dog died two years ago.
I eat lots of cheese now.
I read a newspaper every day now.
I work very hard these days.
I haven't been to a party for ages.
I don't know many people these days.
I haven't played the piano for years.
I work in a bookshop now.
~~I don't go away much these days.~~
Tea's great! I like it now.

Now write sentences about how Karen has changed. Use **used to / didn't use to / never used to** in the first part of your sentence.

1   *She used to travel a lot,*   but   *she doesn't go away much these days.*
2   She used .... but ....
3   .... but ....
4   .... but ....
5   .... but ....
6   .... but ....
7   .... but ....
8   .... but ....
9   .... but ....
10   .... but ....

→ Additional exercise 9 (**page 307**)   **37**

Present tenses (I am doing / I do) for the future

A   *Present continuous* (**I am doing**) with a future meaning

This is Ben's diary for next week.

He **is playing** tennis on Monday afternoon.
He **is going** to the dentist on Tuesday morning.
He **is having** dinner with Kate on Friday.

In all these examples, Ben has already decided and arranged to do these things.

I'm doing something (tomorrow) = I have already decided and arranged to do it:
- ☐ A: What **are** you **doing** on Saturday evening? (*not* What do you do)
  - B: **I'm going** to the theatre. (*not* I go)
- ☐ A: What time **is** Cathy **arriving** tomorrow?
  - B: Half past ten. **I'm meeting** her at the station.
- ☐ **I'm not working** tomorrow, so we can go out somewhere.
- ☐ Ian **isn't playing** football next Saturday. He's hurt his leg.

'I'm **going to** (do)' is also possible in these sentences:
- ☐ What **are** you **going to do** on Saturday evening?

But the present continuous is more natural for arrangements. See also Unit 20B.

Do not use **will** to talk about what you have arranged to do:
- ☐ What **are** you **doing** this evening? (*not* What will you do)
- ☐ Alex **is getting** married next month. (*not* will get)

You can also use the present continuous for an action *just before you begin to do it*. This happens especially with verbs of movement (**go/come/leave** etc.):
- ☐ I'm tired. **I'm going** to bed now. Goodnight. (*not* I go to bed now)
- ☐ 'Tina, are you ready yet?' 'Yes, **I'm coming**.' (*not* I come)

B   *Present simple* (**I do**) with a future meaning

We use the present simple when we talk about timetables, programmes etc. (for public transport, cinemas etc.):
- ☐ My train **leaves** at 11.30, so I need to be at the station by 11.15.
- ☐ What time **does** the film **begin** this evening?
- ☐ It's Wednesday tomorrow. / Tomorrow **is** Wednesday.

You can use the present simple to talk about people if their plans are fixed like a timetable:
- ☐ I **start** my new job on Monday.
- ☐ What time **do** you **finish** work tomorrow?

But the continuous is more usual for personal arrangements:
- ☐ What time **are** you **meeting** Ann tomorrow? (*not* do you meet)

Compare:

Present continuous	*Present simple*
☐ What time **are you arriving**?	☐ What time **does the train arrive**?
☐ **I'm going** to the cinema this evening.	☐ **The film begins** at 8.15 (this evening).

   I'm going to → Units 20, 23   **Will** → Units 21–22   **Present simple after when/if** etc. → Unit 25

Exercises

19.1 A friend of yours is planning to go on holiday soon. You ask her about her plans.
Use the words in brackets to make your questions.

1 (where / go?) _Where are you going?_   Scotland.
2 (how long / go for?) ....   Ten days.
3 (when / leave?) ....   Next Friday.
4 (go / alone?) ....   No, with a friend.
5 (travel / by car?) ....   No, by train.
6 (where / stay?) ....   In a hotel.

19.2 Tom wants you to visit him, but you are very busy. Look at your diary for the next few days and explain to him why you can't come.

TOM: Can you come on Monday evening?
YOU: Sorry, but _I'm playing volleyball_ .... (1)
TOM: What about Tuesday evening then?
YOU: No, not Tuesday. I .... (2)
TOM: And Wednesday evening?
YOU: .... (3)
TOM: Well, are you free on Thursday?
YOU: I'm afraid not. .... (4)

19.3 Have you arranged to do anything at these times? Write sentences about yourself.

1 (this evening) _I'm going out this evening._ or _I'm not doing anything this evening._
2 (tomorrow morning) I ....
3 (tomorrow evening) ....
4 (next Sunday) ....
5 (*choose another day or time*) ....

19.4 Put the verb into the more suitable form, present continuous or present simple.

1 I _'m going_ (go) to the cinema this evening.
2 _Does the film begin_ (the film / begin) at 3.30 or 4.30?
3 We .... (have) a party next Saturday. Would you like to come?
4 The art exhibition .... (finish) on 3 May.
5 I .... (not / go) out this evening. I .... (stay)
   at home.
6 '.. (you / do) anything tomorrow morning?' 'No, I'm free. Why?'
7 We .... (go) to a concert tonight. It .... (start) at 7.30.
8 I .... (leave) now. I've come to say goodbye.
9 A: Have you seen Liz recently?
   B: No, but we .... (meet) for lunch next week.
10 *You are on the train to London and you ask another passenger:*
   Excuse me. What time .... (this train / get) to London?
11 *You are talking to Helen:*
   Helen, I .... (go) to the supermarket. ....
   (you / come) with me?
12 *You and a friend are watching television. You say:*
   I'm bored with this programme. What time .... (it / end)?
13 I .... (not / use) the car this evening, so you can have it.
14 Sue .... (come) to see us tomorrow. She ....
   (travel) by train and her train .... (arrive) at 10.15.

→ Additional exercises 10–13 (pages 308–10)

(I'm) going to (do)

A

I am going to do something = I have already decided to do it, I intend to do it:

- □ A: **Are** you **going to watch** the late film on TV tonight?
  B: No, **I'm going to have** an early night.
- □ A: I hear Sarah has won some money. What **is** she **going to do** with it?
  B: She's **going to buy** a new car.
- □ I'm just **going to make** a quick phone call. Can you wait for me?
- □ This cheese looks horrible. **I'm not going to eat** it.

B

I am doing and **I am going to do**

We use **I am doing** (*present continuous*) when we say what we have *arranged* to do – for example, arranged to meet somebody, arranged to go somewhere:

- □ What time **are** you **meeting** Ann this evening?
- □ **I'm leaving** tomorrow. I've got my plane ticket.

I am going to do something = I've decided to do it (but perhaps not *arranged* to do it):

- □ 'Your shoes are dirty.' 'Yes, I know. **I'm going to clean** them.' (= I've decided to clean them, but I haven't *arranged* to clean them)
- □ I've decided not to stay here any longer. Tomorrow **I'm going to look** for somewhere else to stay.

Often the difference is very small and either form is possible.

C

You can also say that 'something **is going to happen**' in the future. For example:

The man can't see the wall in front of him.

He **is going to walk** into the wall.

When we say that 'something **is going to happen**', the situation *now* makes this clear. The man is walking towards the wall now, so we can see that he **is going to walk** into it.

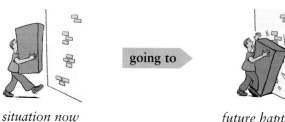

going to

situation now   *future happening*

Some more examples:

- □ Look at those black clouds! It's **going to rain**. (the clouds are there now)
- □ I feel terrible. I think **I'm going to be** sick. (I feel terrible now)
- □ The economic situation is bad now and things **are going to get** worse.

D

I was going to (do something) = I intended to do it, but didn't do it:

- □ We **were going to travel** by train, but then we decided to go by car instead.
- □ Peter **was going to do** the exam, but he changed his mind.
- □ I **was** just **going to cross** the road when somebody shouted 'Stop!'

You can say that 'something **was going to happen**' (but didn't happen):

- □ I thought it **was going to rain**, but it didn't.

I am doing for the future → Unit 19A   **I will** and **I'm going to** → Unit 23

20.1 Write a question with **going to** for each situation.

1 Your friend has won some money. You ask:
(what / do with it?) *What are you going to do with it?*

2 Your friend is going to a party tonight. You ask:
(what / wear?) ....

3 Your friend has just bought a new table. You ask:
(where / put it?) ....

4 Your friend has decided to have a party. You ask:
(who / invite?) ....

20.2 Read the situations and complete the dialogues. Use **going to**.

1 You have decided to tidy your room this morning.
FRIEND: Are you going out this morning?
YOU: No, *I'm going to tidy my room.*

2 You bought a sweater, but it doesn't fit you very well. You have decided to take it back.
FRIEND: That sweater is too big for you.
YOU: I know. ....

3 You have been offered a job, but you have decided not to accept it.
FRIEND: I hear you've been offered a job.
YOU: That's right, but ....

4 You have to phone Sarah. It's morning now, and you have decided to phone her tonight.
FRIEND: Have you phoned Sarah yet?
YOU: No, ...

5 You are in a restaurant. The food is awful and you've decided to complain.
FRIEND: This food is awful, isn't it?
YOU: Yes, it's disgusting. ....

20.3 What is going to happen in these situations? Use the words in brackets.

1 There are a lot of black clouds in the sky.
(rain) *It's going to rain.*

2 It is 8.30. Tom is leaving his house. He has to be at work at 8.45, but the journey takes
30 minutes.
(late) He ....

3 There is a hole in the bottom of the boat. A lot of water is coming in through the hole.
(sink) The boat ....

4 Lucy and Chris are driving. There is very little petrol left in the tank. The nearest petrol
station is a long way away.
(run out) They ....

20.4 Complete the sentences with **was/were going to** + the following verbs:

buy   **give up**   **have**   **phone**   **play**   ~~travel~~

1 We *were going to travel* by train, but then we decided to go by car instead.

2 I .... some new clothes yesterday, but I was very busy and didn't
have time to go to the shops.

3 Martin and I .... tennis last week, but he was injured.

4 I .... Jane, but I decided to email her instead.

5 A: When I last saw Tim, he .... his job.
B: That's right, but in the end he decided to stay where he was.

6 We .... a party last week, but some of our friends couldn't come,
so we cancelled it.

Will/shall 1

A

We use **I'll** (= **I will**) when we decide to do something at the time of speaking:
- □ Oh, I've left the door open. **I'll go** and shut it.
- □ 'What would you like to drink?'   '**I'll have** an orange juice, please.'
- □ 'Did you phone Lucy?'   'Oh no, I forgot. **I'll phone** her now.'

You cannot use the *present simple* (**I do** / **I go** etc.) in these sentences:
- □ **I'll go** and shut the door. (*not* I go and shut)

We often use **I think I'll ...** and **I don't think I'll ...** :
- □ I feel a bit hungry. **I think I'll have** something to eat.
- □ **I don't think I'll go** out tonight. I'm too tired.

In spoken English the negative of **will** is usually **won't** (= **will not**):
- □ I can see you're busy, so I **won't stay** long.

B

Do *not* use **will** to talk about what you have already decided or arranged to do (see Units 19–20):
- □ **I'm going** on holiday next Saturday. (*not* I'll go)
- □ **Are** you **working** tomorrow? (*not* Will you work)

C

We often use **will** in these situations:

Offering to do something
- □ That bag looks heavy. **I'll help** you with it. (*not* I help)

Agreeing to do something
- □ A: Can you give Tim this book?
-   B: Sure, **I'll give** it to him when I see him this afternoon.

Promising to do something
- □ Thanks for lending me the money. **I'll pay** you back on Friday.
- □ I **won't tell** anyone what happened. I promise.

Asking somebody to do something (**Will you ...** ?)
- □ **Will you** please turn the stereo down? I'm trying to concentrate.

You can use **won't** to say that somebody refuses to do something:
- □ I've tried to give her advice, but she **won't listen**.
- □ The car **won't start**. (= the car 'refuses' to start)

D

Shall I ... ?   **Shall we ...** ?

Shall is used mostly in the questions **shall I ...** ? / **shall we ...** ?

We use **shall I ...** ? / **shall we ...** ? to ask somebody's opinion (especially in offers or suggestions):
- □ **Shall I** open the window? (= Do you want me to open the window?)
- □ I've got no money. What **shall I** do? (= What do you suggest?)
- □ '**Shall we** go?' 'Just a minute. I'm not ready yet.'
- □ Where **shall we** go this evening?

Compare **shall I ...** ? and **will you ...** ?:
- □ **Shall I** shut the door? (= Do you want me to shut it?)
- □ **Will you** shut the door? (= I want you to shut it)

21.1 Complete the sentences with **I'll** + a suitable verb.

1 I'm too tired to walk home. I think _____I'll take_____ a taxi.
2 'It's cold in this room.' 'Is it? _____ on the heating then.'
3 A: We haven't got any milk.
   B: Oh, I forgot to buy some. _____ and get some now.
4 'Shall I do the washing-up?' 'No, it's all right. _____ it later.'
5 'I don't know how to use this computer.' 'OK, _____ you.'
6 'Would you like tea or coffee?' '_____ coffee, please.'
7 'Goodbye! Have a nice holiday.' 'Thanks. _____ you a postcard.'
8 Thanks for letting me borrow your camera. _____ it back to you on Monday, OK?
9 'Are you coming with us?' 'No, I think _____ here.'

21.2 Read the situations and write sentences with **I think I'll ...** or **I don't think I'll ...** .

1 It's a bit cold. The window is open and you decide to close it. You say:
   I think I'll close the window.
2 You are feeling tired and it's getting late. You decide to go to bed. You say:
   I think _____
3 A friend of yours offers you a lift in his car, but you decide to walk. You say:
   Thank you, but _____
4 You arranged to play tennis today. Now you decide that you don't want to play. You say:
   I don't think _____
5 You were going to go swimming. Now you decide that you don't want to go. You say:
   _____

21.3 Which is correct? (If necessary, study Units 19–20 first.)

1 'Did you phone Lucy?' 'Oh no, I forgot. ~~I phone~~ / I'll phone her now.' (I'll phone *is correct*)
2 I can't meet you tomorrow. I'm playing / ~~I'll play~~ tennis. (I'm playing *is correct*)
3 'I meet / I'll meet you outside the hotel in half an hour, OK?' 'Yes, that's fine.'
4 'I need some money.' 'OK, I'm lending / I'll lend you some. How much do you need?'
5 I'm having / I'll have a party next Saturday. I hope you can come.
6 'Remember to get a newspaper when you go out.' 'OK. I don't forget / I won't forget.'
7 What time does your train leave / will your train leave tomorrow?
8 I asked Sue what happened, but she doesn't tell / won't tell me.
9 'Are you doing / Will you do anything tomorrow evening?' 'No, I'm free. Why?'
10 I don't want to go out alone. Do you come / Will you come with me?

21.4 What do you say in these situations? Write sentences with **shall I ... ?** or **shall we ... ?**

1 You and a friend want to do something this evening, but you don't know what.
   You ask your friend. _What shall we do this evening?_
2 You try on a jacket in a shop. You are not sure whether to buy it or not. You ask a
   friend for advice. _____ it?
3 It's Helen's birthday next week. You want to give her a present, but you don't know what.
   You ask a friend for advice.
   What _____
4 You and a friend are going on holiday together, but you haven't decided where.
   You ask him/her. _____
5 You and a friend are going out. You haven't decided whether to go by car or to walk. You ask
   him/her. _____ or _____
6 Your friend wants you to phone later. You don't know what time to phone. You ask him/her.

Will/shall 2

A

We do *not* use **will** to say what somebody has already arranged or decided to do:

- □ Diane **is working** next week. (*not* Diane will work)
- □ **Are** you **going to watch** television this evening? (*not* Will you watch)

For '**is working**' and '**Are** you **going to** … ?', see Units 19–20.

But often, when we talk about the future, we are *not* talking about what somebody has decided to do. For example:

Kate is doing an exam next week. Chris and Joe are talking about it.

Do you think Kate **will pass** the exam?

CHRIS

Yes, **she'll pass** easily.

JOE

She'll pass does *not* mean 'she has decided to pass'. Joe is saying what he knows or thinks will happen. He is *predicting* the future.

When we predict a future happening or situation, we use **will/won't**.

Some more examples:

- □ Jill has been away a long time. When she returns, she'll **find** a lot of changes here.
- □ 'Where **will** you **be** this time next year?'   'I'll **be** in Japan.'
- □ That plate is hot. If you touch it, you'll **burn** yourself.
- □ Tom **won't pass** the exam. He hasn't studied hard enough.
- □ When **will** you **get** your exam results?

B

We often use **will** ('**ll**) with:

probably	□ I'll **probably** be home late tonight.
I expect	□ I haven't seen Carol today. **I expect** she'll phone this evening.
(I'm) sure	□ Don't worry about the exam. **I'm sure** you'll pass.
(I) think	□ Do you **think** Sarah **will** like the present we bought her?
(I) don't think	□ I **don't think** the exam **will** be very difficult.
I wonder	□ **I wonder** what **will** happen.

After **I hope**, we generally use the present (**will** is also possible):

- □ I hope Kate **passes** the exam. (*or* I hope Kate **will pass** …)
- □ I hope it **doesn't rain** tomorrow.

C

Generally we use **will** to talk about the future, but sometimes we use **will** to talk about *now*. For example:

- □ Don't phone Ann now. She'll **be** busy. (= she'll be busy *now*)

D

I shall … / we shall …

Normally we use **shall** only with I and we. You can say:

I shall *or* **I will** (**I'll**)   **we shall** *or* **we will** (**we'll**)

- □ **I shall** be late this evening. (*or* **I will** be)
- □ **We shall** probably go to Scotland in the summer. (*or* We **will** probably go)

In spoken English we normally use **I'll** and **we'll**:

- □ **We'll** probably go to Scotland.

The negative of **shall** is **shall not** or **shan't**:

- □ I **shan't** be here tomorrow. (*or* I **won't** be)

Do not use **shall** with **he/she/it/you/they**:

- □ She **will** be very angry. (*not* She shall be)

Will/shall 1 → Unit 21   I will and I'm going to → Unit 23   Will be doing and will have done → Unit 24
The future → Appendix 3   American English → Appendix 7

22.1 Which form of the verb is correct (or more natural) in these sentences? The verbs are underlined.

1 Diane isn't free on Saturday. <u>She'll work / She's working</u>. (<u>She's working</u> *is correct*)
2 <u>I'll go / I'm going</u> to a party tomorrow night. Would you like to come too?
3 I think Jenny <u>will get / is getting</u> the job. She has a lot of experience.
4 I can't meet you this evening. A friend of mine <u>will come / is coming</u> to see me.
5 A: Have you decided where to go for your holidays?
   B: Yes, <u>we'll go / we're going</u> to Italy.
6 There's no need to be afraid of the dog. <u>It won't hurt / It isn't hurting</u> you.

22.2 Complete the sentences with **will ('ll)** + the following verbs:

be   come   get   like   live   look   meet   ~~pass~~

1 Don't worry about the exam. I'm sure you __'ll pass__ .
2 Why don't you try on this jacket? It _____ nice on you.
3 You must meet George sometime. I think you _____ him.
4 It's raining. Don't go out. You _____ wet.
5 Do you think people _____ longer in the future?
6 Goodbye. I expect we _____ again before long.
7 I've invited Sue to the party, but I don't think she _____ .
8 When the new road is finished, my journey to work _____ much shorter.

22.3 Put in **will ('ll)** or **won't**.

1 Can you wait for me? I __won't__ be very long.
2 There's no need to take an umbrella with you. It _____ rain.
3 If you don't eat anything now, you _____ be hungry later.
4 I'm sorry about what happened yesterday. It _____ happen again.
5 I've got some incredible news! You _____ never believe what happened.
6 Don't ask Amanda for advice. She _____ know what to do.

22.4 Where do you think you will be at these times? Write true sentences about yourself. Use:

I'll be ... *or* **I'll probably be ...** *or* **I don't know where I'll be**

1 (next Monday evening at 7.45) __I'll be at home.__
                          or __I'll probably be at home.__
                          or __I don't know where I'll be.__

2 (at 5 o'clock tomorrow morning)
   _____

3 (at 10.30 tomorrow morning)
   _____

4 (next Saturday afternoon at 4.15)
   _____

5 (this time next year)
   _____

22.5 Write questions using **do you think ... will ... ?** + the following:

be back   cost   end   get married   happen   ~~like~~   rain

1 I've bought Rosa this picture. __Do you think she'll like it__ ?
2 The weather doesn't look very good. Do you _____ ?
3 The meeting is still going on. When do you _____ ?
4 My car needs to be repaired. How much _____ ?
5 Sally and David are in love. Do _____ ?
6 'I'm going out now.' 'OK. What time _____ ?'
7 The future situation is uncertain. What _____ ?

→ Additional exercises 10–13 (pages 308–10)

I will and I'm going to

Future actions

Study the difference between **will** and **(be) going to:**

Sue is talking to Helen:

> Let's have a party.

> That's a great idea. We'll **invite** lots of people.

SUE   HELEN

will ('ll): We use **will** when we decide to do something at the time of speaking. The speaker has not decided before. The party is a new idea.

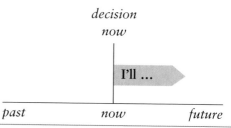

Later that day, Helen meets Dave:

> Sue and I have decided to have a party. We're **going to invite** lots of people.

HELEN   DAVE

(be) going to: We use **(be) going to** when we have *already decided* to do something. Helen had already decided to invite lots of people *before* she spoke to Dave.

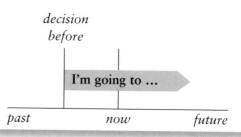

Compare:

☐ 'Gary phoned while you were out.' 'OK. I'll **call** him back.'
  'Gary phoned while you were out.' 'Yes, I know. I'm **going to call** him back.'
☐ 'Ann is in hospital.' 'Oh really? I didn't know. I'll **go** and visit her.'
  'Ann is in hospital.' 'Yes, I know. I'm **going to visit** her this evening.'

Future happenings and situations (predicting the future)

Sometimes there is not much difference between **will** and **going to.** For example, you can say:
  ☐ I think the weather **will** be nice this afternoon.
  ☐ I think the weather **is going to** be nice this afternoon.

When we say something **is going to** happen, we think this is because of the situation *now* (see Unit 20C). For example:
  ☐ Look at those black clouds. It's **going to rain.** (*not* It will rain)
    (We can see that it **is going to rain** from the clouds that are in the sky *now*.)
  ☐ I feel terrible. I think **I'm going to be** sick. (*not* I think I'll be sick)
    (I think **I'm going to be** sick because I feel terrible *now*.)
Do not use **will** in this type of situation.

In other situations, use **will:**
  ☐ Tom **will** probably **get** here at about 8 o'clock.
  ☐ I think Sarah **will like** the present we bought for her.
  ☐ These shoes are very well-made. They'll **last** a long time.

I'm going to → Unit 20   **Will** → Units 21–22   **The future** → Appendix 3

23.1 Complete the sentences using **will ('ll)** or **going to**.

1 A: Why are you turning on the television?
   B: __I'm going to watch__ the news. (I / watch)

2 A: Oh, I've just realised. I haven't got any money.
   B: Haven't you? Well, don't worry. .... you some. (I / lend)

3 A: I've got a headache.
   B: Have you? Wait a second and .... an aspirin for you. (I / get)

4 A: Why are you filling that bucket with water?
   B: .... the car. (I / wash)

5 A: I've decided to repaint this room.
   B: Oh, have you? What colour .... it? (you / paint)

6 A: Where are you going? Are you going shopping?
   B: Yes, ... something for dinner. (I / buy)

7 A: I don't know how to use this camera.
   B: It's easy. .... you. (I / show)

8 A: What would you like to eat?
   B: .... a sandwich, please. (I / have)

9 A: Did you post that letter for me?
   B: Oh, I'm sorry. I completely forgot. .... it now. (I / do)

10 A: The ceiling in this room doesn't look very safe, does it?
   B: No, it looks as if .... down. (it / fall)

11 A: Has George decided what to do when he leaves school?
   B: Yes. Everything is planned. .... a holiday for a few weeks.
   (he / have) Then .... a computer programming course. (he / do)

23.2 Read the situations and complete the sentences using **will ('ll)** or **going to**.

1 The phone rings and you answer. Somebody wants to speak to Jim.
   CALLER: Hello. Can I speak to Jim, please?
   YOU: Just a moment. __I'll get__ him. (I / get)

2 It's a nice day, so you have decided to take a walk. Just before you go, you tell your friend.
   YOU: The weather's too nice to stay in. .... a walk. (I / take)
   FRIEND: Good idea. I think .... you. (I / join)

3 Your friend is worried because she has lost an important letter.
   YOU: Don't worry about the letter. I'm sure .... it. (you / find)
   FRIEND: I hope so.

4 There was a job advertised in the paper recently. At first you were interested, but then you
   decided not to apply.
   FRIEND: Have you decided what to do about that job you were interested in?
   YOU: Yes, ... for it. (I / not / apply)

5 You and a friend come home very late. Other people in the house are asleep. Your friend
   is noisy.
   YOU: Shh! Don't make so much noise. .... everybody up. (you / wake)

6 Paul has to go to the airport to catch a plane tomorrow morning.
   PAUL: Liz, I need somebody to take me to the airport tomorrow morning.
   LIZ: That's no problem. .... you. (I / take) What time is your flight?
   PAUL: 10.50.
   LIZ: OK, ... at about 9 o'clock then. (we / leave)
   Later that day, Joe offers to take Paul to the airport.
   JOE: Paul, do you want me to take you to the airport?
   PAUL: No thanks, Joe. .... me. (Liz / take)

→ Additional exercises 10–13 **(pages 308–10)**

Will be doing and will have done

Study this example situation:

These people are standing in a queue to get into the cinema.

now

Half an hour from now, the cinema will be full. Everyone **will be watching** the film.

half an hour from now

Three hours from now, the cinema will be empty. The film **will have finished**. Everybody **will have gone** home.

three hours from now

I **will be doing** something (*future continuous*) = I will be in the middle of doing it:
- □ This time next week I'll be on holiday. **I'll be lying** on the beach or **swimming** in the sea.
- □ You have no chance of getting the job. You**'ll be wasting** your time if you apply for it.

Compare **will be** (do)**ing** and **will** (do):
- □ Don't phone between 7 and 8. We**'ll be having** dinner.
- □ Let's wait for Liz to arrive and then we**'ll have** dinner.

Compare **will be -ing** with other continuous forms:
- □ At 10 o'clock yesterday, Sally **was** in her office. She **was working**. *(past)*
  It's 10 o'clock now. She **is** in her office. She **is working**. *(present)*
  At 10 o'clock tomorrow, she **will be** in her office. She **will be working**.

We also use **will be -ing** in a different way: to talk about complete actions in the future.
For example:
- □ The government **will be making** a statement about the crisis later today.
- □ **Will** you **be going** away this summer?
- □ Later in the programme, **I'll be talking** to the Minister of Education …
- □ Our best player is injured and **won't be playing** in the game on Saturday.

Later in the programme I'll be talking to …

In these examples **will be -ing** is similar to **(be) going to** … .

We use **will have** (**done**) (*future perfect*) to say that something will already be complete before a time in the future. For example:
- □ Sally always leaves for work at 8.30 in the morning. She won't be at home at 9 o'clock – she**'ll have gone** to work.
- □ We're late. The film **will** already **have started** by the time we get to the cinema.

Compare **will have** (done) with other perfect forms:
- □ Ted and Amy **have been** married for 24 years. *(present perfect)*
  Next year they **will have been** married for 25 years.
  When their son was born, they **had been** married for three years. *(past perfect)*

Exercises

24.1 Read about Colin. Then tick (✓) the sentences which are true. In each group of sentences at least one is true.

Colin goes to work every day. He leaves home at 8 o'clock and arrives at work at about 8.45. He starts work immediately and continues until 12.30 when he has lunch (which takes about half an hour). He starts work again at 1.15 and goes home at exactly 4.30. Every day he follows the same routine and tomorrow will be no exception.

1 **At 7.45**
   a he'll be leaving the house
   b he'll have left the house
   c he'll be at home ✓
   d he'll be having breakfast ✓

4 **At 12.45**
   a he'll have lunch
   b he'll be having lunch
   c he'll have finished his lunch
   d he'll have started his lunch

2 **At 8.15**
   a he'll be leaving the house
   b he'll have left the house
   c he'll have arrived at work
   d he'll be arriving at work

5  **At 4 o'clock**
   a he'll have finished work
   b he'll finish work
   c he'll be working
   d he won't have finished work

3  **At 9.15**
   a he'll be working
   b he'll start work
   c he'll have started work
   d he'll be arriving at work

6 **At 4.45**
   a he'll leave work
   b he'll be leaving work
   c he'll have left work
   d he'll have arrived home

24.2 Put the verb into the correct form, **will be (do)ing** or **will have (done)**.

1 Don't phone between 7 and 8. _We'll be having_ (we / have) dinner then.
2 Phone me after 8 o'clock. .... (we / finish) dinner by then.
3 Tomorrow afternoon we're going to play tennis from 3 o'clock until 4.30. So at 4 o'clock, ... (we / play) tennis.
4 A: Can we meet tomorrow?
  B: Yes, but not in the afternoon. .... (I / work).
5 *B has to go to a meeting which begins at 10 o'clock. It will last about an hour.*
  A: Will you be free at 11.30?
  B: Yes, ... (the meeting / end) by then.
6 Ben is on holiday and he is spending his money very quickly. If he continues like this, ... (he / spend) all his money before the end of his holiday.
7 Do you think .... (you / still / do) the same job in ten years' time?
8 Lisa is from New Zealand. She is travelling around Europe at the moment. So far she has travelled about 1,000 miles. By the end of the trip, ... (she / travel) more than 3,000 miles.
9 If you need to contact me, ... (I / stay) at the Lion Hotel until Friday.
10 A: .... (you / see) Laura tomorrow?
  B: Yes, probably. Why?
  A: I borrowed this CD from her. Can you give it back to her?

A   Study this example:

Will you phone me tomorrow?

Yes, I'll phone you **when I get** home from work.

'I'll phone you when I get home' is a sentence with two parts:

  the main part: 'I'll phone you'
and   *the* **when-***part:*   'when I get home'

The time in the sentence is future ('tomorrow'), but we use a *present* tense (I **get**) in the **when**-part of the sentence.

We do *not* use **will** in the **when**-part of the sentence.

Some more examples:

- We'**ll go** out **when** it **stops** raining. (*not* when it will stop)
- **When** you **are** in London again, come and see us. (*not* When you will be)
- (*said to a child*) What do you want to be **when** you **grow** up? (*not* will grow)

The same thing happens after **while / before / after / as soon as / until** or **till**:

- I'm going to read a lot **while I'm** on holiday. (*not* while I will be)
- I'll probably go back home on Sunday. **Before I go**, I'd like to visit the museum.
- Wait here **until** (*or* **till**) **I come** back.

B   You can also use the present perfect (**have done**) after **when / after / until / as soon as**:

- Can I borrow that book **when** you'**ve finished** with it?
- Don't say anything while Ian is here. Wait **until** he **has gone**.

If you use the present perfect, one thing must be complete *before* the other (so the two things do *not* happen together):

- **When I've phoned** Kate, we can have dinner.
  (= First I'll phone Kate and *after that* we can have dinner.)

Do not use the present perfect if the two things happen together:

- **When I phone** Kate, I'll ask her about the party. (*not* When I've phoned)

It is often possible to use either the present simple or the present perfect:

- I'll come **as soon as I finish**.   *or*   I'll come **as soon as I've finished**.
- You'll feel better **after** you **have**   *or*   You'll feel better **after** you'**ve had**
  something to eat   something to eat.

C   After **if**, we normally use the present simple (**if I do / if I see** etc.) for the future:

- It's raining hard. We'll get wet **if** we **go** out. (*not* if we will go)
- I'll be angry **if** it **happens** again. (*not* if it will happen)
- Hurry up! **If** we **don't hurry**, we'll be late.

D   Compare **when** and **if**:

We use **when** for things which are *sure* to happen:

- I'm going shopping later. (for sure)   **When** I go shopping, I'll buy some food.

We use **if** (*not* when) for things that will *possibly* happen:

- I might go shopping later. (it's possible)   **If** I go shopping, I'll buy some food.
- **If** it is raining this evening, I won't go out. (*not* When it is raining)
- Don't worry **if** I'm late tonight. (*not* when I'm late)
- **If** they don't come soon, I'm not going to wait. (*not* When they don't come)

Exercises

25.1 Complete the sentences using the verbs in brackets. All the sentences are about the future.
Use **will/won't** or the present simple (**I see** / **he plays** / **it is** etc.).

1 I .....'ll phone..... (phone) you when I .....get..... (get) home from work.
2 I want to see Julia before she .... (go) out.
3 We're going on holiday tomorrow. I .... (tell) you all about it when we
.... (come) back.
4 Brian looks very different now. When you .... (see) him again, you
.... (not / recognise) him.
5 .... (you / be) lonely without me while I .... (be) away?
6 We must do something soon before it .... (be) too late.
7 I don't want to go without you. I .... (wait) until you ....
(be) ready.
8 Sue has applied for the job, but she isn't very well-qualified for it. I ....
(be) surprised if she .... (get) it.
9 I hope to play tennis tomorrow if the weather .... (be) nice.
10 I'm going out now. If anybody .... (phone) while I .... (be)
out, can you take a message?

25.2 Make one sentence from two.

1 It will stop raining soon. Then we'll go out.
.....We'll go out..... when .....it stops raining......
2 I'll find somewhere to live. Then I'll give you my address.
I .... when ....
3 I'll do the shopping. Then I'll come straight back home.
.... after ....
4 It's going to get dark. Let's go home before that.
.... before ....
5 She must apologise to me first. I won't speak to her until then.
.... until ....

25.3 Read the situations and complete the sentences.

1 A friend of yours is going on holiday. You want to know what she is going to do.
You ask: What are you going to do when .....you are on holiday.. ?
2 A friend of yours is visiting you. She has to go soon but maybe there's time for some more coffee.
You ask: Would you like some more coffee before .... ?
3 You want to sell your car. Jim is interested in buying it, but he hasn't decided yet.
You ask: Can you let me know as soon as .... ?
4 Your friends are going to New York soon. You want to know where they're going to stay.
You ask: Where are you going to stay when .... ?
5 The traffic is very bad in your town, but they are building a new road at the moment.
You say: I think things will be better when they ....

25.4 Put in **when** or **if**.

1 Don't worry .....if..... I'm late tonight.
2 Tom might phone while I'm out this evening. .... he does, can you take a message?
3 I'm going to Rome next week. .... I'm there, I hope to visit a friend of mine.
4 I think Jill will get the job. I'll be very surprised .... she doesn't get it.
5 I'm going shopping. .... you want anything, I can get it for you.
6 I'm going away for a few days. I'll phone you .... I get back.
7 I want you to come to the party, but .... you don't want to come, that's all right.
8 We can eat at home or, ... you prefer, we can go to a restaurant.

→ Additional exercises 12–15 (**pages 309–11**), 32 (**page 321**)

Can, could and (be) able to

A We use **can** to say that something is possible or allowed, or that somebody has the ability to do something. We use **can** + *infinitive* (**can do** / **can see** etc.):

- ☐ We **can see** the lake from our bedroom window.
- ☐ 'I haven't got a pen.' 'You **can use** mine.'
- ☐ **Can** you **speak** any foreign languages?
- ☐ I **can come** and see you tomorrow if you like.
- ☐ The word 'play' **can be** a noun or a verb.

The negative is **can't** (= **cannot**):

- ☐ I'm afraid I **can't come** to the party on Friday.

B You can say that somebody **is able to** do something, but **can** is more usual:

- ☐ We **are able to see** the lake from our bedroom window.

But **can** has only two forms: **can** (*present*) and **could** (*past*). So sometimes it is necessary to use **(be) able to**. Compare:

☐ I **can't** sleep.	☐ I **haven't been able to** sleep recently.
☐ Tom **can** come tomorrow.	☐ Tom **might be able to** come tomorrow.
☐ Maria **can** speak French, Spanish and English.	☐ Applicants for the job **must be able to** speak two foreign languages.

C Could

Sometimes **could** is the past of **can**. We use **could** especially with:

see   hear   smell   taste   feel   remember   understand

- ☐ We had a lovely room in the hotel. We **could see** the lake.
- ☐ As soon as I walked into the room, I **could smell** gas.
- ☐ I was sitting at the back of the theatre and **couldn't hear** very well.

We also use **could** to say that somebody had the general ability or permission to do something:

- ☐ My grandfather **could speak** five languages.
- ☐ We were totally free. We **could do** what we wanted. (= we were allowed to do)

D Could and was able to

We use **could** for *general* ability. But if you want to say that somebody did something in a specific situation, use **was/were able to** or **managed to** (*not* **could**):

- ☐ The fire spread through the building very quickly, but fortunately everybody **was able to escape** / **managed to escape**. (*not* could escape)
- ☐ We didn't know where David was, but we **managed to find** / **were able to find** him in the end. (*not* could find)

Compare:

- ☐ Mike was an excellent tennis player when he was younger. He **could beat** anybody.
  (= he had the general ability to beat anybody)
- *but*   Mike and Pete played tennis yesterday. Pete played very well, but Mike **managed to beat** him. (= he managed to beat him in this particular game)

The negative **couldn't** (**could not**) is possible in all situations:

- ☐ My grandfather **couldn't swim**.
- ☐ We looked for David everywhere, but we **couldn't find** him.
- ☐ Pete played well, but he **couldn't beat** Mike.

26.1 Complete the sentences using **can** or **(be) able to**. Use **can** if possible; otherwise use **(be) able to.**

1 Gary has travelled a lot. He ....*can*.... speak five languages.
2 I haven't ...*been able to*... sleep very well recently.
3 Nicole .... drive, but she hasn't got a car.
4 I used to .... stand on my head, but I can't do it now.
5 I can't understand Martin. I've never .... understand him.
6 I can't see you on Friday, but I .... meet you on Saturday morning.
7 Ask Catherine about your problem. She might .... help you.

26.2 Write sentences about yourself using the ideas in brackets.

1 (something you used to be able to do)
  I used to be able to sing well.
2 (something you used to be able to do)
  I used ....
3 (something you would like to be able to do)
  I'd ....
4 (something you have never been able to do)
  I've ....

26.3 Complete the sentences with **can/can't/could/couldn't** + the following:

~~come~~   eat   hear   run   sleep   wait

1 I'm afraid I ...*can't come*... to your party next week.
2 When Tim was 16, he .... 100 metres in 11 seconds.
3 'Are you in a hurry?' 'No, I've got plenty of time. I ....'
4 I was feeling sick yesterday. I .... anything.
5 Can you speak a little louder? I .... you very well.
6 'You look tired.' 'Yes, I .... last night.'

26.4 Complete the answers to the questions with **was/were able to** ... .

1 A: Did everybody escape from the fire?
  B: Yes, although the fire spread quickly, everybody ...*was able to escape*........................ .
2 A: Did you finish your work this afternoon?
  B: Yes, there was nobody to disturb me, so I ....
3 A: Did you have difficulty finding our house?
  B: Not really. Your directions were good and we ....
4 A: Did the thief get away?
  B: Yes. No-one realised what was happening and the thief ....

26.5 Complete the sentences using **could, couldn't** or **managed to.**

1 My grandfather travelled a lot. He ...*could*... speak five languages.
2 I looked everywhere for the book, but I ...*couldn't*... find it.
3 They didn't want to come with us at first, but we ...*managed to*... persuade them.
4 Laura had hurt her leg and .... walk very well.
5 Sue wasn't at home when I phoned, but I .... contact her at her office.
6 I looked very carefully and I .... see somebody in the distance.
7 I wanted to buy some tomatoes. The first shop I went to didn't have any, but I
  .... get some in the next shop.
8 My grandmother loved music. She .... play the piano very well.
9 A girl fell into the river, but fortunately we .... rescue her.
10 I had forgotten to bring my camera, so I .... take any photographs.

Could (do) and could have (done)

A

We use **could** in a number of ways. Sometimes **could** is the past of **can** (see Unit 26):

- ☐ Listen. I **can hear** something. *(now)*
- ☐ I listened. I **could hear** something. *(past)*

But **could** is not only used in this way. We also use **could** to talk about possible actions *now* or *in the future* (especially to make suggestions).
For example:

- ☐ A: What shall we do this evening?
  - B: We **could go** to the cinema.
- ☐ A: When you go to Paris next month, you **could stay** with Julia.
  - B: Yes, I suppose I **could**.

> What shall we do this evening?

> We **could go** to the cinema.

Can is also possible in these sentences ('We **can** go to the cinema.' etc.). With **could**, the suggestion is less sure.

B

We also use **could** (*not* **can**) for actions which are not realistic. For example:

- ☐ I'm so tired, I **could sleep** for a week. (*not* I can sleep for a week)

Compare **can** and **could**:

- ☐ I **can stay** with Julia when I go to Paris. (realistic)
- ☐ Maybe I **could stay** with Julia when I go to Paris. (possible, but less sure)
- ☐ This is a wonderful place. I **could stay** here for ever. (unrealistic)

C

We also use **could** (*not* **can**) to say that something is possible now or in the future. The meaning is similar to **might** or **may** (see Unit 29):

- ☐ The story **could be** true, but I don't think it is. (*not* can be true)
- ☐ I don't know what time Liz is coming. She **could get** here at any time.

D

We use **could have** (done) to talk about the past. Compare:

- ☐ I'm so tired, I **could sleep** for a week. *(now)*
  I was so tired, I **could have slept** for a week. *(past)*
- ☐ The situation is bad, but it **could be** worse. *(now)*
  The situation was bad, but it **could have been** worse. *(past)*

Something **could have** happened = it was possible but did *not* happen:

- ☐ Why did you stay at a hotel when you were in Paris? You **could have stayed** with Julia. (you didn't stay with her)
- ☐ I didn't know that you wanted to go to the concert. I **could have got** you a ticket. (I didn't get you a ticket)
- ☐ Dave was lucky. He **could have hurt** himself when he fell, but he's OK.

E

We use **couldn't** to say that something would not be possible now:

- ☐ I **couldn't live** in a big city. I'd hate it. (= it wouldn't be possible for me)
- ☐ Everything is fine right now. Things **couldn't be** better.

For the past we use **couldn't have** (done):

- ☐ We had a really good holiday. It **couldn't have been** better.
- ☐ The trip was cancelled last week. Paul **couldn't have gone** anyway because he was ill. (= it would not have been possible for him to go)

Couldn't have (done) → Unit 28B   **Could and might** → Unit 29C   **Could I/you ... ?** → Unit 37
Could with if → Units 38C, 39E, 40D   **Modal verbs (can/could/will/would etc.)** → Appendix 4

27.1 Answer the questions with a suggestion. Use **could**.

1 Where shall we go for our holidays?
2 What shall we have for dinner tonight?
3 When shall I phone Angela?
4 What shall I give Ann for her birthday?
5 Where shall we hang this picture?

(to Scotland) _We could go to Scotland._
(fish) We ....
(now) You ....
(a book) ....
(in the kitchen) ....

27.2 In some of these sentences, you need **could** (not **can**). Change the sentences where necessary.

1 The story can be true, but I don't think it is.   _could be true_
2 It's a nice day. We can go for a walk.   _OK (could go is also possible)_
3 I'm so angry with him. I can kill him!
4 If you're hungry, we can have dinner now.
5 It's so nice here. I can stay here all day, but unfortunately I have to go.
6 A: Where's my bag. Have you seen it?
   B: No, but it can be in the car.
7 Peter is a keen musician. He plays the flute and he can also play the piano.
8 A: I need to borrow a camera.
   B: You can borrow mine.
9 The weather is nice now, but it can change later.

27.3 Complete the sentences. Use **could** or **could have** + a suitable verb.

1 A: What shall we do this evening?
   B: I don't mind. We _could go_ to the cinema.
2 A: I had a very boring evening at home yesterday.
   B: Why did you stay at home? You .... out with us.
3 A: There's an interesting job advertised in the paper. You .... for it.
   B: What sort of job? Show me the advertisement.
4 A: How was your exam? Was it difficult?
   B: It wasn't so bad. It .... worse.
5 A: I got very wet walking home in the rain last night.
   B: Why did you walk? You .... a taxi.
6 A: Where shall we meet tomorrow?
   B: Well, I .... to your house if you like.

27.4 Complete the sentences. Use **couldn't** or **couldn't have** + these verbs (in the correct form):

~~be~~   be   come   find   get   ~~live~~   wear

1 I _couldn't live_ in a big city. I'd hate it.
2 We had a really good holiday. It _couldn't have been_ better.
3 I .... that hat. I'd look silly and people would laugh at me.
4 We managed to find the restaurant you recommended, but we .... it without the map that you drew for us.
5 Paul has to get up at 4 o'clock every morning. I don't know how he does it. I .... up at that time every day.
6 The staff at the hotel were really nice when we stayed there last summer. They .... more helpful.
7 A: I tried to phone you last week. We had a party and I wanted to invite you.
   B: That was nice of you, but I .... anyway. I was away all last week.

Must and can't

Study this example:

My house is very near the motorway.

It **must be** very noisy.

You can use **must** to say that you believe something is certain:

- You've been travelling all day. You **must be** tired. (Travelling is tiring and you've been travelling all day, so you **must** be tired.)
- 'Jim is a hard worker.' 'Jim? You **must be joking**. He doesn't do anything.'
- Carol **must get** very bored in her job. She does the same thing every day.
- I'm sure Sally gave me her phone number. I **must have** it somewhere.

You can use **can't** to say that you believe something is not possible:

- You've just had lunch. You **can't be** hungry already. (People are not normally hungry just after eating a meal. You've just eaten, so you **can't** be hungry.)
- They haven't lived here for very long. They **can't know** many people.

Study the structure:

I/you/he (etc.)	must can't	be (tired / hungry / at work etc.) be (doing / going / joking etc.) do / get / know / have etc.

For the past we use **must have** (**done**) and **can't have** (**done**).

Study this example:

There's nobody at home. They **must have gone** out.

Martin and Lucy are standing at the door of their friends' house.
They have rung the doorbell twice, but nobody has answered. Lucy says:

They **must have gone** out.

- I didn't hear the phone. I **must have been** asleep.
- 'I've lost one of my gloves.' 'You **must have dropped** it somewhere.'
- Sue hasn't contacted me. She **can't have got** my message.
- Tom walked into a wall. He **can't have been looking** where he was going.

Study the structure:

I/you/he (etc.)	must can't	have	been (asleep / at work etc.) been (doing / looking etc.) gone / got / known etc.

You can use **couldn't have** instead of **can't have**:

- Sue **couldn't have got** my message.
- Tom **couldn't have been looking** where he was going.

Can't ('I can't swim' etc.) → Unit 26   **Must** ('I must go' etc.) → Units 31–32
Modal verbs (can/could/will/would etc.) → Appendix 4   **American English** → Appendix 7

28.1 Put in **must** or **can't**.

1 You've been travelling all day. You ......*must*..... be tired.
2 That restaurant .... be very good. It's always full of people.
3 That restaurant .... be very good. It's always empty.
4 I'm sure I gave you the key. You .... have it. Have you looked in your bag?
5 You're going on holiday next week. You .... be looking forward to it.
6 It rained every day during their holiday, so they .... have had a very nice time.
7 Congratulations on passing your exam. You .... be very pleased.
8 You got here very quickly. You .... have walked very fast.
9 Bill and Sue always travel business class, so they .... be short of money.

28.2 Complete each sentence with a verb (one or two words) in the correct form.

1 I've lost one of my gloves. I must ....*have dropped*.... it somewhere.
2 They haven't lived here for very long. They can't ....*know*.... many people.
3 Ted isn't at work today. He must .... ill.
4 Ted wasn't at work last week. He must .... ill.
5 *(the doorbell rings)* I wonder who that is. It can't .... Mary. She's still at work at this time.
6 Sarah knows a lot about films. She must .... to the cinema a lot.
7 Look. James is putting on his hat and coat. He must .... out.
8 I left my bike outside the house last night and now it has gone. Somebody must .... it.
9 Amy was in a very difficult situation when she lost her job. It can't .... easy for her.
10 There is a man walking behind us. He has been walking behind us for the last twenty minutes. He must .... us.

28.3 Read the situations and use the words in brackets to write sentences with **must have** and **can't have**.

1 The phone rang, but I didn't hear it. (I / asleep)
....*I must have been asleep.*..

2 Sue hasn't contacted me. (she / get / my message)
....*She can't have got my message.*..

3 The jacket you bought is very good quality. (it / very expensive)
....

4 I haven't seen the people next door for ages. (they / go away)
....

5 I can't find my umbrella. (I / leave / it in the restaurant last night)
....

6 Dave, who is usually very friendly, walked past me without speaking. (he / see / me)
....

7 There was a man standing outside the café. (he / wait / for somebody)
....

8 Liz did the opposite of what I asked her to do. (she / understand / what I said)
....

9 When I got back to my car, the door was unlocked. (I / forget / to lock it)
....

10 I was woken up in the night by the noise next door. (the neighbours / have / a party)
....

11 The light was red, but the car didn't stop. (the driver / see / the red light)
....

→ Additional exercises 16–18 **(pages 311–13)**

May and might 1

A Study this example situation:

You are looking for Bob. Nobody is sure where he is, but you get some suggestions.

Where's Bob?

He **may be** in his office. (= perhaps he is in his office)

He **might be having** lunch. (= perhaps he is having lunch)

Ask Ann. She **might know**. (= perhaps she knows)

We use **may** or **might** to say that something is a possibility. Usually you can use **may** or **might**, so you can say:

- ☐ It **may** be true. *or* It **might** be true. (= perhaps it is true)
- ☐ She **might** know. *or* She **may** know.

The negative forms are **may not** and **might not** (*or* **mightn't**):

- ☐ It **may not** be true. (= perhaps it isn't true)
- ☐ She **might not** work here any more. (= perhaps she doesn't work here)

Study the structure:

I/you/he (etc.)	may might	(not)	**be** (true / in his office etc.) **be** (doing / working / having etc.) **know** / **work** / **want** etc.

B For the past we use **may have (done)** or **might have (done)**:

- ☐ A: I wonder why Kate didn't answer the phone.
  B: She **may have been** asleep. (= perhaps she was asleep)
- ☐ A: I can't find my bag anywhere.
  B: You **might have left** it in the shop. (= perhaps you left it in the shop)
- ☐ A: I was surprised that Kate wasn't at the meeting yesterday.
  B: She **might not have known** about it. (= perhaps she didn't know)
- ☐ A: I wonder why David was in such a bad mood yesterday.
  B: He **may not have been feeling** well. (= perhaps he wasn't feeling well)

Study the structure:

I/you/he (etc.)	may might	(not) have	**been** (asleep / at home etc.) **been** (doing / working / feeling etc.) **known** / **had** / **wanted** / **left** etc.

C Could is similar to **may** and **might**:

- ☐ It's a strange story, but it **could be** true. (= it may/might be true)
- ☐ You **could have left** your bag in the shop. (= you may/might have left it)

But **couldn't** (*negative*) is different from **may not** and **might not**. Compare:

- ☐ Sarah **couldn't have** got my message. Otherwise she would have replied.
  (= it is not possible that she got my message)
- ☐ I wonder why Sarah hasn't replied to my message. I suppose she **might not have** got it.
  (= perhaps she didn't get it, and perhaps she did)

Could → Unit 27 **May/might 2** → Unit 30 **May I … ?** → Unit 37C **Might with if** → Units 30B, 38C, 40D
Modal verbs (can/could/will/would etc.) → Appendix 4

29.1 Write these sentences in a different way using **might**.

1 Perhaps Helen is in her office.   _She might be in her office._
2 Perhaps Helen is busy.   ....
3 Perhaps she is working.   ....
4 Perhaps she wants to be alone.   ....
5 Perhaps she was ill yesterday.   ....
6 Perhaps she went home early.   ....
7 Perhaps she had to go home early.   ....
8 Perhaps she was working yesterday.   ....

In sentences 9–11 use **might not**.

9   Perhaps she doesn't want to see me.   ....
10 Perhaps she isn't working today.   ....
11 Perhaps she wasn't feeling well yesterday. ....

29.2 Complete each sentence with a verb in the correct form.

1 'Where's Sam?' 'I'm not sure. He might ....._be having_.... lunch.'
2 'Who is that man with Emily?' 'I'm not sure. It might .... her brother.'
3 A: Who was the man we saw with Anna yesterday?
   B: I'm not sure. It may .... her brother.
4 A: What are those people doing by the side of the road?
   B: I don't know. They might .... for a bus.
5 'Do you have a stamp?' 'No, but ask Simon. He may .... one.'

29.3 Read the situation and make sentences from the words in brackets. Use **might**.

1 I can't find Jeff anywhere. I wonder where he is.
   a (he / go / shopping) ..._He might have gone shopping._.............................
   b (he / play / tennis) ..._He might be playing tennis._..............................
2 I'm looking for Sarah. Do you know where she is?
   a (she / watch / TV / in her room) ....
   b (she / go / out) ....
3 I can't find my umbrella. Have you seen it?
   a (it / be / in the car) ....
   b (you / leave / in the restaurant last night) ....
4 Why didn't Dave answer the doorbell? I'm sure he was at home at the time.
   a (he / go / to bed early) ....
   b (he / not / hear / the doorbell) ....
   c (he / be / in the shower) ....

29.4 Complete the sentences using **might not have …** or **couldn't have …** .

1 A: Do you think Sarah got the message we sent her?
   B: No, she would have contacted us. _She couldn't have got it_ ....
2 A: I was surprised Kate wasn't at the meeting. Perhaps she didn't know about it.
   B: That's possible. _She might not have known about it_ ....
3 A: I wonder why they never replied to our letter. Do you think they received it?
   B: Maybe not. They ....
4 A: I wonder how the fire started. Was it an accident?
   B: No, the police say it ....
5 A: Mike says he needs to see you. He tried to find you yesterday.
   B: Well, he .... very hard. I was in my office all day.
6 A: The man you spoke to – are you sure he was American?
   B: No, I'm not sure. He ....

May and might 2

A We use **may** and **might** to talk about possible actions or happenings in the future:

- ☐ I haven't decided yet where to go for my holidays. I **may go** to Ireland. (= perhaps I will go there)
- ☐ Take an umbrella with you. It **might rain** later. (= perhaps it will rain)
- ☐ The bus isn't always on time. We **might have** to wait a few minutes. (= perhaps we will have to wait)

The negative forms are **may not** and **might not** (**mightn't**):

- ☐ Liz **may not go** out tonight. She isn't feeling well. (= perhaps she will not go out)
- ☐ There **might not be** enough time to discuss everything at the meeting. (= perhaps there will not be enough time)

Compare **will** and **may/might**:

- ☐ **I'll be** late this evening. (for sure)
- ☐ I **may/might** be late this evening. (possible)

B Usually you can use **may** or **might**. So you can say:

- ☐ I **may go** to Ireland.   *or*   I **might go** to Ireland.
- ☐ Jane **might be** able to help you.   *or*   Jane **may be** able to help you.

But we use only **might** (*not* **may**) when the situation is *not real*:

- ☐ If I were in Tom's position, I **might** look for another job.

The situation here is not real because I am *not* in Tom's position (so I'm not going to look for another job). **May** is not possible in this example.

C There is also a continuous form: **may/might be -ing**. Compare this with **will be -ing**:

- ☐ Don't phone at 8.30. **I'll be watching** the film on television.
- ☐ Don't phone at 8.30. I **might be watching** (*or* I **may be watching**) the film on television. (= perhaps I'll be watching it)

We also use **may/might be -ing** for possible plans. Compare:

- ☐ **I'm going** to Ireland in July. (for sure)
- ☐ I **may be going** (*or* I **might be going**) to Ireland in July. (possible)

But you can also say 'I **may go** (*or* I **might go**) ...' with little difference in meaning.

D **Might as well**

Rose and Clare have just missed the bus. The buses run every hour.

> What shall we do? Shall we walk?

> We **might as well**. It's a nice day and I don't want to wait here for an hour.

We **might as well** do something = We should do it because there is no better alternative. There is no reason not to do it.

May as well is also possible.

- ☐ A: What time are you going out?
  B: Well, I'm ready, so I **might as well go** now.
- ☐ Buses are so expensive these days, you **may as well get** a taxi. (= taxis are as good, no more expensive)

30.1 Write sentences with **might**.

1 Where are you going for your holidays? (to Ireland???)
I haven't decided yet. *I might go to Ireland.*
2 What sort of car are you going to buy? (a Mercedes???)
I'm not sure yet. I ....
3 What are you doing this weekend? (go to London???)
I haven't decided yet. ....
4 When is Tom coming to see us? (on Saturday???)
He hasn't said yet. ....
5 Where are you going to hang that picture? (in the dining room???)
I haven't made up my mind yet. ....
6 What is Julia going to do when she leaves school? (go to university???)
She's still thinking about it. ....

30.2 Complete the sentences using **might** + the following:

bite   break   need   ~~rain~~   slip   wake

1 Take an umbrella with you when you go out. It ....*might rain*........ later.
2 Don't make too much noise. You .... the baby.
3 Be careful of that dog. It .... you.
4 I don't think we should throw that letter away. We .... it later.
5 Be careful. The footpath is very icy. You ....
6 Don't let the children play in this room. They .... something.

30.3 Complete the sentences using **might be able to** or **might have to** + a suitable verb.

1 I can't help you, but why don't you ask Jane? She ....*might be able to help*........ you.
2 I can't meet you this evening, but I .... you tomorrow.
3 I'm not working on Saturday, but I .... on Sunday.
4 I can come to the meeting, but I .... before the end.

30.4 Write sentences with **might not**.

1 I'm not sure that Liz will come to the party.
Liz might not come to the party.
2 I'm not sure that I'll go out this evening.
I ....
3 I'm not sure that we'll get tickets for the concert.
We ....
4 I'm not sure that Sue will be able to come out with us this evening.
....

30.5 Read the situations and make sentences with **might as well**.

1 You and a friend have just missed the bus. The buses run every hour.
You say: We'll have to wait an hour for the next bus. *We might as well walk.*
2 You have a free ticket for a concert. You're not very keen on the concert, but you decide to go.
You say: I .... to the concert. It's a pity to waste a free ticket.
3 You've just painted your kitchen. You still have a lot of paint, so why not paint the bathroom too?
You say: We .... There's plenty of paint left.
4 You and a friend are at home. You're bored. There's a film on TV starting in a few minutes.
You say: .... There's nothing else to do.

Have to and must

A

I **have to** do something = it is necessary to do it, I am obliged to do it:

- □ You can't turn right here. You **have to turn** left.
- □ I **have to wear** glasses for reading.
- □ George can't come out with us this evening. He **has to work** late.
- □ Last week Tina broke her arm and **had to go** to hospital.
- □ I haven't **had to go** to the doctor for ages.

> You **have to turn** left here.

We use **do/does/did** in questions and negative sentences (for the present and past simple):

- □ What **do I have to do** to get a new driving licence? (*not* What have I to do?)
- □ Karen **doesn't have to work** Saturdays. (*not* Karen hasn't to)
- □ Why **did** you **have to leave** early?

You can use **have to** with **will** and **might/may**:

- □ If the pain gets worse, you'**ll have to go** to the doctor.
- □ I **might have to work** late tomorrow evening. *or* I **may have to work** …
  (= it's possible that I will have to)

B

Must is similar to **have to**:

- □ It's later than I thought. I **must go**. *or* I **have to go**.

You can use **must** to give your own opinion (for example, to say what *you* think is necessary, or to recommend someone to do something). **Have to** is also possible:

- □ I haven't spoken to Sue for ages. I **must phone** her. (= I say this is necessary)
- □ Mark is a really nice person. You **must meet** him. (I recommend this)

We use **have to** (*not* must) to say what someone is *obliged* to do. The speaker is not giving his/her own opinion:

- □ I **have to work** from 8.30 to 5.30 every day. (a fact, not an opinion)
- □ Jane **has to travel** a lot for her work.

But **must** is often used in written rules and instructions:

- □ Applications for the job **must be received** by 18 May.
- □ *(exam instruction)* You **must write** your answers in ink.

You cannot use **must** to talk about the past:

- □ We **had** to leave early. (*not* we must)

C

Mustn't and **don't have to** are completely different:

You **mustn't** do something = it is necessary that you do *not* do it (so don't do it):	You **don't have to** do something = you don't need to do it (but you can if you want):
□ You **must keep** it a secret. You **mustn't tell** anyone. (= don't tell anyone)	□ You **don't have to tell** him, but you can if you want to.
□ I promised I would be on time. I **mustn't be** late. (= I must be on time)	□ I **don't have to be** at the meeting, but I think I'll go anyway.

D

You can use **have got to** instead of **have to**. So you can say:

- □ I'**ve got to** work tomorrow.   *or*   I **have to** work tomorrow.
- □ When **has** Liz **got to** go?   *or*   When **does** Liz **have to** go?

31.1 Complete the sentences with **have to / has to / had to.**

1 Bill starts work at 5 a.m. <u>He has to get up</u> at four. (he / get up)
2 'I broke my arm last week.' '<u>Did you have to go</u> to hospital?' (you / go)
3 There was a lot of noise from the street. .... the window.
   (we / close)
4 Karen can't stay for the whole meeting. .... early. (she / leave)
5 How old .... to drive in your country? (you / be)
6 I don't have much time. .... (I / hurry)
7 How is Paul enjoying his new job? .... a lot? (he / travel)
8 'I'm afraid I can't stay long.' 'What time .... ?' (you / go)
9 'The bus was late again.' 'How long .... ?' (you / wait)
10 There was nobody to help me. I .... everything by myself. (I / do)

31.2 Complete the sentences using **have to** + the verbs in the list. Some sentences are positive
(**I have to ...** etc.) and some are negative (**I don't have to ...** etc.):

   ask   do   drive   ~~get up~~   go   make   make   pay   ~~show~~

1 I'm not working tomorrow, so I <u>don't have to get up</u> early.
2 Steve didn't know how to use the computer, so I <u>had to show</u> him.
3 Excuse me a moment – I .... a phone call. I won't be long.
4 I'm not so busy. I have a few things to do, but I .... them now.
5 I couldn't find the street I wanted. I .... somebody for directions.
6 The car park is free. You .... to park your car there.
7 A man was injured in the accident, but he .... to hospital because it
   wasn't serious.
8 Sue has a senior position in the company. She .... important decisions.
9 When Patrick starts his new job next month, he .... 50 miles to
   work every day.

31.3 In some of these sentences, **must** is wrong or unnatural. Correct the sentences where necessary.

1 It's later than I thought. I must go.   <u>OK (have to *is also correct*)</u>
2 I must work every day from 8.30 to 5.30.   <u>I have to work</u>
3 You must come and see us again soon.   ....
4 Tom can't meet us tomorrow. He must work.   ....
5 I must work late yesterday evening.   ....
6 I must get up early tomorrow. I have lots to do. ....
7 Julia wears glasses. She must wear glasses   ....
   since she was very young.

31.4 Complete the sentences with **mustn't** or **don't/doesn't have to.**

1 I don't want anyone to know about our plan. You <u>mustn't</u> tell anyone.
2 Richard <u>doesn't have to</u> wear a suit to work, but he usually does.
3 I can stay in bed tomorrow morning because I .... go to work.
4 Whatever you do, you .... touch that switch. It's very dangerous.
5 There's a lift in the building, so we .... climb the stairs.
6 You .... forget what I told you. It's very important.
7 Sue .... get up early, but she usually does.
8 Don't make so much noise. We .... wake the children.
9 I .... eat too much. I'm supposed to be on a diet.
10 You .... be a good player to enjoy a game of tennis.

→ Additional exercise 16 (page 311)

Must   mustn't   needn't

A   Must   mustn't   needn't

You **must** do something = it is necessary that you do it:
- □ Don't tell anybody what I said. You **must** keep it a secret.
- □ We haven't got much time. We **must** hurry.

You **mustn't** do something = it is necessary that you do *not* do it (so don't do it):
- □ You **must** keep it a secret. You **mustn't** tell anybody else. (= don't tell anybody else)
- □ We **must** be very quiet. We **mustn't** make any noise.

You **needn't** do something = you don't need to do it (but you can if you like):
- □ You can come with me if you like, but you **needn't come** if you don't want to. (= it is not necessary for you to come)
- □ We've got plenty of time. We **needn't hurry**. (= it is not necessary to hurry)

B

Instead of **needn't**, you can use **don't/doesn't need to**. So you can say:
- □ We **needn't** hurry.   *or*   We **don't need to** hurry.

Remember that we say **don't need to do**, but **needn't do** (*without* **to**).

C   Needn't have (done)

Study this example situation:

I think it's going to rain. I'll take the umbrella.

I **needn't have brought** the umbrella.

later

Paul had to go out. He thought it was going to rain, so he took the umbrella.

But it didn't rain, so the umbrella was not necessary. So he **needn't have taken** it.

He **needn't have taken** the umbrella = He took the umbrella, but this was not necessary.

Compare **needn't** (do) and **needn't have** (done):
- □ Everything will be OK. You **needn't worry**. (it's not necessary)
- □ Everything was OK. You **needn't have worried**. (you worried, but it was not necessary)

D   Didn't need to (do) and needn't have (done)

I **didn't need to** … = it was not necessary for me to … (and I knew this at the time):
- □ I **didn't need to** get up early, so I didn't.
- □ I **didn't need to** get up early, but it was a lovely morning, so I did.

I **didn't have to** … is also possible in these examples.

I **needn't have done** something = I did it, but *now I know* that it was not necessary:
- □ I got up very early because I had to get ready to go away. But in fact it didn't take me long to get ready. So, I **needn't have got** up so early. I could have stayed in bed longer.

Must ('You must be tired') → Unit 28   **Have to and must** → Unit 31
Modal verbs **(can/could/will/would etc.)** → Appendix 4   **American English** → Appendix 7

32.1 Complete the sentences using **needn't** + the following verbs:

     ask   come   explain   ~~leave~~   tell   walk

1 We've got plenty of time. We ..._needn't leave_... yet.
2 I can manage the shopping alone. You .... with me.
3 We .... all the way home. We can get a taxi.
4 Just help yourself if you'd like more to eat. You .... first.
5 We can keep this a secret between ourselves. We .... anybody else.
6 I understand the situation perfectly. You .... further.

32.2 Complete the sentences with **must**, **mustn't** or **needn't**.

1 We haven't got much time. We ..._must_... hurry.
2 We've got plenty of time. We ..._needn't_... hurry.
3 We have enough food at home, so we .... go shopping today.
4 Gary gave me a letter to post. I .... remember to post it.
5 Gary gave me a letter to post. I .... forget to post it.
6 There's plenty of time for you to make up your mind. You .... decide now.
7 You .... wash those tomatoes. They've already been washed.
8 This is a valuable book. You .... look after it carefully and you .... lose it.
9 A: What sort of house do you want to buy? Something big?
   B: Well, it .... be big – that's not so important. But it .... have a nice garden – that's essential.

32.3 Read the situations and make sentences with **needn't have**.

1 Paul went out. He took an umbrella because he thought it was going to rain. But it didn't rain.
   He needn't have taken an umbrella.
2 Linda bought some eggs when she went shopping. When she got home, she found that she already had plenty of eggs. She ....
3 A colleague got angry with you at work. He shouted at you, which you think was unnecessary. Later you say to him: You ....
4 Brian had money problems, so he sold his car. A few days later he won some money in a lottery. He ....
5 We took a camcorder with us on holiday, but we didn't use it in the end. We ....
6 I thought I was going to miss my train, so I rushed to the station. But the train was late and in the end I had to wait twenty minutes. ....

32.4 Write two sentences for each situation. Use **needn't have** in the first sentence and **could have** in the second (as in the example). For **could have**, see Unit 27.

1 Why did you rush? Why didn't you take your time?
   You needn't have rushed. You could have taken your time.
2 Why did you walk home? Why didn't you take a taxi?
   ....
3 Why did you stay at a hotel? Why didn't you stay with us?
   ....
4 Why did she phone me in the middle of the night? Why didn't she wait until the morning?
   ....
5 Why did you leave without saying anything? Why didn't you say goodbye?
   ....

Should 1

A

You **should do** something = it is a good thing to do or the right thing to do. You can use **should** to give advice or to give an opinion:

- ☐ You look tired. You **should go** to bed.
- ☐ The government **should do** more to reduce crime.
- ☐ 'Should we invite Susan to the party?'   'Yes, I think we **should.**'

We often use **should** with **I think / I don't think / Do you think … ?:**

- ☐ **I think** the government **should do** more to reduce crime.
- ☐ **I don't think** you **should work** so hard.
- ☐ **'Do you think** I **should apply** for this job?'   'Yes, **I think you should.**'

You **shouldn't** do something = it isn't a good thing to do:

- ☐ You **shouldn't believe** everything you read in the newspapers.

Should is not as strong as **must** or **have to:**

- ☐ You **should** apologise.   (= it would be a good thing to do)
- ☐ You **must** apologise. / You **have to** apologise.   (= you have no alternative)

B

You can use **should** when something is not right or what you expect:

- ☐ I wonder where Tina is. She **should be** here by now.
  (= she isn't here yet, and this is not normal)
- ☐ The price on this packet is wrong. It **should be** £2.50, not £3.50.
- ☐ That man on the motorbike **should be wearing** a helmet.

We also use **should** to say that we expect something to happen:

- ☐ She's been studying hard for the exam, so she **should pass.**   (= I expect her to pass)
- ☐ There are plenty of hotels in the town. It **shouldn't be** difficult to find somewhere to stay.
  (= I don't expect it to be difficult)

C

You **should have done** something = you didn't do it, but it would have been the right thing to do:

- ☐ You missed a great party last night. You **should have come.** Why didn't you?
  (= you didn't come, but it would have been good to come)
- ☐ I wonder why they're so late. They **should have arrived** long ago.

You **shouldn't have done** something = you did it, but it was the wrong thing to do:

- ☐ I'm feeling sick. I **shouldn't have eaten** so much.   (= I ate too much)
- ☐ She **shouldn't have been listening** to our conversation. It was private.
  (= she was listening)

Compare **should** (do) and **should have** (done):

- ☐ You look tired. You **should go** to bed now.
- ☐ You went to bed very late last night. You **should have gone** to bed earlier.

D

Ought to …

You can use **ought to** instead of **should** in the sentences on this page. We say 'ought **to** do' (with **to**):

- ☐ Do you think I **ought to apply** for this job?   (= Do you think I **should apply** … ?)
- ☐ Jack **ought not to go** to bed so late.   (= Jack **shouldn't go** …)
- ☐ It was a great party last night. You **ought to have come.**
- ☐ She's been studying hard for the exam, so she **ought to pass.**

33.1 For each situation, write a sentence with **should** or **shouldn't** + the following:

~~go away for a few days~~   go to bed so late   look for another job
put some pictures on the walls   take a photograph   use her car so much

1 Liz needs a change.   _She should go away for a few days._
2 Your salary is very low.   You ....
3 Jack always has difficulty getting up.   He ....
4 What a beautiful view!   You ....
5 Sue drives everywhere. She never walks.   She ....
6 Bill's room isn't very interesting. ....

33.2 Read the situations and write sentences with **I think/I don't think ... should ...** .

1 Peter and Cathy are planning to get married. You think it's a bad idea.
   I don't think they should get married.
2 Jane has a bad cold but plans to go out this evening. You don't think this is a good idea. You say to her: ....
3 Peter needs a job. He's just seen an advertisement for a job which you think would be ideal for him, but he's not sure whether to apply or not. You say to him:
I think ....
4 The government wants to increase taxes, but you don't think this is a good idea.
....

33.3 Complete the sentences with **should (have)** + the verb in brackets.

1 Diane ....._should pass_.... the exam. She's been studying very hard. (pass)
2 You missed a great party last night. ....._You should have come_.... . (come)
3 We don't see you enough. You .... and see us more often. (come)
4 I'm in a difficult position. What do you think I .... ? (do)
5 I'm sorry that I didn't take your advice. I .... what you said. (do)
6 I'm playing tennis with Jane tomorrow. She .... – she's much better than me. (win)
7 We lost the match, but we .... We were the better team. (win)
8 'Is Mike here yet?' 'Not yet, but he .... here soon.' (be)
9 I posted the letter three days ago, so it .... by now. (arrive)

33.4 Read the situations and write sentences with **should/shouldn't**. Some of the sentences are past and some are present.

1 I'm feeling sick. I ate too much. ....._I shouldn't have eaten so much._....
2 That man on the motorbike isn't wearing a helmet. That's dangerous.
He ....._should be wearing a helmet._....
3 When we got to the restaurant, there were no free tables. We hadn't reserved one.
We ....
4 The notice says that the shop is open every day from 8.30. It is 9 o'clock now, but the shop isn't open yet. ....
5 The speed limit is 30 miles an hour, but Kate is doing 50.
She ....
6 Laura gave me her address, but I didn't write it down. Now I can't remember it.
I ....
7 I was driving behind another car. Suddenly, the driver in front stopped without warning and I drove into the back of his car. It wasn't my fault.
The driver in front ....
8 I walked into a wall. I was looking behind me. I wasn't looking where I was going.
....

→ Additional exercises 16–18 (pages 311–13)

Should 2

A

You can use **should** after a number of verbs, especially:

demand   insist   propose   recommend   suggest

- They **insisted** that we **should have** dinner with them.
- I **demanded** that he **should apologise**.
- What do you **suggest** I **should do**?
- I **insist** that something **should be done** about the problem.

We also say '**It's important/vital/necessary/essential** that ... **should** ...':
- It's **essential** that everyone **should be** here on time.

B

You can also leave out **should** in all the sentences in Section A:
- It's **essential** that everyone **be** here on time.   (= that everyone **should be** here)
- I **demanded** that he **apologise**. (= that he **should apologise**)
- What do you **suggest** I **do**?
- I **insist** that something **be done** about the problem.

This form (**be/do/have/apologise** etc.) is sometimes called the *subjunctive*. It is the same as the *infinitive* (without **to**).
You can also use normal present and past tenses:
- It's **essential** that everyone **is** here on time.
- I **demanded** that he **apologised**.

After **suggest**, you cannot use **to** ... ('to do / to buy' etc.). You can say:
- What do you **suggest we should do**?

or   What do you **suggest we do**? (*but not* What do you suggest us to do?)
- Jane **suggested** that I (**should**) **buy** a car.

or   Jane **suggested** that I **bought** a car. (*but not* Jane suggested me to buy)

You can also use **-ing** after **suggest**: What do you **suggest** doing? See Unit 53.

C

You can use **should** after a number of adjectives, especially:

strange   odd   funny   typical   natural   interesting   surprised   surprising

- It's **strange** that he **should be** late. He's usually on time.
- I was **surprised** that he **should say** such a thing.

D

If ... should ...

You can say '**If** something **should** happen ...' . For example:
- **If** Tom **should phone** while I'm out, tell him I'll call him back later.
'**If** Tom **should phone**' is similar to '**If** Tom **phones**'. With **should**, the speaker feels that the possibility is smaller. Another example:
- We have no jobs at present. But **if** the situation **should change**, we'll let you know.

You can also begin these sentences with **should** (**Should** something happen ...):
- **Should** Tom **phone**, tell him I'll call him back later.

E

You can use **I should ... / I shouldn't ...** to give somebody advice. For example:
- 'Shall I leave now?'   'No, **I should** wait a bit longer.'
Here, **I should wait** = I would wait if I were you, I advise you to wait.
Two more examples:
- 'I'm going out now. Is it cold?'   'Yes, **I should wear** a coat.
- **I shouldn't stay** up too late. You'll be tired tomorrow.

Should 1 → Unit 33   **American English** → Appendix 7

Exercises

34.1 Write a sentence (beginning in the way shown) that means the same as the first sentence.

1 'I think it would be a good idea to see a specialist,' the doctor said to me.
The doctor recommended that ..... <u>I should see a specialist</u> ..... .

2 'You really must stay a little longer,' she said to me.
She insisted that I ....

3 'Why don't you visit the museum after lunch?' I said to them.
I suggested that ....

4 'You must pay the rent by Friday,' the landlord said to us.
The landlord demanded that ....

5 'Why don't you go away for a few days?' Jack said to me.
Jack suggested that ....

34.2 Are these sentences right or wrong?

1 a Tom suggested that I should look for another job. <u>OK</u>
  b Tom suggested that I look for another job. ....
  c Tom suggested that I looked for another job. ....
  d Tom suggested me to look for another job. ....
2 a Where do you suggest I go for my holiday? ....
  b Where do you suggest me to go for my holiday? ....
  c Where do you suggest I should go for my holiday? ....

34.3 Complete the sentences using **should** + the following:

ask   ~~be~~   **leave**   **listen**   **say**   **worry**

1 It's strange that he .... <u>should be</u> .... late. He's usually on time.
2 It's funny that you .... that. I was going to say the same thing.
3 It's only natural that parents .... about their children.
4 Isn't it typical of Joe that he .... without saying goodbye to anybody?
5 I was surprised that they .... me for advice. What advice could I give them?
6 I'm going to give you all some essential information, so it's important that everybody
.... very carefully.

34.4 Use the words in brackets to complete these sentences. Use **If ... should ... .**

1 I'm going out now. .... <u>If Tom should phone</u> .... , tell him I'll call him back this evening.
(Tom / phone)
2 I've hung the washing out to dry on the balcony. .... ,
can you bring the washing in, please? (it / rain)
3 I think everything will be OK. .... any problems,
I'm sure we'll be able to solve them. (there / be)
4 I don't want anyone to know where I'm going. .... ,
just say that you don't know. (anyone / ask)

Write sentences 3 and 4 again, this time beginning with **Should.**

5 (3) Should .... , I'm sure we'll be able to solve them.
6 (4) .... , just say that you don't know.

34.5 (Section E) Complete the sentences using **I should** + the following:

buy   **keep**   **phone**   ~~wait~~

1 'Shall I leave now?' 'No, ... <u>I should wait</u> .... a bit longer.'
2 'Shall I throw these things away?' 'No, ... them. You may need them.'
3 'Shall I go and see Paul?' 'Yes, but .... him first.'
4 'Is it worth repairing this TV set?' 'No, ... a new one.'

Had better   It's time ...

Had better (I'd better / you'd better etc.)

I'd better do something = it is advisable to do it. If I don't do it, there will be a problem or a danger:

- ☐ I have to meet Ann in ten minutes. **I'd better go** now or I'll be late.
- ☐ 'Shall I take an umbrella?'   'Yes, **you'd better**. It might rain.'
- ☐ **We'd better stop** for petrol soon. The tank is almost empty.

The negative is **I'd better not** (= I **had** better not):

- ☐ 'Are you going out tonight?'   '**I'd better not.** I've got a lot to do.'
- ☐ You don't look very well. **You'd better not go** to work today.

Remember that:

The form is '**had** better' (usually '**I'd** better / you'**d** better' etc. in spoken English).
- ☐ **I'd better** phone Carol, **hadn't** I?

Had is normally past, but the meaning of **had better** is present or future, *not* past.
- ☐ **I'd better go** to the bank **now / tomorrow**.

We say 'I'd better **do**' (*not* to do).
- ☐ It might rain. We'd better **take** an umbrella. (*not* We'd better to take)

Had better and **should**

Had better is similar to **should** but not exactly the same. We use **had better** only for a specific situation (not for things in general). You can use **should** in all types of situations to give an opinion or give advice:

- ☐ It's late. You'**d better go.** / You **should go.** (a specific situation)
- ☐ You're always at home. You **should go** out more often. (in general – *not* 'had better go')

Also, with **had better**, there is always a danger or a problem if you don't follow the advice. **Should** only means 'it is a good thing to do'. Compare:

- ☐ It's a great film. You **should** go and see it. (but no problem if you don't)
- ☐ The film starts at 8.30. You'**d better** go now or you'll be late.

It's time ...

You can say **It's time** (for somebody) **to ...** :

- ☐ It's time **to go** home. / It's time for us **to go** home.

But you can also say:

- ☐ It's late. It's time **we went** home.

Here we use the past (**went**), but the meaning is present, *not* past:

- ☐ It's 10 o'clock and he's still in bed. **It's time** he **got** up. (*not* It's time he gets up)

It's time you did something = you should have already done it or started it. We often use this structure to criticise or to complain:

- ☐ **It's time** the children **were** in bed. It's long after their bedtime.
- ☐ You're very selfish. **It's time** you **realised** that you're not the most important person in the world.

You can also say **It's about time ...** . This makes the criticism stronger:

- ☐ Jack is a great talker. But **it's about time** he **did** something instead of just talking.

Should 1 → Unit 33

35.1 Read the situations and write sentences with **had better** or **had better not**. Use the words in brackets.

1 You're going out for a walk with Tom. It looks as if it might rain. You say to Tom:
(an umbrella) _We'd better take an umbrella._

2 Michael has just cut himself. It's a bad cut. You say to him:
(a plaster) ....

3 You and Kate plan to go to a restaurant this evening. It's a popular restaurant. You say to Kate:
(reserve) We ....

4 Jill doesn't look very well – not well enough to go to work. You say to her:
(work) ....

5 You received the phone bill four weeks ago, but you haven't paid it yet. If you don't pay soon, you could be in trouble. You say to yourself:
(pay) ....

6 You want to go out, but you're expecting an important phone call. You say to your friend:
(go out) I ....

7 You and Liz are going to the theatre. You've missed the bus and you don't want to be late. You say to Liz: (a taxi) ....

35.2 Put in **had better** where suitable. If **had better** is not suitable, use **should**.

1 I have an appointment in ten minutes. I _'d better_ go now or I'll be late.

2 It's a great film. You _should_ go and see it. You'll really like it.

3 I .... get up early tomorrow. I've got a lot to do.

4 When people are driving, they .... keep their eyes on the road.

5 I'm glad you came to see us. You .... come more often.

6 She'll be upset if we don't invite her to the wedding, so we .... invite her.

7 These biscuits are delicious. You .... try one.

8 I think everybody .... learn a foreign language.

35.3 Complete the sentences. Sometimes you need only one word, sometimes two.

1 a I need some money. I'd better _go_ to the bank.

b John is expecting you to phone him. You .... better phone him now.

c 'Shall I leave the window open?' 'No, you'd better .... it.'

d We'd better leave as soon as possible, ... we?

2 a It's time the government .... something about the problem.

b It's time something .... about the problem.

c I think it's about time you .... about other people instead of only thinking about yourself.

35.4 Read the situations and write sentences with **It's time** (somebody **did** something).

1 You think the children should be in bed. It's already 11 o'clock.
It's time the children were in bed.

2 You haven't had a holiday for a very long time. You need one now.
It's time I ....

3 You're sitting on a train waiting for it to leave the station. It's already five minutes late.

....

4 You enjoy having parties. You haven't had one for a long time.

....

5 The company you work for has been badly managed for a long time. You think some changes should be made.

....

6 Andrew has been doing the same job for the last ten years. He should try something else.

→ Additional exercise 16 (page 311)

Would

A

We use **would** (**'d**) / **wouldn't** when we *imagine* a situation or action (= we think of something that is not real):

- ☐ It **would be** nice to buy a new car, but we can't afford it.
- ☐ I**'d love** to live by the sea.
- ☐ A: Shall I tell Chris what happened?
  B: No, I **wouldn't say** anything.
    (= I wouldn't say anything in your situation)

We use **would have** (**done**) when we imagine situations or actions in the past (= things that didn't happen):

- ☐ They helped us a lot. I don't know what we**'d have done** (= we **would have done**) without their help.
- ☐ I didn't tell Sam what happened. He **wouldn't have been** pleased.

Compare **would** (**do**) and **would have** (**done**):

- ☐ I **would phone** Sue, but I haven't got her number. *(now)*
  I **would have phoned** Sue, but I didn't have her number. *(past)*
- ☐ I'm not going to invite them to the party. They **wouldn't come** anyway.
  I didn't invite them to the party. They **wouldn't have come** anyway.

We often use **would** in sentences with **if** (see Units 38–40):

- ☐ I **would phone** Sue **if** I had her number.
- ☐ I **would have phoned** Sue **if** I'd had her number.

B

Compare **will** (**'ll**) and **would** (**'d**):

- ☐ I**'ll stay** a bit longer. I've got plenty of time.
  I**'d stay** a bit longer, but I really have to go now. (so I can't stay longer)
- ☐ I**'ll phone** Sue. I've got her number.
  I**'d phone** Sue, but I haven't got her number. (so I can't phone her)

Sometimes **would/wouldn't** is the past of **will/won't**. Compare:

present		*past*
☐ TOM: I**'ll phone** you on Sunday.	→	Tom said he**'d phone** me on Sunday.
☐ ANN: I promise I **won't be** late.	→	Ann promised that she **wouldn't be** late.
☐ LIZ: Damn! The car **won't start**.	→	Liz was annoyed because her car **wouldn't start**.

C

Somebody **wouldn't do** something = he/she refused to do it:

- ☐ I tried to warn him, but he **wouldn't listen** to me. (= he refused to listen)
- ☐ The car **wouldn't start**. (= it 'refused' to start)

You can also use **would** when you talk about things that happened regularly in the past:

- ☐ When we were children, we lived by the sea. In summer, if the weather was fine, we **would** all get up early and go for a swim. (= we did this regularly)
- ☐ Whenever Richard was angry, he **would** walk out of the room.

With this meaning, **would** is similar to **used to** (see Unit 18):

- ☐ Whenever Richard was angry, he **used to walk** out of the room.

Will → Units 21–22   **Would you ... ?** → Unit 37A   **Would ... if** → Units 38–40   **Wish ... would** → Unit 41
Would like → Units 37E, 58   **Would prefer / would rather** → Unit 59   **Modal verbs** → Appendix 4

Exercises

36.1 Write sentences about yourself. Imagine things you would like or wouldn't like.

1 (a place you'd love to live)   _I'd love to live by the sea._
2 (a job you wouldn't like to do)   ....
3 (something you would love to do)   ....
4 (something that would be nice to have)   ....
5 (a place you'd like to go to)   ....

36.2 Complete the sentences using **would** + the following verbs (in the correct form):

> **be   be   ~~do~~   do   enjoy   enjoy   have   pass   stop**

1 They helped us a lot. I don't know what we ...._would have done_.... without their help.
2 You should go and see the film. You .... it.
3 It's a pity you couldn't come to the concert yesterday. You .... it.
4 Shall I apply for the job or not? What .... you .... in my position?
5 I was in a hurry when I saw you. Otherwise I .... to talk.
6 We took a taxi home last night but got stuck in the traffic. It ....
   quicker to walk.
7 Why don't you go and see Clare? She .... very pleased to see you.
8 Why didn't you do the exam? I'm sure you .... it.
9 In an ideal world, everybody .... enough to eat.

36.3 Each sentence on the right follows a sentence on the left. Which follows which?

1 ~~I'd like to go to Australia one day.~~	a It wouldn't have been very nice. _1c_
2 I wouldn't like to live on a busy road.	b It would have been fun. ....
3 I'm sorry the trip was cancelled.	c ~~It would be nice.~~ ....
4 I'm looking forward to going out tonight.	d It won't be much fun. ....
5 I'm glad we didn't go out in the rain.	e It wouldn't be very nice. ....
6 I'm not looking forward to the trip.	f It will be fun. ....

36.4 Write sentences using **promised** + would/wouldn't.

1 I wonder why Laura is late.   _She promised she wouldn't be late._
2 I wonder why Steve hasn't phoned. He promised ....
3 Why did you tell Jane what I said? You ....
4 I'm surprised they didn't wait for us. They ....

36.5 Complete the sentences. Use **wouldn't** + a suitable verb.

1 I tried to warn him, but he ...._wouldn't listen_.... to me.
2 I asked Amanda what had happened, but she .... me.
3 Paul was very angry about what I'd said and .... to me for two weeks.
4 Martina insisted on carrying all her luggage. She .... me help her.

36.6 These sentences are about things that often happened in the past. Complete the sentences
using **would** + the following: **forget   help   shake   share   ~~walk~~**

1 Whenever Richard was angry, he ...._would walk_.... out of the room.
2 We used to live next to a railway line. Every time a train went past, the house
   ....
3 George was a very kind man. He .... always .... you if you had a
   problem.
4 Brenda was always very generous. She didn't have much, but she ....
   what she had with everyone else.
5 You could never rely on Joe. It didn't matter how many times you reminded him to do
   something, he .... always ....

→ Additional exercises 16–18 (pages 311–13)

Can/Could/Would you ... ? etc.
(Requests, offers, permission and invitations)

A Asking people to do things (requests)

We use **can** or **could** to ask people to do things:
- □ **Can you** wait a moment, please?
- *or* **Could you** wait a moment, please?
- □ Liz, **can you** do me a favour?
- □ Excuse me, **could you** tell me how to get to the airport?

> **Could you** open the door, please?

Note that we say **Do you think** you **could** ... ? (*not* can):
- □ **Do you think you could** lend me some money until next week?

We also use **will** and **would** to ask people to do things (but **can/could** are more usual):
- □ Liz, **will you** do me a favour?
- □ **Would you** please be quiet? I'm trying to concentrate.

B Asking for things

To ask for something, we use **Can I have ... ?** or **Could I have ... ?**:
- □ *(in a shop)* **Can I have** these postcards, please?
- □ *(during a meal)* **Could I have** the salt, please?

May I have ... ? is also possible:
- □ **May I have** these postcards, please?

C Asking to do things

To ask to do something, we use **can**, **could** or **may**:
- □ *(on the phone)* Hello, **can I** speak to Steve, please?
- □ '**Could I** use your phone?' 'Yes, of course.'
- □ **Do you think I could** borrow your bike?
- □ '**May I** come in?' 'Yes, please do.'

May is more formal than **can** or **could**.

To ask to do something, you can also say **Do you mind if I ... ?** or **Is it all right / Is it OK if I ... ?**:
- □ '**Do you mind if I** use your phone?' 'Sure. Go ahead.'
- □ '**Is it all right if I** come in?' 'Yes, of course.'

D Offering to do things

To offer to do something, you can use **Can I ... ?**:
- □ '**Can I** get you a cup of coffee?' 'That would be nice.'
- □ '**Can I** help you?' 'No, it's all right. I can manage.'

E Offering and inviting

To offer or to invite, we use **Would you like ... ?** (*not* Do you like):
- □ '**Would you like** a cup of coffee?' 'Yes, please.'
- □ '**Would you like** to come to dinner tomorrow evening?' 'I'd love to.'

I'd like ... is a polite way of saying what you want:
- □ *(at a tourist information office)* **I'd like** some information about hotels, please.
- □ *(in a shop)* **I'd like** to try on this jacket, please.

Can and could → Units 26–27   Mind -ing → Unit 53   Would like → Units 55A, 58B
Modal verbs (can/could/will/would etc.) → Appendix 4

37.1   Read the situations and write questions beginning **Can ...** or **Could ...** .

1   You're carrying a lot of things. You can't open the door yourself. There's a man standing near the door. You say to him: _Could you open the door, please?_

2   You phone Sue, but somebody else answers. Sue isn't there. You want to leave a message for her. You say: ....

3   You're a tourist. You want to go to the station, but you don't know how to get there. You ask at your hotel: ....

4   You are in a clothes shop. You see some trousers you like and you want to try them on. You say to the shop assistant: ....

5   You have a car. You have to go the same way as Steve, who is on foot. You offer him a lift. You say to him: ....

37.2   Read the situation and write a question using the word in brackets.

1   You want to borrow your friend's camera. What do you say to him?
(think)   _Do you think I could borrow your camera?_

2   You are at a friend's house and you want to use her phone. What do you say?
(all right)   _Is it all right if I use your phone?_

3   You've written a letter in English. Before you send it, you want a friend to check it for you. What do you ask?
(think) ....

4   You want to leave work early. What do you ask your boss?
(mind) ....

5   The woman in the next room is playing music. It's very loud. You want her to turn it down. What do you say to her?
(think) ....

6   You're on a train. The window is open and you're feeling cold. You'd like to close it, but first you ask the woman next to you.
(OK) ....

7   You're still on the train. The woman next to you has finished reading her newspaper, and you'd like to have a look at it. You ask her.
(think) ....

37.3   What would you say in these situations?

1   Paul has come to see you in your flat. You offer him something to eat.
YOU: _Would you like something to eat_ .... ?
PAUL: No, thank you. I've just eaten.

2   You need help to change the film in your camera. You ask Kate.
YOU: I don't know how to change the film. .... ?
KATE: Sure. It's easy. All you have to do is this.

3   You're on a bus. You have a seat, but an elderly man is standing. You offer him your seat.
YOU: .... ?
MAN: Oh, that's very kind of you. Thank you very much.

4   You're the passenger in a car. Your friend is driving very fast. You ask her to slow down.
YOU: You're making me very nervous. .... ?
DRIVER: Oh, I'm sorry. I didn't realise I was going so fast.

5   You've finished your meal in a restaurant and now you want the bill. You ask the waiter:
YOU: .... ?
WAITER: Right. I'll get it for you now.

6   A friend of yours is interested in one of your books. You invite him to borrow it.
FRIEND: This looks very interesting.
YOU: Yes, it's a good book. .... ?

If I do ... and If I did ...

A

Compare these examples:

(1) Lisa has lost her watch. She tells Sue:

LISA: I've lost my watch. Have you seen it anywhere?
SUE: No, but **if I find** it, I'll tell you.

In this example, Sue feels there is a real possibility that she will find the watch. So she says:
if I find ... , **I'll** ... .

(2) Joe says:

If **I found** a wallet in the street, I'd take it to the police station.

This is a different type of situation. Here, Joe doesn't expect to find a wallet in the street; he is *imagining* a situation that will probably not happen. So he says:
if I found ... , **I'd** (= I **would**) ... . (*not* if I find ... , I'll ...)

When you imagine something like this, you use **if** + *past*
(**if I found** / **if** there **was** / **if** we **didn't** etc.).
But the meaning is *not* past:

If I **won** a million pounds ...

□ What would you do **if** you **won** a million pounds? (we don't really expect this to happen)
□ I don't really want to go to their party, but I probably will go. They'd be upset **if** I **didn't** go.
□ **If** there **was** (*or* **were**) an election tomorrow, who would you vote for?

For **if** ... **was/were**, see Unit 39C.

B

We do not normally use **would** in the **if**-part of the sentence:
□ I'd be very frightened **if** somebody **pointed** a gun at me. (*not* if somebody would point)
□ **If** I **didn't** go to their party, they'd be upset. (*not* If I wouldn't go)

But you can use **if** ... **would** when you ask somebody to do something:
□ *(from a formal letter)* I would be grateful **if** you **would let** me know your decision as soon as possible.

C

In the other part of the sentence (not the **if**-part) we use **would** (**'d**) / **wouldn't**:
□ If you took more exercise, you'd (= you **would**) feel better.
□ I'm not tired. If I went to bed now, I **wouldn't sleep**.
□ **Would** you **mind** if I used your phone?

Could and **might** are also possible:
□ If you took more exercise, you **might feel** better. (= it is possible that you would feel better)
□ If it stopped raining, we **could go** out. (= we would be able to go out)

D

Do not use **when** in sentences like those on this page:
□ They'd be upset **if** I didn't go to their party. (*not* when I didn't go)
□ What would you do **if** you were bitten by a snake? (*not* when you were bitten)

Will → Units 21–22   **If and when** → Unit 25D   **Would** → Unit 36   **If I knew** → Unit 39
If I had known → Unit 40

38.1 Put the verb into the correct form.

1 They would be offended if I ___didn't go___ to their party. (not / go)
2 If you took more exercise, you ___would feel___ better. (feel)
3 If they offered me the job, I think I _____ it. (take)
4 A lot of people would be out of work if the car factory _____ . (close down)
5 If I sold my car, I _____ much money for it. (not / get)
6 *(in a lift)* What would happen if somebody _____ that red button? (press)
7 I don't think there's any chance that Gary and Emma will get married. I'd be absolutely astonished if they _____ . (do)
8 Liz gave me this ring. She _____ very upset if I lost it. (be)
9 Dave and Kate are expecting us. They would be very disappointed if we _____ . (not / come)
10 Would Steve mind if I _____ his bike without asking him? (borrow)
11 What would you do if somebody _____ in here with a gun? (walk)
12 I'm sure Sue _____ if you explained the situation to her. (understand)

38.2 You ask a friend to imagine these situations. You ask **What would you do if ... ?**

1 (imagine – you win a lot of money)
___What would you do if you won a lot of money?___

2 (imagine – you lose your passport)
What _____

3 (imagine – there's a fire in the building)
_____

4 (imagine – you're in a lift and it stops between floors)
_____

38.3 Answer the questions in the way shown.

1 A: Shall we catch the 10.30 train?
   B: No. (arrive too early) ___If we caught the 10.30 train, we'd arrive too early.___
2 A: Is Kevin going to take his driving test?
   B: No. (fail) If he _____
3 A: Why don't we stay at a hotel?
   B: No. (cost too much) If _____
4 A: Is Sally going to apply for the job?
   B: No. (not / get it) If _____
5 A: Let's tell them the truth.
   B: No. (not / believe us) If _____
6 A: Why don't we invite Bill to the party?
   B: No. (have to invite his friends too)
   _____

38.4 Use your own ideas to complete these sentences.

1 If you took more exercise, ___you'd feel better.___
2 I'd be very angry if _____
3 If I didn't go to work tomorrow, _____
4 Would you go to the party if _____
5 If you bought some new clothes, _____
6 Would you mind if _____

If I knew ...   I wish I knew ...

A

Study this example situation:

Sarah wants to phone Paul, but she can't do this because she doesn't know his number.
She says:

If I knew his number, **I would phone** him.

Sarah says: **If I knew** his number ... . This tells us that she *doesn't* know his number. She is imagining the situation. The *real* situation is that she doesn't know his number.

If I knew his number ...

When you imagine a situation like this, you use **if** + *past* (**if I knew** / **if you were** / **if we didn't** etc.). But the meaning is present, *not* past:

□ Tom would read more **if** he **had** more time. (but he doesn't have much time)
□ **If I didn't** want to go to the party, I wouldn't go. (but I want to go)
□ We wouldn't have any money **if** we **didn't** work. (but we work)
□ **If you were** in my position, what would you do?
□ It's a pity you can't drive. It would be useful **if** you **could**.

B

We use the past in the same way after **wish** (**I wish I knew** / **I wish you were** etc.). We use **wish** to say that we regret something, that something is not as we would like it to be:

□ I **wish** I **knew** Paul's phone number.
   (= I don't know it and I regret this)
□ Do you ever **wish** you **could** fly?
   (you can't fly)
□ It rains a lot here. I **wish** it **didn't** rain so often.
□ It's very crowded here. I **wish** there **weren't** so many people. (there are a lot of people)
□ I **wish** I **didn't** have to work tomorrow, but unfortunately I do.

I wish I had an umbrella.

C

If I **were** / if I **was**

After **if** and **wish**, you can use **were** instead of **was** (**if I were** ... / **I wish it were** etc.). **I was** / **it was** are also possible. So you can say:

□ **If I were** you, I wouldn't buy that coat. *or* **If I was** you, ...
□ I'd go out **if it weren't** so cold. *or* ... **if it wasn't** so cold.
□ I **wish** Carol **were** here. *or* I **wish** Carol **was** here.

D

We do not normally use **would** in the **if**-part of the sentence or after **wish**:

□ **If I were** rich, **I would** have a yacht. (*not* If I would be rich)
□ I **wish** I **had** something to read. (*not* I wish I would have)

Sometimes **wish** ... **would** is possible: I **wish you would listen**. See Unit 41.

E

Could sometimes means 'would be able to' and sometimes 'was/were able to':

□ You **could** get a better job (you **could** get = you would be able to get)
   if you **could** use a computer. (you **could** use = you were able to use)

Could → Units 26–27   **If I do / if I did** → Unit 38   **If I had known / I wish I had known** → Unit 40
Wish → Unit 41

Exercises

39.1 Put the verb into the correct form.

1 If I ___knew___ (know) his number, I would phone him.
2 I ___wouldn't buy___ (not / buy) that coat if I were you.
3 I _____ (help) you if I could, but I'm afraid I can't.
4 We would need a car if we _____ (live) in the country.
5 If we had the choice, we _____ (live) in the country.
6 This soup isn't very good. It _____ (taste) better if it wasn't so salty.
7 I wouldn't mind living in England if the weather _____ (be) better.
8 If I were you, I _____ (not / wait). I _____ (go) now.
9 You're always tired. If you _____ (not / go) to bed so late every night, you wouldn't be tired all the time.
10 I think there are too many cars. If there _____ (not / be) so many cars, there _____ (not / be) so much pollution.

39.2 Write a sentence with **if** ... for each situation.

1 We don't see you very often because you live so far away.
   If you didn't live so far away, we'd see you more often.
2 This book is too expensive, so I'm not going to buy it.
   I'd _____ if _____
3 We don't go out very often – we can't afford it.
   We _____
4 I can't meet you tomorrow – I have to work late.
   If _____
5 It's raining, so we can't have lunch outside.
   We _____
6 I don't want his advice, and that's why I'm not going to ask for it.
   If _____

39.3 Write sentences beginning **I wish** ... .

1 I don't know many people (and I'm lonely). _I wish I knew more people._
2 I don't have a mobile phone (and I need one). I wish _____
3 Helen isn't here (and I need to see her). _____
4 It's cold (and I hate cold weather). _____
5 I live in a big city (and I don't like it). _____
6 I can't go to the party (and I'd like to). _____
7 I have to work tomorrow (but I'd like to stay in bed).

   _____
8 I don't know anything about cars (and my car has just broken down).

   _____
9 I'm not feeling well (and it's not nice).

   _____

39.4 Write your own sentences beginning **I wish** ... .

1 (somewhere you'd like to be now – on the beach, in New York, in bed etc.)
   I wish I _____
2 (something you'd like to have – a computer, a job, lots of money etc.)

   _____
3 (something you'd like to be able to do – sing, speak a language, fly etc.)

   _____
4 (something you'd like to be – beautiful, strong, rich etc.)

   _____

If I had known ...   I wish I had known ...

A

Study this example situation:

> Last month Gary was in hospital for a few days. Rachel didn't know this, so she didn't go to visit him. They met a few days ago. Rachel said:
>
> **If I had known** you were in hospital, **I would have gone** to see you.
>
> Rachel said: **If I had known** you were in hospital ... . This tells us that she *didn't* know he was in hospital.

We use **if + had** (**'d**) ... to talk about the past (**if I had known/been/done** etc.):

- ☐ I didn't see you when you passed me in the street. **If I'd seen** you, of course I would have said hello. (but I didn't see you)
- ☐ I decided to stay at home last night. I would have gone out **if I hadn't been** so tired. (but I was tired)
- ☐ **If he had been looking** where he was going, he wouldn't have walked into the wall. (but he wasn't looking)
- ☐ The view was wonderful. **If I'd had** a camera with me, I would have taken some photographs. (but I didn't have a camera)

Compare:

- ☐ I'm not hungry. **If I was** hungry, I would eat something. *(now)*
- ☐ I wasn't hungry. **If I had been** hungry, I would have eaten something. *(past)*

B

Do not use **would** in the **if**-part of the sentence. We use **would** in the other part of the sentence:

- ☐ If I had seen you, I **would have said** hello. (*not* If I would have seen you)

Note that **'d** can be **would** or **had**:

- ☐ If I'd seen you,   (I'd seen = I **had** seen)
  I'd have said hello. (I'd have said = I **would** have said)

C

We use **had** (**done**) in the same way after **wish**. **I wish** something **had happened** = I am sorry that it didn't happen:

- ☐ I wish I'd known that Gary was ill. I would have gone to see him. (but I didn't know)
- ☐ I feel sick. I **wish I hadn't eaten** so much cake. (I ate too much cake)
- ☐ Do you **wish** you **had studied** science instead of languages? (you didn't study science)

Do not use **would have** ... after **wish**:

- ☐ The weather was cold while we were away. I wish it **had been** warmer. (*not* I wish it would have been)

D

Compare **would** (**do**) and **would have** (**done**):

- ☐ If I had gone to the party last night, I **would be** tired now. (I am not tired now – *present*)
- ☐ If I had gone to the party last night, I **would have met** lots of people. (I didn't meet lots of people – *past*)

Compare **would have**, **could have** and **might have**:

- ☐ If the weather hadn't been so bad, {
  - we **would have gone** out.
  - we **could have gone** out.
    (= we would have been able to go out)
  - we **might have gone** out.
    (= perhaps we would have gone out)

Had done → Unit 15   **If I do / if I did** → Unit 38   **If I knew / I wish I knew** → Unit 39   **Wish** → Unit 41

40.1 Put the verb into the correct form.

1 I didn't know you were in hospital. If <u>I'd known</u> (I / know), <u>I would have gone</u> (I / go) to see you.

2 Sam got to the station just in time to catch the train to the airport. If .... (he / miss) the train, ... (he / miss) his flight.

3 I'm glad that you reminded me about Amanda's birthday. .... (I / forget) if .... (you / not / remind) me.

4 Unfortunately I forgot my address book when I went on holiday. If .... (I / have) your address, ... (I / send) you a postcard.

5 A: How was your holiday? Did you have a nice time?
   B: It was OK, but .... (we / enjoy) it more if .... (the weather / be) nicer.

6 I took a taxi to the hotel, but the traffic was bad. .... (it / be) quicker if .... (I / walk).

7 I'm not tired. If .... (I / be) tired, I'd go home now.

8 I wasn't tired last night. If .... (I / be) tired, I would have gone home earlier.

40.2 For each situation, write a sentence beginning with **If**.

1 I wasn't hungry, so I didn't eat anything.
   <u>If I'd been hungry, I would have eaten something.</u>

2 The accident happened because the road was icy.
   If the road ....

3 I didn't know that Joe had to get up early, so I didn't wake him up.
   If I ....

4 I was able to buy the car only because Jane lent me the money.
   ....

5 Karen wasn't injured in the crash because she was wearing a seat belt.
   ....

6 You didn't have any breakfast – that's why you're hungry now.
   ....

7 I didn't get a taxi because I didn't have any money.
   ....

40.3 Imagine that you are in these situations. For each situation, write a sentence with **I wish**.

1 You've eaten too much and now you feel sick.
   You say: <u>I wish I hadn't eaten so much.</u>

2 There was a job advertised in the newspaper. You decided not to apply for it. Now you think that your decision was wrong.
   You say: I wish I ....

3 When you were younger, you never learned to play a musical instrument. Now you regret this.
   You say: ....

4 You've painted the gate red. Now you think that red was the wrong colour.
   You say: ....

5 You are walking in the country. You'd like to take some photographs, but you didn't bring your camera.
   You say: ....

6 You have some unexpected guests. They didn't phone first to say they were coming. You are very busy and you are not prepared for them.
   You say (to yourself): ....

→ Additional exercises 19–21 (pages 313–14)

A

You can say 'I wish you luck / every success / a happy birthday' etc. :
- ☐ I **wish you every success** in the future.
- ☐ I saw Tim before the exam and **he wished me luck**.

We say 'wish somebody *something*' (**luck** / **a happy birthday** etc.). But you cannot 'wish that something *happens*'. We use **hope** in this situation. For example:
- ☐ I **hope** you **get** this letter before you go away. (*not* I wish you get)

Compare I **wish** and I **hope**:
- ☐ I **wish** you **a pleasant stay** here.
- ☐ I **hope** you **have** a pleasant stay here. (*not* I wish you have)

B

We also use **wish** to say that we regret something, that something is not as we would like it. When we use **wish** in this way, we use the *past* (**knew/lived** etc.), but the meaning is *present*:
- ☐ I **wish I knew** what to do about the problem. (I don't know and I regret this)
- ☐ I **wish you didn't** have to go so soon. (you have to go)
- ☐ Do you **wish** you **lived** near the sea? (you don't live near the sea)
- ☐ Jack's going on a trip to Mexico soon. I **wish I was** going too. (I'm not going)

To say that we regret something in the past, we use **wish + had** ... (**had known / had said**) etc. :
- ☐ I **wish I'd known** about the party. I would have gone if I'd known. (I didn't know)
- ☐ It was a stupid thing to say. I **wish I hadn't said** it. (I said it)

For more examples, see Units 39 and 40.

C

I **wish I could** (**do** something) = I regret that I cannot do it:
- ☐ I'm sorry I have to go. I **wish I could stay** longer. (but I can't)
- ☐ I've met that man before. I **wish I could remember** his name. (but I can't)

I **wish I could have** (**done** something) = I regret that I could not do it:
- ☐ I hear the party was great. I **wish I could have gone**. (but I couldn't go)

D

You can say 'I **wish** (somebody) **would** (do something)'. For example:

> I wish it would stop raining.

It's been raining all day. Jill doesn't like it. She says:
I **wish** it **would stop** raining.

Jill would like the rain to stop, but this will probably not happen.

We use I **wish** ... **would** when we would like something to happen or change. Usually, the speaker doesn't expect this to happen.

We often use I **wish** ... **would** to complain about a situation:
- ☐ The phone has been ringing for five minutes. I **wish** somebody **would answer** it.
- ☐ I **wish** you **would do** something instead of just sitting and doing nothing.

You can use I **wish** ... **wouldn't** ... to complain about things that people do repeatedly:
- ☐ I **wish** you **wouldn't keep** interrupting me.

We use I **wish** ... **would** ... for actions and changes, *not* situations. Compare:
- ☐ I **wish** Sarah **would** come. (= I want her to come)

but I **wish** Sarah **was** (*or* **were**) here now. (*not* I wish Sarah would be)

- ☐ I **wish** somebody **would buy** me a car.

but I **wish** I **had** a car. (*not* I wish I would have)

I wish I knew → Unit 39   I wish I was / I wish I were → Unit 39C   I wish I had known → Unit 40

Exercises

41.1 Put in **wish(ed)** or **hope(d)**.

1 I ....._wish_..... you a pleasant stay here.
2 Enjoy your holiday. I .... you have a great time.
3 Goodbye. I .... you all the best.
4 We said goodbye to each other and .... each other luck.
5 We're going to have a picnic tomorrow, so I .... the weather is nice.
6 I .... you luck in your new job. I .... it works out well for you.

41.2 What do you say in these situations? Write sentences with **I wish ... would ... .**

1 It's raining. You want to go out, but not in the rain.
You say: ..._I wish it would stop raining._....................
2 You're waiting for Jane. She's late and you're getting impatient.
You say to yourself: I wish ....
3 You're looking for a job – so far without success. Nobody will give you a job.
You say: I wish somebody ....
4 You can hear a baby crying. It's been crying for a long time and you're trying to study.
You say: ....
5 Brian has been wearing the same clothes for years. You think he needs some new clothes.
You say to Brian: ....

For the following situations, write sentences with **I wish ... wouldn't ... .**

6 Your friend drives very fast. You don't like this.
You say to your friend: I wish you ....
7 Joe leaves the door open all the time. This annoys you.
You say to Joe: ....
8 A lot of people drop litter in the street. You don't like this.
You say: I wish people ....

41.3 Are these sentences right or wrong? Correct them where necessary.

1 I wish Sarah would be here now.   _I wish Sarah were here now._......
2 I wish you would listen to me.   ....
3 I wish I would have more free time.   ....
4 I wish our flat would be a bit bigger.   ....
5 I wish the weather would change.   ....
6 I wish you wouldn't complain all the time.   ....
7 I wish everything wouldn't be so expensive.   ....

41.4 Put the verb into the correct form.

1 It was a stupid thing to say. I wish I ..._hadn't said_.... it. (I / not / say)
2 I'm fed up with this rain. I wish ..._it would stop_.... . (it / stop)
3 It's a difficult question. I wish .... the answer. (I / know)
4 I should have listened to you. I wish .... your advice. (I / take)
5 You're lucky to be going away. I wish .... with you. (I / can / come)
6 I have no energy at the moment. I wish .... so tired. (I / not / be)
7 Aren't they ready yet? I wish .... up. (they / hurry)
8 It would be nice to stay here longer. I wish .... to leave now.
(we / not / have)
9 When we were in London last year, we didn't have time to see all the things we wanted to see.
I wish .... longer. (we / can / stay)
10 It's freezing today. I wish .... so cold. I hate cold weather. (it / not / be)
11 Joe still doesn't know what he wants to do. I wish .... (he / decide)
12 I really didn't enjoy the party. I wish .... (we / not / go)

A Study this example:

This house **was built** in 1935.

Was built is *passive*.

Compare active and passive:

Somebody **built** [this house] in 1935.   *(active)*
       subject   *object*

[This house] **was built** in 1935.   *(passive)*
 subject

When we use an active verb, we say *what the subject does*:
- ☐ My grandfather was a builder. **He built** this house in 1935.
- ☐ It's a big company. **It employs** two hundred people.

When we use a passive verb, we say *what happens to the subject*:
- ☐ This house is quite old. **It was built** in 1935.
- ☐ **Two hundred people are employed** by the company.

B When we use the passive, who or what causes the action is often unknown or unimportant:
- ☐ A lot of money **was stolen** in the robbery. (somebody stole it, but we don't know who)
- ☐ **Is** this room **cleaned** every day? (does somebody clean it? – it's not important who)

If we want to say who does or what causes the action, we use **by** ... :
- ☐ This house was built **by my grandfather.**
- ☐ Two hundred people are employed **by the company.**

C The passive is **be** (is/was etc.) + *past participle* (**done/cleaned/seen** etc.):
  (**be**) **done**   (**be**) **cleaned**   (**be**) **damaged**   (**be**) **built**   (**be**) **seen** etc.

For irregular past participles (**done/seen/known** etc.), see Appendix 1.

Study the active and passive forms of the *present simple* and *past simple*:

Present simple
active: **clean(s) / see(s)** etc.   Somebody **cleans** [this room] every day.

passive: **am/is/are** + **cleaned/seen** etc.   [This room] **is cleaned** every day.

- ☐ Many accidents **are caused** by careless driving.
- ☐ **I'm not** often **invited** to parties.
- ☐ How **is** this word **pronounced**?

Past simple
active: **cleaned/saw** etc.   Somebody **cleaned** [this room] yesterday.

passive: **was/were** + **cleaned/seen** etc.   [This room] **was cleaned** yesterday.

- ☐ We **were woken** up by a loud noise during the night.
- ☐ 'Did you go to the party?' 'No, I **wasn't invited.**'
- ☐ How much money **was stolen** in the robbery?

Exercises

42.1 Complete the sentences using one of these verbs in the correct form, present or past:

cause	damage	hold	invite	make
overtake	show	surround	translate	write

1 Many accidents .....*are caused*..... by dangerous driving.
2 Cheese .... from milk.
3 The roof of the building .... in a storm a few days ago.
4 You .... to the wedding. Why didn't you go?
5 A cinema is a place where films ....
6 In the United States, elections for president .... every four years.
7 Originally the book .... in Spanish, and a few years ago it
.... into English.
8 Although we were driving quite fast, we .... by a lot of other cars.
9 You can't see the house from the road. It .... by trees.

42.2 Write questions using the passive. Some are present and some are past.

1 Ask about glass. (how / make?) *How is glass made?* ....
2 Ask about television. (when / invent?) ....
3 Ask about mountains. (how / form?) ....
4 Ask about Pluto (*the planet*). (when / discover?) ....
5 Ask about silver. (what / use for?) ....

42.3 Put the verb into the correct form, present simple or past simple, active or passive.

1 It's a big factory. Five hundred people .....*are employed*..... (employ) there.
2 .....*Did somebody clean*..... (somebody / clean) this room yesterday?
3 Water .... (cover) most of the earth's surface.
4 How much of the earth's surface .... (cover) by water?
5 The park gates .... (lock) at 6.30 p.m. every evening.
6 The letter .... (post) a week ago and it .... (arrive) yesterday.
7 The boat hit a rock and .... (sink) quickly. Fortunately everybody
.... (rescue).
8 Richard's parents .... (die) when he was very young. He and his sister
.... (bring up) by their grandparents.
9 I was born in London, but I .... (grow up) in Canada.
10 While I was on holiday, my camera .... (steal) from my hotel room.
11 While I was on holiday, my camera .... (disappear) from my hotel room.
12 Why .... (Sue / resign) from her job? Didn't she enjoy it?
13 Why .... (Bill / sack) from his job? What did he do wrong?
14 The company is not independent. It .... (own) by a much larger company.
15 I saw an accident last night. Somebody .... (call) an ambulance but nobody
.... (injure), so the ambulance .... (not / need).
16 Where .... (these photographs / take)? In London?
.... (you / take) them, or somebody else?
17 Sometimes it's quite noisy living here, but it's not a problem for me –
I .... (not / bother) by it.

42.4 Rewrite these sentences. Instead of using **somebody**, **they**, **people** etc., write a passive sentence.

1 Somebody cleans the room every day. *The room is cleaned every day.* ....
2 They cancelled all flights because of fog. All ....
3 People don't use this road much. ....
4 Somebody accused me of stealing money. I ....
5 How do people learn languages? How ....
6 Somebody warned us not to go out alone. ....

Passive 2 (be done / been done / being done)

Study the following active and passive forms:

A

Infinitive

active: (to) **do/clean/see** etc.   Somebody **will clean** [the room] later.

passive: (to) **be + done/cleaned/seen** etc.   [The room] **will be cleaned** later.

- The situation is serious. Something must **be done** before it's too late.
- A mystery is something that can't **be explained**.
- The music was very loud and could **be heard** from a long way away.
- A new supermarket is going **to be built** next year.
- Please go away. I want **to be left** alone.

B

Perfect infinitive

active: (to) **have + done/cleaned/seen** etc.   Somebody **should have cleaned** [the room].

passive: (to) **have been + done/cleaned/seen** etc.   [The room] **should have been cleaned**.

- I haven't received the letter yet. It might **have been sent** to the wrong address.
- If you hadn't left the car unlocked, it wouldn't **have been stolen**.
- There were some problems at first, but they seem **to have been solved**.

C

Present perfect

active: **have/has + done** etc.   The room looks nice. Somebody **has cleaned** [it].

passive: **have/has been + done** etc.   The room looks nice. [It] **has been cleaned**.

- Have you heard? The concert **has been cancelled**.
- **Have** you ever **been bitten** by a dog?
- 'Are you going to the party?' 'No, I **haven't been invited**.'

Past perfect

active: **had + done** etc.   The room looked nice. Somebody **had cleaned** [it].

passive: **had been + done** etc.   The room looked nice. [It] **had been cleaned**.

- The vegetables didn't taste very good. They **had been cooked** too long.
- The car was three years old but **hadn't been used** very much.

D

Present continuous

active: **am/is/are + (do)ing**   Somebody **is cleaning** [the room] at the moment.

passive: **am/is/are + being (done)**   [The room] **is being cleaned** at the moment.

- There's somebody walking behind us. I think we **are being followed**.
- *(in a shop)* 'Can I help you?' 'No, thank you. **I'm being served**.'

Past continuous

active: **was/were + (do)ing**   Somebody **was cleaning** [the room] when I arrived.

passive: **was/were + being (done)**   [The room] **was being cleaned** when I arrived.

- There was somebody walking behind us. We **were being followed**.

Passive 1, 3 → Units 42, 44

43.1 What do these words mean? Use **it can ...** or **it can't ...** . Use a dictionary if necessary.

If something is

1 **washable,** _it can be washed_ .   4 **unusable,** _____ .
2 **unbreakable,** it _____ .   5 **invisible,** _____ .
3 **edible,** _____ .   6 **portable,** _____ .

43.2 Complete these sentences with the following verbs (in the correct form):

     arrest   carry   cause   ~~do~~   make   repair   ~~send~~   spend   wake up

Sometimes you need **have** (**might have, should have** etc.).

1 The situation is serious. Something must _be done_ before it's too late.
2 I haven't received the letter. It might _have been sent_ to the wrong address.
3 A decision will not _____ until the next meeting.
4 Do you think that more money should _____ on education?
5 This road is in very bad condition. It should _____ a long time ago.
6 The injured man couldn't walk and had to _____ .
7 It's not certain how the fire started, but it might _____ by an electrical fault.
8 I told the hotel receptionist I wanted to _____ at 6.30 the next morning.
9 If you hadn't pushed the policeman, you wouldn't _____ .

43.3 Rewrite these sentences. Instead of using **somebody** or **they** etc., write a passive sentence.

1 Somebody has cleaned the room.   _The room has been cleaned._
2 They have postponed the meeting.   The _____
3 Somebody is using the computer at the moment.
    The computer _____
4 I didn't realise that somebody was recording our conversation.
    I didn't realise that _____
5 When we got to the stadium, we found that they had cancelled the game.
    When we got to the stadium, we found that _____
6 They are building a new ring road round the city.
    _____
7 They have built a new hospital near the airport.
    _____

43.4 Make sentences from the words in brackets. Sometimes the verb is active, sometimes passive.

1 There's somebody behind us. (I think / we / follow) _I think we're being followed._
2 This room looks different. (you / paint / the walls?) _Have you painted the walls?_
3 My car has disappeared. (it / steal!) It _____
4 My umbrella has disappeared. (somebody / take) Somebody _____
5 Sam gets a higher salary now. (he / promote) He _____
6 Ann can't use her office at the moment. (it / redecorate) It _____
7 The photocopier broke down yesterday, but now it's OK. (it / work / again ; it / repair)
    It _____ It _____
8 When I went into the room, I saw that the table and chairs were not in the same place.
    (the furniture / move) The _____
9 The man next door disappeared six months ago. (he / not / see / since then)
    He _____
10 I wonder how Jane is these days. (I / not / see / for ages)
    I _____
11 A friend of mine was mugged on his way home a few nights ago. (you / ever / mug?)
    _____

A I was offered … / we were given … etc.

Some verbs can have two objects. For example, **give**:

□ Somebody gave **the police the information**. (= Somebody gave the information to the police)

object 1   object 2

So it is possible to make two passive sentences:

□ **The police** were given the information. *or*
The information was given to the police.

Other verbs which can have two objects are:

    ask   offer   pay   show   teach   tell

When we use these verbs in the passive, most often we begin with the *person*:

□ **I was offered** the job, but I refused it. (= they offered me the job)
□ **You will be given** plenty of time to decide. (= we will give you plenty of time)
□ **Have you been shown** the new machine? (= has anybody shown you?)
□ **The men were paid** £400 to do the work. (= somebody paid the men £400)

B I don't like being …

The passive of **doing/seeing** etc. is **being done / being seen** etc. Compare:

active: I don't like **people telling me** what to do.
passive: I don't like **being told** what to do.

□ I remember **being taken** to the zoo when I was a child.
(= I remember somebody taking me to the zoo)
□ Steve hates **being kept** waiting. (= he hates people keeping him waiting)
□ We managed to climb over the wall without **being seen**. (= without anybody seeing us)

C I was born …

We say 'I **was born** …' (*not* I am born):

□ I **was born** in Chicago.
□ Where **were** you **born**? (*not* Where are you born?) } *past*

but

□ How many babies **are born** every day?   *present*

D Get

You can use **get** instead of **be** in the passive:

□ There was a fight at the party, but nobody **got hurt**. (= nobody **was** hurt)
□ I don't often **get invited** to parties. (= I'm not often invited)
□ I'm surprised Liz **didn't get offered** the job. (= Liz **wasn't offered** the job)

You can use **get** only when things *happen*. For example, you cannot use **get** in the following sentences:

□ Jill **is liked** by everybody. (*not* gets liked – this is not a 'happening')
□ He was a mystery man. Very little **was known** about him. (*not* got known)

We use **get** mainly in informal spoken English. You can use **be** in all situations.

We also use **get** in the following expressions (which are not passive in meaning):

get married, get divorced   **get lost** (= not know where you are)
get dressed (= put on your clothes)   **get changed** (= change your clothes)

44.1 Write these sentences in another way, beginning in the way shown.

1 They didn't give me the information I needed.
I <u>wasn't given the information I needed.</u>

2 They asked me some difficult questions at the interview.
I ....

3 Linda's colleagues gave her a present when she retired.
Linda ....

4 Nobody told me about the meeting.
I wasn't ....

5 How much will they pay you for your work?
How much will you ....

6 I think they should have offered Tom the job.
I think Tom ....

7 Has anybody shown you what to do?
Have you ....

44.2 Complete the sentences using **being** + the following (in the correct form):

give   invite   ~~keep~~   knock down   stick   treat

1 Steve hates ....<u>being kept</u>.... waiting.

2 We went to the party without ....

3 I like giving presents and I also like .... them.

4 It's a busy road and I don't like crossing it. I'm afraid of ....

5 I'm an adult. I don't like .... like a child.

6 You can't do anything about .... in a traffic jam.

44.3 When were they born? Choose five of these people and write a sentence for each.
(Two of them were born in the same year.)

Beethoven	Galileo	Elvis Presley	1452	1869	1929
Agatha Christie	Mahatma Gandhi	Leonardo da Vinci	1564	1890	1935
~~Walt Disney~~	Martin Luther King	William Shakespeare	1770	~~1901~~	

1 <u>Walt Disney was born in 1901.</u>

2 ....

3 ....

4 ....

5 ....

6 ....

7 And you? I ....

44.4 Complete the sentences using **get/got** + the following verbs (in the correct form):

ask   damage   ~~hurt~~   pay   steal   sting   stop   use

1 There was a fight at the party, but nobody ....<u>got hurt</u>... .

2 Alex .... by a bee while he was sitting in the garden.

3 These tennis courts don't .... very often. Not many people want to play.

4 I used to have a bicycle, but it .... a few months ago.

5 Rachel works hard but doesn't .... very much.

6 Last night I .... by the police as I was driving home. One of the lights on my car wasn't working.

7 Please pack these things very carefully. I don't want them to ....

8 People often want to know what my job is. I often .... that question.

Unit 45

It is said that ... He is said to ...
He is supposed to ...

A Study this example situation:

Henry is very old. Nobody knows exactly how old he is, but:

It is said that he is 108 years old.

or   He **is said to be** 108 years old.

Both these sentences mean: 'People say that he is 108 years old.'

You can use these structures with a number of other verbs, especially:

alleged   believed   considered   expected   known   reported   thought   understood

Compare the two structures:

☐ Cathy works very hard.
   It is said that she works 16 hours a day.   *or*   She **is said to work** 16 hours a day.
☐ The police are looking for a missing boy.
   It is believed that the boy is wearing   *or*   The boy **is believed to be wearing**
   a white pullover and blue jeans.   a white pullover and blue jeans.
☐ The strike started three weeks ago.
   It is expected that it will end soon.   *or*   The strike **is expected to end** soon.
☐ A friend of mine has been arrested.
   It is alleged that he hit a policeman.   *or*   He **is alleged to have hit** a policeman.
☐ The two houses belong to the same family.
   It is said that there is a secret tunnel   *or*   There **is said to be** a secret tunnel
   between them.   between them.

These structures are often used in news reports. For example, in a report about an accident:

☐ **It is reported that** two people were   *or*   Two people **are reported to have**
   injured in the explosion.   **been injured** in the explosion.

B **(Be) supposed to**

Sometimes (**it is**) **supposed to** ... = (it is) said to ... :

☐ I want to see that film. It's **supposed to be** good. (= it is said to be good)
☐ Mark **is supposed to have hit** a policeman, but I don't believe it.

But sometimes **supposed to** has a different meaning. We use **supposed to** to say what is intended, arranged or expected. Often this is different from the real situation:

☐ The plan **is supposed to be** a secret, but everybody seems to know about it.
   (= the plan is intended to be a secret)
☐ What are you doing at work? You're **supposed to be** on holiday.
   (= you arranged to be on holiday)
☐ Our guests **were supposed to come** at 7.30, but they were late.
☐ Jane **was supposed to phone** me last night, but she didn't.
☐ I'd better hurry. I'm **supposed to be meeting** Chris in ten minutes.

You're **not supposed to** do something = it is not allowed or advisable:

☐ You're **not supposed to park** your car here. It's private parking only.
☐ Jeff is much better after his illness, but he's still **not supposed to do** any heavy work.

Exercises

45.1 Write these sentences in another way, beginning as shown. Use the <u>underlined</u> word each time.

1 It is <u>expected</u> that the strike will end soon. The strike _is expected to end soon._

2 It is <u>expected</u> that the weather will be good tomorrow.
The weather is ....

3 It is <u>believed</u> that the thieves got in through a window in the roof.
The thieves ....

4 It is <u>reported</u> that many people are homeless after the floods.
Many people ....

5 It is <u>thought</u> that the prisoner escaped by climbing over a wall.
The prisoner ....

6 It is <u>alleged</u> that the man was driving at 110 miles an hour.
The man ....

7 It is <u>reported</u> that the building has been badly damaged by the fire.
The building ....

8 a It is <u>said</u> that the company is losing a lot of money.
The company ....

b It is <u>believed</u> that the company lost a lot of money last year.
The company ....

c It is <u>expected</u> that the company will make a loss this year.
The company ....

45.2 There are a lot of rumours about Alan. Here are some of the things people say about him:

1 (Alan speaks ten languages.)   2 (He knows a lot of famous people.)

3 (He is very rich.) 4 (He has twelve children.) 5 (He was an actor when he was younger.)

Alan

Nobody is sure whether these things are true. Write sentences about Alan using **supposed to.**

1 _Alan is supposed to speak ten languages._

2 He ....

3 ....

4 ....

5 ....

45.3 Complete the sentences using **supposed to be** + the following:

on a diet   a flower   my friend   a joke   ~~a secret~~   working

1 Everybody seems to know about the plan, but it _is supposed to be a secret._

2 You shouldn't criticise me all the time. You ....

3 I shouldn't be eating this cake really. I ....

4 I'm sorry for what I said. I was trying to be funny. It ....

5 What's this drawing? Is it a tree? Or maybe it ....

6 You shouldn't be reading the paper now. You ....

45.4 Write sentences with **supposed to** + the following verbs:

arrive   block   ~~park~~   phone   start

Use the negative (**not supposed to**) where necessary.

1 You _'re not supposed to park_ here. It's private parking only.

2 We .... work at 8.15, but we rarely do anything before 8.30.

3 Oh, I .... Helen, but I completely forgot.

4 This door is a fire exit. You .... it.

5 My train .... at 11.30, but it was an hour late.

→ Additional exercises 22–24 (pages 314–15)

A Study this example situation:

LISA

The roof of Lisa's house was damaged in a storm. Yesterday a workman came and repaired it.

Lisa **had** the roof **repaired** yesterday.

This means: Lisa arranged for somebody else to repair the roof. She didn't repair it herself.

We use **have something done** to say that we arrange for somebody else to do something for us. Compare:

- ☐ Lisa **repaired** the roof. (= she repaired it herself)
  Lisa **had** the roof **repaired**. (= she arranged for somebody else to repair it)
- ☐ 'Did you **make** those curtains yourself?' 'Yes, I enjoy making things.'
  'Did you **have** those curtains **made**?' 'No, I made them myself.'

B Be careful with word order. The *past participle* (**repaired/cut** etc.) is after the *object*:

	have	*object*	*past participle*
Lisa	**had**	the roof	**repaired** yesterday.
Where did you	**have**	your hair	**cut**?
Your hair looks nice. Have you	**had**	it	**cut**?
Our neighbour has just	**had**	a garage	**built**.
We are	**having**	the house	**painted** at the moment.
How often do you	**have**	your car	**serviced**?
I think you should	**have**	that coat	**cleaned**.
I don't like	**having**	my photograph	**taken**.

C **Get something done**

You can also say '**get** something done' instead of '**have** something done' (mainly in informal spoken English):

- ☐ When are you going to **get the roof repaired**? (= have the roof repaired)
- ☐ I think you should **get your hair cut** really short.

D Sometimes **have something done** has a different meaning. For example:

- ☐ Paul and Karen **had all their money stolen** while they were on holiday.

This does not mean that they arranged for somebody to steal their money. 'They **had all their money stolen**' means only: 'All their money was stolen from them'.

With this meaning, we use **have something done** to say that something happens to somebody or their belongings. Usually what happens is not nice:

- ☐ Gary **had** his nose **broken** in a fight. (= his nose was broken)
- ☐ Have you ever **had** your passport **stolen**?

Exercises

46.1 Tick (✓) the correct sentence, (a) or (b), for each picture.

1 	2 	3 	4 
SARAH	BILL	JOHN	SUE
(a) Sarah is cutting her hair.	(a) Bill is cutting his hair.	(a) John is cleaning his shoes.	(a) Sue is taking a photograph.
(b) Sarah is having her hair cut.	(b) Bill is having his hair cut.	(b) John is having his shoes cleaned.	(b) Sue is having her photograph taken.

46.2 Answer the questions using **To have something done**. Choose from the boxes:

~~my car~~	my eyes	my jacket	my watch		clean	repair	~~service~~	test

1 Why did you go to the garage?   _To have my car serviced._
2 Why did you go to the cleaner's?   To ....
3 Why did you go to the jeweller's?   ....
4 Why did you go to the optician's?   ....

46.3 Write sentences in the way shown.

1 Lisa didn't repair the roof herself. She _had it repaired._
2 I didn't cut my hair myself. I ....
3 They didn't paint the house themselves. They ....
4 John didn't build that wall himself. ....
5 I didn't deliver the flowers myself. ....

46.4 Use the words in brackets to complete the sentences. Use the structure **have something done**.

1 We _are having the house painted_ (the house / paint) at the moment.
2 I lost my key. I'll have to .... (another key / make).
3 When was the last time you .... (your hair / cut)?
4 .... (you / a newspaper / deliver) to your house every day, or do you go out and buy one?
5 A: What are those workmen doing in your garden?
   B: Oh, we .... (a garage / build).
6 A: Can I see the photographs you took when you were on holiday?
   B: I'm afraid I .... (not / the film / develop) yet.
7 This coat is dirty. I must .... (it / clean).
8 If you want to wear earrings, why don't you ....
   (your ears / pierce)?
9 A: I heard your computer wasn't working.
   B: That's right, but it's OK now. I .... (it / repair).

In these items, use 'have something done' with its second meaning (see Section D).

10 Gary was in a fight last night. He _had his nose broken_ (his nose / break).
11 Did I tell you about Jane? She ....
   (her handbag / steal) last week.
12 Did you hear about Pete? He .... (his car / vandalise)
   a few nights ago.

A Study this example situation:

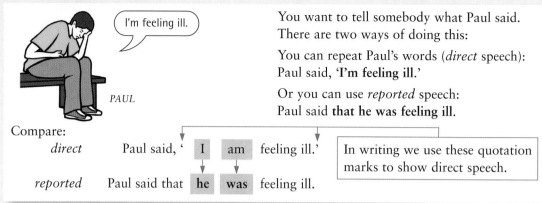

I'm feeling ill.

PAUL

You want to tell somebody what Paul said. There are two ways of doing this:

You can repeat Paul's words (*direct* speech): Paul said, '**I'm feeling ill.**'

Or you can use *reported* speech: Paul said **that he was feeling ill.**

Compare:

direct   Paul said, ' **I** **am** feeling ill.'

reported   Paul said that **he** **was** feeling ill.

> In writing we use these quotation marks to show direct speech.

B When we use reported speech, the main verb of the sentence is usually past (Paul **said** that ... / I **told** her that ... etc.). The rest of the sentence is usually past too:

- ☐ Paul **said** that he **was feeling** ill.
- ☐ I **told** Lisa that I **didn't have** any money.

You can leave out **that**. So you can say:

- ☐ Paul **said that** he was feeling ill.   *or*   Paul **said** he was feeling ill.

In general, the *present* form in direct speech changes to the *past* form in reported speech:

am/is → **was**	do/does → **did**	will → **would**
are → **were**	have/has → **had**	can → **could**
want/like/know/go etc. → **wanted/liked/knew/went** etc.		

Compare direct speech and reported speech:

You met Jenny. Here are some of the things she said in *direct* speech:

JENNY

'My parents **are** very well.'

'**I'm** going to learn to drive.'

'I **want** to buy a car.'
'John **has** a new job.'
'I **can't** come to the party on Friday.'

'I **don't** have much free time.'

'**I'm** going away for a few days. **I'll** phone you when I **get** back.'

Later you tell somebody what Jenny said. You use *reported* speech:

- ☐ Jenny said that her parents **were** very well.
- ☐ She said that she **was** going to learn to drive.
- ☐ She said that she **wanted** to buy a car.
- ☐ She said that John **had** a new job.
- ☐ She said that she **couldn't** come to the party on Friday.
- ☐ She said she **didn't** have much free time.
- ☐ She said that she **was** going away for a few days and **would** phone me when she **got** back.

C The *past simple* (**did/saw/knew** etc.) can usually stay the same in reported speech, or you can change it to the *past perfect* (**had done / had seen / had known** etc.):

- ☐ *direct*   Paul said: 'I **woke** up feeling ill, so I **didn't go** to work.'
  reported   Paul said (that) he **woke** up feeling ill, so he **didn't go** to work.   *or*
  Paul said (that) he **had woken** up feeling ill, so he **hadn't gone** to work.

47.1 Yesterday you met a friend of yours, Steve. You hadn't seen him for a long time. Here are some of the things Steve said to you:

1 I'm living in London.

2 My father isn't very well.

3 Rachel and Mark are getting married next month.

4 My sister has had a baby.

5 I don't know what Frank is doing.

6 I saw Helen at a party in June and she seemed fine.

Steve

7 I haven't seen Diane recently.

8 I'm not enjoying my job very much.

9 You can come and stay at my place if you're ever in London.

10 My car was stolen a few days ago.

11 I want to go on holiday, but I can't afford it.

12 I'll tell Chris I saw you.

Later that day you tell another friend what Steve said. Use reported speech.

1 _Steve said that he was living in London._
2 He said that ....
3 He ....
4 ....
5 ....
6 ....
7 ....
8 ....
9 ....
10 ....
11 ....
12 ....

47.2 Somebody says something to you which is the opposite of what they said earlier. Complete the answers.

1 A: That restaurant is expensive.
  B: Is it? I thought you said ...._it was cheap_.............................. .

2 A: Sue is coming to the party tonight.
  B: Is she? I thought you said she ....

3 A: Sarah likes Paul.
  B: Does she? Last week you said ....

4 A: I know lots of people.
  B: Do you? I thought you said ....

5 A: Jane will be here next week.
  B: Will she? But didn't you say .... ?

6 A: I'm going out this evening.
  B: Are you? But you said ....

7 A: I can speak a little French.
  B: Can you? But earlier you said ....

8 A: I haven't been to the cinema for ages.
  B: Haven't you? I thought you said ....

→ Additional exercise 25 (page 316)

Reported speech 2

A

It is not always necessary to change the verb in reported speech. If you report something and the situation *hasn't changed*, you do not need to change the verb to the past:

- □ *direct*   Paul said, 'My new job **is** very interesting.'
  reported   Paul said that his new job **is** very interesting.
  (The situation hasn't changed. His job **is** still interesting.)

- □ *direct*   Helen said, '**I want** to go to New York next year.'
  reported   Helen told me that **she wants** to go to New York next year.
  (Helen still wants to go to New York next year.)

You can also change the verb to the past:

- □ Paul said that his new job **was** very interesting.
- □ Helen told me that she **wanted** to go to New York next year.

But if you are reporting a finished situation, you *must* use a past verb:

- □ Paul left the room suddenly. He said **he had** to go. (*not* has to go)

B

You need to use a past form when there is a difference between what was said and what is really true. For example:

You met Sonia a few days ago.
She said: '**Joe is in hospital**.' *(direct speech)*

Later that day you meet Joe in the street. You say:
'I didn't expect to see you, Joe. Sonia said you **were** in hospital.'
(*not* 'Sonia said you are in hospital', because clearly he is not)

SONIA

Have you heard? Joe is in hospital.

Sonia said you **were** in hospital.

JOE

C

Say and **tell**

If you say *who* somebody is talking to, use **tell**:

- □ Sonia **told me** that you were in hospital. (*not* Sonia said me)
- □ What did you **tell the police**? (*not* say the police)

TELL SOMEBODY

Otherwise use **say**:

- □ Sonia **said** that you were in hospital. (*not* Sonia told that ...)
- □ What did you **say**?

SAY ~~SOMEBODY~~

But you can '**say** something **to** somebody':

- □ Ann **said** goodbye **to** me and left. (*not* Ann said me goodbye)
- □ What did you **say to** the police?

D

Tell/ask somebody **to** do something

We also use the infinitive (**to do** / **to stay** etc.) in reported speech, especially with **tell** and **ask** (for orders and requests):

- □ *direct*   '**Stay** in bed for a few days,' the doctor said to me.
  reported   The doctor **told me to** stay in bed for a few days.
- □ *direct*   '**Don't shout**,' I said to Jim.
  reported   I **told Jim not to** shout.
- □ *direct*   'Please **don't tell** anybody what happened,' Jackie said to me.
  reported   Jackie **asked me not to** tell anybody what (had) happened.

You can also say 'Somebody **said** (not) **to** do something':

- □ Jackie **said** not **to tell** anyone. (*but not* Jackie said me)

Reported speech → Unit 47   Reported questions → Unit 50B

Exercises

48.1 Here are some things that Sarah said to you:

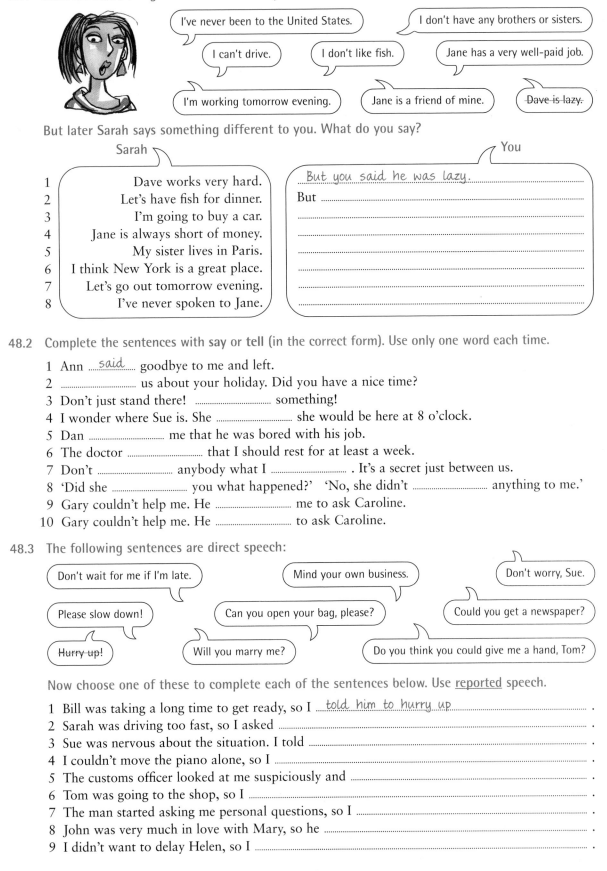

I've never been to the United States.

I don't have any brothers or sisters.

I can't drive.

I don't like fish.

Jane has a very well-paid job.

I'm working tomorrow evening.

Jane is a friend of mine.

~~Dave is lazy.~~

But later Sarah says something different to you. What do you say?

	Sarah	You
1	Dave works very hard.	But you said he was lazy.
2	Let's have fish for dinner.	But ....
3	I'm going to buy a car.	
4	Jane is always short of money.	
5	My sister lives in Paris.	
6	I think New York is a great place.	
7	Let's go out tomorrow evening.	
8	I've never spoken to Jane.	

48.2 Complete the sentences with **say** or **tell** (in the correct form). Use only one word each time.

1 Ann ...*said*... goodbye to me and left.
2 .... us about your holiday. Did you have a nice time?
3 Don't just stand there! .... something!
4 I wonder where Sue is. She .... she would be here at 8 o'clock.
5 Dan .... me that he was bored with his job.
6 The doctor .... that I should rest for at least a week.
7 Don't .... anybody what I .... It's a secret just between us.
8 'Did she .... you what happened?' 'No, she didn't .... anything to me.'
9 Gary couldn't help me. He .... me to ask Caroline.
10 Gary couldn't help me. He .... to ask Caroline.

48.3 The following sentences are direct speech:

Don't wait for me if I'm late.

Mind your own business.

Don't worry, Sue.

Please slow down!

Can you open your bag, please?

Could you get a newspaper?

~~Hurry up!~~

Will you marry me?

Do you think you could give me a hand, Tom?

Now choose one of these to complete each of the sentences below. Use <u>reported</u> speech.

1 Bill was taking a long time to get ready, so I ...*told him to hurry up*... .
2 Sarah was driving too fast, so I asked ....
3 Sue was nervous about the situation. I told ....
4 I couldn't move the piano alone, so I ....
5 The customs officer looked at me suspiciously and ....
6 Tom was going to the shop, so I ....
7 The man started asking me personal questions, so I ....
8 John was very much in love with Mary, so he ....
9 I didn't want to delay Helen, so I ....

→ Additional exercise 25 (page 316)

Questions 1

A

In questions we usually put the subject after the first verb:

subject + verb   *verb + subject*

Tom	will	→	will	Tom?
you	have	→	have	you?
the house	was	→	was	the house?

□ **Will Tom** be here tomorrow?
□ **Have you** been working hard?
□ When **was the house** built?

Remember that the subject comes after the *first* verb:
   □ **Is Catherine** working today? (*not* Is working Catherine)

B

In *present simple* questions, we use **do/does**:

you	live	→	**do**	you live?
the film	begins	→	**does**	the film begin?

□ **Do you live** near here?
□ What time **does** the film **begin**?

In *past simple* questions, we use **did**:

you	sold	→	**did**	you sell?
the train	stopped	→	**did**	the train stop?

□ **Did** you **sell** your car?
□ Why **did** the train **stop**?

But do not use **do/does/did** if **who/what** etc. is the subject of the sentence. Compare:

who *object*

Emma telephoned somebody .

├── *object* ──┤

 Who did Emma **telephone**?

who *subject*

 Somebody telephoned Emma.

├ *subject* ──┤

 Who **telephoned** Emma?

In these examples, **who/what** etc. is the *subject*:
   □ **Who wants** something to eat? (*not* Who does want)
   □ **What happened** to you last night? (*not* What did happen)
   □ **How many people came** to the meeting? (*not* did come)
   □ **Which bus goes** to the centre? (*not* does go)

C

Note the position of prepositions in questions beginning **Who/What/Which/Where ... ?**:
   □ **Who** do you want to speak **to**?
   □ **Which** job has Ann applied **for**?
   □ **What** was the weather **like** yesterday?
   □ **Where** are you **from**?

You can use *preposition* + **whom** in formal style:
   □ **To whom** do you wish to speak?

D

Isn't it ... ? / Didn't you ... ? etc. (negative questions)

We use negative questions especially to show surprise:
   □ **Didn't you** hear the doorbell? I rang it three times.
or when we expect the listener to agree with us:
   □ '**Haven't we** met somewhere before?'   'Yes, I think we have.'

Note the meaning of **yes** and **no** in answers to negative questions:
   □ **Don't you** want to go to the party? { **Yes.** (= Yes, I want to go)
                                              { **No.** (= No, I don't want to go)

Note the word order in negative questions beginning **Why ... ?**:
   □ **Why don't we** go out for a meal tonight? (*not* Why we don't go)
   □ **Why wasn't Mary** at work yesterday? (*not* Why Mary wasn't)

Questions 2 → Unit 50   Question tags (do you? isn't it? etc.) → Unit 52

Exercises

49.1 Ask Joe questions. (Look at his answers before you write the questions.)

1 (where / live?) _Where do you live?_ .... In Manchester.
2 (born there?) .... No, I was born in London.
3 (married?) .... Yes.
4 (how long / married?) .... 17 years.
   ....
5 (children?) .... Yes, two boys.
   ....
6 (how old / they?) .... 12 and 15.
7 (what / do?) .... I'm a journalist.
8 (what / wife / do?) .... She's a doctor.

Joe

49.2 Make questions with **who** or **what**.

1 Somebody hit me.   _Who hit you?_
2 I hit somebody.   _Who did you hit?_
3 Somebody paid the bill.   Who ....
4 Something happened.   What ....
5 Diane said something.   ....
6 This book belongs to somebody. ....
7 Somebody lives in that house.   ....
8 I fell over something.   ....
9 Something fell on the floor.   ....
10 This word means something.   ....
11 I borrowed the money from somebody. ....
12 I'm worried about something.   ....

49.3 Put the words in brackets in the correct order. All the sentences are questions.

1 (when / was / built / this house) _When was this house built?_
2 (how / cheese / is / made) ....
3 (when / invented / the computer / was) ....
4 (why / Sue / working / isn't / today) ....
5 (what time / coming / your friends / are) ....
6 (why / was / cancelled / the concert) ....
7 (where / your mother / was / born) ....
8 (why / you / to the party / didn't / come) ....
9 (how / the accident / did / happen) ....
10 (why / this machine / doesn't / work) ....

49.4 Write negative questions from the words in brackets. In each situation you are surprised.

1 A: We won't see Liz this evening.
   B: Why not? (she / not / come / to the party?) _Isn't she coming to the party?_
2 A: I hope we don't meet David tonight.
   B: Why? (you / not / like / him?) ....
3 A: Don't go and see that film.
   B: Why not? (it / not / good?) ....
4 A: I'll have to borrow some money.
   B: Why? (you / not / have / any?) ....

Questions 2 (Do you know where ... ? / He asked me where ...)

A

Do you know where ... ? / I don't know why ... / Could you tell me what ... ? etc.

We say: Where **has Tom** gone?

but   **Do you know** where **Tom has** gone? (*not* Do you know where has Tom gone?)

When the question (**Where has Tom gone?**) is part of a longer sentence (**Do you know ... ? /
I don't know ... / Can you tell me ... ?** etc.), the word order changes. We say:

□ What time **is it**?	*but* **Do you know** what time **it is**?
□ Who **are those people**?	**I don't know** who **those people are**.
□ Where **can I** find Linda?	**Can you tell me** where **I can** find Linda?
□ How much **will it** cost?	**Do you have any idea** how much **it will** cost?

Be careful with **do/does/did** questions. We say:

□ What time **does the film begin**?	*but* **Do you know** what time **the film begins**?
	(*not* does the film begin)
□ What **do you mean**?	**Please explain** what **you mean**.
□ Why **did she leave** early?	**I wonder** why **she left** early.

Use **if** or **whether** where there is no other question word (**what, why** etc.):

□ Did anybody see you?	*but* **Do you know if** anybody saw you?
	or ... **whether** anybody saw you?

B

He asked me where ... (reported questions)

The same changes in word order happen in reported questions. Compare:

□ *direct*	The police officer said to us, 'Where	are you going ?'
reported	The police officer asked us where	we were going .
□ *direct*	Clare said, 'What time	do the banks close ?'
reported	Clare wanted to know what time	the banks closed .

In reported speech the verb usually changes to the past (**were, closed** etc.). See Unit 47.

Study these examples. You had an interview for a job and these were some of the questions the
interviewer asked you:

Are you willing to travel?

What **do you do** in your spare time?

How long **have you** been
working in your present job?

Why **did you apply** for the job?

Can you speak any foreign languages?

Do you have a driving licence?

Later you tell a friend what the interviewer asked you. You use *reported* speech:
□ She asked if (*or* whether) **I was** willing to travel.
□ She wanted to know what **I did** in my spare time.
□ She asked how long **I had** been working in my present job.
□ She asked why **I had** applied for the job. (*or* ... why **I applied**)
□ She wanted to know if (*or* whether) **I could** speak any foreign languages.
□ She asked if (*or* whether) **I had** a driving licence.

Reported speech → Units 47–48

Exercises

50.1 Make a new sentence from the question in brackets.

1 (Where has Tom gone?) Do you know ...where Tom has gone?...
2 (Where is the post office?) Could you tell me where ....
3 (What's the time?) I wonder ....
4 (What does this word mean?) I want to know ....
5 (What time did they leave?) Do you know ....
6 (Is Sue going out tonight?) I don't know ....
7 (Where does Caroline live?) Do you have any idea ....
8 (Where did I park the car?) I can't remember ....
9 (Is there a bank near here?) Can you tell me ....
10 (What do you want?) Tell me ....
11 (Why didn't Kate come to the party?) I don't know ....
12 (How much does it cost to park here?) Do you know ....
13 (Who is that woman?) I have no idea ....
14 (Did Liz get my letter?) Do you know ....
15 (How far is it to the airport?) Can you tell me ....

50.2 You are making a phone call. You want to speak to Sue, but she isn't there. Somebody else answers the phone. You want to know three things:
(1) **Where has she gone?** (2) **When will she be back?** and (3) **Did she go out alone?**
Complete the conversation:

A: Do you know where ....? (1)
B: Sorry, I've got no idea.
A: Never mind. I don't suppose you know .... (2)
B: No, I'm afraid not.
A: One more thing. Do you happen to know ....? (3)
B: I'm afraid I didn't see her go out.
A: OK. Well, thank you anyway. Goodbye.

50.3 You have been away for a while and have just come back to your home town. You meet Tony, a friend of yours. He asks you a lot of questions:

1 (How are you?)
5 (Why did you come back?)
6 (Where are you living?)
2 (Where have you been?)
7 (Are you glad to be back?)
3 (How long have you been back?)
8 (Do you have any plans to go away again?)
4 (What are you doing now?)
9 (Can you lend me some money?)

Tony

Now you tell another friend what Tony asked you. Use reported speech.

1 ...He asked me how I was....
2 He asked me ....
3 He ....
4 ....
5 ....
6 ....
7 ....
8 ....
9 ....

→ Additional exercise 25 (page 316)

Auxiliary verbs (have/do/can etc.)
I think so / I hope so etc.

A

In each of these sentences there is an auxiliary verb and a main verb:

I	have	lost	my keys.
She	can't	come	to the party.
The hotel	was	built	ten years ago.
Where	do you	live?	

In these examples **have/can't/was/do** are auxiliary (= helping) verbs.

You can use an auxiliary verb when you don't want to repeat something:
- □ 'Have you locked the door?' 'Yes, I **have**.' (= I have *locked the door*)
- □ George wasn't working, but Janet **was**. (= Janet was *working*)
- □ She could lend me the money, but she **won't**. (= she won't *lend me the money*)

Use **do/does/did** for the present and past simple:
- □ 'Do you like onions?' 'Yes, I **do**.' (= I *like onions*)
- □ 'Does Simon live in London?' 'He **did**, but he **doesn't** any more.'

You can use auxiliary verbs to deny what somebody says (= say it is not true):
- □ 'You're sitting in my place.' 'No, I'm **not**.' (= I'm not *sitting in your place*)
- □ 'You didn't lock the door before you left.' 'Yes, I **did**.' (= I *locked the door*)

B

We use **have you?** / **isn't she?** / **do they?** etc. to show interest in what somebody has said or to show surprise:
- □ 'I've just seen Simon.' 'Oh, **have you**? How is he?'
- □ 'Liz isn't very well today.' 'Oh, **isn't she**? What's wrong with her?'
- □ 'It rained every day during our holiday.' '**Did it**? What a pity!'
- □ 'Jim and Nora are getting married.' '**Are they**? Really?'

C

We use auxiliary verbs with **so** and **neither**:
- □ 'I'm feeling tired.' '**So am I**.' (= I'm feeling tired too)
- □ 'I never read newspapers.' '**Neither do I**.' (= I never read newspapers either)
- □ Sue hasn't got a car and **neither has Martin**.

Note the word order after **so** and **neither** (verb before subject):
- □ I passed the exam and **so did Paul**. (*not* so Paul did)

Instead of **neither**, you can use **nor**. You can also use **not ... either**:
- □ 'I don't know.' '**Neither** do I.' *or* '**Nor** do I.' *or* 'I **don't** either.'

D

I think so / I hope so etc.

After some verbs you can use **so** when you don't want to repeat something:
- □ 'Are those people English?' 'I **think so**.' (= I think *they are English*)
- □ 'Will you be at home this evening?' 'I **expect so**. (= I expect *I'll be at home ...*)
- □ 'Do you think Kate has been invited to the party?' 'I **suppose so**.'

In the same way we say: **I hope so, I guess so** and **I'm afraid so**.

The usual negative forms are:

I think so / I expect so	→	I don't think so / I don't expect so
I hope so / I'm afraid so / I guess so	→	I hope not / I'm afraid not / I guess not
I suppose so	→	I don't suppose so *or* I suppose not

- □ 'Is that woman American?' 'I **think so**. / I **don't think so**.'
- □ 'Do you think it will rain?' 'I **hope so**. / I **hope not**.' (*not* I don't hope so)

51.1 Complete each sentence with an auxiliary verb (**do/was/could** etc.). Sometimes the verb must be negative (**don't/wasn't** etc.).

1 I wasn't tired, but my friends _____were_____ .

2 I like hot weather, but Ann _____ .

3 'Is Colin here?' 'He _____ five minutes ago, but I think he's gone home now.'

4 Liz said she might phone later this evening, but I don't think she _____ .

5 'Are you and Chris coming to the party?' 'I _____ , but Chris _____ .'

6 I don't know whether to apply for the job or not. Do you think I _____ ?

7 'Please don't tell anybody what I said.' 'Don't worry. I _____ .'

8 'You never listen to me.' 'Yes, I _____ !'

9 'Can you play a musical instrument?' 'No, but I wish I _____ .'

10 'Please help me.' 'I'm sorry. I _____ if I _____ , but I _____ .'

51.2 You never agree with Sue. Answer in the way shown.

	Sue	You
1	I'm hungry.	Are you? I'm not.
2	I'm not tired.	Aren't you? I am.
3	I like football.	
4	I didn't enjoy the film.	
5	I've never been to Australia.	
6	I thought the exam was easy.	

51.3 You are talking to Tina. If you're in the same position as Tina, reply with **So ...** or **Neither ...** as in the first example. Otherwise, ask questions as in the second example.

	Tina	You
1	I'm feeling tired.	So am I.
2	I work hard.	Do you? What do you do?
3	I watched television last night.	
4	I won't be at home tomorrow.	
5	I like reading. I read a lot.	
6	I'd like to live somewhere else.	
7	I can't go out tonight.	

51.4 In these conversations, you are B. Read the information in brackets and then answer with **I think so, I hope not** etc.

1 (You don't like rain.)
   A: Do you think it will rain? B: (hope) ___I hope not.___

2 (You need more money quickly.)
   A: Do you think you'll get a pay rise soon? B: (hope) _____

3 (You think Diane will probably get the job that she applied for.)
   A: Do you think Diane will get the job? B: (expect) _____

4 (You're not sure whether Barbara is married – probably not.)
   A: Is Barbara married? B: (think) _____

5 (You are the receptionist at a hotel. The hotel is full.)
   A: Have you got a room for tonight? B: (afraid) _____

6 (You're at a party. You have to leave early.)
   A: Do you have to leave already? B: (afraid) _____

7 (Ann normally works every day, Monday to Friday. Tomorrow is Wednesday.)
   A: Is Ann working tomorrow? B: (suppose) _____

8 (You are going to a party. You can't stand John.)
   A: Do you think John will be at the party? B: (hope) _____

9 (You're not sure what time the concert is – probably 7.30.)
   A: Is the concert at 7.30? B: (think) _____

Question tags (do you? isn't it? etc.)

A Study these examples:

You haven't seen Kate today, **have you**?

No, I'm afraid not.

It was a good film, **wasn't it**?

Yes, it was great.

Have you? and **wasn't it?** are *question tags* (= mini-questions that we often put on the end of a sentence in spoken English). In question tags, we use an auxiliary verb (**have/was/will** etc.). We use **do/does/did** for the present and past simple (see Unit 51):

- ☐ 'Karen plays the piano, **doesn't** she?' 'Well, yes, but not very well.'
- ☐ 'You didn't lock the door, **did** you?' 'No, I forgot.'

B Normally we use a *negative* question tag after a *positive* sentence:

... and a *positive* question tag after a *negative* sentence:

	positive sentence +	*negative tag*
	Kate **will** be here soon,	**won't she?**
	There **was** a lot of traffic,	**wasn't there?**
	Michael **should** pass the exam,	**shouldn't he?**

	negative sentence +	*positive tag*
	Kate **won't** be late,	**will she?**
	They **don't** like us,	**do they?**
	You **haven't** got a car,	**have you?**

Notice the meaning of **yes** and **no** in answer to a negative sentence:

- ☐ You're **not** going out today, **are you?**
  - **Yes.** (= Yes, I am going out)
  - **No.** (= No, I am not going out)

C The meaning of a question tag depends on how you say it. If your voice goes *down*, you are not really asking a question; you are only inviting the listener to agree with you:

- ☐ 'It's a nice day, **isn't it?**' 'Yes, beautiful.'
- ☐ 'Tim doesn't look well today, **does he?**' 'No, he looks very tired.'
- ☐ She's very funny. She's got a great sense of humour, **hasn't she?**

But if the voice goes *up*, it is a real question:

- ☐ 'You haven't seen Lisa today, **have you?**' 'No, I'm afraid I haven't.'
  (= Have you by chance seen Lisa today?)

You can use a *negative sentence + positive tag* to ask for things or information, or to ask somebody to do something. The voice goes *up* at the end of the tag in sentences like these:

- ☐ 'You haven't got a pen, **have you?**' 'Yes, here you are.'
- ☐ 'You couldn't do me a favour, **could you?**' 'It depends what it is.'
- ☐ 'You don't know where Karen is, **do you?**' 'Sorry, I have no idea.'

D After **Let's** ... the question tag is **shall we**:

- ☐ **Let's** go for a walk, **shall we?** (the voice goes *up*)

After **Don't** ... , the question tag is **will you**:

- ☐ **Don't** be late, **will you?** (the voice goes *down*)

After **I'm** ... , the negative question tag is **aren't I?** (= am I not?):

- ☐ **I'm** right, **aren't I?** 'Yes, you are.'

Auxiliary verbs (have/do/can etc.) → Unit 51

52.1 Put a question tag on the end of these sentences.

1	Kate won't be late, _will she_ ?	No, she's never late.
2	You're tired, _aren't you_ ?	Yes, a little.
3	You've got a camera, ... ?	Yes, I've got two actually.
4	You weren't listening, ... ?	Yes, I was!
5	Sue doesn't know Ann, ... ?	No, they've never met.
6	Jack's on holiday, ... ?	Yes, he's in Portugal.
7	Kate's applied for the job, ... ?	Yes, but she won't get it.
8	You can speak German, ... ?	Yes, but not very fluently.
9	He won't mind if I use his phone, ... ?	No, of course he won't.
10	There are a lot of people here, ... ?	Yes, more than I expected.
11	Let's go out tonight, ... ?	Yes, that would be great.
12	This isn't very interesting, ... ?	No, not very.
13	I'm too impatient, ... ?	Yes, you are sometimes.
14	You wouldn't tell anyone, ... ?	No, of course not.
15	Helen has lived here a long time, ... ?	Yes, 20 years.
16	I shouldn't have lost my temper, ... ?	No, but never mind.
17	He'd never met her before, ... ?	No, that was the first time.
18	Don't drop that vase, ... ?	No, don't worry.

52.2 Read the situation and write a sentence with a question tag. In each situation you are asking your friend to agree with you.

1 You look out of the window. The sky is blue and the sun is shining. What do you say to your friend? (nice day) _It's a nice day, isn't it?_

2 You're with a friend outside a restaurant. You're looking at the prices, which are very high. What do you say? (expensive) It ....

3 You and a colleague have just finished a training course. You really enjoyed it. What do you say to your colleague? (great) The course ....

4 Your friend's hair is much shorter than when you last met. What do you say to her/him? (have / your hair / cut) You ....

5 You and a friend are listening to a woman singing. You like her voice very much. What do you say to your friend? (a good voice) She ....

6 You are trying on a jacket in a shop. You look in the mirror and you don't like what you see. What do you say to your friend? (not / look / very good)
It ....

7 You and a friend are walking over a small wooden bridge. The bridge is very old and some parts are broken. What do you say? (not / very safe)
This bridge ....

52.3 In these situations you are asking for information, asking people to do things etc.

1 You need a pen. Perhaps Jane has got one. Ask her.
Jane, you haven't got a pen, have you?

2 Joe is just going out. You want him to get some stamps. Ask him.
Joe, you ....

3 You're looking for Diane. Perhaps Kate knows where she is. Ask her.
Kate, you ....

4 You need a bicycle pump. Perhaps Helen has got one. Ask her.
Helen, ...

5 Ann has a car and you need a lift to the station. Perhaps she'll take you. Ask her.
Ann, ...

6 You're looking for your keys. Perhaps Robert has seen them. Ask him.
Robert, ...

Verb + -ing (enjoy doing / stop doing etc.)

A

Look at these examples:

- □ I **enjoy** read**ing**. (*not* I enjoy to read)
- □ Would you **mind** clos**ing** the door?
  (*not* mind to close)
- □ Chris **suggested** go**ing** to the cinema.
  (*not* suggested to go)

> Would you mind closing the door?

After **enjoy, mind** and **suggest**, we use **-ing** (*not* **to** …).

Some more verbs that are followed by **-ing**:

stop	postpone	admit	avoid	imagine
finish	consider	deny	risk	fancy

- □ Suddenly everybody **stopped** talk**ing**. There was silence.
- □ I'll do the shopping when I've **finished** clean**ing** the flat.
- □ He tried to **avoid** answer**ing** my question.
- □ I don't **fancy** go**ing** out this evening. (= I'm not enthusiastic about it)
- □ Have you ever **considered** go**ing** to live in another country?

The negative form is **not -ing**:

- □ When I'm on holiday, I **enjoy not** hav**ing** to get up early.

B

We also use **-ing** after:

give up (= stop)
put off (= postpone)
go on / carry on (= continue)
keep *or* **keep on** (= do something continuously or repeatedly)

- □ I've **given up** read**ing** newspapers. I think it's a waste of time.
- □ Jenny doesn't want to retire. She wants to **go on** work**ing**. (*or* … to **carry on** work**ing**.)
- □ You **keep** interrupt**ing** when I'm talking! *or* You **keep on** interrupt**ing** …

C

With some verbs you can use the structure *verb* + somebody + **-ing**:

- □ I can't **imagine** George rid**ing** a motorbike.
- □ You can't **stop me** do**ing** what I want.
- □ 'Sorry to **keep you** wait**ing** so long.' 'That's all right.'

Note the passive form (**being done/seen/kept** etc.):

- □ I don't **mind being kept** waiting. (= I don't mind **people** keep**ing** me …)

D

When you are talking about finished actions, you can say **having done/stolen/said** etc. :

- □ They admitted **having stolen** the money.

But it is not necessary to use **having** (done). You can also say:

- □ They admitted **stealing** the money.
- □ I now regret **saying** (*or* **having said**) what I said.

For **regret**, see Unit 56B.

E

After some of the verbs on this page (especially **admit/deny/suggest**) you can also use **that** … :

- □ They **denied that** they had stolen the money. (*or* They **denied** stealing …)
- □ Sam **suggested that** we went to the cinema. (*or* Sam **suggested** going …)

Suggest → Unit 34 **Being done (passive)** → Unit 44B **Verb + to …** → Unit 54 **Verb + to … and -ing** → Units 55C, 56–58 **Regret / go on** → Unit 56B **Go on / carry on / keep on** → Unit 141A

Exercises

53.1 Complete each sentence with one of the following verbs (in the correct form):

~~answer~~   apply   be   forget   listen   live   lose   make   read   try   use   write

1 He tried to avoid ....*answering*.... my question.
2 Could you please stop .... so much noise?
3 I enjoy .... to music.
4 I considered .... for the job, but in the end I decided against it.
5 Have you finished .... the newspaper yet?
6 We need to change our routine. We can't go on .... like this.
7 I don't mind you .... the phone as long as you pay for all your calls.
8 My memory is getting worse. I keep .... things.
9 I've put off .... the letter so many times. I really must do it today.
10 What a stupid thing to do! Can you imagine anybody .... so stupid?
11 I've given up .... to lose weight – it's impossible.
12 If you invest your money on the stock market, you risk .... it.

53.2 Complete the sentences for each situation using -ing.

1 What shall we do? / We could go to the zoo.
She suggested ...*going to the zoo*... .

2 Do you want to play tennis? / No, not really.
He didn't fancy ....

3 You were driving too fast. / Yes, it's true. Sorry!
She admitted ....

4 Why don't we go for a swim? / Good idea!
She suggested ....

5 You broke the CD player. / No, I didn't!
He denied ....

6 Can you wait a few minutes? / Sure, no problem.
They didn't mind ....

53.3 Complete the sentences so that they mean the same as the first sentence. Use -ing.

1 I can do what I want and you can't stop me.
   You ...*can't stop me doing what I want*... .
2 It's not a good idea to travel during the rush hour.
   It's better to avoid ....
3 Shall we paint the kitchen next weekend instead of this weekend?
   Shall we postpone .... until .... ?
4 Could you turn the radio down, please?
   Would you mind .... ?
5 Please don't interrupt me all the time.
   Would you mind .... ?

53.4 Use your own ideas to complete these sentences. Use -ing.

1 She's a very interesting person. I always enjoy ...*talking to her*... .
2 I'm not feeling very well. I don't fancy ....
3 I'm afraid there aren't any chairs. I hope you don't mind ....
4 It was a beautiful day, so I suggested ....
5 It was very funny. I couldn't stop ....
6 My car isn't very reliable. It keeps ....

A

offer	decide	hope	deserve	promise
agree	plan	manage	afford	threaten
refuse	arrange	fail	forget	learn

After these verbs you can use **to ...** (*infinitive*):
- ☐ It was late, so we **decided to take** a taxi home.
- ☐ Simon was in a difficult situation, so I **agreed to help** him.
- ☐ How old were you when you **learnt to drive**? (*or* learnt **how** to drive)
- ☐ I waved to Karen but **failed to attract** her attention.

The negative is **not to ...** :
- ☐ We **decided not to go** out because of the weather.
- ☐ I **promised not to be** late.

After some verbs **to ...** is not possible. For example, **enjoy/think/suggest**:
- ☐ I **enjoy** reading. (*not* enjoy to read)
- ☐ Tom **suggested** going to the cinema. (*not* suggested to go)
- ☐ Are you **thinking of** buying a car? (*not* thinking to buy)

For verb + **-ing**, see Unit 53. For verb + preposition + **-ing**, see Unit 62.

B

We also use **to ...** after:

seem   appear   tend   pretend   claim

For example:
- ☐ They **seem to have** plenty of money.
- ☐ I like Dan, but I think he **tends to talk** too much.
- ☐ Ann **pretended not to see** me when she passed me in the street.

There is also a *continuous* infinitive (**to be doing**) and a *perfect* infinitive (**to have done**):
- ☐ I **pretended to be** reading the newspaper. (= I pretended that I **was** reading)
- ☐ You **seem to have lost** weight. (= it seems that you **have lost** weight)
- ☐ Martin **seems to be** enjoying his new job. (= it seems that he **is** enjoying it)

C

After **dare** you can use the infinitive with or without **to**:
- ☐ I wouldn't **dare to tell** him. *or* I wouldn't **dare tell** him.

But after **dare not** (*or* **daren't**), you must use the infinitive without **to**:
- ☐ I **daren't tell** him what happened. (*not* I daren't to tell him)

D

After some verbs you can use a question word (**what/whether/how** etc.) + **to ...** . We use this structure especially after:

ask   decide   know   remember   forget   explain   learn   understand   wonder

We **asked**	how	to get	to the station.
Have you **decided**	where	to go	for your holidays?
I don't **know**	whether	to apply	for the job or not.
Do you **understand**	what	to do?	

Also **show/tell/ask/advise/teach** somebody **what/how/where** to do something:
- ☐ Can somebody **show me how to change** the film in this camera?
- ☐ Ask Jack. He'll **tell you what to do**.

Verb + **-ing** → Unit 53   Verb + object + **to ...** (want etc.) → Unit 55
Verb + **to ...** and **-ing** → Units 55C, 56–58

54.1 Complete the sentences for these situations.

1 *Shall we get married?* — *Yes, let's.* They decided __to get married__ .

2 *Please help me.* — *OK.* She agreed _____ .

3 *Can I carry your bag for you?* — *No, thanks. I can manage.* He offered _____ .

4 *Let's meet at 8 o'clock.* — *OK, fine.* They arranged _____ .

5 *What's your name?* — *I'm not going to tell you.* She refused _____ .

6 *Please don't tell anyone.* — *I won't. I promise.* She promised _____ .

54.2 Complete each sentence with a suitable verb.

1 Don't forget __to post__ the letter I gave you.
2 There was a lot of traffic, but we managed _____ to the airport in time.
3 Jill has decided not _____ a car.
4 We've got a new computer in our office. I haven't learnt _____ it yet.
5 Karen failed _____ a good impression at the job interview.
6 We were all afraid to speak. Nobody dared _____ anything.

54.3 Put the verb into the correct form, **to ...** or **–ing**. (See Unit 53 for verbs + **–ing**.)

1 When I'm tired, I enjoy __watching__ television. It's relaxing. (watch)
2 It was a nice day, so we decided _____ for a walk. (go)
3 It's a nice day. Does anyone fancy _____ for a walk? (go)
4 I'm not in a hurry. I don't mind _____ . (wait)
5 They don't have much money. They can't afford _____ out very often. (go)
6 I wish that dog would stop _____ . It's driving me mad. (bark)
7 Our neighbour threatened _____ the police if we didn't stop the noise. (call)
8 We were hungry, so I suggested _____ dinner early. (have)
9 Hurry up! I don't want to risk _____ the train. (miss)
10 I'm still looking for a job, but I hope _____ something soon. (find)

54.4 Make a new sentence using the verb in brackets.

1 You've lost weight.   (seem)   __You seem to have lost weight.__
2 Tom is worried about something. (appear) Tom appears _____
3 You know a lot of people.   (seem)   You _____
4 My English is getting better. (seem)   _____
5 That car has broken down.   (appear) _____
6 David forgets things.   (tend)   _____
7 They have solved the problem. (claim)   _____

54.5 Complete each sentence using **what/how/whether** + the following verbs:

do ~~get~~ **go** **ride** **say** **use**

1 Do you know __how to get__ to John's house?
2 Can you show me _____ this washing machine?
3 Would you know _____ if there was a fire in the building?
4 You'll never forget _____ a bicycle once you've learnt.
5 I was really astonished. I didn't know _____ .
6 I've been invited to the party, but I haven't decided _____ or not.

→ Additional exercises 26–28 (pages 317–19)

Verb (+ object) + to ...
(I want you to ... etc.)

A

want	ask	help		would like
expect	beg	mean (= intend)		would prefer

These verbs are followed by **to ...** (*infinitive*). The structure can be:

verb + **to ...**   *or*   *verb* + *object* + **to ...**

- ☐ We **expected to be** late.
- ☐ **Would** you **like to go** now?
- ☐ He doesn't **want to know**.

- ☐ We expected **Dan to be** late.
- ☐ Would you like **me to go** now?
- ☐ He doesn't want **anybody to know**.

Do not say 'want that':
- ☐ Do you **want me to come** with you? (*not* Do you want that I come)

After **help** you can use the infinitive with or without **to**. So you can say:
- ☐ Can you help me **to move** this table? *or* Can you help me **move** this table?

B

tell	remind	force	encourage	teach	enable
order	warn	invite	persuade	get (= persuade, arrange for)	

These verbs have the structure *verb* + *object* + **to ...** :
- ☐ Can you **remind me to phone** Sam tomorrow?
- ☐ Who **taught you to drive**?
- ☐ I didn't move the piano by myself. I **got somebody to help** me.
- ☐ Jim said the switch was dangerous and **warned me not to touch** it.

In the next example, the verb is *passive* (**I was warned / we were told** etc.):
- ☐ I **was warned not to touch** the switch.

You cannot use **suggest** with the structure *verb* + *object* + **to ...** :
- ☐ Jane **suggested that I should ask** your advice. (*not* Jane suggested me to ask)

C

After **advise, recommend** and **allow**, two structures are possible. Compare:

verb + **-ing** (without an object)   *verb* + *object* + **to ...**

- ☐ I wouldn't **advise/recommend** staying in that hotel.
- ☐ They don't **allow** parking in front of the building.

- ☐ I wouldn't **advise/recommend anybody to stay** in that hotel.
- ☐ They don't **allow people to park** in front of the building.

Study these examples with (**be**) **allowed** (*passive*):
- ☐ **Parking isn't allowed** in front of the building.
- ☐ You **aren't allowed to park** in front of the building.

D

Make and **let**

These verbs have the structure *verb* + *object* + *infinitive* (without **to**):
- ☐ I **made him promise** that he wouldn't tell anybody what happened. (*not* to promise)
- ☐ Hot weather **makes me feel** tired. (= causes me to feel tired)
- ☐ Her parents wouldn't **let her go** out alone. (= wouldn't allow her to go out)
- ☐ **Let me carry** your bag for you.

We say '**make** somebody **do**' (*not* to do), but the *passive* is '(**be**) **made to do**' (with **to**):
- ☐ We **were made to wait** for two hours. (= They **made us wait** ...)

Suggest → Units 34, 53   **Tell/ask somebody to ...** → Unit 48D   **Verb + -ing** → Unit 53
Verb + to ... → Unit 54   **Verb + to ... and -ing** → Units 56–58   **Help** → Unit 57C

55.1 Complete the questions. Use **do you want me to ... ?** or **would you like me to ... ?** with these verbs (+ any other necessary words):

~~come~~ lend repeat show shut wait

1 Do you want to go alone, or _do you want me to come with you_ ?
2 Do you have enough money, or do you want .... ?
3 Shall I leave the window open, or would you .... ?
4 Do you know how to use the machine, or would .... ?
5 Did you hear what I said, or do .... ?
6 Can I go now, or do .... ?

55.2 Complete the sentences for these situations.

1 Lock the door. / OK.   She told _him to lock the door_ .

2 Why don't you come and stay with us? / That would be nice.   They invited him ....
....

3 Can I use your phone? / No!   She wouldn't let ....
....

4 Be careful. / Don't worry. I will.   She warned ....
....

5 Can you give me a hand? / Sure.   He asked ....
....

55.3 Complete each second sentence so that the meaning is similar to the first sentence.

1 My father said I could use his car.   My father allowed _me to use his car._
2 I was surprised that it rained.   I didn't expect ....
3 Don't stop him doing what he wants.   Let ....
4 Tim looks older when he wears glasses.   Tim's glasses make ....
5 I think you should know the truth.   I want ....
6 Don't let me forget to phone my sister.   Remind ....
7 At first I didn't want to apply for the job, but Sarah persuaded me.   Sarah persuaded ....
8 My lawyer said I shouldn't say anything to the police.   My lawyer advised ....
9 I was told that I shouldn't believe everything he says.   I was warned ....
10 If you've got a car, you are able to get around more easily.   Having a car enables ....

55.4 Put the verb into the correct form: infinitive (**do/make/eat** etc.), **to** + infinitive, or **-ing**.

1 They don't allow people _to park_ in front of the building. (park)
2 I've never been to Iceland, but I'd like .... there. (go)
3 I'm in a difficult position. What do you advise me .... ? (do)
4 The film was very sad. It made me .... (cry)
5 Diane's parents always encouraged her .... hard at school. (study)
6 I don't recommend .... in that restaurant. The food is terrible. (eat)
7 She said the letter was personal and wouldn't let me .... it. (read)
8 We are not allowed .... personal phone calls at work. (make)
9 'I don't think Alex likes me.' 'What makes you .... that?' (think)

Verb + -ing or to ... 1 (remember/regret etc.)

A

Some verbs are followed by -ing and some are followed by to ... .

Verbs usually followed by -ing:		
admit	fancy	postpone
avoid	finish	risk
consider	imagine	stop
deny	keep (on)	suggest
enjoy	mind	

For examples, see Unit 53.

Verbs usually followed by to ... :		
afford	fail	offer
agree	forget	plan
arrange	hope	promise
decide	learn	refuse
deserve	manage	threaten

For examples, see Unit 54.

B

Some verbs can be followed by -ing or to ... with a difference of meaning:

remember

I **remember doing** something = I did it and now I remember this.
You **remember doing** something *after* you have done it.
- □ I know I locked the door. I clearly **remember locking** it.
  (= I locked it, and now I remember this)
- □ He could **remember driving** along the road just before the accident, but he couldn't remember the accident itself.

I **remembered to do** something = I remembered that I had to do it, so I did it.
You **remember to do** something *before* you do it.
- □ I **remembered to lock** the door, but I forgot to shut the windows.
  (= I remembered that I had to lock it, and so I locked it)
- □ Please **remember to post** the letter.
  (= don't forget to post it)

regret

I **regret doing** something = I did it and now I'm sorry about it:
- □ I now **regret saying** what I said. I shouldn't have said it.
- □ It began to get cold and he **regretted not wearing** his coat.

I **regret to say / to tell** you / **to inform** you = I'm sorry that I have to say (etc.):
- □ *(from a formal letter)* We **regret to inform** you that we cannot offer you the job.

go on

Go on doing something = continue with the same thing:
- □ The president paused for a moment and then **went on talking**.
- □ We need to change. We can't **go on living** like this.

Go on to do something = do or say something new:
- □ After discussing the economy, the president then **went on to talk** about foreign policy.

C

The following verbs can be followed by -ing or to ... :
begin   start   continue   intend   bother

So you can say:
- □ It has **started raining**. *or* It has **started to rain**.
- □ John **intends buying** a house. *or* John **intends to buy** ...
- □ Don't **bother locking** the door. *or* Don't **bother to lock** ...

But normally we do not use -ing after -ing:
- □ It's starting **to rain**. (*not* It's starting raining)

Verb + -ing → Unit 53   Verb + to ... → Units 54–55   Other verbs + -ing or to ... → Units 57–58

56.1 Put the verb into the correct form, **-ing** or **to** ... . Sometimes either form is possible.

1 They denied ....*stealing*.... the money. (steal)
2 I don't enjoy .... very much. (drive)
3 I don't want .... out tonight. I'm too tired. (go)
4 I can't afford .... out tonight. I don't have enough money. (go)
5 Has it stopped .... yet? (rain)
6 Our team was unlucky to lose the game. We deserved .... (win)
7 Why do you keep .... me questions? Can't you leave me alone? (ask)
8 Please stop .... me questions! (ask)
9 I refuse .... any more questions. (answer)
10 One of the boys admitted .... the window. (break)
11 The boy's father promised .... for the window to be repaired. (pay)
12 If the company continues .... money, the factory may be closed. (lose)
13 'Does Sarah know about the meeting?' 'No, I forgot .... her.' (tell)
14 The baby began .... in the middle of the night. (cry)
15 Julia has been ill, but now she's beginning .... better. (get)
16 I've enjoyed .... you. I hope .... you again soon. (meet, see)

56.2 Here is some information about Tom when he was a child.

1 He was in hospital when he was four.
2 He went to Paris when he was eight.
3 He cried on his first day at school.
4 Once he fell into the river.
5 He said he wanted to be a doctor.
6 Once he was bitten by a dog.

He can still remember 1, 2 and 4. But he can't remember 3, 5 and 6. Write sentences beginning
He can remember ... or **He can't remember ...** .

1 ...*He can remember being in hospital when he was four.*..
2 ....
3 ....
4 ....
5 ....
6 ....

56.3 Complete each sentence with a verb in the correct form, **-ing** or **to** ... .

1 a Please remember ...*to lock*.... the door when you go out.
   b A: You lent me some money a few months ago.
     B: Did I? Are you sure? I don't remember .... you any money.
   c A: Did you remember .... your sister?
     B: Oh no, I completely forgot. I'll phone her tomorrow.
   d When you see Steve, remember .... him my regards.
   e Someone must have taken my bag. I clearly remember .... it by the
     window and now it has gone.

2 a I believe that what I said was fair. I don't regret .... it.
   b I knew they were in trouble, but I regret .... I did nothing to help them.

3 a Ben joined the company nine years ago. He became assistant manager after two
     years, and a few years later he went on .... manager of the company.
   b I can't go on .... here any more. I want a different job.
   c When I came into the room, Liz was reading a newspaper. She looked up and said hello,
     and then went on .... her newspaper.

→ Additional exercises 26–28 (pages 317–19)

A Try to ... and try -ing

Try to do = attempt to do, make an effort to do:
- ☐ I was very tired. I **tried to keep** my eyes open, but I couldn't.
- ☐ Please **try to be** quiet when you come home. Everyone will be asleep.

Try also means 'do something as an experiment or test'. For example:
- ☐ These cakes are delicious. You should **try** one. (= you should have one to see if you like it)
- ☐ We couldn't find anywhere to stay. We **tried** every hotel in the town, but they were all full. (= we went to every hotel to see if they had a room)

If **try** (with this meaning) is followed by a verb, we say **try -ing**:
- ☐ A: The photocopier doesn't seem to be working.
  B: **Try pressing** the green button.
  (= press the green button – perhaps this will help to solve the problem)

Compare:
- ☐ I **tried to move** the table, but it was too heavy. (so I couldn't move it)
- ☐ I didn't like the way the furniture was arranged, so I **tried moving** the table to the other side of the room. But it still didn't look right, so I moved it back again.

B Need to ... and need -ing

I **need to do** something = it is necessary for me to do it:
- ☐ I **need to take** more exercise.
- ☐ He **needs to work** harder if he wants to make progress.
- ☐ I don't **need to come** to the meeting, do I?

This room **needs tidying**.

Something **needs doing** = it needs to be done:
- ☐ The batteries in the radio **need changing**.
  (= they need to be changed)
- ☐ Do you think my jacket **needs cleaning**?
  (= ... needs to be cleaned)
- ☐ It's a difficult problem. It **needs thinking** about very carefully. (= it needs to be thought about)

C Help and can't help

You can say **help to do** or **help do** (with or without **to**):
- ☐ Everybody **helped to clean** up after the party. *or*
  Everybody **helped clean** up ...
- ☐ Can you **help** me **to move** this table? *or*
  Can you **help** me **move** ...

I **can't help doing** something = I can't stop myself doing it:
- ☐ I don't like him, but he has a lot of problems. I **can't help feeling** sorry for him.
- ☐ She tried to be serious, but she **couldn't help laughing**.
  (= she couldn't stop herself laughing)
- ☐ I'm sorry I'm so nervous. I **can't help it**.
  (= I can't help **being** nervous)

57.1 Make suggestions. Each time use **try** + one of the following suggestions:

    phone his office   move the aerial   ~~change the batteries~~

    turn it the other way   take an aspirin

1   The radio isn't working. I wonder what's wrong with it.   Have you _tried changing the batteries?_

2   I can't open the door. The key won't turn.   Try ....

3   The TV picture isn't very good. What can I do about it?   Have you tried ....

4   I can't contact Fred. He's not at home. What shall I do?   Why don't you ....

5   I've got a terrible headache. I wish it would go.   Have you ....

57.2 For each picture, write a sentence with **need(s)** + one of the following verbs:

~~clean~~   cut   empty   paint   tighten

1	2	3	4	5

1 This jacket is dirty.   _It needs cleaning._

2 The room isn't very nice. ....

3 The grass is very long. It ....

4 The screws are loose. ....

5 The bin is full. ....

57.3 Put the verb into the correct form.

1 a   I was very tired. I tried _to keep_ (keep) my eyes open, but I couldn't.

   b   I rang the doorbell, but there was no answer. Then I tried .... (knock) on the door, but there was still no answer.

   c   We tried .... (put) the fire out but without success. We had to call the fire brigade.

   d   Sue needed to borrow some money. She tried .... (ask) Gerry, but he was short of money too.

   e   I tried .... (reach) the shelf, but I wasn't tall enough.

   f   Please leave me alone. I'm trying .... (concentrate).

2 a   I need a change. I need .... (go) away for a while.

   b   My grandmother isn't able to look after herself any more. She needs .... (look) after.

   c   The windows are dirty. They need .... (clean).

   d   Your hair is getting very long. It needs .... (cut).

   e   You don't need .... (iron) that shirt. It doesn't need .... (iron).

3 a   They were talking very loudly. I couldn't help .... (overhear) what they said.

   b   Can you help me .... (get) the dinner ready?

   c   He looks so funny. Whenever I see him, I can't help .... (smile).

   d   The fine weather helped .... (make) it a very enjoyable holiday.

Verb + -ing or to ... 3 (like / would like etc.)

A   Like / love / hate

When you talk about repeated actions, you can use **-ing** or **to** ... after these verbs.
So you can say:

- □ Do you **like** gett**ing** up early? *or* Do you **like to get** up early?
- □ Stephanie **hates** fly**ing**. *or* Stephanie **hates to fly**.
- □ I **love** meet**ing** people. *or* I **love to meet** people.
- □ I don't **like** be**ing** kept waiting. *or* ... **like to be** kept waiting.
- □ I don't **like** friends call**ing** me at work. *or* ... friends **to call** me at work.

but

(1) We use **-ing** (*not* **to** ...) when we talk about a situation that already exists (or existed).
   For example:
   - □ Paul lives in Berlin now. He **likes** liv**ing** there. (He **likes** liv**ing** in Berlin = He lives there and he likes it)
   - □ Do you **like** be**ing** a student? (You are a student – do you like it?)
   - □ The office I worked in was horrible. I **hated** work**ing** there. (I worked there and I hated it)

(2) There is sometimes a difference between **I like to do** and **I like doing**:

   I like doing something = I do it and I enjoy it:
   - □ I **like** clean**ing** the kitchen. (= I enjoy it.)

   I like to do something = I think it is a good thing to do, but I don't necessarily enjoy it:
   - □ It's not my favourite job, but I **like to clean** the kitchen as often as possible.

Note that **enjoy** and **mind** are always followed by **-ing** (*not* **to** ...):
   - □ I **enjoy** clean**ing** the kitchen. (*not* I enjoy to clean)
   - □ I don't **mind** clean**ing** the kitchen. (*not* I don't mind to clean)

B   Would like / would love / would hate / would prefer

Would like / would love etc. are usually followed by **to** ... :
   - □ I'd **like** (= would like) **to go** away for a few days.
   - □ Would you **like to come** to dinner on Friday?
   - □ I wouldn't **like to go** on holiday alone.
   - □ I'd **love to meet** your family.
   - □ Would you **prefer to have** dinner now or later?

Compare **I like** and **I would like** (**I'd** like):
   - □ I **like** play**ing** tennis. / I **like to play** tennis. (= I like it in general)
   - □ I'd **like to play** tennis today. (= I want to play today)

Would mind is always followed by **-ing** (*not* **to** ...):
   - □ Would you **mind** clos**ing** the door, please?

C

I would like **to have done** something = I regret now that I didn't or couldn't do it:
   - □ It's a pity we didn't see Val when we were in London. I **would like to have seen** her again.
   - □ We'd **like to have gone** away, but we were too busy at home.

You can use the same structure after **would love / would hate / would prefer**:
   - □ Poor old David! I **would hate to have been** in his position.
   - □ I'd **love to have gone** to the party, but it was impossible.

58.1 Write sentences about yourself. Say whether you like or don't like these activities. Choose one of these verbs for each sentence:

      like / don't like   **love**   **hate**   **enjoy**   **don't mind**

1 (fly) _I don't like flying._ or _I don't like to fly._

2 (play cards) ....

3 (be alone) ....

4 (go to museums) ....

5 (cook) ....

58.2 Make sentences from the words in brackets. Use **-ing** or **to** ... . Sometimes either form is possible.

1 Paul lives in Berlin now. It's nice. He likes it.
  (he / like / live / there) _He likes living there._

2 Jane is a biology teacher. She likes her job.
  (she / like / teach / biology) She ....

3 Joe always carries his camera with him and takes a lot of photographs.
  (he / like / take / photographs) ....

4 I used to work in a supermarket. I didn't like it much.
  (I / not / like / work / there) ....

5 Rachel is studying medicine. She likes it.
  (she / like / study / medicine) ....

6 Dan is famous, but he doesn't like it.
  (he / not / like / be / famous) ....

7 Jennifer is a very cautious person. She doesn't take many risks.
  (she / not / like / take / risks) ....

8 I don't like surprises.
  (I / like / know / things / in advance) ....

58.3 Complete each sentence with a verb in the correct form, **-ing** or **to** ... . In one sentence either form is possible.

1 It's good to visit other places – I enjoy _travelling_ .

2 'Would you like .... down?' 'No, thanks. I'll stand.'

3 I'm not quite ready yet. Would you mind .... a little longer?

4 When I was a child, I hated .... to bed early.

5 When I have to catch a train, I'm always worried that I'll miss it. So I like .... to the station in plenty of time.

6 I enjoy .... busy. I don't like it when there's nothing to do.

7 I would love .... to your wedding, but I'm afraid it isn't possible.

8 I don't like .... in this part of town. I want to move somewhere else.

9 Do you have a minute? I'd like .... to you about something.

10 If there's bad news and good news, I like .... the bad news first.

58.4 Write sentences using **would ... to have (done)**. Use the verbs in brackets.

1 It's a pity I couldn't go to the wedding. (like) _I would like to have gone to the wedding._

2 It's a pity I didn't see the programme. (like) ....

3 I'm glad I didn't lose my watch. (hate) ....

4 It's a pity I didn't meet your parents. (love) ....

5 I'm glad I wasn't alone. (not / like) ....

6 It's a pity I couldn't travel by train. (prefer) ....

Prefer and would rather

A Prefer to do and prefer doing

You can use 'prefer to (do)' or 'prefer -ing' to say what you prefer in general:

☐ I don't like cities. I prefer to live in the country.   or   I prefer living in the country.

Study the differences in structure after prefer. We say:

	I prefer	something	to something else.
	I prefer	doing something	to doing something else.
but	I prefer	to do something	rather than (do) something else.

☐ I prefer this coat to the coat you were wearing yesterday.
☐ I prefer driving to travelling by train.
but ☐ I prefer to drive rather than travel by train.
☐ Sarah prefers to live in the country rather than (live) in a city.

B Would prefer (I'd prefer …)

We use would prefer to say what somebody wants in a specific situation (not in general):

☐ 'Would you prefer tea or coffee?'   'Coffee, please.'

We say 'would prefer to do something' (*not* doing):

☐ 'Shall we go by train?'   'I'd prefer to drive.' (*not* I'd prefer driving)
☐ I'd prefer to stay at home tonight rather than go to the cinema.

C Would rather (I'd rather …)

Would rather (do) = would prefer (to do). We use would rather + *infinitive* (without to).
Compare:

☐ 'Shall we go by train?' { 'I'd prefer to drive.'
                            { 'I'd rather drive.' (*not* to drive)
☐ 'Would you rather have tea or coffee?'   'Coffee, please.'

The negative is 'I'd rather not (do something)':

☐ I'm tired. I'd rather not go out this evening, if you don't mind.
☐ 'Do you want to go out this evening?'   'I'd rather not.'

We say 'would rather do something than do something else':

☐ I'd rather stay at home tonight than go to the cinema.

D I'd rather you did something

We say 'I'd rather you did something' (*not* I'd rather you do). For example:

☐ 'Shall I stay here?'   'I'd rather you came with us.' (= I would prefer this)
☐ 'I'll repair your bike tomorrow, OK?'   'I'd rather you did it today.'
☐ 'Are you going to tell them what happened?'   'No. I'd rather they didn't know.'
☐ Shall I tell them, or would you rather they didn't know?

In this structure we use the *past* (came, did etc.), but the meaning is present *not* past.
Compare:

☐ I'd rather make dinner now.
  I'd rather you made dinner now. (*not* I'd rather you make)

I'd rather you didn't (do something) = I'd prefer you not to do it:

☐ I'd rather you didn't tell anyone what I said.
☐ 'Shall I tell Linda what happened?'   'I'd rather you didn't.'

Would prefer → Unit 58B   Prefer (one thing) to (another) → Unit 136D

59.1 Which do you prefer? Write sentences using 'I prefer (something) to (something else)'. Put the verb into the correct form where necessary.

1 (drive / travel by train) _I prefer driving to travelling by train._

2 (basketball / football)
   I prefer ....

3 (phone people / send emails)
   I .... to ....

4 (go to the cinema / watch videos at home)
   ....

Now rewrite sentences 3 and 4 using the structure 'I prefer to (do something)'.

5 (1) _I prefer to drive rather than travel by train._

6 (3) I prefer to ....

7 (4) ....

59.2 Write sentences using I'd prefer ... and I'd rather ... + the following:

| eat at home | ~~get a taxi~~ | go alone | wait a few minutes | listen to some music |
| stand | go for a swim | ~~wait till later~~ | think about it for a while | |

1	Shall we walk home?	(prefer)	_I'd prefer to get a taxi._
2	Do you want to eat now?	(rather)	_I'd rather wait till later._
3	Would you like to watch TV?	(rather)	....
4	Do you want to go to a restaurant?	(prefer)	....
5	Let's leave now.	(rather)	....
6	Shall we play tennis?	(rather)	....
7	I think we should decide now.	(prefer)	....
8	Would you like to sit down?	(rather)	....
9	Do you want me to come with you?	(prefer)	....

Now use the same ideas to complete these sentences using **than** and **rather than**.

10 I'd prefer to get a taxi _rather than walk home._

11 I'd prefer to go for a swim ....

12 I'd rather eat at home ....

13 I'd prefer to think about it for a while ....

14 I'd rather listen to some music ....

59.3 Complete the sentences using **would you rather I** ... .

1 Are you going to make dinner or _would you rather I made it_ .... ?

2 Are you going to tell Liz what happened or would you rather .... ?

3 Are you going to do the shopping or .... ?

4 Are you going to phone Diane or .... ?

59.4 Use your own ideas to complete these sentences.

1 'Shall I tell Ann the news?'   'No, I'd rather she _didn't_ know.'

2 Do you want me to go now or would you rather I .... here?

3 Do you want to go out this evening or would you rather .... at home?

4 This is a private letter addressed to me. I'd rather you .... read it.

5 I don't really like these shoes. I'd rather they .... a different colour.

6 A: Do you mind if I turn on the radio?
   B: I'd rather you .... I'm trying to study.

A

If a preposition (**in/for/about** etc.) is followed by a verb, the verb ends in **-ing**:

	preposition	*verb* (**-ing**)	
Are you interested	**in**	working	for us?
I'm not very good	**at**	learning	languages.
Sue must be fed up	**with**	studying.	
What are the advantages	**of**	having	a car?
Thanks very much	**for**	inviting	me to your party.
How	**about**	meeting	for lunch tomorrow?
Why don't you go out	**instead of**	sitting	at home all the time?
Carol went to work	**in spite of**	feeling	ill.

You can also say 'instead of **somebody** doing something', 'fed up with **people** doing something' etc. :

☐ I'm fed up with **people** telling me what to do.

B

Note the use of the following prepositions + **-ing**:

before -ing and **after -ing**:

☐ **Before going** out, I phoned Sarah. (*not* Before to go out)
☐ What did you do **after leaving** school?

You can also say '**Before I went** out …' and '… **after you left** school'.

by -ing (to say *how* something happens):

☐ The burglars got into the house **by breaking** a window and climbing in.
☐ You can improve your English **by reading** more.
☐ She made herself ill **by not eating** properly.
☐ Many accidents are caused **by** people driving too fast.

without -ing:

☐ We ran ten kilometres **without stopping**.
☐ It was a stupid thing to say. I said it **without thinking**.
☐ She needs to work **without** people disturbing her. (*or* … **without** being disturbed.)
☐ I have enough problems of my own **without having** to worry about yours.

C

To -ing (look forward **to doing** something etc.)

To is often part of the *infinitive* (**to do** / **to see** etc.):

☐ We decided **to go** out.
☐ Would you like **to meet** for lunch tomorrow?

But **to** is also a *preposition* (like **in/for/about/from** etc.). For example:

☐ We drove from London **to Edinburgh**.
☐ I prefer tea **to coffee**.
☐ Are you looking forward **to the weekend**?

If a preposition is followed by a verb, the verb ends in **-ing**:

in doing   **about** meeting   **without** stopping (etc.)

So, when **to** is a preposition and it is followed by a verb, you must say **to -ing**:

☐ I prefer driving **to travelling** by train. (*not* to travel)
☐ Are you looking forward **to going** on holiday? (*not* looking forward to go)

Be/get used to –ing → Unit 61   **Verb + preposition + –ing** → Unit 62   **While/when –ing** → Unit 68B
In spite of → Unit 113   **Prepositions** → Units 121–136

60.1 Complete the second sentence so that it means the same as the first.

1 Why is it useful to have a car?
What are the advantages of <u>having a car</u> ?

2 I don't intend to apply for the job.
I have no intention of _____ .

3 Helen has a good memory for names.
Helen is good at _____ .

4 Mark won't pass the exam. He has no chance.
Mark has no chance of _____ .

5 Did you get into trouble because you were late?
Did you get into trouble for _____ ?

6 We didn't eat at home. We went to a restaurant instead.
Instead of _____ .

7 We got into the exhibition. We didn't have to queue.
We got into the exhibition without _____ .

8 Our team played well, but we lost the game.
Our team lost the game despite _____ .

60.2 Complete the sentences using **by -ing**. Use the following (with the verb in the correct form):

borrow too much money	~~break a window~~	drive too fast
put some pictures on the walls	stand on a chair	turn a key

1 The burglars got into the house <u>by breaking a window</u> .
2 I was able to reach the top shelf _____ .
3 You start the engine of a car _____ .
4 Kevin got himself into financial trouble _____ .
5 You can put people's lives in danger _____ .
6 We made the room look nicer _____ .

60.3 Complete the sentences with a suitable word. Use only one word each time.

1 We ran ten kilometres without <u>stopping</u> .
2 He left the hotel without _____ his bill.
3 It's a nice morning. How about _____ for a walk?
4 We were able to translate the letter into English without _____ a dictionary.
5 Before _____ to bed, I like to have a hot drink.
6 It was a long journey. I was very tired after _____ on a train for 36 hours.
7 I was annoyed because the decision was made without anybody _____ me.
8 After _____ the same job for ten years, I felt I needed a change.
9 We lost our way because we went straight on instead of _____ left.
10 I like these photographs you took. You're good at _____ photographs.

60.4 For each situation, write a sentence with **I'm (not) looking forward to**.

1 You are going on holiday next week. How do you feel?
<u>I'm looking forward to going on holiday.</u>

2 Diane is a good friend of yours and she is coming to visit you soon. So you will see her again soon. How do you feel? I'm _____

3 You are going to the dentist tomorrow. You don't enjoy going to the dentist. How do you feel?
I'm not _____

4 Carol is a student at school. She hates it, but she is leaving school next summer.
How does she feel? _____

5 You've arranged to play tennis tomorrow. You like tennis a lot. How do you feel?
_____

Be/get used to something (I'm used to ...)

A Study this example situation:

Lisa is American, but she lives in Britain. When she first drove a car in Britain, she found it very difficult because she had to drive on the left, not on the right. Driving on the left was strange and difficult for her because:

She **wasn't used to it.**
She **wasn't used to driving** on the left.

But after a lot of practice, driving on the left became less strange. So:
She **got used to driving** on the left.

Now it's no problem for Lisa:
She **is used to driving** on the left.

B **I'm used to** something = it is not new or strange for me:
   ☐ Frank lives alone. He doesn't mind this because he has lived alone for 15 years. It is not strange for him. He **is used to it.** He **is used to living** alone.
   ☐ I bought some new shoes. They felt a bit strange at first because I **wasn't used to them.**
   ☐ Our new flat is on a very busy street. I expect we'll **get used to the noise,** but at the moment it's very disturbing.
   ☐ Diane has a new job. She has to get up much earlier now than before – at 6.30. She finds this difficult because she **isn't used to getting** up so early.
   ☐ Barbara's husband is often away from home. She doesn't mind this. She **is used to him being** away.

C After **be/get used** you cannot use the infinitive (**to do / to drive** etc.). We say:
   ☐ She is used **to driving** on the left. (*not* She is used to drive)

When we say 'I am used **to** something', **to** is a *preposition*, not a part of the infinitive.
So we say:
   ☐ Frank is used **to living** alone. (*not* Frank is used to live)
   ☐ Lisa had to get used **to driving** on the left. (*not* get used to drive)

D Do not confuse **I am used to doing** and **I used to do:**

I am used **to** (**doing**) something = it isn't strange or new for me:
   ☐ I am used **to the weather** in this country.
   ☐ I am used **to driving** on the left because I've lived in Britain a long time.

I used **to do** something = I did it regularly in the past but no longer do it. You can use this only for the past, not for the present.
The structure is 'I **used** to do' (*not* 'I **am** used to do'):
   ☐ I **used to drive** to work every day, but these days I usually go by bike.
   ☐ We **used to live** in a small village, but now we live in London.

Used to (do) → Unit 18   **To + -ing** → Unit 60C

Exercises

61.1 Look again at the situation in Section A on the opposite page ('Lisa is American ...').
The following situations are similar. Complete the sentences using **used to**.

1 Juan is Spanish and went to live in England. In Spain he usually had dinner late in the evening, but in England dinner was at 6 o'clock. This was very early for him and he found it very strange at first.
When Juan first went to England, he .... dinner so early, but after some time he .... it. Now he finds it normal. He .... at 6 o'clock.

2 Julia is a nurse. A year ago she started working nights. At first she found it hard and didn't like it.
She .... nights and it took her a few months to .... it. Now, after a year, she's quite happy. She .... nights.

61.2 What do you say in these situations? Use **I'm (not) used to ...** .

1 You live alone. You don't mind this. You have always lived alone.
FRIEND: Do you get a bit lonely sometimes?
YOU: No, _I'm used to living alone._

2 You sleep on the floor. You don't mind this. You have always slept on the floor.
FRIEND: Wouldn't you prefer to sleep in a bed?
YOU: No, I ....

3 You have to work long hours in your job. This is not a problem for you. You have always worked long hours.
FRIEND: You have to work very long hours in your job, don't you?
YOU: Yes, but I don't mind that. I ....

4 You usually go to bed early. Last night you went to bed very late (for you) and as a result you are very tired this morning.
FRIEND: You look tired this morning.
YOU: Yes, ...

61.3 Read the situations and complete the sentences using **used to**.

1 Some friends of yours have just moved into a flat on a busy street. It is very noisy.
They'll have to _get used to the noise._

2 The children at school had a new teacher. She was different from the teacher before her, but this wasn't a problem for the children. They soon ....

3 Sue moved from a big house to a much smaller one. She found it strange at first. She had to .... in a much smaller house.

4 Some people you know from Britain are going to live in your country. What will they have to get used to?
They'll have to ....

61.4 Complete the sentences using only one word each time (see Section C).

1 Lisa had to get used to _driving_ on the left.
2 We used to _live_ in a small village, but now we live in London.
3 Dan used to .... a lot of coffee. Now he prefers tea.
4 I feel very full after that meal. I'm not used to .... so much.
5 I wouldn't like to share an office. I'm used to .... my own office.
6 I used to .... a car, but I sold it a few months ago
7 When we were children, we used to .... swimming very often.
8 There used to .... a cinema here, but it was knocked down a few years ago.
9 I'm the boss here! I'm not used to .... told what to do.

→ Additional exercises 26–28 (pages 317–19)   **123**

Unit 62

Verb + preposition + -ing (succeed in -ing / accuse somebody of -ing etc.)

A

Many verbs have the structure *verb + preposition* (**in/for/about** etc.) *+ object*.
For example:

	verb +	preposition	+ object
We **talked**	about	the problem.
You must **apologise**	for	what you said.

If the *object* is another verb, it ends in **-ing**:

	verb +	preposition	+ -ing (*object*)
We **talked**	about	going to America.
You must **apologise**	for	not telling the truth.

Some more verbs with this structure:

succeed (in)	Have you **succeeded**	in	finding a job yet?
insist (on)	They **insisted**	on	paying for the meal.
think (of)	I'm **thinking**	of	buying a house.
dream (of)	I wouldn't **dream**	of	asking them for money.
approve (of)	He doesn't **approve**	of	swearing.
decide (against)	We have **decided**	against	moving to London.
feel (like)	Do you **feel**	like	going out tonight?
look forward (to)	I'm **looking forward**	to	meeting her.

You can also say 'approve of **somebody** doing something', 'look forward to **somebody** doing something':

- ☐ I don't approve **of people** killing animals for fun.
- ☐ We are all looking forward **to Peter** coming home.

B

The following verbs can have the structure *verb + object + preposition + -ing*:

	verb +	object +	preposition	+ -ing (*object*)
congratulate (on)	I **congratulated**	Liz	on	getting a new job.
accuse (of)	They **accused**	us	of	telling lies.
suspect (of)	Nobody **suspected**	the general	of	being a spy.
prevent (from)	What **prevented**	you	from	coming to see us?
stop (from)	The rain didn't **stop**	us	from	enjoying our holiday.
thank (for)	I forgot to **thank**	them	for	helping me.
excuse (for)	Excuse	me	for	being so late.
forgive (for)	Please **forgive**	me	for	not writing to you.

You can say '**stop** somebody doing' or '**stop** somebody **from** doing':

- ☐ You can't **stop** me doing what I want. *or* You can't **stop** me **from** doing what I want.

Some of these verbs are often used in the *passive*. For example:

- ☐ We **were accused of** telling lies.
- ☐ The general **was suspected of** being a spy.

Note that we say 'apologise **to somebody** for …':

- ☐ I apologised **to them** for keeping them waiting. (*not* I apologised them)

Decide to ... → Unit 54A   **Preposition + -ing** → Unit 60   **Verb + preposition** → Units 132–136

62.1 Complete each sentence using only one word.

1 Our neighbours apologised for ......*making*...... so much noise.
2 I feel lazy. I don't feel like .... any work.
3 I wanted to go out alone, but Joe insisted on .... with me.
4 I'm fed up with my job. I'm thinking of .... something else.
5 We have decided against .... a new car because we can't really afford it.
6 I hope you get in touch with me soon. I'm looking forward to ....
   from you.
7 The weather was extremely bad and this prevented us from .... out.
8 The man who has been arrested is suspected of .... a false passport.
9 I think you should apologise to Sue for .... so rude to her.
10 Some parents don't approve of their children .... a lot of television.
11 I'm sorry I can't come to your party, but thank you very much for .... me.

62.2 Complete each sentence using a preposition + one of the following verbs (in the correct form):

   carry   cause   escape   ~~go~~   interrupt   live   see   solve   spend   walk

1 Do you feel ......*like going*...... out this evening?
2 It took us a long time, but we finally succeeded .... the problem.
3 I've always dreamed .... in a small house by the sea.
4 The driver of the other car accused me .... the accident.
5 There's a fence around the lawn to stop people .... on the grass.
6 Excuse me .... you, but may I ask you something?
7 Where are you thinking .... your holiday this year?
8 The guards weren't able to prevent the prisoner ....
9 My bag wasn't very heavy, but Dan insisted .... it for me.
10 It's a pity Paul can't come to the party. I was really looking forward
   .... him.

62.3 Complete the sentences on the right.

1   YOU   KEVIN
    It was nice of you to help me. Thanks very much.
    Kevin thanked ......*me for helping him*...... .

2   ANN   TOM
    I'll drive you to the station. I insist.
    Tom insisted ....
    ....

3   YOU   DAN
    I hear you got married. Congratulations!
    Dan congratulated me ....
    ....

4   SUE   JENNY
    It was nice of you to come to see me. Thank you.
    Jenny thanked ....
    ....

5   YOU   KATE
    I'm sorry I didn't phone earlier.
    Kate apologised ....
    ....

6   YOU   JANE
    You're selfish.
    Jane accused ....
    ....

→ Additional exercises 27-28 (pages 318–19)

Expressions + -ing

A

When these expressions are followed by a verb, the verb ends in **-ing**:

It's no use / It's no good
- □ There's nothing you can do about the situation, so **it's no use** worrying about it.
- □ **It's no good** trying to persuade me. You won't succeed.

There's no point in
- □ **There's no point in** having a car if you never use it.
- □ **There was no point in** waiting any longer, so we went.

But we usually say 'the point of doing something':
- □ **What's the point of** having a car if you never use it?

It's (not) worth
- □ I live only a short walk from here, so **it's not worth** taking a taxi.
- □ Our flight was very early in the morning, so **it wasn't worth** going to bed.

You can say that a film is **worth seeing**, a book is **worth reading** etc. :
- □ What was the film like? Was it **worth seeing**?
- □ Thieves broke into the house but didn't take anything. There was nothing **worth stealing**.

B

Have difficulty -ing, have trouble -ing

We say 'have difficulty doing something' (*not* to do):
- □ I had no **difficulty** finding a place to live. (*not* difficulty to find)
- □ Did you have any **difficulty** getting a visa?
- □ People often have **difficulty** reading my writing.

You can also say 'have **trouble** doing something':
- □ I had no **trouble** finding a place to live.

C

We use **-ing** after:

a waste of money / a waste of time
- □ It was a **waste of time** reading that book. It was rubbish.
- □ It's a **waste of money** buying things you don't need.

spend/waste (time)
- □ He **spent** hours trying to repair the clock.
- □ I **waste** a lot of time day-dreaming.

(be) busy
- □ She said she couldn't see me. She was too **busy** doing other things.

D

Go swimming / go fishing etc.

We use **go -ing** for a number of activities (especially sports). For example, you can say:

go swimming   go sailing   go fishing   go climbing   go skiing   go jogging

Also **go** shopping, **go** sightseeing

- □ How often do you **go** swimming?
- □ I'd like to **go** skiing.
- □ When did you last **go** shopping?
- □ I've never **been** sailing. (For **gone** and **been**, see Unit 7D.)

63.1 Make sentences beginning **There's no point ... .**

1 Why have a car if you never use it?
  There's no point in having a car if you never use it.

2 Why work if you don't need money?
  ....

3 Don't try to study if you feel tired.
  ....

4 Why hurry if you've got plenty of time?
  ....

63.2 Complete the sentences on the right.

1	Shall we get a taxi home?	No, it isn't far. It's not worth *getting a taxi* .
2	If you need help, why don't you ask Dave?	It's no use .... He won't be able to do anything.
3	I don't really want to go out tonight.	Well, stay at home! There's no point .... if you don't want to.
4	Shall I phone Liz now?	No, it's no good .... now. She won't be at home.
5	Are you going to complain about what happened?	No, it's not worth .... Nobody will do anything about it.
6	Do you ever read newspapers?	No, I think it's a waste ....
7	Do you want to keep these old clothes?	No, let's throw them away. They're not worth ....

63.3 Write sentences using **difficulty**.

1 I managed to get a visa, but it was difficult. I had difficulty *getting a visa* .
2 I find it hard to remember people's names.
  I have difficulty ....
3 Lucy managed to get a job without difficulty.
  She had no ....
4 It won't be difficult to get a ticket for the game.
  You won't have any ....

63.4 Complete the sentences. Use only one word each time.

1 It's a waste of money ....*buying*.... things you don't need.
2 Every morning I spend about an hour .... the newspaper.
3 'What's Sue doing?' 'She's going away tomorrow, so she's busy ....'
4 I think you waste too much time .... television.
5 There's a beautiful view from that hill. It's worth .... to the top.
6 It's no use .... for the job. I know I wouldn't get it.
7 Just stay calm. There's no point in .... angry.

63.5 Complete these sentences with the following (with the verb in the correct form):

  go riding   ~~go sailing~~   **go shopping**   **go skiing**   **go swimming**

1 Barry lives by the sea and he's got a boat, so he often ....*goes sailing*.... .
2 It was a very hot day, so we .... in the lake.
3 There's plenty of snow in the mountains, so we'll be able to ....
4 Helen has got two horses. She .... regularly.
5 'Where's Dan?' 'He's .... There were a few things he needed to buy.'

→ Additional exercises 27–28 (pages 318–19)

To ... , for ... and so that ... (purpose)

A

We use **to ...** to say why somebody does something (= the purpose of an action):

☐ 'Why are you going out?' 'To post a letter.'
☐ A friend of mine phoned **to invite** me to a party.
☐ We shouted **to warn** everybody of the danger.

We use **to ...** to say why something exists (= its purpose):

☐ This wall is **to keep** people out of the garden.
☐ The president has a team of bodyguards **to protect** him.

B

We use **to ...** to say what can be done or must be done with something:

☐ It's difficult to find **a place to park** in the centre. (= a place where you can park)
☐ Would you like **something to eat**?
☐ Have you got **much work to do**? (= work that you must do)
☐ I get lonely if there's **nobody to talk to**.
☐ I need **something to open** this bottle **with**.

Also **money/time/chance/opportunity/energy/courage** etc. to (do something):

☐ They gave us **some money to buy** some food.
☐ Do you have **much opportunity to practise** your English?
☐ I need **a few days to think** about your proposal.

C

For ... and to ...

Compare:

for + *noun*	to + *verb*
☐ I'm going to Spain **for a holiday**.	☐ I'm going to Spain **to learn** Spanish. (*not* for learn, *not* for learning)
☐ What would you like **for dinner**?	☐ What would you like **to eat**?
☐ Let's go to the pool **for a swim**.	☐ Let's go to the pool **to have** a swim.

You can say '**for** (somebody) **to** (do something)':

☐ There weren't any chairs **for us to sit on**, so we had to sit on the floor.

You can use **for -ing** or **to ...** to talk about the general purpose of something, or what it is generally used for:

☐ Do you use this brush **for** washing the dishes? (*or* ... **to wash** the dishes?)

You can use **What ... for?** to ask about purpose:

☐ **What** is this switch **for**?
☐ **What** did you do that **for**?

D

So that

Sometimes you have to use **so that** for purpose.

We use **so that** (*not* to ...) especially

when the purpose is *negative* (**so that ... won't/wouldn't**):

☐ I hurried **so that I wouldn't** be late. (= because I didn't want to be late)
☐ Leave early **so that** you **won't** (*or* **don't**) miss the bus.

with **can** and **could** (**so that ... can/could**):

☐ She's learning English **so that** she **can** study in Canada.
☐ We moved to London **so that** we **could** see our friends more often.

64.1 Choose from Box A and Box B to make a new sentence with **to** ... .

A

1 ~~I shouted~~
2 I had to go to the bank
3 I'm saving money
4 I went into hospital
5 I'm wearing two sweaters
6 I phoned the police

B

I want to keep warm
I wanted to report that my car had been stolen
I want to go to Canada
I had to have an operation
I needed to get some money
~~I wanted to warn people of the danger~~

1   I shouted to warn people of the danger.

2 I had to go to the bank ....

3 I ....

4 ....

5 ....

6 ....

64.2 Complete these sentences using a suitable verb.

1 The president has a team of bodyguards ...to protect... him.

2 I didn't have enough time .... the newspaper today.

3 I came home by taxi. I didn't have the energy ....

4 'Would you like something .... ?' 'Yes, please. A cup of coffee.'

5 We need a bag .... these things in.

6 There will be a meeting next week .... the problem.

7 I wish we had enough money .... another car.

8 I saw Helen at the party, but we didn't have a chance .... to each other.

9 I need some new clothes. I don't have anything nice ....

10 They've just passed their exams. They're having a party ....

11 I can't do all this work alone. I need somebody .... me.

64.3 Put in **to** or **for**.

1 I'm going to Spain ...for... a holiday.

2 You need a lot of experience .... this job.

3 You need a lot of experience .... do this job.

4 We'll need more time .... make a decision.

5 I went to the dentist .... a check-up.

6 I had to put on my glasses .... read the letter.

7 Do you have to wear glasses .... reading?

8 I wish we had a garden .... the children .... play in.

64.4 Write sentences with **so that**.

1 I hurried. I didn't want to be late.   I hurried so that I wouldn't be late.

2 I wore warm clothes. I didn't want to be cold.
   I wore ....

3 I left Dave my phone number. I wanted him to be able to contact me.
   I ....

4 We whispered. We didn't want anybody else to hear our conversation.
   .... nobody ....

5 Please arrive early. We want to be able to start the meeting on time.
   Please ....

6 Jennifer locked the door. She didn't want to be disturbed.
   ....

7 I slowed down. I wanted the car behind me to be able to overtake.
   ....

Adjective + to ...

A Difficult to understand etc.

Compare sentences (a) and (b):

☐ Jim doesn't speak very clearly.
- (a) **It** is **difficult to understand** him .
- (b) He is **difficult to understand**.

Sentences (a) and (b) have the same meaning. Note that we say:
☐ He is difficult **to understand**. (*not* He is difficult to understand him.)

You can use the same structures with:

easy	hard	impossible	dangerous	safe	expensive	cheap	nice
good	interesting	exciting					

☐ Do you think it is **safe** (for us) **to drink this water**?
  Do you think this water is **safe** (for us) **to drink**? (*not* to drink it)
☐ The questions in the exam were very difficult. It was **impossible to answer them**.
  The questions in the exam were very difficult. They were **impossible to answer**.
  (*not* to answer them)
☐ Jill has lots of interesting ideas. It's **interesting to talk** to her.
  Jill is **interesting to talk to**. (*not* to talk to her.)

You can also use this structure with *adjective + noun*:
☐ This is a **difficult question** (for me) **to answer**. (*not* to answer it)

B (It's) nice of (you) to ...

You can say 'It's **nice of** somebody **to** do something':
☐ It was **nice of you to take** me to the airport. Thank you very much.

You can use many other adjectives in this way. For example:

kind   clever   sensible   mean   silly   stupid   careless   unfair   considerate:

☐ It's **silly of Mary to give** up her job when she needs the money.
☐ I think it was very **unfair of him to criticise** me.

C I'm sorry to ... / I was surprised to ... etc.

You can use *adjective + to* ... to say how somebody reacts to something:
☐ I was **sorry to hear** that your father is ill.

You can use many other adjectives in this way. For example:

happy   glad   pleased   sad   disappointed   surprised   amazed   astonished   relieved

☐ Was Julia **surprised to see** you?
☐ It was a long and tiring journey. We were **glad to get** home.

D The first / the next (etc.) + to ...

You can use **to** ... after **the first/the last, the next, the only, the second** (etc.):
☐ If I have any more news, you will be **the first** (person) **to know**.
☐ **The next** train **to arrive** at platform 4 will be the 10.50 to Cardiff.
☐ Everybody was late except me. I was **the only** one **to arrive** on time.

E

You can say that something is **sure/certain/likely/bound to** happen:
☐ Carla is a very good student. She's **bound to pass** the exam. (= she is sure to pass)
☐ I'm **likely to be** late home this evening. (= I will probably be late home)

Exercises

65.1 (Section A) Write these sentences in another way, beginning as shown.

1 It's difficult to understand him.   He _is difficult to understand._
2 It's easy to use this machine.   This machine is ....
3 It was very difficult to open the window.   The window ....
4 It's impossible to translate some words.   Some words ....
5 It's expensive to maintain a car.   A ....
6 It's not safe to stand on that chair.   That ....

65.2 (Section A) Complete the second sentence. Use the adjective in brackets and **to ...** as in the example.

1 I couldn't answer the question.   (difficult) It was a _difficult question to answer._
2 Everybody makes that mistake.   (easy)   It's an ....
3 I like living in this place.   (nice)   It's a ....
4 We enjoyed watching the game.   (good)   It was a ....

65.3 (Section B) Make a new sentence beginning **It ...** . Use one of these adjectives each time:

careless   inconsiderate   ~~kind~~   nice

1 Sue has offered to help me.   _It's kind of Sue to offer to help me._
2 You make the same mistake again and again.
  It ....
3 Dan and Jenny invited me to stay with them.
  ....
4 The neighbours make so much noise at night.
  ....

65.4 (Section C) Use the following words to complete these sentences:

sorry / hear   glad / hear   ~~pleased / get~~   surprised / see

1 We _were pleased to get_ your letter last week.
2 I got your message. I .... that you're keeping well.
3 We .... Paula at the party. We didn't expect her to come.
4 I .... that your mother isn't well. I hope she gets better soon.

65.5 (Section D) Complete the second sentence using the words in brackets + **to ...** .

1 Nobody left before me. (the first) I was _the first person to leave._
2 Everybody else arrived before Paul.
  (the last) Paul was the ....
3 Fiona passed the exam. All the other students failed.
  (the only) Fiona was ....
4 I complained to the restaurant manager about the service. Another customer had already complained.
  (the second) I was ....
5 Neil Armstrong walked on the moon in 1969. Nobody had done this before him.
  (the first) Neil Armstrong was ....

65.6 (Section E) Complete these sentences using the words in brackets and a suitable verb.

1 Diane is a very good student. She _is bound to pass_ the exam. (bound)
2 I'm not surprised you're tired. After such a long journey you .... tired. (bound)
3 Andy has a very bad memory. He .... what you tell him. (sure)
4 I don't think you need to take an umbrella. It .... (not likely)
5 The holidays begin this weekend. There .... a lot of traffic on the roads. (likely)

To ... (afraid to do) and preposition + -ing (afraid of -ing)

A

Afraid to (do) and afraid of (do)ing

I am **afraid to do** something = I don't want to do it because it is dangerous or the result could be bad.
We use **afraid to do** for things we do intentionally; we can choose to do them or not:
□ This part of town is dangerous. People are **afraid to walk** here at night.
  (= they don't want to walk here because it is dangerous – so they don't)
□ James was **afraid to tell** his parents what had happened.
  (= he didn't want to tell them because he knew they would be angry, worried etc.)

I am **afraid of** something **happening** = it is possible that something bad will happen (for example, an accident).
We do not use **afraid of -ing** for things we do intentionally:
□ The path was icy, so we walked very carefully. We were **afraid of falling**.
  (= it was possible that we would fall – *not* we were afraid to fall)
□ I don't like dogs. I'm always **afraid of being** bitten. (*not* afraid to be bitten)

So, you are **afraid to do** something because you are **afraid of something happening** as a result:
□ I was **afraid to go** near the dog because I **was afraid of being** bitten.

B

Interested in (do)ing and interested to (do)

I'm **interested in doing** something = I'm thinking of doing it, I would like to do it:
□ Let me know if you're **interested in joining** the club. (*not* to join)
□ I tried to sell my car, but nobody was **interested in buying** it. (*not* to buy)

We use **interested to ...** to say how somebody reacts to what they **hear/see/read/learn/know/find**.
For example, 'I was **interested to hear** it' = I heard it and it was interesting for me:
□ I was **interested to hear** that Tanya has left her job.
□ Ask Mike for his opinion. I would be **interested to know** what he thinks. (= it would be interesting for me to know it)
This structure is the same as **surprised to ... / glad to ...** etc. (see Unit 65C):
□ I was **surprised to hear** that Tanya has left her job.

C

Sorry to (do) and sorry for/about (do)ing

We use **sorry to ...** to say we regret something that happens (see Unit 65C):
□ I was **sorry to hear** that Nicky lost her job. (= I was sorry when I heard that ...)
□ I've enjoyed my stay here. I'll be **sorry to leave**.
We also say **sorry to ...** to apologise at the time we do something:
□ I'm **sorry to phone** you so late, but I need to ask you something.

You can use **sorry for** or **sorry about** (doing something) to apologise for something you did before:
□ I'm **sorry for** (*or* about) **shouting** at you yesterday. (*not* sorry to shout)
You can also say:
□ I'm **sorry I shouted** at you yesterday.

D

We say:

I **want to** (do) / I'd **like to** (do)	*but*	I'm **thinking of** (do)ing / I **dream of** (do)ing
I **failed to** (do)	*but*	I **succeeded in** (do)ing
I **allowed** them **to** (do)	*but*	I **prevented** them **from** (do)ing
		I **stopped** them **from** (do)ing

For examples, see Units 54–55 and 62.

Verb + preposition + –ing → Unit 62   Adjective + preposition → Units 130–131   **Sorry about/for** → Unit 130

66.1 Use the words in brackets to write sentences. Use **afraid to ...** or **afraid of –ing.**

1 The streets are unsafe at night.
(a lot of people / afraid / go / out) _A lot of people are afraid to go out._

2 We walked very carefully along the icy path.
(we / afraid / fall) _We were afraid of falling._

3 I don't usually carry my passport with me.
(I / afraid / lose / it) ....

4 I thought she would be angry if I told her what had happened.
(I / afraid / tell / her) ....

5 We rushed to the station.
(we / afraid / miss / our train) ....

6 In the middle of the film there was an especially horrifying scene.
(we / afraid / look) ....

7 The vase was very valuable, so I held it carefully.
(I / afraid / drop / it) ....

8 I thought the food on my plate didn't look fresh.
a (I / afraid / eat / it) ....
b (I / afraid / get / sick) ....

66.2 Complete the sentences using **in ...** or **to ... .** Use these verbs:

~~buy~~   get   know   look   read   start

1 I'm trying to sell my car, but nobody is interested _in buying_ it.
2 Julia is interested .... her own business.
3 I was interested .... your letter in the newspaper last week.
4 Ben wants to stay single. He's not interested .... married.
5 I met Mark a few days ago. You'll be interested .... that he's just got a job in Paris.
6 I don't enjoy sightseeing. I'm not interested .... at old buildings.

66.3 Complete each sentence using **sorry for/about ...** or **sorry to ... .** Use the verb in brackets.

1 I'm _sorry to phone_ you so late, but I need to ask you something. (phone)
2 I was .... that you didn't get the job you applied for. (hear)
3 I'm .... all those bad things about you. I didn't mean them. (say)
4 I'm .... you, but do you have a pen I could borrow? (disturb)
5 I'm .... the book you lent me. I'll buy you another one. (lose)

66.4 Complete each sentence using the verb in brackets.

1 a We wanted _to leave_ the building. (leave)
   b We weren't allowed .... the building. (leave)
   c We were prevented .... the building. (leave)

2 a Peter failed .... the problem. (solve)
   b Chris succeeded .... the problem. (solve)

3 a I'm thinking .... away next week. (go)
   b I'm hoping .... away next week. (go)
   c I'd like .... away next week. (go)
   d I'm looking forward .... away next week. (go)

4 a Helen wanted .... me lunch. (buy)
   b Helen promised .... me lunch. (buy)
   c Helen insisted .... me lunch. (buy)
   d Helen wouldn't dream .... me lunch. (buy)

→ Additional exercise 27 **(page 318)**   **133**

See somebody do and see somebody doing

A Study this example situation:

> Tom got into his car and drove away. You saw this.
> You can say:
>   ☐ I saw Tom **get** into his car and **drive** away.
>
> In this structure we use **get/drive/do** etc.
> (*not* to get / to drive / to do).
>
> | Somebody **did** something | + | I saw this |
>
>   I **saw** somebody **do** something
>
>
>
> *TOM*
>
> But after a *passive* ('he **was seen**' etc.), we use **to**:
>   ☐ He was seen **to get** in the car.

B Study this example situation:

> Yesterday you saw Kate. She was waiting for a bus.
> You can say:
>   ☐ I saw Kate **waiting** for a bus.
>
> In this structure we use **-ing** (wait**ing**/do**ing** etc.):
>
> | Somebody **was doing** something | + | I saw this |
>
>   I **saw** somebody **doing** something
>
>
>
> *KATE*

C Study the difference in meaning between the two structures:

> I saw him **do** something = he **did** something (*past simple*) and I saw this. I saw the complete action from beginning to end:
>   ☐ He **fell** off the wall. I saw this. → I saw him **fall** off the wall.
>   ☐ The accident **happened**. Did you see it? → Did you see the accident **happen**?
>
> I saw him **doing** something = he **was doing** something (*past continuous*) and I saw this. I saw him when he was in the middle of doing it. This does not mean that I saw the complete action:
>   ☐ He **was walking** along the street.
>   I saw this when I drove past in my car. } I saw him **walking** along the street.
>
> Sometimes the difference is not important and you can use either form:
>   ☐ I've never seen her **dance**. *or* I've never seen her **dancing**.

D We use these structures with **see** and **hear,** and a number of other verbs:
>   ☐ I didn't **hear** you **come** in. (you came in – I didn't hear this)
>   ☐ Liz suddenly **felt** somebody **touch** her on the shoulder.
>   ☐ Did you **notice** anyone **go** out?
>
>   ☐ I could **hear** it **raining**. (it was raining – I could hear it)
>   ☐ The missing children were last **seen playing** near the river.
>   ☐ **Listen to** the birds **singing**!
>   ☐ Can you **smell** something **burning**?
>   ☐ I **found** Sue in my room **reading** my letters.

67.1 Complete the answers to the questions.

1	Did anybody go out?	I don't think so. I didn't see _anybody go out_ .
2	Has Sarah arrived yet?	Yes, I think I heard her _____ .
3	How do you know I took the money?	I know because I saw you _____ .
4	Did the doorbell ring?	I don't think so. I didn't hear _____ .
5	Can Tom play the piano?	I've never heard _____ .
6	Did I lock the door when I went out?	Yes, I saw _____ .
7	How did the woman fall?	I don't know. I didn't see _____ .

67.2 In each of these situations you and a friend saw, heard or smelt something. Look at the pictures and complete the sentences.

1   _We saw Kate waiting for a bus_ _____ .
2 We saw Dave and Helen _____ .
3 We saw _____ in a restaurant.
4 We heard _____ .
5 We could _____ .
6 _____ .

67.3 Complete these sentences. Use the following verbs (in the correct form):

     climb   ~~**come**~~   **crawl**   **cry**   **explode**   **ride**   **run**   **say**   ~~**sing**~~   **slam**   **sleep**   **tell**

1 Listen to the birds _singing_ !
2 I didn't hear you _come_ in.
3 We listened to the old man _____ his story from beginning to end.
4 Listen! Can you hear a baby _____ ?
5 I looked out of the window and saw Dan _____ his bike along the road.
6 I thought I heard somebody _____ 'Hi', so I looked round.
7 We watched two men _____ across the garden and _____ through an open window into the house.
8 Everybody heard the bomb _____ . It was a tremendous noise.
9 Oh! I can feel something _____ up my leg! It must be an insect.
10 I heard somebody _____ the door in the middle of the night. It woke me up.
11 When we got home, we found a cat _____ on the kitchen table.

-ing clauses
(Feeling tired, I went to bed early.)

A Study these situations:

Joe was playing football. He hurt his knee.
You can say:
  □ Joe hurt his knee **playing football**.

You were feeling tired. So you went to bed early.
You can say:
  □ **Feeling tired**, I went to bed early.

'**Playing tennis**' and '**feeling tired**' are **-ing** clauses.
If the **-ing** clause is at the beginning of the sentence (as in the second example), we write a comma (,) after it.

B When two things happen at the same time, you can use an **-ing** clause.
  □ Kate is in the kitchen **making coffee**.
    (= she is in the kitchen *and* she is making coffee)
  □ A man ran out of the house **shouting**.
    (= he ran out of the house *and* he was shouting)
  □ Do something! Don't just stand there **doing nothing**!

We also use **-ing** when one action happens during another action. We use **-ing** for the longer action:
  □ Joe hurt his knee **playing football**. (= while he was playing)
  □ Did you cut yourself **shaving**? (= while you were shaving)

You can also use **-ing** after **while** or **when**:
  □ Jim hurt his knee **while playing** football.
  □ Be careful **when crossing** the road. (= when you are crossing)

C When one action happens before another action, we use **having** (**done**) for the first action:
  □ **Having found** a hotel, we looked for somewhere to have dinner.
  □ **Having finished** her work, she went home.
You can also say **after -ing**:
  □ **After finishing** her work, she went home.

If one short action follows another short action, you can use the simple **-ing** form (**doing** instead of **having done**) for the first action:
  □ **Taking** a key out of his pocket, he opened the door.

These structures are used more in written English than in spoken English.

D You can use an **-ing** clause to explain something, or to say why somebody does something.
The **-ing** clause usually comes at the beginning of the sentence:
  □ **Feeling** tired, I went to bed early. (= because I felt tired)
  □ **Being** unemployed, he hasn't got much money. (= because he is unemployed)
  □ **Not having** a car, she finds it difficult to get around.
    (= because she doesn't have a car)
  □ **Having** already **seen** the film twice, I didn't want to go to the cinema.
    (= because I had already seen it twice)

These structures are used more in written English than in spoken English.

-ing and -ed clauses → Unit 97

68.1 Choose from Box A and Box B to make sentences. Use an **-ing** clause.

A
1 ~~Kate was in the kitchen.~~
2 Diane was sitting in an armchair.
3 Sue opened the door carefully.
4 Sarah went out.
5 Linda was in London for two years.
6 Mary walked around the town.

B
She was trying not to make a noise.
She looked at the sights and took photographs.
She said she would be back in an hour.
She was reading a book.
~~She was making coffee.~~
She worked as a tourist guide.

1 *Kate was in the kitchen making coffee.*
2 Diane was sitting ....
3 Sue ....
4 ....
5 ....
6 ....

68.2 Make one sentence from two using an **-ing** clause.

1 Joe was playing football. He hurt his knee.   *Joe hurt his knee playing football.*
2 I was watching television. I fell asleep.
   I ....
3 A friend of mine slipped and fell. He was getting off a bus.
   A friend of mine ....
4 I was walking home in the rain. I got very wet.
   I ....
5 Laura was driving to work yesterday. She had an accident.

   ....
6 Two firefighters were overcome by smoke. They were trying to put out the fire.

   ....

68.3 Make sentences beginning **Having** ... .

1 She finished her work. Then she went home.   *Having finished her work, she went home.*
2 We bought our tickets. Then we went into the theatre.

   ....
3 They had dinner and then they continued their journey.

   ....
4 After I'd done the shopping, I went for a cup of coffee.

   ....

68.4 Make sentences beginning **-ing** or **Not -ing** (like those in Section D). Sometimes you need to begin with **Having** (done something).

1 I felt tired. So I went to bed early.
   Feeling tired, I went to bed early.
2 I thought they might be hungry. So I offered them something to eat.

   ....
3 She is a foreigner. So she needs a visa to work in this country.

   ....
4 I didn't know his phone number. So I wasn't able to contact him.

   ....
5 Sarah has travelled a lot. So she knows a lot about other countries.

   ....
6 I wasn't able to speak the local language. So I had trouble communicating.

   ....
7 We had spent nearly all our money. So we couldn't afford to stay at a hotel.

   ....

137

Countable and uncountable 1

A A noun can be *countable* or *uncountable*:

Countable
- ☐ I eat **a banana** every day.
- ☐ I like **bananas**.

Banana is a *countable* noun.

A countable noun can be singular (**banana**) or plural (**bananas**).

We can use numbers with countable nouns. So we can say 'one banana', 'two bananas' etc.

Examples of nouns usually countable:
- ☐ Kate was singing **a song**.
- ☐ There's **a** nice **beach** near here.
- ☐ Do you have **a** ten-pound **note**?
- ☐ It wasn't your fault. It was **an accident**.
- ☐ There are no **batteries** in the radio.
- ☐ We haven't got enough **cups**.

Uncountable
- ☐ I eat **rice** every day.
- ☐ I like **rice**.

Rice is an *uncountable* noun.

An uncountable noun has only one form (**rice**).

We cannot use numbers with uncountable nouns. We cannot say 'one rice', 'two rices' etc.

Examples of nouns usually uncountable:
- ☐ Kate was listening to (some) **music**.
- ☐ There's **sand** in my shoes.
- ☐ Do you have any **money**?
- ☐ It wasn't your fault. It was bad **luck**.
- ☐ There is no **electricity** in this house.
- ☐ We haven't got enough **water**.

B You can use **a/an** with singular countable nouns:

a beach   a student   an umbrella

You cannot use singular countable nouns alone (without **a/the/my** etc.):
- ☐ I want **a banana**. (*not* I want banana)
- ☐ There's been **an accident**. (*not* There's been accident)

You can use *plural* countable nouns alone:
- ☐ I like **bananas**. (= bananas in general)
- ☐ **Accidents** can be prevented.

You cannot normally use **a/an** with uncountable nouns. We do not say 'a sand', 'a music', 'a rice'.
But you can often use **a ... of**. For example:
a bowl / a packet / a grain of rice

You can use uncountable nouns alone (without **the/my/some** etc.):
- ☐ I eat **rice** every day.
- ☐ There's **blood** on your shirt.
- ☐ Can you hear **music**?

C You can use **some** and **any** with plural countable nouns:
- ☐ We sang **some songs**.
- ☐ Did you buy **any apples**?

We use **many** and **few** with plural countable nouns:
- ☐ We didn't take **many photographs**.
- ☐ I have a **few things** to do.

You can use **some** and **any** with uncountable nouns:
- ☐ We listened to **some music**.
- ☐ Did you buy **any** apple **juice**?

We use **much** and **little** with uncountable nouns:
- ☐ We didn't do **much shopping**.
- ☐ I have a **little work** to do.

Countable and uncountable 2 → Unit 70   **Some and any** → Unit 85   **Many/much/few/little** → Unit 87
Children / the children → Unit 75

Exercises

69.1 Some of these sentences need **a/an**. Correct the sentences where necessary.

1 Joe goes everywhere by bike. He hasn't got car.   *He hasn't got a car.*
2 Helen was listening to music when I arrived.   *OK*
3 We went to very nice restaurant last weekend.   ....
4 I clean my teeth with toothpaste.   ....
5 I use toothbrush to clean my teeth.   ....
6 Can you tell me if there's bank near here?   ....
7 My brother works for insurance company in London.   ....
8 I don't like violence.   ....
9 Can you smell paint?   ....
10 When we were in Rome, we stayed in big hotel.   ....
11 We need petrol. I hope we come to petrol station soon.   ....
12 I wonder if you can help me. I have problem.   ....
13 I like your suggestion. It's very interesting idea.   ....
14 John has got interview for job tomorrow.   ....
15 I like volleyball. It's good game.   ....
16 Liz doesn't usually wear jewellery.   ....
17 Jane was wearing beautiful necklace.   ....

69.2 Complete the sentences using the following words. Use **a/an** where necessary.

~~accident~~	biscuit	blood	coat	decision	electricity
interview	key	moment	~~music~~	question	sugar

1 It wasn't your fault. It was ..... *an accident* .
2 Listen! Can you hear ..... *music* ?
3 I couldn't get into the house because I didn't have ....
4 It's very warm today. Why are you wearing .... ?
5 Do you take .... in your coffee?
6 Are you hungry? Would you like .... with your coffee?
7 Our lives would be very difficult without ....
8 'I had .... for a job yesterday.' 'Did you? How did it go?'
9 The heart pumps .... through the body.
10 Excuse me, but can I ask you .... ?
11 I'm not ready yet. Can you wait .... , please?
12 We can't delay much longer. We have to make .... soon.

69.3 Complete the sentences using the following words. Sometimes the word needs to be plural (**-s**), and sometimes you need to use **a/an**.

air	day	friend	language	letter	meat
patience	people	~~photograph~~	queue	space	umbrella

1 I had my camera, but I didn't take any ..... *photographs* .
2 There are seven .... in a week.
3 A vegetarian is a person who doesn't eat ....
4 Outside the cinema there was .... of people waiting to see the film.
5 I'm not very good at writing ....
6 Last night I went out with some .... of mine.
7 There were very few .... in town today. The streets were almost empty.
8 I'm going out for a walk. I need some fresh ....
9 Gary always wants things quickly. He hasn't got much ....
10 I think it's going to rain. Do you have .... I could borrow?
11 Do you speak any foreign .... ?
12 Our flat is very small. We haven't got much ....

Countable and uncountable 2

A Many nouns can be used as countable or uncountable nouns, usually with a difference in meaning. Compare:

Countable	Uncountable
□ Did you hear **a noise** just now? (= a specific noise)	□ I can't work here. There's too much **noise**. (*not* too many noises)
□ I bought **a paper** to read. (= a newspaper)	□ I need **some paper** to write on. (= material for writing on)
□ There's **a hair** in my soup! (= one single hair)	□ You've got very long **hair**. (*not* hairs) (= all the hair on your head)
□ You can stay with us. There is **a** spare **room**. (= a room in a house)	□ You can't sit here. There isn't **room**. (= space)
□ I had some interesting **experiences** while I was travelling. (= things that happened to me)	□ They offered me the job because I had a lot of **experience**. (*not* experiences)
□ Enjoy your trip. Have **a** good **time**!	□ I can't wait. I haven't got **time**.

Coffee/tea/juice/beer etc. (drinks) are normally uncountable:
  □ I don't like **coffee** very much.

But you can say **a coffee** (= a cup of coffee), **two coffees** (= two cups) etc. :
  □ **Two** coffees and **an orange juice**, please.

B The following nouns are usually uncountable:

accommodation	behaviour	damage	luck	permission	traffic
advice	bread	furniture	luggage	progress	weather
baggage	chaos	information	news	scenery	work

You cannot use **a/an** with these nouns:
  □ I'm going to buy **some bread**. *or* ... **a loaf of bread**. (*not* a bread)
  □ Enjoy your holiday! I hope you have good **weather**. (*not* a good weather)

These nouns are not usually plural (so we do not say 'breads', 'furnitures' etc.):
  □ Where are you going to put all your **furniture**? (*not* furnitures)
  □ Let me know if you need more **information**. (*not* informations)

News is uncountable, not plural:
  □ The **news was** very depressing. (*not* The news were)

Travel (*noun*) means 'travelling in general' (uncountable). We do not say 'a travel' to mean **a trip** or **a journey**:
  □ They spend a lot of money on **travel**.
  □ We had **a** very good **trip/journey**. (*not* a good travel)

Compare these countable and uncountable nouns:

Countable	Uncountable
□ I'm looking for **a job**.	□ I'm looking for **work**. (*not* a work)
□ What **a** beautiful **view**!	□ What beautiful **scenery**!
□ It's **a** nice **day** today.	□ It's nice **weather** today.
□ We had a lot of **bags** and **cases**.	□ We had a lot of **baggage/luggage**
□ **These chairs** are mine.	□ **This furniture** is mine.
□ That's **a** good **suggestion**.	□ That's good **advice**.

Countable and uncountable 1 → Unit 69   **American English** → Appendix 7

Exercises

70.1 Which of the underlined parts of these sentences is correct?

1 'Did you hear ~~noise~~ / a noise just now?' 'No, I didn't hear anything.' (a noise *is correct*).
2 a If you want to know the news, you can read paper / a paper.
  b I want to print some documents, but the printer is out of paper / papers.
3 a I thought there was somebody in the house because there was light / a light on inside.
  b Light / A light comes from the sun.
4 a I was in a hurry this morning. I didn't have time / a time for breakfast.
  b 'Did you enjoy your holiday?' 'Yes, we had wonderful time / a wonderful time.'
5 This is nice room / a nice room. Did you decorate it yourself?
6 Sue was very helpful. She gave us some very useful advice / advices.
7 Did you have nice weather / a nice weather when you were away?
8 We were very unfortunate. We had bad luck / a bad luck.
9 Is it difficult to find a work / job at the moment?
10 Our travel / journey from Paris to Moscow by train was very tiring.
11 When the fire alarm rang, there was total chaos / a total chaos.
12 I had to buy a / some bread because I wanted to make some sandwiches.
13 Bad news don't / doesn't make people happy.
14 Your hair is / Your hairs are too long. You should have it / them cut.
15 The damage / the damages caused by the storm will cost a lot to repair.

70.2 Complete the sentences using the following words. Use the plural (–s) where necessary.

advice	chair	experience	experience	furniture	hair
information	job	~~luggage~~	permission	progress	work

1 I didn't have much ……*luggage*…… – just two small bags.
2 They'll tell you all you want to know. They'll give you plenty of …………………………………… .
3 There is room for everybody to sit down. There are plenty of …………………………………… .
4 We have no …………………………………… , not even a bed or a table.
5 'What does Alan look like?' 'He's got a long beard and very short …………………………………… .'
6 Carla's English is better than it was. She's made …………………………………… .
7 Mike is unemployed. He can't get a …………………………………… .
8 Mike is unemployed. He can't get …………………………………… .
9 If you want to leave early, you have to ask for …………………………………… .
10 I didn't know what to do. So I asked Chris for …………………………………… .
11 I don't think Dan will get the job. He doesn't have enough …………………………………… .
12 Paul has done many interesting things. He could write a book about his …………………………………… .

70.3 What do you say in these situations? Complete each sentence using one of the words from Section B.

1 Your friends have just arrived at the station. You can't see any cases or bags. You ask them:
Have ……*you got any luggage*……………………………… ?
2 You go into the tourist office. You want to know about places to see in the town. You say:
I'd like …………………………………… .
3 You are a student. You want your teacher to advise you about which courses to do. You say:
Can you give me …………………………………… ?
4 You want to watch the news on TV, but you don't know when it is on. You ask your friend:
What time …………………………………… ?
5 You are at the top of a mountain. You can see a very long way. It's beautiful. You say:
It …………………………………… , isn't it?
6 You look out of the window. The weather is horrible: cold, wet and windy. You say:
What …………………………………… !

Countable nouns with a/an and some

Countable nouns can be *singular* or *plural*:

a **dog**	a **child**	the **evening**	this **party**	an **umbrella**
dogs	some **children**	the **evenings**	these **parties**	two **umbrellas**

Before singular countable nouns you can use **a/an**:
- ☐ Goodbye! Have **a** nice **evening**.
- ☐ Do you need **an umbrella**?

You cannot use singular countable nouns alone (without **a/the/my** etc.):
- ☐ She never wears **a** hat. (*not* She never wears hat)
- ☐ Be careful of **the** dog. (*not* Be careful of dog)
- ☐ What **a** beautiful day!
- ☐ I've got **a** headache.

We use **a/an** ... to say what kind of thing or person something/somebody is:
- ☐ That's **a nice table**.

In the plural we use the noun alone (*not* some ...):
- ☐ Those are **nice chairs**. (*not* some nice chairs)

Compare singular and plural:

☐ A dog is **an animal**.	☐ Dogs are **animals**.
☐ I'm **an optimist**.	☐ We're **optimists**.
☐ Tim's father is **a doctor**.	☐ Most of my friends are **students**.
☐ Are you **a good driver**?	☐ Are they **good students**?
☐ Jill is **a really nice person**.	☐ Jill's parents are **really nice people**.
☐ What **a lovely dress**!	☐ What **awful shoes**!

We say that somebody has **a long nose / a nice face / blue eyes / small hands** etc. :

☐ Jack has got **a long nose**.	☐ Jack has got **blue eyes**.
(*not* the long nose)	(*not* the blue eyes)

Remember to use **a/an** when you say what somebody's job is:
- ☐ Sandra is **a nurse**. (*not* Sandra is nurse)
- ☐ Would you like to be **an English teacher**?

You can use **some** with plural countable nouns. We use **some** in two ways.

(1) **Some** = a number of / a few of / a pair of:
- ☐ I've seen **some** good **films** recently. (*not* I've seen good films)
- ☐ **Some friends** of mine are coming to stay at the weekend.
- ☐ I need **some** new **sunglasses**. (= a new pair of sunglasses)

Do *not* use **some** when you are talking about things in general (see Unit 75):
- ☐ I love **bananas**. (*not* some bananas)
- ☐ My aunt is a writer. She writes **books**. (*not* some books)

Sometimes you can make sentences with or without **some** (with no difference in meaning):
- ☐ There are (**some**) eggs in the fridge if you're hungry.

(2) **Some** = some but not all:
- ☐ **Some children** learn very quickly. (but not all children)
- ☐ Tomorrow there will be rain in **some places**, but most of the country will be dry.

71.1 What are these things? Use a dictionary if necessary.

1 an ant? _It's an insect._
2 ants and bees? _They're insects._
3 a cauliflower? ....
4 chess? ....
5 a violin, a trumpet and a flute? ....

6 a skyscraper? ....

7 Earth, Mars, Venus and Jupiter? ....

8 a tulip? ....
9 the Nile, the Rhine and the Mississippi? ....

10 a pigeon, an eagle and a crow? ....

Who were these people?

11 Beethoven? _He was a composer._
12 Shakespeare? ....
13 Albert Einstein? ....

14 Washington, Lincoln and Kennedy? ....

15 Marilyn Monroe? ....

16 Elvis Presley and John Lennon? ....

17 Van Gogh, Renoir and Picasso? ....

71.2 Read about what these people do, and say what their jobs are. Choose from:

chef   interpreter   journalist   ~~nurse~~   plumber   surgeon   travel agent   waiter

1 Sarah looks after patients in hospital. _She's a nurse._
2 Gary works in a restaurant. He brings the food to the tables. He ....
3 Martina arranges people's holidays for them. She ....
4 Kevin works in a hospital. He operates on people. ....
5 Jonathan cooks in a restaurant. ....
6 Jane writes articles for a newspaper. ....
7 Dave installs and repairs water pipes. ....
8 Linda translates what people are saying from one language into another, so that they can understand each other. ....

71.3 Put in **a/an** or **some** where necessary. If no word is necessary, leave the space empty.

1 I've seen _some_ good films recently.
2 What's wrong with you? Have you got _a_ headache?
3 I know a lot of people. Most of them are _-_ students.
4 When I was .... child, I used to be very shy.
5 Would you like to be .... actor?
6 Do you collect .... stamps?
7 What .... beautiful garden!
8 .... birds, for example the penguin, cannot fly.
9 Do you enjoy going to .... concerts?
10 I've been walking for three hours. I've got .... sore feet.
11 I don't feel very well this morning. I've got .... sore throat.
12 Maria speaks .... English, but not very much.
13 It's a pity we don't have .... camera. I'd like to take .... photograph of that house.
14 Those are .... nice shoes. Where did you get them?
15 I'm going shopping. I want to buy .... new shoes.
16 You need .... visa to visit .... countries, but not all of them.
17 Jane is .... teacher. Her parents were .... teachers too.
18 I don't believe him. He's .... liar. He's always telling .... lies.

A/an and the

A

Study this example:

> I had **a** sandwich and **an** apple for lunch.
>
> **The** sandwich wasn't very good, but **the** apple was nice.

JOE   KAREN

Joe says '**a** sandwich', '**an** apple' because this is the first time he talks about them.

Joe now says '**the** sandwich', '**the** apple' because Karen knows which sandwich and which apple he means – **the** sandwich and **the** apple that he had for lunch.

Compare **a** and **the** in these examples:
- **A** man and **a** woman were sitting opposite me. **The** man was American, but I think **the** woman was British.
- When we were on holiday, we stayed at **a** hotel. Sometimes we ate at **the** hotel and sometimes we went to **a** restaurant.

B

We use **the** when we are thinking of a specific thing. Compare **a/an** and **the**:
- Tim sat down on **a** chair. (perhaps one of many chairs in the room)
  Tim sat down on **the** chair **nearest the door**. (a specific chair)
- Paula is looking for **a** job. (not a specific job)
  Did Paula get **the** job **she applied for**? (a specific job)
- Have you got **a** car? (not a specific car)
  I cleaned **the** car yesterday. (= my car)

C

We use **the** when it is clear in the situation which thing or person we mean. For example, in a room we talk about **the** light / **the** floor / **the** ceiling / **the** door / **the** carpet etc. :
- Can you turn off **the** light, please? (= the light in this room)
- I took a taxi to **the** station. (= the station in that town)
- *(in a shop)* I'd like to speak to **the** manager, please. (= the manager of this shop)

In the same way, we say (go to) **the bank**, **the post office**:
- I have to go to **the bank** and then I'm going to **the post office**. (The speaker is usually thinking of a specific bank or post office.)

We also say (go to) **the doctor** / **the dentist**:
- Caroline isn't very well. She's gone to **the doctor**. (= her usual doctor)
- I don't like going to **the dentist**.

Compare **the** and **a**:
- I have to go to **the bank** today.
  Is there **a bank** near here?
- I don't like going to **the dentist**.
  My sister is **a dentist**.

D

We say 'once **a** week / three times **a** day / £1.50 **a** kilo' etc. :
- 'How often do you go to the cinema?' 'About once **a** month.'
- 'How much are those potatoes?' '£1.50 **a** kilo.'
- Helen works eight hours **a** day, six days **a** week.

A/an → Unit 71   The → Units 73–78

Exercises

72.1 Put in a/an or the.

1 This morning I bought ....*a*.... newspaper and .... magazine. .... newspaper is in my bag, but I can't remember where I put .... magazine.

2 I saw .... accident this morning. .... car crashed into .... tree. .... driver of .... car wasn't hurt, but .... car was badly damaged.

3 There are two cars parked outside: .... blue one and .... grey one. .... blue one belongs to my neighbours; I don't know who .... owner of .... grey one is.

4 My friends live in .... old house in .... small village. There is .... beautiful garden behind .... house. I would like to have .... garden like that.

72.2 Put in a/an or the.

1 a This house is very nice. Has it got .... garden?
  b It's a beautiful day. Let's sit in .... garden.
  c I like living in this house, but it's a pity that .... garden is so small.

2 a Can you recommend .... good restaurant?
  b We had dinner in .... very nice restaurant.
  c We had dinner in .... best restaurant in town.

3 a She has .... French name, but in fact she's English, not French.
  b What's .... name of that man we met yesterday?
  c We stayed at a very nice hotel – I can't remember .... name now.

4 a There isn't .... airport near where I live. .... nearest airport is 70 miles away.
  b Our flight was delayed. We had to wait at .... airport for three hours.
  c Excuse me, please. Can you tell me how to get to .... airport?

5 a 'Are you going away next week?' 'No, ... week after next.'
  b I'm going away for .... week in September.
  c Gary has a part-time job. He works three mornings .... week.

72.3 Put in a/an or the where necessary.

1 Would you like apple?   *Would you like an apple?*
2 How often do you go to dentist?   ....
3 Could you close door, please?   ....
4 I'm sorry. I didn't mean to do that. It was mistake.   ....
5 Excuse me, where is bus station, please?   ....
6 I have problem. Can you help me?   ....
7 I'm just going to post office. I won't be long.   ....
8 There were no chairs, so we sat on floor.   ....
9 Have you finished with book I lent you?   ....
10 My sister has just got job in bank in Manchester.   ....
11 We live in small flat in city centre.   ....
12 There's supermarket at end of street I live in.   ....

72.4 Answer these questions about yourself. Where possible, use the structure in Section D (once a week / three times a day etc.).

1 How often do you go to the cinema?   *Three or four times a year.*
2 How much does it cost to hire a car in your country?   *About £20 a day.*
3 How often do you go to the cinema?   ....
4 How often do you go away on holiday?   ....
5 What's the usual speed limit in towns in your country?   ....
6 How much sleep do you need?   ....
7 How often do you go out in the evening?   ....
8 How much television do you watch (on average)?   ....

→ Additional exercise 29 (page 319)

A

We use **the** when there is only one of something:
- □ What is **the** longest river in **the** world? (there is only one longest river)
- □ **The** earth goes round **the** sun and **the** moon goes round **the** earth.
- □ Have you ever crossed **the** equator?
- □ I'm going away at **the** end of this month.

Don't forget **the**:
- □ Paris is **the** capital of France. (*not* Paris is capital of …)

But we use **a/an** to say what kind of thing something is (see Unit 71B). Compare **the** and **a**:
- □ **The** sun is **a** star. (= one of many stars)
- □ **The** hotel we stayed at was **a** very nice hotel.

B

We say: **the sky, the sea, the ground, the country, the environment.**
- □ We looked up at all the stars in **the sky**. (*not* in sky)
- □ Would you like to live in **the country**? (= not in a town)
- □ We must do more to protect **the environment**. (= the natural world around us)

But we say **space** (without **the**) when we mean 'space in the universe'. Compare:
- □ There are millions of stars **in space**. (*not* in the space)
- □ I tried to park my car, but **the space** was too small.

C

We use **the** before **same** (**the same**):
- □ Your pullover is **the same** colour as mine. (*not* is same colour)
- □ 'Are these keys **the same**?' 'No, they're different.'

D

We say: (go to) **the cinema, the theatre.**
- □ I go to **the cinema** a lot, but I haven't been to **the theatre** for ages.

When we say **the cinema / the theatre**, we do not necessarily mean a specific cinema or theatre.

We usually say **the radio**, but **television** (without **the**). Compare:
- □ I listen to **the radio** a lot.   *but*   I watch **television** a lot.
- □ We heard the news on **the radio**.   *but*   We watched the news on **television**.

The television = the television set:
- □ Can you turn off **the television**, please?

E

Breakfast   lunch   dinner

We do *not* normally use **the** with the names of meals (**breakfast, lunch** etc.):
- □ What did you have for **breakfast**?
- □ We had **lunch** in a very nice restaurant.
- □ What time is **dinner**?

But we use **a** if there is an adjective before **breakfast, lunch** etc. :
- □ We had **a** very **nice lunch**. (*not* We had very nice lunch)

F

Platform 5   Room 126 etc.

We do *not* use **the** before *noun + number*. For example, we say:
- □ Our train leaves from **Platform 5**. (*not* the Platform 5)
- □ *(in a shop)* Have you got these shoes in **size 43**? (*not* the size 43)

In the same way, we say: **Room 126** (in a hotel), **page 29** (of a book), **question 3** (in an exam), **Gate 10** (at an airport) etc.

A/an and the → Unit 72   The 2–4 → Units 74–76   Names with and without the → Units 77–78

73.1 Put in **the** or **a/an** where necessary. If no word is necessary, leave the space empty.

  1 A: Where did you have _____–_____ lunch?

     B: We went to ___a___ restaurant.

  2 A: Did you have _____ nice holiday?

     B: Yes, it was _____ best holiday I've ever had.

  3 A: Where's _____ nearest shop?

     B: There's one at _____ end of this street.

  4 A: Do you often listen to _____ radio?

     B: No. In fact I haven't got _____ radio.

  5 A: Would you like to travel in _____ space?

     B: Yes, I'd love to go to _____ moon.

  6 A: Do you go to _____ cinema very often?

     B: No, not very often. But I watch a lot of films on _____ television.

  7 A: It was _____ nice day yesterday, wasn't it?

     B: Yes, it was beautiful. We went for a walk by _____ sea.

  8 A: What did you have for _____ breakfast this morning?

     B: Nothing. I never eat _____ breakfast.

  9 A: Excuse me, where is _____ Room 25, please?

     B: It's on _____ second floor.

 10 A: We spent all our money because we stayed at _____ most expensive hotel in town.

     B: Why didn't you stay at _____ cheaper hotel?

73.2 Put in **the** where necessary. If you don't need **the**, leave the space empty.

  1 I haven't been to ___the___ cinema for ages.

  2 I lay down on _____ ground and looked up at _____ sky.

  3 Sarah spends most of her free time watching _____ television.

  4 _____ television was on, but nobody was watching it.

  5 Lisa and I arrived at _____ same time.

  6 Have you had _____ dinner yet?

  7 You'll find _____ information you need at _____ top of _____ page 15.

  8 What's _____ capital city of Canada?

73.3 Put in **the** or **a/an** where necessary. (See Unit 72 for **a/an** and **the** if necessary.)

  1 Sun is star. ___The sun is a star.___

  2 Paul lives in small village in country. _____

  3 Moon goes round earth every 27 days. _____

  4 I'm fed up with doing same thing every day. _____

  5 It was very hot day. It was hottest day of year. _____

  6 I don't usually have lunch, but I always eat good breakfast. _____

  7 If you live in foreign country, you should try and learn language. _____

  8 We missed our train because we were waiting on wrong platform. _____

  9 Next train to London leaves from Platform 3. _____

73.4 Complete the sentences using the following. Use **the** where necessary.

    breakfast   cinema   ~~dinner~~   gate   Gate 21   question 8   sea

  1 'Are you going out this evening?' 'Yes, after ___dinner___ .'

  2 There was no wind, so _____ was very calm.

  3 The test wasn't too difficult, but I couldn't answer _____ .

  4 'I'm going to _____ tonight.' 'Are you? What are you going to see?'

  5 I didn't have time for _____ this morning because I was in a hurry.

  6 Oh, _____ is open. I must have forgotten to shut it.

  7 *(airport announcement)* Flight AB123 to Rome is now boarding at _____ .

→ Additional exercise 29 (page 319)

A Compare **school** and **the school**:

ALISON

Alison is ten years old. Every day she goes to **school**. She's at **school** now. **School** begins at 9 and finishes at 3.

We say a child goes to **school** or is at **school** (as a pupil). We are not necessarily thinking of a specific school. We are thinking of **school** as a general idea.

Today Alison's mother wants to speak to her daughter's teacher. So she has gone to **the school** to see her. She's at **the school** now.

Alison's mother is not a pupil. She is not 'at school', she doesn't 'go to school'. If she wants to see Alison's teacher, she goes to **the school** (= Alison's school, a specific building).

B We use **prison, hospital, university, college** and **church** in a similar way. We do not use **the** when we are thinking of the general idea of these places and what they are used for. Compare:

- ☐ Ken's brother is in **prison** for robbery. (He is a prisoner. We are not thinking of a specific prison.)
- ☐ Joe had an accident last week. He was taken to **hospital**. He's still in **hospital** now. (as a patient)
- ☐ When I leave **school**, I want to go to **university/college**.
- ☐ Sally's father goes to **church** every Sunday. (to a religious service)

- ☐ Ken went to **the prison** to visit his brother. (He went as a visitor, not as a prisoner.)
- ☐ Jane has gone to **the hospital** to visit Joe. She's at **the hospital** now. (as a visitor)

- ☐ Excuse me, where is **the university**, please? (= the university buildings)
- ☐ Some workmen went to **the church** to repair the roof. (not for a religious service)

With most other places, you need **the**. For example, **the cinema, the bank** (see Units 72C and 73D).

C Bed   work   home

We say **go to bed / be in bed** etc. (*not* the bed):
- ☐ It's time to go to **bed** now.
- ☐ Do you ever have breakfast **in bed**?
but ☐ I sat down on **the bed**. (a specific piece of furniture)

go to work / be at work / start work / finish work etc. (*not* the work):
- ☐ Chris didn't go to **work** yesterday.
- ☐ What time do you usually finish **work**?

go home / come home / arrive home / get home / be at home etc. :
- ☐ It's late. Let's go **home**.
- ☐ Will you be at **home** tomorrow afternoon?

D We say **go to sea / be at sea** (without **the**) when the meaning is 'go/be on a voyage':
- ☐ Keith works on ships. He is **at sea** most of the time.
but ☐ I'd like to live near **the sea**.
- ☐ It can be dangerous to swim in **the sea**.

The → Units 72–73, 75–78   **Prepositions (at school / in hospital etc.)** → Units 123–125   **Home** → Unit 126D
American English → Appendix 7

74.1 Complete each sentence using a preposition (**to/at/in** etc.) + one of these words:

    bed   home   ~~hospital~~   hospital   prison   school   university   work

1 Two people were injured in the accident and were taken ...._to hospital_..... .
2 In Britain, children from the age of five have to go ....
3 Mark didn't go out last night. He stayed ....
4 There is a lot of traffic in the morning when everybody is going ....
5 Cathy's mother has just had an operation. She is still ....
6 When Julia leaves school, she wants to study economics ....
7 Bill never gets up before 9 o'clock. It's 8.30 now, so he is still ....
8 If you commit a serious crime, you could be sent ....

74.2 Complete the sentences with the word given (**school** etc.). Use **the** where necessary.

1 (**school**)
    a Every term parents are invited to ...._the school_.... to meet the teachers.
    b Why aren't your children at ...._school_.... today? Are they ill?
    c When he was younger, Ted hated ....
    d What time does ....usually start in the mornings in your country?
    e A: How do your children get home from .... ? By bus?
          B: No, they walk. .... isn't very far.
    f What sort of job does Jenny want to do when she leaves .... ?
    g There were some people waiting outside .... to meet their children.

2 (**university**)
    a In your country do many people go to .... ?
    b If you want to get a degree, you normally have to study at ....
    c This is only a small town, but .... is one of the biggest in the country.

3 (**hospital**)
    a My brother has always been very healthy. He's never been in ....
    b When Ann was ill, I went to .... to visit her. When I was there,
        I met Lisa who is a nurse at ....
    c Peter was injured in an accident and was kept in .... for a few days.

4 (**church**)
    a John's mother is a regular churchgoer. She goes to .... every Sunday.
    b John himself doesn't go to ....
    c John went to .... to take some photographs of the building.

5 (**prison**)
    a In some places people are in .... because of their political beliefs.
    b A few days ago the fire brigade were called to .... to put out a fire.
    c The judge decided to fine the man £500 instead of sending him to ....

6 (**home/work/bed**)
    a I like to read in .... before I go to sleep.
    b It's nice to travel around, but there's no place like .... !
    c Shall we meet after .... tomorrow evening?
    d If I'm feeling tired, I go to .... early.
    e What time do you usually start .... in the morning?
    f The economic situation was very bad. Many people were out of ....

7 (**sea**)
    a There's a nice view from the window. You can see ....
    b It was a long voyage. We were at .... for four weeks.
    c I love swimming in ....

→ Additional exercise 29 (page 319)   **149**

The 3 (children / the children)

A When we are talking about things or people in general, we do *not* use **the**:

- ☐ I'm afraid of **dogs**. (*not* the dogs)
  (**dogs** = dogs in general, not a specific group of dogs)
- ☐ **Doctors** are paid more than **teachers**.
- ☐ Do you collect **stamps**?
- ☐ **Crime** is a problem in most big cities. (*not* The crime)
- ☐ **Life** has changed a lot in the last thirty years. (*not* The life)
- ☐ Do you like **classical music / Chinese food / fast cars**?
- ☐ My favourite sport is **football/skiing/athletics**.
- ☐ My favourite subject at school was **history/physics/English**.

We say '**most** people / **most** books / **most** cars' etc. (*not* the most ...):

- ☐ **Most hotels** accept credit cards. (*not* The most hotels)

B We use **the** when we mean specific things or people.
Compare:

In general (without **the**)	*Specific people or things* (with **the**)
☐ **Children** learn from playing. (= children in general)	☐ We took **the children** to the zoo. (= a specific group, perhaps the speaker's children)
☐ I couldn't live without **music**.	☐ The film wasn't very good, but I liked **the music**. (= the music in the film)
☐ All **cars** have wheels.	☐ All **the cars** in this car park belong to people who work here.
☐ **Sugar** isn't very good for you.	☐ Can you pass **the sugar**, please? (= the sugar on the table)
☐ **English people** drink a lot of tea. (= English people in general)	☐ **The English people I know** drink a lot of tea. (= only the English people I know, not English people in general)

C The difference between 'something in general' and 'something specific' is not always very clear.
Compare:

In general (without **the**)	*Specific people or things* (with **the**)
☐ I like working with **people**. (= people in general)	
☐ I like working with **people who are lively**. (not all people, but 'people who are lively' is still a general idea)	☐ I like **the people I work with**. (= a specific group of people)
☐ Do you like **coffee**? (= coffee in general)	
☐ Do you like **strong black coffee**? (not all coffee, but 'strong black coffee' is still a general idea)	☐ Did you like **the coffee we had after dinner last night**? (= specific coffee)

The 1–2 → Units 73–74   **The + adjective (the young / the English etc.)** → Unit 76

75.1 Choose four of these things and write whether you like them or not:

boxing	cats	fast food restaurants	football	~~hot weather~~
maths	opera	small children	rock music	zoos

Begin each sentence with one of these:

I like ... / I don't like ...   **I don't mind ...**
I love ... / I hate ...   **I'm interested in ... / I'm not interested in ...**

1   *I don't like hot weather very much.*
2
3
4
5

75.2 Complete the sentences using the following. Use **the** where necessary.

~~(the) basketball~~	(the) **grass**	(the) **patience**	(the) **people**
(the) **questions**	(the) **meat**	~~(the) information~~	(the) **shops**
(the) **history**	(the) **water**	(the) **spiders**	(the) **lies**

1 My favourite sport is ..... *basketball* .
2 ..... *The information* ..... we were given wasn't correct.
3 Some people are afraid of ....
4 A vegetarian is somebody who doesn't eat ....
5 The test wasn't very difficult. I answered .... without difficulty.
6 Do you know .... who live next door?
7 .... is the study of the past.
8 George always tells the truth. He never tells ....
9 It was late when we arrived in the town, and .... were shut.
10 .... in the pool didn't look very clean, so we didn't go for a swim.
11 Don't sit on .... It's wet after the rain.
12 You need .... to teach young children.

75.3 Choose the correct form, with or without **the**.

1 I'm afraid of <u>dogs</u> / <s>the dogs.</s> (<u>dogs</u> *is correct*)
2 Can you pass <s>salt</s> / <u>the salt</u>, please? (<u>the salt</u> *is correct*)
3 <u>Apples</u> / <u>The apples</u> are good for you.
4 Look at <u>apples</u> / <u>the apples</u> on that tree! They're very big.
5 <u>Women</u> / <u>The women</u> live longer than <u>men</u> / <u>the men</u>.
6 I don't drink <u>tea</u> / <u>the tea</u>. I don't like it.
7 We had a very good meal. <u>Vegetables</u> / <u>The vegetables</u> were especially good.
8 <u>Life</u> / <u>The life</u> is strange sometimes. Some very strange things happen.
9 I like <u>skiing</u> / <u>the skiing</u>, but I'm not very good at it.
10 Who are <u>people</u> / <u>the people</u> in this photograph?
11 What makes <u>people</u> / <u>the people</u> violent? What causes <u>aggression</u> / <u>the aggression</u>?
12 <u>All books</u> / <u>All the books</u> on the top shelf belong to me.
13 Don't stay in that hotel. It's very noisy and <u>beds</u> / <u>the beds</u> are very uncomfortable.
14 A pacifist is somebody who is against <u>war</u> / <u>the war</u>.
15 <u>First World War</u> / <u>The First World War</u> lasted from 1914 until 1918.
16 I'd like to go to Egypt and see <u>Pyramids</u> / <u>the Pyramids</u>.
17 Someone gave me a book about <u>history</u> / <u>the history</u> of <u>modern art</u> / <u>the modern art</u>.
18 Ron and Brenda got married, but <u>marriage</u> / <u>the marriage</u> didn't last very long.
19 <u>Most people</u> / <u>The most people</u> believe that <u>marriage</u> / <u>the marriage</u> and
    <u>family life</u> / <u>the family life</u> are the basis of <u>society</u> / <u>the society</u>.

→ Additional exercise 29 **(page 319)**

A

Study these sentences:

- **The giraffe** is the tallest of all animals.
- **The bicycle** is an excellent means of transport.
- When was **the telephone** invented?
- **The dollar** is the currency (= the money) of the United States.

In these examples, **the** ... does not mean one specific thing. **The giraffe** = a specific type of animal, not a specific giraffe. We use **the** (+ singular countable noun) in this way to talk about a type of animal, machine etc.

In the same way we use **the** for musical instruments:

- Can you play **the** guitar?
- **The** piano is my favourite instrument.

Compare **a** and **the**:

- I'd like to have **a piano**.   *but*   I can't play **the piano**.
- We saw **a giraffe** at the zoo.   *but*   **The giraffe** is my favourite animal.

Note that we use **man** (= human beings in general / the human race) without **the**:

- What do you know about the origins of **man**? (*not* the man)

B

The + adjective

We use **the** + adjective (without a noun) to talk about groups of people, especially:

the young	the rich	the sick	the blind	the injured
the old	the poor	the disabled	the deaf	the dead
the elderly	the homeless	the unemployed		

The young = young people, **the rich** = rich people etc. :

- Do you think **the rich** should pay higher taxes?
- The government has promised to provide more money to help **the homeless**.

These expressions are always *plural* in meaning. For example, you cannot say 'a young' or 'the injured' for one person. You must say 'a young **person**', '**the** injured **woman**' etc.

Note that we say 'the **poor**' (*not* the poors), 'the **young**' (*not* the youngs) etc.

C

The + nationality

You can use **the** + nationality adjectives that end in -ch or -sh (**the French / the English / the Spanish** etc.) The meaning is 'the people of that country':

- **The French** are famous for their food. (= the people of France)

The French / the English etc. are plural in meaning. We do not say 'a French / an English'. You have to say **a Frenchman / an Englishwoman** etc.

You can also use **the** + nationality words ending in -ese (**the Chinese / the Sudanese / the Japanese** etc.):

- **The Chinese** invented printing.

But these words can also be singular (**a Japanese, a Sudanese** etc.).
Also **a Swiss** (singular) and **the Swiss** (= the people of Switzerland)

With other nationalities, the plural noun ends in -s. For example:

    an Italian → **Italians**   **a Mexican** → **Mexicans**   **a Turk** → **Turks**

With these words (**Italians** etc.), we do not normally use **the** to talk about the people in general (see Unit 75).

A/an and the → Unit 72   The 1–3 → Units 73–75   Names with and without the → Units 77–78

76.1 Answer the questions. Choose the right answer from the box. Don't forget **the**. Use a dictionary if necessary.

| 1 | 2 | 3 | 4 |

animals	*birds*	*inventions*	*currencies*
tiger elephant	eagle penguin	telephone wheel	dollar peso
rabbit cheetah	swan owl	telescope laser	euro rupee
giraffe kangaroo	parrot robin	helicopter typewriter	rouble yen

1 a Which of the animals is tallest? .... the giraffe ....
   b Which animal can run fastest? ....
   c Which of these animals is found in Australia? ....
2 a Which of these birds has a long neck? ....
   b Which of these birds cannot fly? ....
   c Which bird flies at night? ....
3 a Which of these inventions is oldest? ....
   b Which one is most recent? ....
   c Which one was especially important for astronomy? ....
4 a What is the currency of India? ....
   b What is the currency of Canada? ....
   c And the currency of your country? ....

76.2 Put in **the** or **a**.
1 When was .....the..... telephone invented?
2 Can you play .... musical instrument?
3 Jill plays .... violin in an orchestra.
4 There was .... piano in the corner of the room.
5 Can you play .... piano?
6 Our society is based on .... family.
7 Martin comes from .... large family.
8 .... computer has changed the way we live.

76.3 Complete these sentences using **the** + the following:

   injured   **poor**   **rich**   **sick**   **unemployed**   ~~**young**~~

1 .....The young..... have the future in their hands.
2 Ambulances arrived at the scene of the accident and took .... to hospital.
3 Life is all right if you have a job, but things are not so easy for ....
4 Julia has been a nurse all her life. She has spent her life caring for ....
5 In England there is an old story about a man called Robin Hood. It is said that he robbed .... and gave the money to ....

76.4 What do you call the people of these countries?

	one person (**a/an** ...)	*the people in general*
1 Canada	a Canadian	Canadians
2 Germany		
3 France		
4 Russia		
5 China		
6 Brazil		
7 England		
8 and your country		

A

We do *not* use **the** with names of people ('Helen', 'Helen Taylor' etc.). In the same way, we do *not* normally use **the** with names of places. For example:

continents	Africa (*not* the Africa), Europe, South America
countries, states etc.	France (*not* the France), Japan, Switzerland, Texas
islands	Sicily, Bermuda, Tasmania
cities, towns etc.	Cairo, New York, Bangkok
mountains	Everest, Etna, Kilimanjaro

But we use **the** in names with **Republic, Kingdom, States** etc. :

the Czech **Republic**   the United **Kingdom** (the UK)
the Dominican **Republic**   the United **States** of America (**the USA**)

Compare:
    ☐ Have you been to **Canada** or **the United States**?

B

When we use **Mr/Mrs/Captain/Doctor** etc. + a name, we do not use **the**. So we say:

Mr Johnson / **Doctor** Johnson / **Captain** Johnson / **President** Johnson etc. (*not* the ...)
Uncle Robert / **Saint** Catherine / **Princess** Maria etc. (*not* the ...)

Compare:
    ☐ We called **the doctor**.
       We called **Doctor** Johnson. (*not* the Doctor Johnson)

We use **mount** (= mountain) and **lake** in the same way (without **the**):

Mount Everest (*not* the ...) **Mount** Etna **Lake** Superior **Lake** Constance
    ☐ They live near **the lake**.
       They live near **Lake Constance**. (*not* the Lake Constance)

C

We use **the** with the names of oceans, seas, rivers and canals:

the Atlantic (Ocean)	the Red Sea	the Amazon
the Indian Ocean	the Channel (between	the Nile
the Mediterranean (Sea)	France and Britain)	the Suez Canal

We use **the** with the names of deserts:

the Sahara (Desert)   the Gobi Desert

D

We use **the** with *plural* names of people and places:

people	**the** Taylors (= the Taylor family), **the** Johnsons
countries	**the** Netherlands, **the** Philippines, **the** United States
groups of islands	**the** Canaries / **the** Canary Islands, **the** Bahamas
mountain ranges	**the** Rocky Mountains / **the** Rockies, **the** Andes, **the** Alps

    ☐ The highest mountain in **the Alps** is **Mont Blanc**.

E

We say:

    the north (of Brazil)   *but*   **northern** Brazil (*without* the)
    the south-east (of Spain)   *but*   **south-eastern** Spain

Compare:
    ☐ Sweden is in **northern Europe**; Spain is in **the south**.

Also **the** Middle East, **the** Far East

We also use **north/south** etc. (without **the**) in the names of some regions and countries:

    North America   **South Africa**

Note that on maps, **the** is not usually included in the name.

77.1 Put in **the** where necessary. Leave the space empty if the sentence is already complete.

1 Who is ....‒........ Doctor Johnson? (*the sentence is complete without* the)
2 I was ill, so I went to see .... doctor.
3 The most powerful person in .... United States is .... president.
4 .... President Kennedy was assassinated in 1963.
5 Do you know .... Wilsons? They're a very nice couple.
6 Do you know .... Professor Brown's phone number?

77.2 Some of these sentences are correct, but some need **the** (sometimes more than once). Correct the sentences where necessary.

1 Everest was first climbed in 1953.   *OK*
2 Milan is in north of Italy.   *in the north of Italy*
3 Africa is much larger than Europe.
4 Last year I visited Mexico and United States.
5 South of England is warmer than north.
6 Portugal is in western Europe.
7 France and Britain are separated by Channel.
8 Jim has travelled a lot in Middle East.
9 Chicago is on Lake Michigan.
10 Next year we're going skiing in Swiss Alps.
11 UK consists of Great Britain and Northern Ireland.
12 Seychelles are a group of islands in Indian Ocean.
13 Africa's highest mountain is Kilimanjaro (5895 metres).
14 River Volga flows into Caspian Sea.

77.3 Here are some geography questions. Choose the right answer from one of the boxes and write **the** if necessary. You do not need all the names in the boxes. Use an atlas if necessary.

continents	countries	oceans and seas	mountains	rivers and canals	
Africa	Canada	~~Atlantic~~	Alps	Amazon	Rhine
Asia	Denmark	Indian Ocean	Andes	Danube	Thames
Australia	Indonesia	Pacific	Himalayas	Nile	Volga
Europe	Sweden	Black Sea	Rockies	Suez Canal	
North America	Thailand	Mediterranean	Urals	Panama Canal	
South America	United States	Red Sea			

1 What do you have to cross to travel from Europe to America?   *the Atlantic*
2 Where is Argentina? ....
3 Which is the longest river in Africa? ....
4 Of which country is Stockholm the capital? ....
5 Of which country is Washington the capital? ....
6 What is the name of the mountain range in the west of North America? ....
7 What is the name of the sea between Africa and Europe? ....
8 Which is the smallest continent in the world? ....
9 What is the name of the ocean between North America and Asia? ....
10 What is the name of the ocean between Africa and Australia? ....
11 Which river flows through London? ....
12 Which river flows through Vienna, Budapest and Belgrade? ....
13 Of which country is Bangkok the capital? ....
14 What joins the Atlantic and Pacific Oceans? ....
15 Which is the longest river in South America? ....

Names with and without **the** 2

A Names without **the**

We do not use **the** with names of most city streets/roads/squares/parks etc. :

Wall **Street** (*not* the …)	Fifth **Avenue**	Hyde **Park**
Queens **Road**	**Broadway**	Times **Square**

Names of important public buildings and institutions (for example, airports, stations, universities) are often two words:

Manchester Airport   **Harvard University**

The first word is the name of a place ('Manchester') or a person ('Harvard'). These names are usually without **the**. In the same way, we say:

Victoria Station (*not* the …)	**Canterbury Cathedral**	**Edinburgh Castle**
Buckingham Palace	**Cambridge University**	**Sydney Harbour**

Compare:

Buckingham Palace (*not* the …)   *but*   **the Royal Palace**
('Royal' is an adjective – it is not a name like 'Buckingham'.)

B Most other buildings have names with **the**. For example:

hotels/restaurants	**the** Sheraton Hotel, **the** Bombay Restaurant, **the** Holiday Inn
theatres/cinemas	**the** Palace Theatre, **the** Odeon (cinema)
museums/galleries	**the** Guggenheim Museum, **the** Hayward Gallery
other buildings	**the** Empire State (Building), **the** White House, **the** Eiffel Tower

We often leave out the noun:

the Sheraton (Hotel)   **the Palace** (Theatre)   **the Guggenheim** (Museum)

Some names are only **the** + *noun*, for example:

the Acropolis   **the Kremlin**   **the Pentagon**

C Names with **of** usually have **the**. For example:

the Bank **of** England	**the** Museum **of** Modern Art
the Great Wall **of** China	**the** Tower **of** London

Note that we say:

the University **of** Cambridge   *but*   **Cambridge University** (*without* **the**)

D Many shops, restaurants, hotels, banks etc. are named after the people who started them. These names end in -'s or -s. We do not use **the** with these names:

Lloyds Bank (*not* the …)   **Brown's Restaurant**   **Macy's** (department store)

Churches are often named after saints:

St John's Church (*not* the St Johns Church)   **St Patrick's Cathedral**

E Most newspapers and many organisations have names with **the**:

newspapers	**the** Washington Post, **the** Financial Times, **the** Sun
organisations	**the** European Union, **the** BBC (= British Broadcasting Corporation), **the** Red Cross

Names of companies, airlines etc. are usually without **the**:

Fiat (*not* the Fiat)	**Sony**	**British Airways**
Kodak	**IBM**	**Yale University Press**

78.1 Use the map to answer the questions. Write the name of the place and the street it is in.
Use **the** if necessary. (Remember that on maps we do not normally use **the**.)

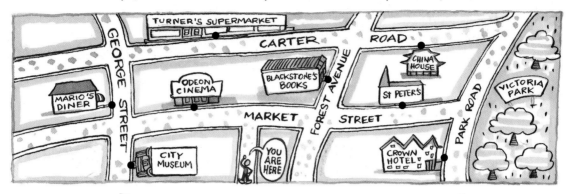

1	Is there a cinema near here?	Yes, the Odeon in Market Street .... .
2	Is there a supermarket near here?	Yes, ... in ....
3	Is there a hotel near here?	Yes, ... in ....
4	Is there a church near here?	Yes, ...
5	Is there a museum near here?	Yes, ...
6	Is there a bookshop near here?	Yes, ...
7	Is there a park near here?	Yes, ... at the end of ....
8	Is there a restaurant near here?	There are two. .... or ....

78.2 Where are the following? Use **the** where necessary.

Acropolis	Broadway	Buckingham Palace	Eiffel Tower
Kremlin	White House	Gatwick Airport	~~Times Square~~

1 ... Times Square ... is in New York.
2 .... is in Paris.
3 .... is in London.
4 .... is in Washington.
5 .... is in Moscow.
6 .... is in New York.
7 .... is in Athens.
8 .... is near London.

78.3 Choose the correct form, with or without **the**.

1 Have you ever been to ~~British Museum~~ / the British Museum? (*the British Museum is correct*)
2 Hyde Park / The Hyde Park is a very large park in central London.
3 Another park in central London is St James's Park / the St James's Park.
4 Grand Hotel / The Grand Hotel is in Baker Street / the Baker Street.
5 Dublin Airport / The Dublin Airport is situated about 12 kilometres from the city centre.
6 Frank is a student at Liverpool University / the Liverpool University.
7 If you're looking for a department store, I would recommend Harrison's / the Harrison's.
8 If you're looking for a place to have lunch, I would recommend Ship Inn / the Ship Inn.
9 Statue of Liberty / The Statue of Liberty is at the entrance to New York Harbour / the New York Harbour.
10 You should go to Science Museum / the Science Museum. It's very interesting.
11 John works for IBM / the IBM now. He used to work for British Telecom / the British Telecom.
12 'Which cinema are you going to this evening?' 'Classic / The Classic.'
13 I'd like to go to China and see Great Wall / the Great Wall.
14 'Which newspaper do you want?' 'Herald / The Herald.'
15 This book is published by Cambridge University Press / the Cambridge University Press.

→ Additional exercise 29 (page 319)

Singular and plural

A Sometimes we use a *plural* noun for one thing that has two parts. For example:

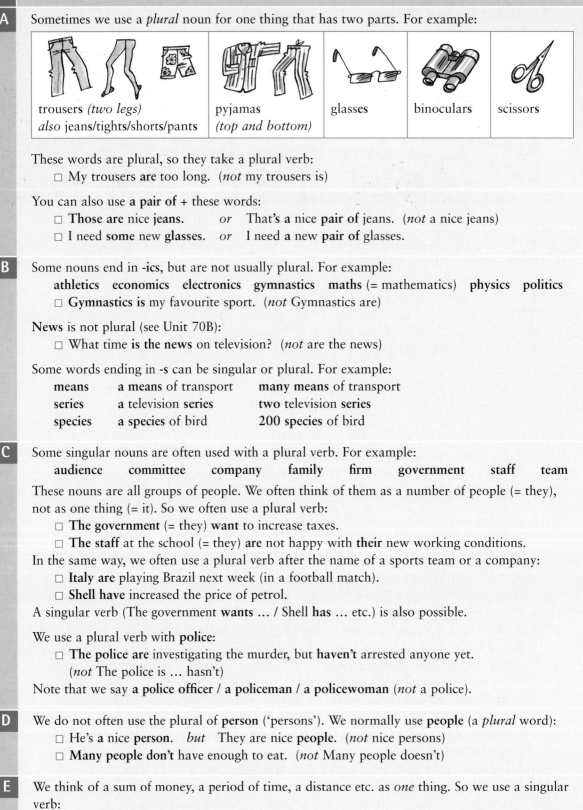

trousers *(two legs)* also jeans/tights/shorts/pants	pyjamas *(top and bottom)*	glasses	binoculars	scissors

These words are plural, so they take a plural verb:
- ☐ My trousers **are** too long. (*not* my trousers is)

You can also use **a pair of** + these words:
- ☐ **Those are** nice **jeans.** *or* That's a nice **pair of** jeans. (*not* a nice jeans)
- ☐ I need **some** new **glasses.** *or* I need a new **pair of** glasses.

B Some nouns end in -ics, but are not usually plural. For example:

athletics economics electronics gymnastics maths (= mathematics) **physics politics**
- ☐ **Gymnastics is** my favourite sport. (*not* Gymnastics are)

News is not plural (see Unit 70B):
- ☐ What time **is the news** on television? (*not* are the news)

Some words ending in -s can be singular or plural. For example:

means	**a means** of transport	**many means** of transport
series	**a** television **series**	**two** television **series**
species	**a species** of bird	**200 species** of bird

C Some singular nouns are often used with a plural verb. For example:

audience committee company family firm government staff team

These nouns are all groups of people. We often think of them as a number of people (= they), not as one thing (= it). So we often use a plural verb:
- ☐ The government (= they) **want** to increase taxes.
- ☐ The staff at the school (= they) **are** not happy with **their** new working conditions.

In the same way, we often use a plural verb after the name of a sports team or a company:
- ☐ **Italy are** playing Brazil next week (in a football match).
- ☐ **Shell have** increased the price of petrol.

A singular verb (The government **wants** ... / Shell **has** ... etc.) is also possible.

We use a plural verb with **police**:
- ☐ The police **are** investigating the murder, but **haven't** arrested anyone yet.
  (*not* The police is ... hasn't)

Note that we say **a police officer / a policeman / a policewoman** (*not* a police).

D We do not often use the plural of **person** ('persons'). We normally use **people** (a *plural* word):
- ☐ He's **a** nice **person.** *but* They are nice **people.** (*not* nice persons)
- ☐ **Many people don't** have enough to eat. (*not* Many people doesn't)

E We think of a sum of money, a period of time, a distance etc. as *one* thing. So we use a singular verb:
- ☐ **Twenty thousand pounds** (= it) **was** stolen in the robbery. (*not* were stolen)
- ☐ **Three years** (= it) **is** a long time to be without a job. (*not* Three years are)
- ☐ **Six miles is** a long way to walk every day.

American English → Appendix 7

79.1 Complete each sentence using a word from Sections A or B. Sometimes you need a or some.

1 My eyesight isn't very good. I need ....glasses.... .
2 ....A species.... is a group of animals or plants that have the same characteristics.
3 Footballers don't wear trousers when they play. They wear ....
4 The bicycle is .... of transport.
5 The bicycle and the car are .... of transport.
6 I want to cut this piece of material. I need ....
7 A friend of mine is writing .... of articles for the local newspaper.
8 There are a lot of American TV .... shown on British television.
9 While we were out walking, we saw many different .... of bird.

79.2 In each example the words on the left are connected with an activity (for example, a sport or an academic subject). Write the name of the activity. The beginning of the word is given.

1 calculate   algebra   equation   ....mathematics....
2 government   election   minister   p...
3 finance   trade   employment   e...
4 running   jumping   throwing   a...
5 light   heat   gravity   ph...
6 exercises   somersault   parallel bars   gy...
7 computer   silicon chip   video games   el...

79.3 Choose the correct form of the verb, singular or plural. In one sentence either the singular or plural verb is possible.

1 Gymnastics is / are my favourite sport. (is *is correct*)
2 The trousers you bought for me doesn't / don't fit me.
3 The police want / wants to interview two men about the robbery last week.
4 Physics was / were my best subject at school.
5 Can I borrow your scissors? Mine isn't / aren't sharp enough.
6 Fortunately the news wasn't / weren't as bad as we expected.
7 Where does / do your family live?
8 Three days isn't / aren't long enough for a good holiday.
9 I can't find my binoculars. Do you know where it is / they are?
10 It's a nice place to visit. The people is / are very friendly.
11 Does / Do the police know how the accident happened?
12 I don't like very hot weather. Thirty degrees is / are too hot for me.

79.4 Most of these sentences are wrong. Correct them where necessary.

1 Three years are a long time to be without a job.   Three years is a long time
2 The government want to increase taxes.   OK (wants *is also correct*)
3 Susan was wearing a black jeans.   ....
4 Brazil are playing Italy in a football match next week.   ....
5 I like Martin and Jane. They're very nice persons.   ....
6 I need more than ten pounds. Ten pounds aren't enough.   ....
7 I'm going to buy a new pyjama.   ....
8 The committee haven't made a decision yet.   ....
9 There was a police directing traffic in the street.   ....
10 What is the police going to do?   ....
11 This scissors isn't very sharp.   ....

Noun + noun (a **tennis ball** / a **headache**)

You can use two nouns together (*noun + noun*) to mean *one* thing/person/idea etc. For example:

a **tennis ball**   a **bank manager**   a **road accident**   **income tax**   the **city centre**

The first noun is like an adjective. It tells us what kind of thing/person/idea etc. For example:

> a **tennis ball** = a **ball** used to play **tennis**
> a **road accident** = an **accident** that happens on the **road**
> **income tax** = **tax** that you pay on your **income**
> the **water temperature** = the **temperature** of the **water**
> a **London doctor** = a **doctor** from **London**
> my **life story** = the **story** of my **life**

So you can say:

a **television** camera   a **television** programme   a **television** studio   a **television** producer
(these are all different things or people to do with television)
language **problems**   marriage **problems**   health **problems**   work **problems**
(these are all different kinds of problems)

Compare:

garden vegetables (= vegetables that are grown in a garden)
a **vegetable garden** (= a garden where vegetables are grown)

Sometimes the first word ends in **-ing**. Usually these are things used for doing something:

a **frying** pan (= a pan for frying)   a **washing** machine   a **swimming** pool   a **dining** room

Sometimes there are more than two nouns together:

> ☐ I waited at the **hotel reception desk**.
> ☐ We watched the **World Swimming Championships** on television.
> ☐ If you want to play **table tennis** (= a game), you need a **table tennis table** (= a table).

When two nouns are together like this, sometimes we write them as one word and sometimes as two separate words. For example:

a **headache**   **toothpaste**   a **weekend**   a **car park**   a **road sign**

There are no clear rules for this. If you are not sure, write two words.

Note the difference between:

a **sugar bowl** (perhaps empty) and a **bowl of sugar** (= a bowl with sugar in it)
a **shopping bag** (perhaps empty) and a **bag of shopping** (= a bag full of shopping)

When we use *noun + noun*, the first noun is like an *adjective*. It is normally singular, but the meaning is often plural. For example: a **book**shop is a shop where you can buy **books**, an **apple** tree is a tree that has **apples**.

In the same way we say:

a **three-hour** journey (= a journey that takes three **hours**)
a **ten-pound** note (*not* pounds)
a **four-week** course (*not* weeks)
two **14-year**-old girls (*not* years)
a **six-page** letter (*not* pages)

Compare:

> ☐ It was **a four-week** course. *but* The course lasted four **weeks**.

Exercises

80.1 What do we call these things and people?

1 A ticket for a concert is _a concert ticket_ .
2 Problems concerning health are _health problems_ .
3 A magazine about computers is ....
4 Photographs taken on your holiday are your ....
5 Chocolate made with milk is ....
6 Somebody whose job is to inspect factories is ....
7 A horse that runs in races is ....
8 A race for horses is ....
9 A hotel in central London is ....
10 The results of your exams are your ....
11 The carpet in the dining room is ....
12 A scandal involving an oil company is ....
13 Workers at a car factory are ....
14 A scheme to improve a road is ....
15 A course that lasts five days is ....
16 A question that has two parts is ....
17 A girl who is seven years old is ....

80.2 Answer the questions using two of the following words each time:

~~accident~~	belt	card	credit	editor	forecast	newspaper
number	~~road~~	room	seat	shop	weather	window

1 This can be caused by bad driving.   _a road accident_
2 If you're staying at a hotel, you need to remember this.   your ....
3 You should wear this when you're in a car.   a ....
4 You can often use this to pay for things instead of cash.   a ....
5 If you want to know if it's going to rain, you can read or listen to this.   the ....
6 This person is a top journalist.   a ....
7 You might stop to look in this when you're walking along a street.   a ....

80.3 Complete the sentences using the following:

15 minute(s)	60 minute(s)	two hour(s)	five day(s)	two year(s)	500 year(s)
six mile(s)	six mile(s)	20 pound(s)	five course(s)	~~ten page(s)~~	~~450 page(s)~~

Sometimes you need the singular (day/page etc.) and sometimes the plural (days/pages etc.).

1 It's quite a long book. There are _450 pages_ .
2 A few days ago I received a _ten-page_ letter from Julia.
3 I didn't have any change. I only had a .... note.
4 At work in the morning I usually have a .... break for coffee.
5 There are .... in an hour.
6 It's only a .... flight from London to Madrid.
7 It was a very big meal. There were ....
8 Mary has just started a new job. She's got a .... contract.
9 The oldest building in the city is the .... castle.
10 I work .... a week. Saturday and Sunday are free.
11 We went for a long walk in the country. We must have walked ....
12 We went for a .... walk in the country.

-'s (your sister's name) and of ... (the name of the book)

A

We use **-'s** (*apostrophe* + **s**) mostly for people or animals:
- □ **Tom's** computer isn't working. (*not* the computer of Tom)
- □ How old are **Chris's** children? (*not* the children of Chris)
- □ What's (= What is) **your sister's** name?
- □ What's **Tom's sister's** name?
- □ Be careful. Don't step on **the cat's** tail.

Note that you can use **-'s** without a following noun:
- □ This isn't my book. It's **my sister's**. (= my sister's book)

We do not always use **-'s** for people. For example, we would use **of ...** in this sentence:
- □ What was the name **of the man who phoned you?** ('the man who phoned you' is too long to be followed by **-'s**)

Note that we say **a woman's hat** (= a hat for a woman), **a boy's name** (= a name for a boy), **a bird's egg** (= an egg laid by a bird) etc.

B

With a *singular* noun we use **-'s**:
  my **sister's** room (= **her** room – one sister)   **Mr Carter's** house (= **his** house)

With a *plural* noun (sisters, friends etc.) we put an apostrophe at the end of the word (**-s'**):
  my **sisters'** room (= **their** room – *two or more* sisters)
  the **Carters'** house (= **their** house – Mr and Mrs Carter)

If a plural noun does not end in **-s** (for example **men/women/children/people**) we use **-'s**:
  the **men's** changing room   a **children's** book (= a book for children)

Note that you can use **-'s** after more than one noun:
  Jack and Karen's wedding   **Mr and Mrs Carter's** house

C

For things, ideas etc., we normally use **of** (**... of the book** / **... of the restaurant** etc.):
  the door **of the garage** (*not* the garage's door)
  the name **of the book**   the owner **of the restaurant**
Sometimes the structure *noun + noun* is possible (see Unit 80):
  the **garage door**   the **restaurant owner**

We say **the beginning/end/middle of ...** , **the top/bottom of ...** , **the front/back/side of ...** :
  the beginning of the month (*not* the month's beginning)
  the top of the hill   **the back of** the car

D

You can usually use **-'s** or **of ...** for an organisation (= a group of people). So you can say:
  the government's decision *or* the decision **of the government**
  the company's success *or* the success **of the company**

It is also possible to use **-'s** for places. So you can say:
  the city's streets   **the world's** population   **Italy's** prime minister

E

You can also use **-'s** with time expressions (**yesterday** / **next week** etc.):
- □ Do you still have **yesterday's** newspaper?
- □ **Next week's** meeting has been cancelled.

In the same way, you can say **today's** / **tomorrow's** / **this evening's** / **Monday's** etc.

We also use **-'s** (or **-s'** with plural words) with periods of time:
- □ I've got **a week's** holiday starting on Monday.
- □ Julia has got **three weeks'** holiday.
- □ I live near the station – it's only about **ten minutes'** walk.

The garage door (noun + noun) → Unit 80   A three-hour journey, a ten-pound note → Unit 80D

Exercises

81.1 In some of these sentences, it would be more natural to use –'s or –'. Change the underlined parts where necessary.

1 Who is the owner of this restaurant?   *OK*
2 Where are the children of Chris?   *Chris's children*
3 Is this the umbrella of your friend?
4 Write your name at the top of the page.
5 I've never met the daughter of Charles.
6 Have you met the son of Mary and Dan?
7 We don't know the cause of the problem.
8 Do we still have the newspaper of yesterday?
9 What's the name of this street?
10 What is the cost of a new computer?
11 The friends of your children are here.
12 The garden of our neighbours is very nice.
13 I work on the ground floor of the building.
14 The hair of Bill is very long.
15 I couldn't go to the party of Catherine.
16 What's the name of the woman who lives next door?
17 Have you seen the car of the parents of Mike?
18 What's the meaning of this expression?
19 Do you agree with the economic policy of the government?

81.2 What is another way of saying these things? Use –'s.

1 a hat for a woman   *a woman's hat*
2 a name for a boy
3 clothes for children
4 a school for girls
5 a nest for a bird
6 a magazine for women

81.3 Read each sentence and write a new sentence beginning with the <u>underlined</u> words.

1 The meeting <u>tomorrow</u> has been cancelled.
    Tomorrow's meeting has been cancelled.
2 The storm <u>last week</u> caused a lot of damage.
    Last
3 The only cinema in <u>the town</u> has closed down.
    The
4 The weather in <u>Britain</u> is very changeable.

5 Tourism is the main industry in <u>the region</u>.

81.4 Use the information given to complete the sentences.

1 If I leave my house at 9 o'clock and drive to the airport, I arrive at about 11.
    So it's about   *two hours' drive*   from my house to the airport. (drive)
2 If I leave my house at 8.40 and walk to the centre, I get there at 9 o'clock.
    So it's   from my house to the centre. (walk)
3 I'm going on holiday on the 12th. I have to be back at work on the 26th.
    So I've got   . (holiday)
4 I went to sleep at 3 o'clock this morning and woke up an hour later. After that I couldn't sleep. So last night I only had   . (sleep)

Myself/yourself/themselves etc.

A

Study this example:

Hi, I'm Steve.

STEVE

Steve **introduced himself** to the other guests.

We use **myself/yourself/himself** etc. (*reflexive pronouns*) when the *subject* and *object* are the same:

Steve	introduced	himself
subject		*object*

The reflexive pronouns are:

singular: myself   yourself *(one person)*   himself/herself/itself

plural: ourselves   yourselves *(more than one person)*   themselves

- ☐ I don't want you to pay for me. I'll pay for **myself**.   (*not* I'll pay for me)
- ☐ Julia had a great holiday. **She** really enjoyed **herself**.
- ☐ Do **you** talk to **yourself** sometimes? *(said to one person)*
- ☐ If you want more to eat, help **yourselves**. *(said to more than one person)*

Compare:

- ☐ It's not our fault. **You** can't blame **us**.
- ☐ It's our own fault. **We** should blame **ourselves**.

B

We do not use **myself** etc. after feel/relax/concentrate/meet:

- ☐ I **feel** nervous. I can't **relax**.
- ☐ You must try and **concentrate**. (*not* concentrate yourself)
- ☐ What time shall we **meet**? (*not* meet ourselves, *not* meet us)

We normally use **wash/shave/dress** *without* **myself** etc. :

- ☐ He got up, **washed**, **shaved** and **dressed**. (*not* washed himself etc.)

You can also say **get dressed** (He **got dressed**).

C

Compare -selves and each other:

- ☐ Kate and Joe stood in front of the mirror and looked at **themselves**. (= *Kate and Joe* looked at *Kate and Joe*)
- ☐ Kate looked at Joe; Joe looked at Kate. They looked at **each other**.

themselves

each other

You can use **one another** instead of **each other**:

- ☐ How long have you and Bill known **each other**?   *or*   ... known **one another**?
- ☐ Sue and Ann don't like **each other**.   *or*   ... don't like **one another**.
- ☐ Do you and Sarah live near **each other**?   *or*   ... near **one another**?

D

We also use **myself/yourself** etc. in another way. For example:

- ☐ 'Who repaired your bike for you?'   'I repaired it **myself**.'

I repaired it myself = I repaired it, not anybody else. Here, **myself** is used to emphasise 'I' (= it makes it stronger). Some more examples:

- ☐ I'm not going to do your work for you. **You** can do it **yourself**. (= you, not me)
- ☐ Let's paint the house **ourselves**. It will be much cheaper.
- ☐ **The film itself** wasn't very good, but I loved the music.
- ☐ I don't think Liz will get the job. **Liz herself** doesn't think she'll get it. (*or* Liz doesn't think she'll get it **herself**.)

Get dressed / get married etc. → Unit 44D   **By myself / by yourself etc.** → Unit 83C

82.1 Complete the sentences using **myself/yourself** etc. + the following verbs (in the correct form):

> blame   burn   enjoy   express   hurt   ~~introduce~~   put

1 Steve __introduced himself__ to the other guests at the party.
2 Bill fell down some steps, but fortunately he didn't ....
3 It isn't Sue's fault. She really shouldn't ....
4 Please try and understand how I feel. .... in my position.
5 The children had a great time at the beach. They really ....
6 Be careful! That pan is very hot. Don't ....
7 Sometimes I can't say exactly what I mean. I wish I could .... better.

82.2 Put in **myself/yourself/ourselves** etc. or **me/you/us** etc.

1 Julia had a great holiday. She enjoyed __herself__ .
2 It's not my fault. You can't blame ....
3 What I did was really bad. I'm ashamed of ....
4 We've got a problem. I hope you can help ....
5 'Can I take another biscuit?' 'Of course. Help .... !'
6 You must meet Sarah. I'll introduce .... to her.
7 Don't worry about us. We can look after ....
8 I gave them a key to our house so that they could let .... in.
9 I didn't want anybody to see the letters, so I burned ....

82.3 Complete these sentences. Use **myself/yourself** etc. only where necessary. Use the following verbs (in the correct form):

> concentrate   defend   dry   feel   meet   relax   ~~shave~~   wash

1 Martin decided to grow a beard because he was fed up with __shaving__ .
2 I wasn't very well yesterday, but I .... much better today.
3 I climbed out of the swimming pool and .... with a towel.
4 I tried to study, but I couldn't ....
5 If somebody attacks you, you need to be able to ....
6 I'm going out with Chris this evening. We're .... at 7.30.
7 You're always rushing around. Why don't you sit down and .... ?
8 There was no water, so we couldn't ....

82.4 Complete the sentences with **–selves** or **each other**.

1 How long have you and Bill known __each other__ ?
2 If people work too hard, they can make .... ill.
3 I need you and you need me. We need ....
4 In Britain friends often give .... presents at Christmas.
5 Some people are very selfish. They only think of ....
6 Tracy and I don't see .... very often these days.
7 We couldn't get back into the house. We had locked .... out.
8 They've had an argument. They're not speaking to .... at the moment.
9 We'd never met before, so we introduced .... to ....

82.5 Complete the answers to the questions using **myself/yourself/itself** etc.

1	Who repaired the bike for you?	Nobody. I __repaired it myself.__
2	Who cuts Brian's hair for him?	Nobody. He cuts ....
3	Do you want me to post that letter for you?	No, I'll ....
4	Who told you that Linda was going away?	Linda ....
5	Can you phone John for me?	Why can't you .... ?

→ Additional exercise 30 (page 320)

A **A friend of mine / a friend of Tom's etc.**

We say '(a friend) **of mine/yours/his/hers/ours/theirs**':
- □ I'm going to a wedding on Saturday. **A friend of mine** is getting married. (*not* a friend of me)
- □ We went on holiday with **some friends of ours**. (*not* some friends of us)
- □ Michael had an argument with **a neighbour of his**.
- □ It was **a good idea of yours** to go to the cinema.

In the same way we say '(a friend) **of my sister's** / (a friend) **of Tom's**' etc. :
- □ That woman over there is **a friend of my sister's**.
- □ It was **a good idea of Tom's** to go to the cinema.

B **My own … / your own … etc.**

We use **my/your/his/her/its/our/their** before **own**:
    my own house   **your own** car   **her own** room
    (*not* an own house, an own car etc.)

My own … / your own … etc. = something that is only mine/yours, not shared or borrowed:
- □ I don't want to share a room with anybody. I want **my own room**.
- □ Vicky and George would like to have **their own house**.
- □ It's a pity that the flat hasn't got **its own parking space**.
- □ It's **my own fault** that I've got no money. I buy too many things I don't need.
- □ Why do you want to borrow my car? Why don't you use **your own**? (= your own car)

You can also use **own** to say that you do something yourself instead of somebody else doing it for you. For example:
- □ Brian usually cuts **his own hair**.
  (= he cuts it himself; he doesn't
  go to the hairdresser's)
- □ I'd like to have a garden so that
  I could grow **my own vegetables**.
  (= grow them myself instead of
  buying them from shops)

BRIAN

C **On my own / by myself**

On my own and **by myself** both mean 'alone'. We say:

on	my/your his/her/its our/their	own	=	by	myself / yourself (*singular*) himself / herself / itself ourselves / yourselves (*plural*) / themselves

- □ I like living **on my own / by myself**.
- □ 'Did you go on holiday **on your own / by yourself**?' 'No, with a friend.'
- □ David was sitting **on his own / by himself** in a corner of the café.
- □ Learner drivers are not allowed to drive **on their own / by themselves**.

83.1 Write new sentences with the same meaning. Change the <u>underlined</u> words and use the structure in Section A (**a friend of mine** etc.).

1 I am meeting <u>one of my friends</u> tonight.   *I'm meeting a friend of mine tonight.*
2 We met <u>one of your relatives</u>.   We met a ....
3 Henry borrowed <u>one of my books</u>.   Henry ....
4 Liz invited <u>some of her friends</u> to her flat.   Liz ....
5 We had dinner with <u>one of our neighbours</u>.   ....
6 I went on holiday with <u>two of my friends</u>.   ....
7 Is that man <u>one of your friends</u>?   ....
8 I met <u>one of Jane's friends</u> at the party.   ....

83.2 Complete the sentences using **my own / your own** etc. + the following:

~~bedroom~~   business   opinions   private beach   words

1 I share a kitchen and bathroom, but I have ...*my own bedroom*........................ .
2 Gary doesn't think the same as me. He's got ....
3 Julia is fed up with working for other people. She wants to start ....
4 We stayed at a luxury hotel by the sea. The hotel had ....
5 In the test we had to read a story, and then write it in ....

83.3 Complete the sentences using **my own / your own** etc.

1 Why do you want to borrow my car?   *Why don't you use your own car*........................ ?
2 How can you blame me? It's not my fault. It's ....
3 She's always using my ideas. Why can't she use .... ?
4 Please don't worry about my problems. You've got ....
5 I can't make his decisions for him. He must make ....

83.4 Complete the sentences using **my own / your own** etc. Use the following verbs:

bake   ~~cut~~   make   write

1 Brian never goes to the hairdresser.
   He ....*cuts his own hair*.. .
2 Mary doesn't often buy clothes.
   She usually ....
3 We don't often buy bread.
   We usually ....
4 Paul is a singer. He sings songs written by other people, but he also
   ....

83.5 Complete the sentences using on **my own / by myself** etc.

1 Did you go on holiday on ....*your own*.... ?
2 I'm glad I live with other people. I wouldn't like to live on ....
3 The box was too heavy for me to lift by ....
4 'Who was Tom with when you saw him?'   'Nobody. He was by ....'
5 Very young children should not go swimming by ....
6 I don't think she knows many people. When I see her, she is always by ....
7 I don't like strawberries with cream. I like them on ....
8 Do you like working with other people or do you prefer working by .... ?
9 We had no help decorating the flat. We did it completely on ....
10 I went out with Sally because she didn't want to go out on ....

There ... and it ...

A

There and **it**

> There's a new restaurant in King Street.

> Yes, I know. I went there last night. It's very good.

We use **there** ... when we talk about something for the first time, to say that it exists:

☐ **There's** a new restaurant in King Street. (*not* A new restaurant is in King Street)
☐ I'm sorry I'm late. **There was** a lot of traffic. (*not* It was a lot of traffic)
☐ Things are more expensive now. **There has been** a big rise in the cost of living.

It = a specific thing, place, fact, situation etc. (but see also section C):

☐ We went to the new restaurant. **It's** very good. (**It** = the restaurant)
☐ I wasn't expecting them to come. **It** was a complete surprise. (**It** = that they came)

Compare **there** and **it**:

☐ I don't like this town. **There's** nothing to do here. **It's** a boring place.

There also means 'to/at/in that place':

☐ The new restaurant is very good. I went **there** (= to the restaurant) last night.
☐ When we got to the party, there were already a lot of people **there** (= at the party).

B

You can say **there will be / there must be / there might be / there used to be** etc. :

☐ **Will there be** many people at the party?
☐ 'Is there a flight to Paris this evening?' '**There might be**. I'll phone the airport.'
☐ If people drove more carefully, **there wouldn't be** so many accidents.

Also **there must have been, there should have been** etc. :

☐ There was a light on. **There must have been** somebody at home.

Compare **there** and **it**:

☐ They live on a busy road. **There must be** a lot of noise from the traffic.
  They live on a busy main road. **It must be** very noisy.
☐ **There used to be** a cinema in King Street, but it closed a few years ago.
  That building is now a supermarket. **It used to be** a cinema.

You can also say **there is sure/certain/likely/bound** to be ... :

☐ **There is bound** (= sure) **to be** a flight to Paris this evening.

C

We also use **it** in sentences like this:

☐ **It's** dangerous **to walk in the road.**

We do not usually say 'To walk in the road is dangerous'. Normally we begin with **It** ... .
Some more examples:

☐ **It** didn't take us long **to get here.**
☐ **It's** a pity (**that**) **Sandra can't come to the party.**
☐ Let's go. **It's** not worth **waiting any longer.**

We also use **it** to talk about distance, time and weather:

☐ How far is **it** from here to the airport.
☐ What day is **it** today?
☐ **It's** a long time since we saw you last.
☐ **It** was windy yesterday. (*but* **There** was **a cold wind.**)

It's worth / it's no use / there's no point → Unit 63A   **Sure to / bound to ...** etc. → Unit 65E
There is + -ing/-ed → Unit 97

84.1 Put in **there is/was** or **it is/was**. Some sentences are questions (is there ... ? / is it ... ? etc.) and some are negative (isn't/wasn't).

1 The journey took a long time. _There was_ a lot of traffic.
2 What's the new restaurant like? _Is it_ good?
3 '............................ a bookshop near here?' 'Yes, ... one in Hill Street.'
4 When we got to the cinema, ... a queue outside. .... a very long queue, so we decided not to wait.
5 I couldn't see anything. .... completely dark.
6 .... trouble at the club last night. They had to call the police.
7 How far .... from Milan to Rome?
8 .... Keith's birthday yesterday. We had a party.
9 .... three years since I last went to the theatre.
10 I wanted to visit the museum, but .... enough time.
11 '............................ time to leave?' 'Yes, ... nearly midnight.'
12 A few days ago .... a storm. .... a lot of damage.
13 .... a beautiful day yesterday. We had a picnic.
14 .... anything on television, so I turned it off.
15 .... an accident in King Street, but .... very serious.

84.2 Read the first sentence and then write a sentence beginning **There ... .**

1 The roads were busy today.   _There was a lot of traffic._
2 This soup is very salty.   There .... in the soup.
3 The box was empty.   .... in the box.
4 The film was very violent.   ....
5 The shops were very crowded.   ....
6 I like this town – it's lively. ....

84.3 Complete the sentences. Use **there will be, there would be** etc. Choose from:

will   may   ~~would~~   wouldn't   should   used to   (be) going to

1 If people drove more carefully, _there would be_ fewer accidents.
2 'Do we have any eggs?' 'I'm not sure. .... some in the fridge.'
3 I think everything will be OK. I don't think .... any problems.
4 Look at the sky. .... a storm.
5 'Is there a school in the village?' 'Not now. .... one, but it closed.'
6 People drive too fast on this road. I think .... a speed limit.
7 If people weren't aggressive, ... any wars.

84.4 Are these sentences right or wrong? Change **it** to **there** where necessary.

1 They live on a busy road. <u>It must be</u> a lot of noise.   _There must be a lot of noise._
2 Last winter it was very cold and it was a lot of snow.   ....
3 It used to be a church here, but it was knocked down.   ....
4 Why was she so unfriendly? It must have been a reason.   ....
5 It's a long way from my house to the nearest shop.   ....
6 A: Where can we park the car?
  B: Don't worry. It's sure to be a car park somewhere.   ....
7 After the lecture it will be an opportunity to ask questions.   ....
8 I like the place where I live, but it would be nicer to live by the sea.   ....
9 I was told that it would be somebody to meet me at the station, but it wasn't anybody.   ....
10 The situation is still the same. It has been no change.   ....
11 I don't know who'll win, but it's sure to be a good game.   ....

Unit 85 — Some and any

A

In general we use **some** (*also* **somebody/someone/something**) in positive sentences and **any** (*also* **anybody** etc.) in negative sentences:

some	any
☐ We bought **some** flowers.	☐ We did**n't** buy **any** flowers.
☐ He's busy. He's got **some** work to do.	☐ He's lazy. He **never** does **any** work.
☐ There's **somebody** at the door.	☐ There is**n't anybody** at the door.
☐ I'm hungry. I want **something** to eat.	☐ I'm not hungry. I do**n't** want **anything** to eat.

We use **any** in the following sentences because the meaning is negative:
- ☐ She went out **without any** money. (she did**n't** take **any** money with her)
- ☐ He **refused** to eat **anything**. (he did**n't** eat **anything**)
- ☐ **Hardly anybody** passed the examination. (= almost **nobody** passed)

B

We use both **some** and **any** in questions. We use **some** to talk about a person or thing that we know exists, or we think exists:
- ☐ Are you waiting for **somebody**? (I think you are waiting for somebody)

We use **some** in questions when we offer or ask for things:
- ☐ Would you like **something** to eat? (there is something to eat)
- ☐ Can I have **some** sugar, please? (there is probably some sugar I can have)

But in most questions, we use **any**. We do not know if the thing or person exists:
- ☐ 'Have you got **any** luggage?' 'No, I haven't.'
- ☐ I can't find my bag. Has **anybody** seen it?

C

We often use **any** after **if**:
- ☐ **If** there are **any** letters for me, can you send them on to this address?
- ☐ **If anyone** has any questions, I'll be pleased to answer them.
- ☐ Let me know **if** you need **anything**.

The following sentences have the idea of **if**:
- ☐ I'm sorry for **any** trouble I've caused. (= if I have caused any trouble)
- ☐ **Anyone** who wants to do the exam must tell me by Friday. (= if there is anyone)

D

We also use **any** with the meaning 'it doesn't matter which':
- ☐ You can take **any** bus. They all go to the centre. (= it doesn't matter which bus you take)
- ☐ 'Sing a song.' 'Which song shall I sing?' '**Any** song. I don't mind.' (= it doesn't matter which song)
- ☐ Come and see me **any** time you want.
- ☐ 'Let's go out somewhere.' 'Where shall we go?' '**Anywhere**. I just want to go out.'
- ☐ We left the door unlocked. **Anybody** could have come in.

Compare **something** and **anything**:
- ☐ A: I'm hungry. I want **something** to eat.
  B: What would you like?
  A: I don't mind. **Anything**. (= it doesn't matter what)

E

Somebody/someone/anybody/anyone are singular words:
- ☐ **Someone** is here to see you.

But we often use **they/them/their** after these words:
- ☐ **Someone** has forgotten **their** umbrella. (= his or her umbrella)
- ☐ If **anybody** wants to leave early, **they** can. (= he or she can)

Not … any → Unit 86   Some of / any of … → Unit 88   Hardly any → Unit 101C

85.1 Put in **some** or **any**.

1 We didn't buy ......*any*...... flowers.
2 This evening I'm going out with .... friends of mine.
3 A: Have you seen .... good films recently?
   B: No, I haven't been to the cinema for ages.
4 I didn't have .... money, so I had to borrow ....
5 Can I have .... milk in my coffee, please?
6 I was too tired to do .... work.
7 You can cash these traveller's cheques at .... bank.
8 Can you give me .... information about places of interest in the town?
9 With the special tourist train ticket, you can travel on .... train you like.
10 If there are .... words you don't understand, use a dictionary.

85.2 Complete the sentences with **some-** or **any-** + **-body/-thing/-where**.

1 I was too surprised to say ......*anything*...... .
2 There's .... at the door. Can you go and see who it is?
3 Does .... mind if I open the window?
4 I wasn't feeling hungry, so I didn't eat ....
5 You must be hungry. Would you like .... to eat?
6 Quick, let's go! There's .... coming and I don't want .... to see us.
7 Sarah was upset about .... and refused to talk to ....
8 This machine is very easy to use. .... can learn to use it very quickly.
9 There was hardly .... on the beach. It was almost deserted.
10 'Do you live .... near Joe?' 'No, he lives in another part of town.'
11 'Where shall we go on holiday?' 'Let's go .... warm and sunny.'
12 They stay at home all the time. They never seem to go ....
13 I'm going out now. If .... phones while I'm out, can you tell them I'll be back at 11.30?
14 Why are you looking under the bed? Have you lost .... ?
15 The police have asked that .... who saw the accident should contact them.
16 'Can I ask you .... ?' 'Sure. What do you want to ask?'
17 Sue is very secretive. She never tells .... (*2 words*)

85.3 Complete the sentences. Use **any** (+ noun) or **anybody/anything/anywhere**.

1	Which bus do I have to catch?	......*Any bus*...... . They all go to the centre.
2	Which day shall I come?	I don't mind. ....
3	What do you want to eat?	.... I don't mind. Whatever you have.
4	Where shall I sit?	It's up to you. You can sit .... you like.
5	What sort of job are you looking for?	.... It doesn't matter.
6	What time shall I phone tomorrow?	.... I'll be in all day.
7	Who shall I invite to the party?	I don't mind. .... you like.
8	Which newspaper shall I buy?	.... Whatever they have in the shop.

A   No and none

We use **no** + *noun*. **No** = **not a** or **not any**:
- ☐ We had to walk home because there was **no bus**. (= there wasn't a bus)
- ☐ Sue will have **no difficulty** finding a job. (= Sue won't have **any** difficulty …)
- ☐ There were **no shops** open. (= There weren't **any** shops open.)

You can use **no** + *noun* at the beginning of a sentence:
- ☐ **No reason** was given for the change of plan.

We use **none** *without* a noun:
- ☐ 'How much money do you have?' '**None**.' (= no money)
- ☐ All the tickets have been sold. There are **none** left. (= no tickets left)

Or we use **none of** … :
- ☐ This money is all yours. **None of it** is mine.

After **none of** + *plural* (none of **the students**, none of **them** etc.) the verb can be singular or plural. A plural verb is more usual:
- ☐ None of the shops **were** (*or* **was**) open.

B   Nothing   nobody/no-one   nowhere

You can use these negative words at the beginning of a sentence or alone (as answers to questions):
- ☐ **Nobody** (*or* **No-one**) came to visit me while I was in hospital.
- ☐ 'What happened?' '**Nothing**.'
- ☐ 'Where are you going?' '**Nowhere**. I'm staying here.'

You can also use these words after a verb, especially after **be** and **have**:
- ☐ The house is empty. There's **nobody** living there.
- ☐ We **had nothing** to eat.

Nothing/nobody etc. = **not** + **anything/anybody** etc. :
- ☐ I didn't say **anything**. (= I said **nothing**.)
- ☐ Jane didn't tell **anybody** about her plans. (= Jane told **nobody** …)
- ☐ They haven't got **anywhere** to live. (= They've got **nowhere** to live.)

With **nothing/nobody** etc., do *not* use a negative verb (**isn't, didn't** etc.):
- ☐ I **said** nothing. (*not* I didn't say nothing)
- ☐ Nobody **tells** me anything. (*not* Nobody doesn't tell me)

C

We also use **any/anything/anybody** etc. (*without* not) to mean 'it doesn't matter which/what/who' (see Unit 85D). Compare **no-** and **any-**:
- ☐ There was **no** bus, so we walked home.
  You can take **any** bus. They all go to the centre. (= it doesn't matter which)
- ☐ 'What do you want to eat?' '**Nothing**. I'm not hungry.'
  I'm so hungry. I could eat **anything**. (= it doesn't matter what)
- ☐ The exam was extremely difficult. **Nobody** passed. (= everybody failed)
  The exam was very easy. **Anybody** could have passed. (= it doesn't matter who)

D

After **nobody/no-one** you can use **they/them/their** (see also Unit 85E):
- ☐ **Nobody** phoned, did **they**? (= did he or she)
- ☐ **No-one** did what I asked **them** to do. (= him or her)
- ☐ **Nobody** in the class did **their** homework. (= his or her homework)

Some and any → Unit 85   **None of …** → Unit 88   **Any bigger / no better etc.** → Unit 106B

Exercises

86.1 Complete these sentences with **no, none** or **any**.

1 It was a public holiday, so there were ....no.... shops open.
2 I haven't got ....any.... money. Can you lend me some?
3 We had to walk home because there were .... taxis.
4 We had to walk home because there weren't .... taxis.
5 'How many eggs have we got?' '........................ . Do you want me to get some?'
6 We took a few photographs, but .... of them were very good.
7 What a stupid thing to do! .... intelligent person would do such a thing.
8 I'll try and answer .... questions you ask me.
9 I couldn't answer .... of the questions they asked me.
10 We cancelled the party because .... of the people we invited were able to come.
11 I tried to phone Chris, but there was .... answer.

86.2 Answer these questions using **none/nobody/nothing/nowhere**.

1 What did you do? — Nothing.
2 Who were you talking to? — ....
3 How much luggage have you got? — ....
4 Where are you going? — ....
5 How many mistakes did you make? — ....
6 How much did you pay? — ....

Now answer the same questions using complete sentences with **any/anybody/anything/ anywhere**.

7 (1) ...I didn't do anything. ....
8 (2) I ....
9 (3) ....
10 (4) ....
11 (5) ....
12 (6) ....

86.3 Complete these sentences with **no-** or **any-** + **-body/-thing/-where**.

1 I don't want ....anything.... to drink. I'm not thirsty.
2 The bus was completely empty. There was .... on it.
3 'Where did you go for your holidays?' '........................ . I stayed at home.'
4 I went to the shops, but I didn't buy ....
5 'What did you buy?' '........................ . I couldn't find .... I wanted.'
6 The town is still the same as it was years ago. .... has changed.
7 Have you seen my watch? I can't find it ....
8 There was complete silence in the room. .... said ....

86.4 Choose the right word.

1 She didn't tell ~~nobody~~ / anybody about her plans. (anybody *is correct*)
2 The accident looked serious, but fortunately nobody / anybody was badly injured.
3 I looked out of the window, but I couldn't see no-one / anyone.
4 My job is very easy. Nobody / Anybody could do it.
5 'What's in that box?' 'Nothing / Anything. It's empty.'
6 The situation is uncertain. Nothing / Anything could happen.
7 I don't know nothing / anything about economics.

→ Additional exercise 30 (page 320)

Much, many, little, few, a lot, plenty

A

We use **much** and **little** with *uncountable* nouns:

much time   much luck   little energy   little money

We use **many** and **few** with *plural* nouns:

many friends   many people   few cars   few countries

B

We use **a lot of** / **lots of** / **plenty of** with both *uncountable* and *plural* nouns:

a lot of luck   lots of time   plenty of money
a lot of friends   lots of people   plenty of ideas

Plenty = more than enough:

☐ There's no need to hurry. We've got **plenty of time**.

C

Much is unusual in positive sentences (especially in spoken English). Compare:

☐ We did**n't** spend **much** money.

but   We spent **a lot of** money. (*not* We spent much money)

☐ Do you see David **much**?

but   I see David **a lot**. (*not* I see David much)

We use **many** and **a lot** of in all kinds of sentences:

☐ **Many** people drive too fast.   *or*   **A lot of** people drive too fast.
☐ Do you know **many** people?   *or*   Do you know **a lot of** people?
☐ There aren't **many** tourists here.   *or*   There aren't **a lot of** tourists here.

Note that we say **many years** / **many weeks** / **many days** (*not* a lot of …):

☐ We've lived here for **many years**. (*not* a lot of years)

D

Little and **few** (*without* a) are negative ideas (= not much / not many):

☐ Gary is very busy with his job. He has **little time** for other things. (= not much time, less time than he would like)
☐ Vicky doesn't like living in London. She has **few** friends there. (= not many, not as many as she would like)

You can say **very little** and **very few**:

☐ Gary has **very little** time for other things.
☐ Vicky has **very few** friends in London.

E

A little and **a few** have a more positive meaning.

A little = some, a small amount:

☐ Let's go and have a coffee. We have **a little** time before the train leaves.
(a little time = some time, enough time to have a coffee)
☐ 'Do you speak English?' '**A little**.' (so we can talk a bit)

A few = some, a small number:

☐ I enjoy my life here. I have **a few** friends and we meet quite often.
(a few friends = not many but enough to have a good time)
☐ 'When was the last time you saw Clare?' '**A few** days ago.' (= some days ago)

Compare:

☐ He spoke **little** English, so it was difficult to communicate with him.
He spoke **a little** English, so we were able to communicate with him.
☐ She's lucky. She has **few** problems. (= not many problems)
Things are not going so well for her. She has **a few** problems. (= some problems)

You can say **only a little** and **only a few**:

☐ Hurry! We **only** have **a little** time. (*not* only little time)
☐ The village was very small. There were **only a few** houses. (*not* only few houses)

87.1 In some of these sentences **much** is incorrect or unnatural. Change **much** to **many** or **a lot (of)** where necessary. Write 'OK' if the sentence is correct.

1 We didn't spend much money. _____OK_____
2 Sue drinks <u>much</u> tea. _____a lot of tea_____
3 Joe always puts much salt on his food. ....
4 We'll have to hurry. We haven't got much time. ....
5 It cost much to repair the car. ....
6 Did it cost much to repair the car? ....
7 I don't know much people in this town. ....
8 I use the phone much at work. ....
9 There wasn't much traffic this morning. ....
10 You need much money to travel round the world. ....

87.2 Complete the sentences using **plenty (of)** + the following:

hotels	money	room	things to see	~~time~~	to learn

1 There's no need to hurry. There's ....plenty of time.....................................
2 He's got no financial problems. He's got ....
3 Come and sit with us. There's ....
4 She knows a lot, but she still has ....
5 It's an interesting town to visit. There ....
6 I'm sure we'll find somewhere to stay. ....

87.3 Put in **much/many/few/little** (one word only).

1 She isn't very popular. She has .....few..... friends.
2 Ann is very busy these days. She has .... free time.
3 Did you take .... photographs when you were on holiday?
4 I'm not very busy today. I haven't got .... to do.
5 This is a very modern city. There are .... old buildings.
6 The weather has been very dry recently. We've had .... rain.
7 'Do you know Rome?' 'No, I haven't been there for .... years.'

87.4 Put in **a** where necessary. Write 'OK' if the sentence is already complete.

1 She's lucky. She has <u>few problems</u>. _____OK_____
2 Things are not going so well for her. She has <u>few problems</u>. _____a few problems_____
3 Can you lend me <u>few dollars</u>? ....
4 There was <u>little traffic</u>, so the journey didn't take very long. ....
5 I can't give you a decision yet. I need <u>little time</u> to think. ....
6 It was a surprise that he won the match. <u>Few people</u> expected him to win. ....
7 I don't know much Spanish – <u>only few words</u>. ....
8 I wonder how Sam is. I haven't seen him for <u>few months</u>. ....

87.5 Put in **little / a little / few / a few**.

1 Gary is very busy with his job. He has .....little..... time for other things.
2 Listen carefully. I'm going to give you .... advice.
3 Do you mind if I ask you .... questions?
4 It's not a very interesting place to visit, so .... tourists come here.
5 I don't think Jill would be a good teacher. She's got .... patience.
6 'Would you like milk in your coffee?' 'Yes, ...'
7 This is a very boring place to live. There's .... to do.
8 'Have you ever been to Paris?' 'Yes, I've been there .... times.'

Unit 88

All / all of   most / most of   no / none of etc.

A

all	some	any	most	much/many	little/few	no

You can use the words in the box with a noun (**some food** / **few books** etc.):
- **All cars** have wheels.
- **Some cars** can go faster than others.
- *(on a notice)* **NO CARS.** (= no cars allowed)
- **Many people** drive too fast.
- I don't go out very often. I'm at home **most days**.

NO CARS

You cannot say 'all of cars', 'some of people' etc. (see also Section B):
- **Some people** learn languages more easily than others. (*not* Some of people)

Note that we say **most** (*not* the most):
- **Most tourists** don't visit this part of the town. (*not* The most tourists)

B

all	some	any	most	much/many	little/few	half	none

You can use the words in the box with **of** (**some of** / **most of** etc.).
We use **some of** / **most of** / **none of** etc. + the/this/that/these/those/my ... etc. So you can say
'some **of the people**', 'some **of those people**' (*but not* 'some of people'):
- **Some of the people I work with** are not very friendly.
- **None of this money** is mine.
- Have you read **any of these books**?
- I was sick yesterday. I spent **most of the day** in bed.

You don't need **of** after **all** or **half**. So you can say:
- **All my friends** live in Los Angeles. *or* All of my friends ...
- **Half this money** is mine. *or* Half of this money ...

Compare:
- **All flowers** are beautiful. (= all flowers in general)
  All (of) the flowers in this garden are beautiful. (= a specific group of flowers)
- **Most problems** have a solution. (= most problems in general)
  We were able to solve **most of the problems we had**. (= a specific group of problems)

C

You can use **all of** / **some of** / **none of** etc. + it/us/you/them:
- 'How many of these people do you know?' '**None of them. / A few of them.**'
- Do **any of you** want to come to a party tonight?
- 'Do you like this music?' '**Some of it. Not all of it.**'

We say: **all of us** / **all of you** / **half of it** / **half of them** etc. You cannot leave out **of** before
it/us/you/them:
- **All of us** were late. (*not* all us)
- I haven't finished the book yet. I've only read **half of it**. (*not* half it)

D

You can also use **some/most** etc. alone, *without* a noun:
- Some cars have four doors and **some** have two.
- A few of the shops were open, but **most** (of them) were closed.
- Half this money is mine, and **half** (of it) is yours. (*not* the half)

Some and any → Unit 85   **No and none** → Unit 86   **Much/many/little/few** → Unit 87
All → Units 90, 110C   **All of whom** / **most of which** etc. → Unit 96B

Exercises

88.1 Put in **of** where necessary. Leave the space empty if the sentence is already complete.

1 All _____–_____ cars have wheels. (*the sentence is already complete*)
2 None __of__ this money is mine.
3 Some _____ films are very violent.
4 Some _____ the films I've seen recently have been very violent.
5 Joe never goes to museums. He says that all _____ museums are boring.
6 I think some _____ people watch too much television.
7 'Are any _____ those letters for me?'   'No, they're all for me.'
8 Kate has lived in London most _____ her life.
9 Jim has lived in Chicago all _____ his life.
10 Most _____ days I get up before 7 o'clock.

88.2 Choose from the list and complete the sentences. Use **of** (some of / most of etc.) where necessary.

accidents	European countries	my dinner	the players
birds	her friends	my spare time	the population
~~cars~~	her opinions	the buildings	~~these books~~

1 I haven't read many __of these books__ .
2 All __cars__ have wheels.
3 I spend much _____ gardening.
4 Many _____ are caused by bad driving.
5 It's a historic town. Many _____ are over 400 years old.
6 When she got married, she kept it a secret. She didn't tell any _____ .
7 Not many people live in the north of the country. Most _____ live in the south.
8 Not all _____ can fly. For example, the penguin can't fly.
9 Our team played badly and lost the game. None _____ played well.
10 Julia and I have very different ideas. I don't agree with many _____ .
11 Sarah travels a lot in Europe. She has been to most _____ .
12 I had no appetite. I could only eat half _____ .

88.3 Use your own ideas to complete these sentences.

1 The building was damaged in the explosion. All __the windows__ were broken.
2 We had a very lazy holiday. We spent most of _____ on the beach.
3 I went to the cinema by myself. None of _____ wanted to come.
4 The test was difficult. I could only answer half _____ .
5 Some of _____ you took at the wedding were very good.
6 'Have you spent all _____ I gave you?'   'No, there's still some left.'

88.4 Complete the sentences. Use:
all of / some of / none of + it/them/us (all of it / some of them etc.)

1 These books are all Jane's. __None of them__ belong to me.
2 'How many of these books have you read?'   '_____ . Every one.'
3 We all got wet in the rain because _____ had an umbrella.
4 Some of this money is yours and _____ is mine.
5 I asked some people for directions, but _____ was able to help me.
6 She invented the whole story from beginning to end. _____ was true.
7 Not all the tourists in the group were Spanish. _____ were French.
8 I watched most of the film, but not _____ .

Both / both of   neither / neither of
either / either of

A

We use **both/neither/either** for *two* things. You can use these words with a *noun* (**both books**, **neither book** etc.).

For example, you are going out to eat. There are two possible restaurants. You say:

- □ **Both restaurants** are very good. (*not* The both restaurants)
- □ **Neither restaurant** is expensive.
- □ We can go to **either restaurant**. I don't mind.
  (**either** = one or the other, it doesn't matter which one)

B

Both of ... / neither of ... / either of ...

We use **both of / neither of / either of** + **the/these/my/Tom's** ... etc. So we say 'both of **the** restaurants', 'both of **those** restaurants' etc. (*but not* both of restaurants):

- □ **Both of these** restaurants are very good.
- □ **Neither of the** restaurants we went to was (*or* were) expensive.
- □ I haven't been to **either of those** restaurants. (= I haven't been to one or the other)

You don't need **of** after **both**. So you can say:

- □ **Both my parents** are from London. *or* Both **of** my parents ...

You can use **both of / neither of / either of** + **us/you/them**:

- □ *(talking to two people)* Can **either of you** speak Spanish?
- □ I asked two people the way to the station, but **neither of them** could help me.

You must say 'both **of**' before **us/you/them**:

- □ **Both of us** were very tired. (*not* Both us were ...)

After **neither of** ... a *singular* or a *plural* verb is possible:

- □ Neither of the children **wants** (*or* **want**) to go to bed.

C

You can also use **both/neither/either** alone, *without* a noun:

- □ I couldn't decide which of the two shirts to buy. I liked **both**. (*or* I liked **both** of them.)
- □ 'Is your friend British or American?' '**Neither**. She's Australian.'
- □ 'Do you want tea or coffee?' '**Either**. I don't mind.'

D

You can say:

both ... and ...	□ **Both** Chris **and** Pat were late. □ I was **both** tired **and** hungry when I arrived home.
neither ... nor ...	□ **Neither** Chris **nor** Pat came to the party. □ Tom said he would contact me, but he **neither** wrote **nor** phoned.
either ... or ...	□ I'm not sure where Maria's from. She's **either** Spanish **or** Italian. □ **Either** you apologise **or** I'll never speak to you again.

E

Compare **either/neither/both** (two things) and **any/none/all** (more than two):

□ There are **two** good hotels here. You could stay at **either** of them.	□ There are **many** good hotels here. You could stay at **any** of them.
□ We tried **two** hotels. { **Neither** of them had any rooms. { **Both** of them were full.	□ We tried **a lot of** hotels. { **None** of them had any rooms. { **All** of them were full.

Neither do I / I don't either → Unit 51C   **Both of whom / neither of which** → Unit 96B   **Both** → Unit 110C

89.1 Complete the sentences with **both/neither/either**.

1 'Do you want tea or coffee?' ' __Either__ . I really don't mind.'
2 'What day is it today – the 18th or the 19th?' ' _____ . It's the 20th.'
3 A: Where did you go for your holidays – Scotland or Ireland?
   B: We went to _____ . A week in Scotland and a week in Ireland.
4 'When shall I phone, in the morning or afternoon?' ' _____ . I'll be in all day.'
5 'Where's Liz? Is she at work or at home?' ' _____ . She's away on holiday.'

89.2 Complete the sentences with **both/neither/either**. Use **of** where necessary.

1 __Both__ my parents are from London.
2 To get to the town centre, you can go along the footpath by the river or you can go along the road. You can go _____ way.
3 I tried twice to phone George, but _____ times he was out.
4 _____ Tom's parents is English. His father is Polish and his mother is Italian.
5 I saw an accident this morning. One car drove into the back of another. Fortunately _____ driver was injured, but _____ cars were badly damaged.
6 I've got two sisters and a brother. My brother is working, but _____ my sisters are still at school.

89.3 Complete the sentences with **both/neither/either + of us/them**.

1 I asked two people the way to the station, but __neither of them__ could help me.
2 I was invited to two parties last week, but I couldn't go to _____ .
3 There were two windows in the room. It was very warm, so I opened _____ .
4 Sarah and I play tennis together regularly, but _____ can play very well.
5 I tried two bookshops for the book I wanted, but _____ had it.

89.4 Write sentences with **both ... and ... / neither ... nor ... / either ... or ...** .

1 Chris was late. So was Pat. __Both Chris and Pat were late.__
2 He didn't write and he didn't phone. __He neither wrote nor phoned.__
3 Joe is on holiday and so is Sam. _____
4 Joe hasn't got a car. Sam hasn't got one either. _____
5 Brian doesn't watch TV and he doesn't read newspapers.
_____
6 It was a boring film. It was long too.
The film _____
7 Is that man's name Richard? Or is it Robert? It's one of the two.
That man's name _____
8 I haven't got time to go on holiday. And I haven't got the money.
I've got _____
9 We can leave today or we can leave tomorrow – whichever you prefer.
We _____

89.5 Complete the sentences with **neither/either/none/any**.

1 We tried a lot of hotels, but __none__ of them had any rooms.
2 I took two books with me on holiday, but I didn't read _____ of them.
3 I took five books with me on holiday, but I didn't read _____ of them.
4 There are a few shops at the end of the street, but _____ of them sells newspapers.
5 You can phone me at _____ time during the evening. I'm always at home.
6 I can meet you next Monday or Friday. Would _____ of those days be convenient for you?
7 John and I couldn't get into the house because _____ of us had a key.

A All and everybody/everyone

We do not normally use **all** to mean **everybody/everyone**:
- **Everybody** enjoyed the party. (*not* All enjoyed)

But we say **all of us/you/them** (*not* everybody of ...):
- **All of us** enjoyed the party. (*not* Everybody of us)

B All and everything

Sometimes you can use **all** or **everything**:
- I'll do **all I can** to help.   *or*   I'll do **everything I can** to help.

You can say 'all **I can**' / 'all **you need**' etc., but we do not normally use **all** *alone*:
- He thinks he knows **everything**. (*not* he knows all)
- Our holiday was a disaster. **Everything** went wrong. (*not* All went wrong)
But you can say **all about**:
- He knows **all about** computers.

We also use **all** (*not* everything) to mean 'the only thing(s)':
- **All** I've eaten today is a sandwich. (= the only thing I've eaten today)

C

Every / everybody / everyone / everything are *singular* words, so we use a *singular* verb:
- **Every seat** in the theatre **was** taken.
- **Everybody has** arrived. (*not* have arrived)
But you can use **they/them/their** after **everybody/everyone**:
- **Everybody** said **they** enjoyed **themselves**. (= he or she enjoyed himself or herself)

D Whole and all

Whole = complete, entire. Most often we use **whole** with *singular* nouns:
- Did you read **the whole book**? (= all the book, not just a part of it)
- Emily has lived **her whole life** in Scotland.
- I was so hungry, I ate **a whole packet** of biscuits. (= a complete packet)

We use **the/my/her** etc. before **whole**. Compare **whole** and **all**:
the **whole** book / **all** the book   her **whole** life / **all** her life

We do not normally use **whole** with *uncountable* nouns. We say:
- I've spent **all the money** you gave me. (*not* the whole money)

E Every/all/whole with time words

We use **every** to say how often something happens (**every day** / **every Monday** / **every ten minutes** / **every three weeks** etc.):
- When we were on holiday, we went to the beach **every day**. (*not* all days)
- The bus service is excellent. There's a bus **every ten minutes**.
- We don't see each other very often – about **every six months**.

All day / **the whole day** = the complete day from beginning to end:
- We spent **all day** / **the whole day** on the beach.
- Dan was very quiet. He didn't say a word **all evening** / **the whole evening**.
Note that we say **all day** (*not* all the day), **all week** (*not* all the week) etc.

Compare **all the time** and **every time**:
- They never go out. They are at home **all the time**. (= always, continuously)
- **Every time** I see you, you look different. (= each time, on every occasion)

Countable and uncountable → Units 69–70   **All / all of** → Unit 88   **Each and every** → Unit 91
Every one → Unit 91D   **All (word order)** → Unit 110C

90.1 Complete these sentences with **all, everything** or **everybody/everyone**.

1 It was a good party. .....Everybody..... enjoyed it.
2 ...All.... I've eaten today is a sandwich.
3 .... has their faults. Nobody is perfect.
4 Nothing has changed. .... is the same as it was.
5 Kate told me .... about her new job. It sounds quite interesting.
6 Can .... write their names on a piece of paper, please?
7 Why are you always thinking about money? Money isn't ....
8 I didn't have much money with me. .... I had was ten pounds.
9 When the fire alarm rang, ... left the building immediately.
10 Sue didn't say where she was going. .... she said was that she was going away.
11 We have completely different opinions. I disagree with .... she says.
12 We all did well in the examination. .... in our class passed.
13 We all did well in the examination. .... of us passed.
14 Why are you so lazy? Why do you expect me to do .... for you?

90.2 Write sentences with **whole**.

1 I read the book from beginning to end. .....I read the whole book.....
2 Everyone in the team played well.
  The ....
3 Paul opened a box of chocolates. When he finished eating, there were no chocolates left in the box. He ate ....
4 The police came to the house. They were looking for something. They searched everywhere, every room. They ....
5 Everyone in Dave and Jane's family plays tennis. Dave and Jane play, and so do all their children. The ....
6 Ann worked from early in the morning until late in the evening.
  ....
7 Jack and Jill went on holiday to the seaside for a week. It rained from the beginning of the week to the end. It ....

Now write sentences 6 and 7 again using **all** instead of **whole**.

8 (6) Ann ....
9 (7) ....

90.3 Complete these sentences using **every** with the following:

> **five minutes** ~~**ten minutes**~~ **four hours** **six months** **four years**

1 The bus service is very good. There's a bus .....every ten minutes..... .
2 Tom is ill. He has some medicine. He has to take it ....
3 The Olympic Games take place ....
4 We live near a busy airport. A plane flies over our house ....
5 Martin has a check-up with his dentist ....

90.4 Which is the correct alternative?

1 I've spent ~~the whole money~~ / all the money you gave me. (all the money *is correct*)
2 Sue works every day / all days except Sunday.
3 I'm tired. I've been working hard all the day / all day.
4 It was a terrible fire. Whole building / The whole building was destroyed.
5 I've been trying to phone her, but every time / all the time I phone the line is busy.
6 I don't like the weather here. It rains every time / all the time.
7 When I was on holiday, all my luggage / my whole luggage was stolen.

→ Additional exercise 30 **(page 320)**

Each and every

A

Each and every are similar in meaning. Often it is possible to use each or every:

- □ **Each** time (*or* **Every** time) I see you, you look different.
- □ There's a telephone in **each** room (*or* **every** room) of the house.

But **each** and **every** are not exactly the same. Study the difference:

We use **each** when we think of things separately, one by one. □ Study **each sentence** carefully. (= study the sentences one by one) each = ✗ + ✗ + ✗ + ✗ **Each** is more usual for a small number: □ There were four books on the table. **Each book** was a different colour. □ *(in a card game)* At the beginning of the game, **each player** has three cards.	We use **every** when we think of things as a group. The meaning is similar to **all**. □ **Every sentence** must have a verb. (= all sentences in general) every = (✗✗✗✗✗✗✗✗✗✗✗✗✗✗✗✗✗✗✗✗✗✗✗✗) **Every** is more usual for a large number: □ Kate loves reading. She has read **every book** in the library. (= all the books) □ I would like to visit **every country** in the world. (= all the countries)

Each (but not **every**) can be used for two things:

- □ In a football match, **each team** has eleven players. (*not* every team)

We use **every** (not **each**) to say how often something happens:

- □ 'How often do you use your computer?' '**Every day.**' (*not* Each day)
- □ There's a bus **every ten minutes**. (*not* each ten minutes)

B

Compare the structures we use with **each** and **every**:

You can use **each** with a noun: **each book** **each student** You can use **each** alone (without a noun): □ None of the rooms was the same. **Each** (= each room) was different. Or you can use **each one**: □ **Each one** was different. You can say **each of** (the ... / these ... / them etc.): □ Read **each of these** sentences carefully. □ **Each of the** books is a different colour. □ **Each of them** is a different colour.	You can use **every** with a noun: **every book** **every student** You can't use **every** alone, but you can say **every one**: □ A: Have you read all these books? B: Yes, **every one**. You can say **every one of** ... (*but not* every of): □ I've read **every one of those** books. (*not* every of those books) □ I've read **every one of them**.

C

You can also use **each** in the middle or at the end of a sentence. For example:

- □ The students were **each** given a book. (= Each student was given a book.)
- □ These oranges cost 15 pence **each**.

D

Everyone and every one

Everyone (one word) is only for people (= everybody).
Every one (two words) is for things or people, and is similar to **each one** (see Section B).

- □ **Everyone** enjoyed the party. (= **Everybody** ...)
- □ Sarah is invited to lots of parties and she goes to **every one**. (= to every party)

Each other → Unit 82C   All and every → Unit 90

91.1 Look at the pictures and complete the sentences with **each** or **every**.

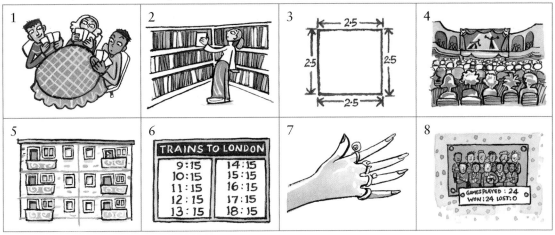

1 <u>Each</u> player has three cards.
2 Kate has read <u>every</u> book in the library.
3 .... side of a square is the same length.
4 .... seat in the theatre was taken.
5 There are six apartments in the building. .... one has a balcony.
6 There's a train to London .... hour.
7 She was wearing four rings – one on .... finger.
8 Our football team is playing well. We've won .... game this season.

91.2 Put in **each** or **every**.

1 There were four books on the table. <u>Each</u> book was a different colour.
2 The Olympic Games are held <u>every</u> four years.
3 .... parent worries about their children.
4 In a game of tennis there are two or four players. .... player has a racket.
5 Nicola plays volleyball .... Thursday evening.
6 I understood most of what they said but not .... word.
7 The book is divided into five parts and .... of these has three sections.
8 I get paid .... four weeks.
9 We had a great weekend. I enjoyed .... minute of it.
10 I tried to phone her two or three times, but .... time there was no reply.
11 Car seat belts save lives. .... driver should wear one.
12 *(from an exam)* Answer all five questions. Write your answer to .... question on a separate sheet of paper.

91.3 Complete the sentences using **each**.

1 The price of one of those oranges is 30 pence. Those <u>oranges are 30 pence each</u> .
2 I had ten pounds and so did Sonia. Sonia and I ....
3 One of those postcards costs 80 pence. Those ....
4 The hotel was expensive. I paid £120 and so did you. We ....

91.4 Put in **everyone** (1 word) or **every one** (2 words).

1 Sarah is invited to a lot of parties and she goes to <u>every one</u> .
2 As soon as .... had arrived, we began the meeting.
3 I asked her lots of questions and she answered .... correctly.
4 She's very popular. .... likes her.
5 I dropped a tray of glasses. Unfortunately .... broke.

Relative clauses 1: clauses with who/that/which

A Look at this example sentence:

The woman │ who lives next door │ is a doctor.
└── *relative clause* ──┘

A *clause* is a part of a sentence. A *relative clause* tells us which person or thing (or what kind of person or thing) the speaker means:

☐ The woman **who lives next door** … ('who lives next door' tells us which woman)
☐ People **who live in the country** … ('who live in the country' tells us what kind of people)

We use **who** in a relative clause when we are talking about people (not things):

> the woman – she lives next door – is a doctor
>
> ──→ The woman **who lives next door** is a doctor.
>
> we know a lot of people – they live in the country
>
> ──→ We know a lot of people **who live in the country.**

☐ An architect is someone **who designs buildings.**
☐ What was the name of the person **who phoned you?**
☐ Anyone **who wants to apply for the job** must do so by Friday.

You can also use **that** (instead of **who**), but you can't use **which** for people:

☐ The woman **that lives next door** is a doctor. (*not* the woman which)

Sometimes you must use **who** (*not* that) for people – see Unit 95.

B When we are talking about things, we use **that** or **which** (*not* who) in a relative clause:

> where is the cheese? – it was in the fridge
>
> ──→ Where is the cheese { that / which } was in the fridge?

☐ I don't like stories **that have unhappy endings.** (*or* stories **which** have …)
☐ Barbara works for a company **that makes furniture.** (*or* a company **which** makes furniture)
☐ The machine **that broke down** is working again now. (*or* The machine **which** broke down)

That is more usual than **which**, but sometimes you must use **which** – see Unit 95.

C **What** = 'the thing(s) that'. Compare **what** and **that**:

☐ **What** happened was my fault. (= the thing that happened)
☐ Everything **that happened** was my fault. (*not* Everything what happened)
☐ The machine **that broke down** is now working again. (*not* The machine what broke down)

D Remember that in relative clauses we use **who/that/which**, not **he/she/they/it**:

☐ I've never spoken to the woman **who lives** next door. (*not* the woman she lives)

92.1 In this exercise you have to explain what some words mean. Choose the right meaning from the box and then write a sentence with **who**. Use a dictionary if necessary.

he/she	steals from a shop	he/she	buys something from a shop
	~~designs buildings~~		pays rent to live in a house or flat
	doesn't believe in God		breaks into a house to steal things
	is not brave		expects the worst to happen

1 (an architect) <u>An architect is someone who designs buildings.</u>
2 (a burglar) A burglar is someone ....
3 (a customer) ....
4 (a shoplifter) ....
5 (a coward) ....
6 (an atheist) ....
7 (a pessimist) ....
8 (a tenant) ....

92.2 Make one sentence from two. Use **who/that/which**.

1 A girl was injured in the accident. She is now in hospital.
  <u>The girl who was injured in the accident is now in hospital.</u>
2 A waitress served us. She was impolite and impatient.
  The ....
3 A building was destroyed in the fire. It has now been rebuilt.
  The ....
4 Some people were arrested. They have now been released.
  The ....
5 A bus goes to the airport. It runs every half hour.
  The ....

92.3 Complete the sentences. Choose the best ending from the box and change it into a relative clause.

he invented the telephone	~~it makes furniture~~
she runs away from home	it gives you the meaning of words
they stole my car	it can support life
they were on the wall	it cannot be explained

1 Barbara works for a company <u>that makes furniture</u> ....
2 The book is about a girl ....
3 What happened to the pictures .... ?
4 A mystery is something ....
5 The police have caught the men ....
6 A dictionary is a book ....
7 Alexander Bell was the man ....
8 It seems that the earth is the only planet ....

92.4 Are these sentences right or wrong? Correct them where necessary.

1 I don't like stories <u>who have</u> unhappy endings.   <u>stories that have</u>
2 What was the name of the person who phoned you?   <u>OK</u>
3 Where's the nearest shop who sells newspapers?   ....
4 The driver which caused the accident was fined £500.   ....
5 Do you know the person that took these photographs?   ....
6 We live in a world what is changing all the time.   ....
7 Dan said some things about me that were not true.   ....
8 What was the name of the horse it won the race?   ....

Relative clauses 2:
clauses with and without **who/that/which**

A Look at these example sentences from Unit 92:

☐ The woman who **lives next door** is a doctor. (*or* The woman **that** lives ...)

The woman lives next door. **who** (= the woman) is the *subject*

☐ Where is the cheese that **was in the fridge?** (*or* the cheese **which** was ...)

The cheese was in the fridge. **that** (= the cheese) is the *subject*

You must use **who/that/which** when it is the subject of the relative clause. So you cannot say 'The woman lives next door is a doctor' or 'Where is the cheese was in the fridge?'.

B Sometimes **who/that/which** is the *object* of the verb. For example:

☐ The woman who **I wanted to see** was away on holiday.

I wanted to see the woman **who** (= the woman) is the *object*
I is the *subject*

☐ Have you found the keys that **you lost?**

You lost the keys. **that** (= the keys) is the *object*
you is the *subject*

When **who/that/which** is the object, you can leave it out. So you can say:

☐ **The woman I wanted to see** was away. *or* The woman **who** I wanted to see ...
☐ Have you found **the keys you lost**? *or* ... the keys **that** you lost?
☐ **The dress Liz bought** doesn't fit her very well. *or* The dress **that** Liz bought ...
☐ Is there **anything I can do**? *or* ... anything **that** I can do?

Note that we say:
the keys you lost (*not* the keys you lost them)
the dress Liz bought (*not* the dress Liz bought it)

C Note the position of prepositions (**in/to/for** etc.) in relative clauses:

Tom is talking to **a woman – do you know her?**

⟶ Do you know the woman (who/that) **Tom is talking** to ?

I slept in **a bed last night – it wasn't very comfortable**

⟶ The bed (that/which) **I slept** in **last night** wasn't very comfortable.

☐ Are these the books **you were looking for**? *or* ... the books **that/which** you were ...
☐ The woman **he fell in love with** left him after a month. *or* The woman **who/that** he ...
☐ The man **I was sitting next to on the plane** talked all the time. *or*
The man **who/that** I was sitting next to ...

Note that we say:
the books you were looking for (*not* the books you were looking for them)

D You cannot use **what** in sentences like these (see also Unit 92C):

☐ Everything (**that**) **they said** was true. (*not* Everything what they said)
☐ I gave her all the money (**that**) **I had**. (*not* all the money what I had)

What = 'the thing(s) that':
☐ Did you hear **what they said**? (= the things that they said)

Relative clauses 1 → Unit 92   Relative clauses 3–5 → Units 94–96   Whom → Unit 94B

93.1 In some of these sentences you need **who** or **that**. Correct the sentences where necessary.

1 The woman lives next door is a doctor.   _The woman who lives next door_
2 Have you found the keys you lost?   _OK_
3 The people we met last night were very nice.   ....
4 The people work in the office are very nice.   ....
5 The people I work with are very nice.   ....
6 What have you done with the money I gave you?   ....
7 What happened to the money was on the table?   ....
8 What's the worst film you've ever seen?   ....
9 What's the best thing it has ever happened to you?   ....

93.2 What do you say in these situations? Complete each sentence with a relative clause.

1 Your friend lost some keys. You want to know if he has found them. You say:
   Have you found _the keys you lost_ ?
2 A friend is wearing a dress. You like it. You tell her:
   I like the dress ....
3 A friend is going to see a film. You want to know the name of the film. You say:
   What's the name of the film .... ?
4 You wanted to visit a museum. It was shut when you got there. You tell a friend:
   The museum .... was shut when we got there.
5 You invited some people to your party. Some of them couldn't come. You tell someone:
   Some of the people .... couldn't come.
6 Your friend had to do some work. You want to know if she has finished. You say:
   Have you finished the work .... ?
7 You hired a car. It broke down after a few miles. You tell a friend:
   The car .... broke down after a few miles.
8 You stayed at a hotel. Tom had recommended it to you. You tell a friend:
   We stayed at a hotel ....

93.3 Complete each sentence using a relative clause with a preposition. Choose from the box.

we went to a party last night	you can rely on Gary	we were invited to a wedding
I work with some people	I applied for a job	you told me about a hotel
~~you were looking for some books~~	I saw you with a man	

1 Are these the books _you were looking for_ ?
2 Unfortunately we couldn't go to the wedding ....
3 I enjoy my job. I like the people ....
4 What's the name of that hotel .... ?
5 The party .... wasn't very enjoyable.
6 I didn't get the job ....
7 Gary is a good person to know. He's somebody ....
8 Who was that man .... in the restaurant?

93.4 Put in **that** or **what** where necessary. If the sentence is already complete, leave the space empty.

1 I gave her all the money ...–... I had. (all the money **that** I had *is also correct*)
2 Did you hear _what_ they said?
3 They give their children everything .... they want.
4 Tell me .... you want and I'll try to get it for you.
5 Why do you blame me for everything .... goes wrong?
6 I won't be able to do much, but I'll do .... I can.
7 I won't be able to do much, but I'll do the best .... I can.
8 I don't agree with .... you've just said.
9 I don't trust him. I don't believe anything .... he says.

A Whose

We use **whose** in relative clauses instead of **his/her/their**:

> we saw some people – their car had broken down
>
> ⟶ We saw some people whose **car had broken down.**

We use **whose** mostly for people:

- A widow is a woman **whose husband is dead.** (**her** husband is dead)
- What's the name of the man **whose car you borrowed?** (you borrowed **his** car)
- I met someone **whose brother I went to school with.** (I went to school with **his/her** brother)

Compare **who** and **whose**:

- I met a man **who** knows you. (**he** knows you)
- I met a man **whose sister** knows you. (**his sister** knows you)

B Whom

Whom is possible instead of **who** when it is the *object* of the verb in the relative clause (like the sentences in Unit 93B):

- The woman **whom I wanted to see** was away. (I wanted to see **her**)

You can also use **whom** with a preposition (**to whom / from whom / with whom** etc.):

- The people **with whom I work** are very nice. (I work **with them**)

But we do not often use **whom** in spoken English. We usually prefer **who** or **that,** or nothing (see Unit 93). So we usually say:

- The woman **I wanted to see** …   *or*   The woman **who/that** I wanted to see …
- The people **I work with** …   *or*   The people **who/that** I work with …

C Where

You can use **where** in a relative clause to talk about a place:

> the restaurant – we had dinner there – it was near the airport
>
> ⟶ The restaurant where **we had dinner** was near the airport.

- I recently went back to **the town where I grew up.**
  (*or* … the town I grew up in *or* … the town **that** I grew up in)
- I would like to live in **a place where there is plenty of sunshine.**

D We say:

the day / the year / the time etc. { something happens   *or*
{ **that** something happens

- Do you remember **the day (that) we went to the zoo?**
- **The last time (that) I saw her,** she looked fine.
- I haven't seen them since **the year (that) they got married.**

E We say:

the reason { something happens   *or*
{ **that/why** something happens

- **The reason I'm phoning you** is to ask your advice.
  (*or* The reason **that** I'm phoning / The reason **why** I'm phoning)

Relative clauses 1–2 → Units 92–93   Relative clauses 4–5 → Units 95–96   Whom → Unit 96

94.1 You met these people at a party:

The next day you tell a friend about these people. Complete the sentences using **who** or **whose**.

1 I met somebody ___whose mother writes detective stories___ .
2 I met a man _____ .
3 I met a woman _____ .
4 I met somebody _____ .
5 I met a couple _____ .
6 I met somebody _____ .

94.2 Read the situations and complete the sentences using **where**.

1 You grew up in a small town. You went back there recently. You tell someone this.
   I recently went back to the small town ___where I grew up___ .
2 You want to buy some postcards. You ask a friend where you can do this.
   Is there a shop near here _____ ?
3 You work in a factory. The factory is going to close down next month. You tell a friend:
   The factory _____ is going to close down next month.
4 Sue is staying at a hotel. You want to know the name of the hotel. You ask a friend:
   Do you know the name of the hotel _____ ?
5 You play football in a park on Sundays. You show a friend the park. You say:
   This is the park _____ on Sundays.

94.3 Complete each sentence using **who/whom/whose/where**.

1 What's the name of the man ___whose___ car you borrowed?
2 A cemetery is a place _____ people are buried.
3 A pacifist is a person _____ believes that all wars are wrong.
4 An orphan is a child _____ parents are dead.
5 What was the name of the person to _____ you spoke on the phone?
6 The place _____ we spent our holidays was really beautiful.
7 This school is only for children _____ first language is not English.
8 The woman with _____ he fell in love left him after a month.

94.4 Use your own ideas to complete these sentences. They are like the examples in Sections D and E.

1 I'll always remember the day ___I first met you___ .
2 I'll never forget the time _____ .
3 The reason _____ was that I didn't know your address.
4 Unfortunately I wasn't at home the evening _____ .
5 The reason _____ is that they don't need one.
6 _____ was the year _____ .

A There are two types of relative clause. In these examples, the relative clauses are <u>underlined</u>. Compare:

Type 1	Type 2
□ The woman <u>who lives next door</u> is a doctor. □ Barbara works for a company <u>that makes furniture</u>. □ We stayed at the hotel <u>(that) you recommended</u>.	□ My brother Rob, <u>who lives in Australia</u>, is a doctor. □ Colin told me about his new job, <u>which he's enjoying very much</u>. □ We stayed at the Park Hotel, <u>which a friend of ours recommended</u>.
In these examples, the relative clause tells you which person or thing (or what kind of person or thing) the speaker means: 'The woman **who lives next door**' tells us *which* woman. 'A company **that makes furniture**' tells us *what kind* of company. 'The hotel (**that**) **Ann recommended**' tells us *which* hotel.	In these examples, the relative clauses do not tell you which person or thing the speaker means. We already know which thing or person is meant: 'My brother Rob', 'Colin's new job' and 'the Park Hotel'. The relative clauses in these sentences give us *extra information* about the person or thing.
We do not use commas (,) with these clauses: □ We know a lot of people <u>who live in London</u>.	We use commas (,) with these clauses: □ My brother Rob, <u>who lives in London</u>, is a doctor.

B In both types of relative clause we use **who** for people and **which** for things. But:

Type 1	Type 2
You can use **that**: □ Do you know anyone **who/that** speaks French and Italian? □ Barbara works for a company **which/that** makes furniture.	You cannot use **that**: □ John, **who** (*not* that) speaks French and Italian, works as a tourist guide. □ Colin told me about his new job, **which** (*not* that) he's enjoying very much.
You can leave out **who/which/that** when it is the object (see Unit 93): □ We stayed at the hotel (that/which) you recommended. □ This morning I met somebody (who/that) I hadn't seen for ages.	You cannot leave out **who** or **which**: □ We stayed at the Park Hotel, **which** a friend of ours recommended. □ This morning I met Chris, **who** I hadn't seen for ages.
We do not often use **whom** in this type of clause (see Unit 94B).	You can use **whom** for people (when it is the object): □ This morning I met Chris, **whom** I hadn't seen for ages.

In both types of relative clause you can use **whose** and **where**:

□ We met some people **whose** car had broken down. □ What's the name of the place **where** you went on holiday?	□ Liz, **whose** car had broken down, was in a very bad mood. □ Jill has just been to Sweden, **where** her daughter lives.

95.1 Make one sentence from two. Use the sentence in brackets to make a relative clause (Type 2). You will need to use **who(m)/whose/which/where**.

1 Catherine is very friendly. (She lives next door.)
  Catherine, who lives next door, is very friendly.

2 We stayed at the Park Hotel. (A friend of ours had recommended it.)
  We stayed at the Park Hotel, which a friend of ours had recommended.

3 We often go to visit our friends in Bristol. (It is not very far away.)
  ....

4 I went to see the doctor. (He told me to rest for a few days.)
  ....

5 John is one of my closest friends. (I have known him for a very long time.)
  John ....

6 Sheila is away from home a lot. (Her job involves a lot of travelling.)
  ....

7 The new stadium will be opened next month. (It can hold 90,000 people.)
  ....

8 Glasgow is the largest city in Scotland. (My brother lives there.)
  ....

9 A friend of mine helped me to get a job. (His father is the manager of a company.)
  ....

95.2 Read the information and complete each sentence. Use a relative clause of Type 1 or Type 2. Use commas where necessary.

1 There's a woman living next door to me. She's a doctor.
  The woman *who lives next door to me is a doctor.*

2 I've got a brother called Rob. He lives in Australia. He's a doctor.
  My brother Rob *, who lives in Australia, is a doctor.*

3 There was a strike at the car factory. It began ten days ago. It is now over.
  The strike at the car factory ....

4 I was looking for a book this morning. I've found it now.
  I've found ....

5 London was once the largest city in the world, but the population is now falling.
  The population of London ....

6 A job was advertised. A lot of people applied for it. Few of them had the necessary qualifications.
  Few of ....

7 Amy has a son. She showed me a photograph of him. He's a policeman.
  Amy showed me ....

95.3 Correct the sentences that are wrong and put in commas where necessary. If the sentence is correct, write 'OK'.

1 Colin told me about his <u>new job that</u> he's enjoying very much.
  Colin told me about his new job, which he's enjoying very much.

2 My office that is on the second floor is very small.
  ....

3 The office I'm using at the moment is very small.
  ....

4 Ben's father that used to be a teacher now works for a TV company.
  ....

5 The doctor that examined me couldn't find anything wrong.
  ....

6 The sun that is one of millions of stars in the universe provides us with heat and light.
  ....

A *Prepositions + whom/which*

You can use a *preposition* before **whom** (for people) and **which** (for things). So you can say:
to whom / with whom / about which / without which etc. :

- ☐ Mr Lee, **to whom** I spoke at the meeting, is very interested in our proposal.
- ☐ Fortunately we had a map, **without which** we would have got lost.

In informal English we often keep the preposition after the verb in the relative clause. When we do this, we normally use **who** (*not* whom) for people:

- ☐ This is my friend from Canada, **who** I was telling you **about**.
- ☐ Yesterday we visited the City Museum, **which** I'd never been **to** before.

B **All of / most of** etc. + **whom/which**

Study these examples:

> Mary has three brothers. All of them are married. *(2 sentences)*
>
> → Mary has three brothers, **all of whom** are married. *(1 sentence)*
>
> They asked me a lot of questions. I couldn't answer most of them . *(2 sentences)*
>
> → They asked me a lot of questions, **most of which** I couldn't answer. *(1 sentence)*

In the same way you can say:

none of / neither of / any of / either of
some of / many of / much of / (a) few of
both of / half of / each of / one of / two of etc.
} + **whom** (people)
+ **which** (things)

- ☐ Martin tried on three jackets, **none of which** fitted him.
- ☐ Two men, **neither of whom** I had seen before, came into the office.
- ☐ They've got three cars, **two of which** they rarely use.
- ☐ Sue has a lot of friends, **many of whom** she was at school with.

You can also say **the cause of which / the name of which** etc. :

- ☐ The building was destroyed in a fire, **the cause of which** was never established.
- ☐ We stayed at a beautiful hotel, **the name of which** I can't remember now.

C **Which** (*not* what)

Study this example:

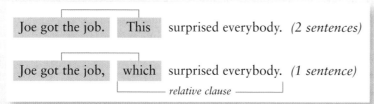

> Joe got the job. This surprised everybody. *(2 sentences)*
>
> Joe got the job, which surprised everybody. *(1 sentence)*
> ——— relative clause ———

In this example, **which** = 'the fact that he got the job'. You must use **which** (*not* what) in sentences like these:

- ☐ Sarah couldn't meet us, **which** was a pity. (*not* what was a pity)
- ☐ The weather was good, **which** we hadn't expected. (*not* what we hadn't expected)

For **what**, see Units 92C and 93D.

Exercises

96.1 Write the relative clauses in a more formal way using a preposition + **whom/which**.

1 Yesterday we visited the City Museum, which I'd never been to before.
Yesterday we visited the City Museum, <u>to which I'd never been before</u>.

2 My brother showed us his new car, which he's very proud of.
My brother showed us his new car, ...

3 This is a photograph of our friends Chris and Sam, who we went on holiday with.
This is a photograph of our friends Chris and Sam, ...

4 The wedding, which only members of the family were invited to, took place on Friday.
The wedding, ... ,
took place on Friday.

96.2 Use the information in the first sentence to complete the second sentence. Use **all of / most of** etc. or **the … of + whom/which**.

1 All of Mary's brothers are married.
Mary has three brothers, <u>all of whom are married</u>.

2 Most of the information we were given was useless.
We were given a lot of information, ...

3 Jane has received neither of the letters I sent her.
I sent Jane two letters, ...

4 None of the ten people who applied for the job was suitable.
Ten people applied for the job, ...

5 Kate hardly ever uses one of her computers.
Kate has got two computers, ...

6 Mike gave half of the £50,000 he won to his parents.
Mike won £50,000, ...

7 Both of Julia's sisters are teachers.
Julia has two sisters, ...

8 I went to a party – I knew only a few of the people there.
There were a lot of people at the party, ...

9 The sides of the road we drove along were lined with trees.
We drove along the road, the ....

10 The aim of the company's new business plan is to save money.
The company has a new business plan, ...

96.3 Join sentences from the boxes to make new sentences. Use **which**.

1 ~~Laura couldn't come to the party.~~
2 Jane doesn't have a phone.
3 Neil has passed his exams.
4 Our flight was delayed.
5 Kate offered to let me stay at her house.
6 The street I live in is very noisy at night.
7 Our car has broken down.

This was very kind of her.
This means we can't go away tomorrow.
This makes it difficult to contact her.
This makes it difficult to sleep sometimes.
~~This was a pity.~~
This is good news.
This meant we had to wait three hours at the airport.

1 Laura couldn't come to the party, <u>which was a pity.</u> ....
2 Jane ....
3 ....
4 ....
5 ....
6 ....
7 ....

A

A *clause* is a part of a sentence. Some clauses begin with **-ing** or **-ed**. For example:

Do you know the woman **talking to Tom** ?
└── -ing *clause* ──┘

TOM

the woman talking to Tom

The boy **injured in the accident** was taken to hospital.
└────── -ed *clause* ──────┘

the boy injured in the accident

B

We use **-ing** clauses to say what somebody (or something) is (or was) doing at a particular time:

- ☐ Do you know the woman **talking to Sam**? (the woman **is talking** to Sam)
- ☐ Police **investigating the crime** are looking for three men. (police **are investigating** the crime)
- ☐ Who were those people **waiting outside**? (they **were waiting**)
- ☐ I was woken up by a bell **ringing**. (a bell **was ringing**)

You can also use an **-ing** clause to say what happens all the time, not just at a particular time. For example:

- ☐ The road **connecting the two villages** is very narrow. (the road **connects** the two villages)
- ☐ I have a large room **overlooking the garden**. (the room **overlooks** the garden)
- ☐ Can you think of the name of a flower **beginning with T**? (the name **begins** with T)

C

-ed clauses have a *passive* meaning:

- ☐ The boy **injured in the accident** was taken to hospital. (he **was injured** in the accident)
- ☐ George showed me some pictures **painted by his father**. (they **had been painted** by his father)

Injured and **invited** are *past participles*. Note that many past participles are irregular and do not end in **-ed** (**stolen/made/written** etc.):

- ☐ The police never found the money **stolen in the robbery**.
- ☐ Most of the goods **made in this factory** are exported.

You can use **left** in this way, with the meaning 'not used, still there':

- ☐ We've eaten nearly all the chocolates. There are only a few **left**.

D

We often use **-ing** and **-ed** clauses after **there is / there was** etc. :

- ☐ **There were** some children **swimming** in the river.
- ☐ **Is there** anybody **waiting**?
- ☐ **There was** a big red car **parked** outside the house.

194

See/hear **somebody doing something** → Unit 67   **-ing clauses** → Unit 68   **There (is)** → Unit 84
Irregular past participles (made/stolen etc.) → Appendix 1

97.1 Make one sentence from two. Complete the sentences with an **-ing** clause.

1 A bell was ringing. I was woken up by it.
I was woken up by .....*a bell ringing*.. .

2 A man was sitting next to me on the plane. I didn't talk much to him.
I didn't talk much to the ....

3 A taxi was taking us to the airport. It broke down.
The .... broke down.

4 There's a path at the end of this street. The path leads to the river.
At the end of the street there's a ....

5 A factory has just opened in the town. It employs 500 people.
A .... has just opened in the town.

6 The company sent me a brochure. It contained the information I needed.
The company sent me ....

97.2 Make one sentence from two, beginning as shown. Each time make an **-ed** clause.

1 A boy was injured in the accident. He was taken to hospital.
The boy .....*injured in the accident*..... was taken to hospital.

2 A gate was damaged in the storm. It has now been repaired.
The gate .... has now been repaired.

3 A number of suggestions were made at the meeting. Most of them were not very practical.
Most of the .... were not very practical.

4 Some paintings were stolen from the museum. They haven't been found yet.
The .... haven't been found yet.

5 A man was arrested by the police. What was his name?
What was the name of .... ?

97.3 Complete the sentences using the following verbs in the correct form:

blow   call   ~~invite~~   live   offer   read   ~~ring~~   sit   study   work

1 I was woken up by a bell .....*ringing*..... .
2 Some of the people .....*invited*..... to the party can't come.
3 Life must be very unpleasant for people .... near busy airports.
4 A few days after the interview, I received a letter .... me the job.
5 Somebody .... Jack phoned while you were out.
6 There was a tree .... down in the storm last night.
7 The waiting room was empty except for a young man .... by the window
.... a magazine.
8 Ian has a brother .... in a bank in London and a sister ....
economics at university in Manchester.

97.4 Use the words in brackets to make sentences using **There is / There was** etc.

1 That house is empty. (nobody / live / in it)   *There's nobody living in it.*
2 The accident wasn't serious. (nobody / injure)   *There was nobody injured.*
3 I can hear footsteps. (somebody / come)
There ....
4 The train was full. (a lot of people / travel)
....
5 We were the only guests at the hotel. (nobody else / stay there)
....
6 The piece of paper was blank. (nothing / write / on it)
....
7 The college offers English courses in the evening. (a course / begin / next Monday)
....

Adjectives ending in **-ing** and **-ed** (boring/bored etc.)

There are many adjectives ending in **-ing** and **-ed**, for example: **boring** and **bored**. Study this example situation:

bored

boring

Jane has been doing the same job for a very long time. Every day she does exactly the same thing again and again. She doesn't enjoy her job any more and would like to do something different.

Jane's job is **boring**.

Jane is **bored** (with her job).

Somebody is **bored** if something (or somebody else) is **boring**. Or, if something is **boring**, it makes you **bored**. So:

- ☐ Jane is **bored** because her job is **boring**.
- ☐ Jane's job is **boring**, so Jane is **bored**. (*not* Jane is boring)

If a person is **boring**, this means that they make other people **bored**:

- ☐ George always talks about the same things. He's really **boring**.

Compare adjectives ending in **-ing** and **-ed**:

☐ My job is {
boring.
interesting.
tiring.
satisfying.
depressing. etc.
}

- ☐ I'm **bored** with my job.
- ☐ I'm not **interested** in my job any more.
- ☐ I get very **tired** doing my job.
- ☐ I'm not **satisfied** with my job.
- ☐ My job makes me **depressed**. etc.

In these examples, the **-ing** adjective tells you about the job.

In these examples, the **-ed** adjective tells you how somebody feels (about the job).

Compare these examples:

interesting
- ☐ Julia thinks politics is **interesting**.

- ☐ Did you meet anyone **interesting** at the party?

surprising
- ☐ It was **surprising** that he passed the exam.

disappointing
- ☐ The film was **disappointing**. We expected it to be much better.

shocking
- ☐ The news was **shocking**.

interested
- ☐ Julia is **interested** in politics. (*not* interesting in politics)
- ☐ Are you **interested** in buying a car? I'm trying to sell mine.

surprised
- ☐ Everybody was **surprised** that he passed the exam.

disappointed
- ☐ We were **disappointed** with the film. We expected it to be much better.

shocked
- ☐ I was **shocked** when I heard the news.

98.1 Complete the sentences for each situation. Use the word in brackets + -ing or -ed.

1 The film wasn't as good as we had expected. (**disappoint...**)
    a The film was ....._disappointing_..... .
    b We were ....._disappointed_..... with the film.

2 Donna teaches young children. It's a very hard job, but she enjoys it. (**exhaust...**)
    a She enjoys her job, but it's often ....
    b At the end of a day's work, she is often ....

3 It's been raining all day. I hate this weather. (**depress...**)
    a This weather is ....
    b This weather makes me ....
    c It's silly to get .... because of the weather.

4 Clare is going to Mexico next month. She has never been there before. (**excit...**)
    a It will be an .... experience for her.
    b Going to new places is always ....
    c She is really .... about going to Mexico.

98.2 Choose the correct word.

1 I was ~~disappointing~~ / disappointed with the film. I had expected it to be better.
    (disappointed *is correct*)
2 Are you <u>interesting / interested</u> in football?
3 The football match was very <u>exciting / excited</u>. I enjoyed it.
4 It's sometimes <u>embarrassing / embarrassed</u> when you have to ask people for money.
5 Do you easily get <u>embarrassing / embarrassed</u>?
6 I had never expected to get the job. I was really <u>amazing / amazed</u> when I was offered it.
7 She has really learnt very fast. She has made <u>astonishing / astonished</u> progress.
8 I didn't find the situation funny. I was not <u>amusing / amused</u>.
9 It was a really <u>terrifying / terrified</u> experience. Afterwards everybody was very <u>shocking / shocked</u>.
10 Why do you always look so <u>boring / bored</u>? Is your life really so <u>boring / bored</u>?
11 He's one of the most <u>boring / bored</u> people I've ever met. He never stops talking and he never says anything <u>interesting / interested</u>.

98.3 Complete each sentence using a word from the box.

amusing/amused	annoying/annoyed	boring/bored
confusing/confused	disgusting/disgusted	exciting/excited
exhausting/exhausted	interesting/interested	~~surprising~~/surprised

1 He works very hard. It's not ....._surprising_..... that he's always tired.
2 I've got nothing to do. I'm ....
3 The teacher's explanation was .... Most of the students didn't understand it.
4 The kitchen hadn't been cleaned for ages. It was really ....
5 I seldom visit art galleries. I'm not particularly .... in art.
6 There's no need to get .... just because I'm a few minutes late.
7 The lecture was .... I fell asleep.
8 I've been working very hard all day and now I'm ....
9 I'm starting a new job next week. I'm very .... about it.
10 Steve is very good at telling funny stories. He can be very ....
11 Liz is a very .... person. She knows a lot, she's travelled a lot and she's done lots of different things.

Adjectives: a **nice new** house, you look **tired**

A

Sometimes we use two or more adjectives together:

☐ My brother lives in a **nice new** house.
☐ In the kitchen there was a **beautiful large round wooden** table.

Adjectives like **new/large/round/wooden** are *fact* adjectives. They give us factual information about age, size, colour etc.
Adjectives like **nice/beautiful** are *opinion* adjectives. They tell us what somebody thinks of something or somebody.
Opinion adjectives usually go before fact adjectives.

	opinion	fact	
a	nice	long	summer holiday
an	interesting	young	man
	delicious	hot	vegetable soup
a	beautiful	large round wooden	table

B

Sometimes we use two or more fact adjectives together. Usually (but not always) we put fact adjectives in this order:

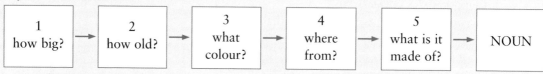

| 1 how big? | → | 2 how old? | → | 3 what colour? | → | 4 where from? | → | 5 what is it made of? | → | NOUN |

a **tall young** man (1 → 2)   a **large wooden** table (1 → 5)
big blue eyes (1 → 3)   an **old Russian** song (2 → 4)
a **small black plastic** bag (1 → 3 → 5)   an **old white cotton** shirt (2 → 3 → 5)

Adjectives of size and length (**big/small/tall/short/long** etc.) usually go before adjectives of shape and width (**round/fat/thin/slim/wide** etc.):

a **large round** table   a **tall thin** girl   a **long narrow** street

When there are two or more colour adjectives, we use **and**:

a **black and white** dress   a **red, white and green** flag

This does not usually happen with other adjectives before a noun:

a **long black** dress (*not* a long and black dress)

C

We use adjectives after **be/get/become/seem**:

☐ **Be careful**!
☐ **I'm tired** and **I'm getting hungry**.
☐ As the film went on, it **became** more and more **boring**.
☐ Your friend **seems** very **nice**.

We also use adjectives to say how somebody/something looks, feels, sounds, tastes or smells:

☐ You **look tired**. / I **feel tired**. / She **sounds tired**.
☐ The dinner **smells good**.
☐ This tea **tastes** a bit **strange**.

But to say *how* somebody does something you must use an *adverb* (see Units 100–101):

☐ Drive **carefully**! (*not* Drive careful)
☐ Susan plays the piano very **well**. (*not* plays … very good)

D

We say 'the **first two** days / the **next few** weeks / the **last ten** minutes' etc. :

☐ I didn't enjoy the **first two** days of the course. (*not* the two first days)
☐ They'll be away for the **next few** weeks. (*not* the few next weeks)

Adverbs → Units 100–101   **Comparison (cheaper etc.)** → Units 105–107
Superlatives (cheapest etc.) → Unit 108

Exercises

99.1 Put the adjectives in brackets in the correct position.

1 a beautiful table (wooden / round)   _a beautiful round wooden table_
2 an unusual ring (gold) ....
3 an old house (beautiful) ....
4 black gloves (leather) ....
5 an American film (old) ....
6 a long face (thin) ....
7 big clouds (black) ....
8 a sunny day (lovely) ....
9 an ugly dress (yellow) ....
10 a wide avenue (long) ....
11 a red car (old / little) ....
12 a new sweater (green / nice) ....
13 a metal box (black / small) ....
14 a big cat (fat / black) ....
15 a little village (old / lovely) ....
16 long hair (black / beautiful) ....
17 an old painting (interesting / French) ....
18 an enormous umbrella (red / yellow) ....

99.2 Complete each sentence with a verb (in the correct form) and an adjective from the boxes.

feel	look	~~seem~~		awful	fine	interesting
smell	sound	taste		nice	~~upset~~	wet

1 Helen ....._seemed upset_.... this morning. Do you know what was wrong?
2 I can't eat this. I've just tried it and it ....
3 I wasn't very well yesterday, but I .... today.
4 What beautiful flowers! They .... too.
5 You .... Have you been out in the rain?
6 Jim was telling me about his new job. It .... – much better than his old job.

99.3 Put in the correct word.

1 This tea tastes a bit ....._strange_.... . (strange / strangely)
2 I always feel .... when the sun is shining. (happy / happily)
3 The children were playing .... in the garden. (happy / happily)
4 The man became .... when the manager of the restaurant asked him to leave. (violent / violently)
5 You look .... ! Are you all right? (terrible / terribly)
6 There's no point in doing a job if you don't do it .... (proper / properly)
7 The soup tastes .... (good / well)
8 Hurry up! You're always so .... (slow / slowly)

99.4 Write the following in another way using **the first ... / the next ... / the last ...** .

1 the first day and the second day of the course   _the first two days of the course_
2 next week and the week after   _the next two weeks_
3 yesterday and the day before yesterday ....
4 the first week and the second week of May ....
5 tomorrow and a few days after that ....
6 questions 1, 2 and 3 in the exam ....
7 next year and the year after ....
8 the last day of our holiday and the two days before that ....

→ Additional exercise 31 (page 320)

Adjectives and adverbs 1 (quick/quickly)

Look at these examples:
- □ Our holiday was too short – the time passed very **quickly**.
- □ Two people were **seriously** injured in the accident.

Quickly and **seriously** are *adverbs*. Many adverbs are formed from an adjective + **-ly**:

adjective: quick   serious   careful   quiet   heavy   bad

adverb: quickly   seriously   carefully   quietly   heavily   badly

For spelling, see Appendix 6.

Not all words ending in **-ly** are adverbs. Some *adjectives* end in **-ly** too, for example:

    friendly   **lively**   **elderly**   **lonely**   **silly**   **lovely**

Adjective or adverb?

Adjectives (**quick/careful** etc.) tell us about a *noun* (somebody or something). We use adjectives before nouns: □ Sam is a **careful driver**. (*not* a carefully driver) □ We didn't go out because of the **heavy rain**.	Adverbs (**quickly/carefully** etc.) tell us about a *verb* (*how* somebody does something or *how* something happens): □ Sam **drove carefully** along the narrow road. (*not* drove careful) □ We didn't go out because it was **raining heavily**. (*not* raining heavy)

Compare:

□ She speaks **perfect English**.
    adjective + noun
	□ She **speaks** English **perfectly**.
	    verb + noun + adverb

We also use adjectives after some verbs, especially **be**, and also **look/feel/sound** etc.
Compare:

□ Please **be quiet**. □ I was disappointed that my exam results **were** so **bad**. □ Why do you always **look** so **serious**? □ I **feel happy**.	□ Please **speak quietly**. □ I was unhappy that I **did** so **badly** in the exam. (*not* did so bad) □ Why do you never **take** me **seriously**? □ The children were **playing happily**.

We also use adverbs before *adjectives* and *other adverbs*. For example:

    reasonably cheap   (*adverb + adjective*)

    terribly sorry   (*adverb + adjective*)

    incredibly quickly   (*adverb + adverb*)

- □ It's a **reasonably cheap** restaurant and the food is **extremely good**.
- □ I'm **terribly sorry**. I didn't mean to push you. (*not* terrible sorry)
- □ Maria learns languages **incredibly quickly**.
- □ The examination was **surprisingly easy**.

You can also use an adverb before a *past participle* (**injured/organised/written** etc.):

- □ Two people were **seriously injured** in the accident. (*not* serious injured)
- □ The meeting was very **badly organised**.

Adjectives after be/look/feel etc. → Unit 99C   Adjectives and adverbs 2 → Unit 101

100.1 Complete each sentence with an adverb. The first letters of the adverb are given.

1 We didn't go out because it was raining he _avily_ .
2 Our team lost the game because we played very ba............................ .
3 I had little difficulty finding a place to live. I found a flat quite ea............................ .
4 We had to wait for a long time, but we didn't complain. We waited pat............................ .
5 Nobody knew Steve was coming to see us. He arrived unex............................ .
6 Mike keeps fit by playing tennis reg............................ .
7 I don't speak French very well, but I can understand per............................ if people speak
   sl............................ and cl............................ .

100.2 Put in the correct word.

1 Two people were ....._seriously_.... injured in the accident. (serious / seriously)
2 The driver of the car had ....._serious_.... injuries. (serious / seriously)
3 I think you behaved very .... (selfish / selfishly)
4 Rose is .... upset about losing her job. (terrible / terribly)
5 There was a .... change in the weather. (sudden / suddenly)
6 Everybody at the party was .... dressed. (colourful / colourfully)
7 Linda likes wearing .... clothes. (colourful / colourfully)
8 Liz fell and hurt herself quite .... (bad / badly)
9 Joe says he didn't do well at school because he was .... taught. (bad / badly)
10 Don't go up that ladder. It doesn't look .... (safe / safely)

100.3 Complete each sentence using a word from the box. Sometimes you need the adjective (**careful** etc.) and sometimes the adverb (**carefully** etc.).

careful(ly)	complete(ly)	continuous(ly)	financial(ly)	fluent(ly)
happy/happily	nervous(ly)	perfect(ly)	~~quick(ly)~~	special(ly)

1 Our holiday was too short. The time passed very ..._quickly_.. .
2 Steve doesn't take risks when he's driving. He's always ....
3 Sue works .... She never seems to stop.
4 Rachel and Patrick are very .... married.
5 Maria's English is very .... although she makes quite a lot of mistakes.
6 I cooked this meal .... for you, so I hope you like it.
7 Everything was very quiet. There was .... silence.
8 I tried on the shoes and they fitted me ....
9 Do you usually feel .... before examinations?
10 I'd like to buy a car, but it's .... impossible for me at the moment.

100.4 Choose two words (one from each box) to complete each sentence.

absolutely	badly	completely
~~reasonably~~	seriously	slightly
unnecessarily	unusually	

changed	~~cheap~~	damaged
enormous	ill	long
planned	quiet	

1 I thought the restaurant would be expensive, but it was ..._reasonably cheap_.. .
2 Steve's mother is .... in hospital.
3 What a big house! It's ....
4 It wasn't a serious accident. The car was only ....
5 The children are normally very lively, but they're .... today.
6 When I returned home after 20 years, everything had ....
7 The film was .... It could have been much shorter.
8 A lot went wrong during our holiday because it was ....

→ Additional exercise 31 (page 320)

Adjectives and adverbs 2 (well/fast/late, hard/hardly)

A Good/well

Good is an *adjective*. The *adverb* is **well**:
- ☐ Your English is **good**. *but* You **speak** English **well**.
- ☐ Susan is a **good** pianist. *but* Susan **plays** the piano **well**.

We use **well** (*not* good) with *past participles* (**dressed/known** etc.):

well-dressed   well-known   well-educated   well-paid
- ☐ Gary's father is a **well-known** writer.

But **well** is also an adjective with the meaning 'in good health':
- ☐ 'How are you today? 'I'm very **well**, thanks.'

B Fast/hard/late

These words are both adjectives and adverbs:

adjective	*adverb*
☐ Darren is a very **fast runner**.	Darren can **run** very **fast**.
☐ Kate is a **hard worker**.	Kate **works hard**. (*not* works hardly)
☐ I was **late**.	I **got up late** this morning.

Lately = recently:
- ☐ Have you seen Tom **lately**?

C Hardly

Hardly = very little, almost not. Study these examples:
- ☐ Sarah wasn't very friendly at the party. She **hardly** spoke to me.
  (= she spoke to me very little, almost not at all)
- ☐ We've only met once or twice. We **hardly** know each other.

Hard and **hardly** are different. Compare:
- ☐ He tried **hard** to find a job, but he had no luck. (= he tried a lot, with a lot of effort)
- ☐ I'm not surprised he didn't find a job. He **hardly** tried to find one. (= he tried very little)

You can use **hardly + any/anybody/anyone/anything/anywhere**:
- ☐ A: How much money have we got?
  B: **Hardly any.** (= very little, almost none)
- ☐ These two cameras are very similar. There's **hardly any** difference between them.
- ☐ The exam results were very bad. **Hardly anybody** in our class passed. (= very few students passed)

> There's **hardly anything** in the fridge.

Note that you can say:
- ☐ She said **hardly anything**.   *or*   She **hardly** said **anything**.
- ☐ We've got **hardly any** money.   *or*   We've **hardly** got **any** money.

I can hardly do something = it's very difficult for me, almost impossible:
- ☐ Your writing is terrible. I **can hardly** read it. (= it is almost impossible to read it)
- ☐ My leg was hurting me. I **could hardly** walk.

Hardly ever = almost never:
- ☐ I'm nearly always at home in the evenings. I **hardly ever** go out.

Hardly also means 'certainly not'. For example:
- ☐ It's **hardly surprising** that you're tired. You haven't slept for three days.
  (= it's certainly not surprising)
- ☐ The situation is serious, but it's **hardly a crisis**. (= it's certainly not a crisis)

Adjectives after verbs ('You look tired' etc.) → Unit 99C   Adjectives and adverbs 1 → Unit 100

101.1 Put in **good** or **well**.

1 I play tennis but I'm not very _good_ .
2 Your exam results were very _____ .
3 You did _____ in your exams.
4 The weather was _____ while we were on holiday.
5 I didn't sleep _____ last night.
6 How are you? Are you _____ ?
7 Lucy speaks German very _____ .
8 Lucy's German is very _____ .
9 Our new business isn't doing very _____ at the moment.
10 I like your hat. It looks _____ on you.
11 I've met her a few times, but I don't know her _____

101.2 Complete these sentences using **well** + the following words:

~~behaved~~   dressed   informed   kept   known   paid   written

1 The children were very good. They were _well-behaved_ .
2 I'm surprised you haven't heard of her. She is quite _____ .
3 Our neighbours' garden is neat and tidy. It is very _____ .
4 I enjoyed the book you lent me. It's a great story and it's very _____ .
5 Tania knows a lot about many things. She is very _____ .
6 Mark's clothes are always smart. He is always _____ .
7 Jane has a lot of responsibility in her job, but she isn't very _____ .

101.3 Are the <u>underlined</u> words right or wrong? Correct them where necessary.

1 I'm tired because I've been working <u>hard</u>.   _OK_
2 I tried <u>hard</u> to remember her name, but I couldn't.   _____
3 This coat is practically unused. I've <u>hardly</u> worn it.   _____
4 Judy is a good tennis player. She hits the ball <u>hardly</u>.   _____
5 Don't walk so <u>fast</u>! I can't keep up with you.   _____
6 I had plenty of time, so I was walking <u>slow</u>.   _____

101.4 Complete the sentences. Use **hardly** + the following verbs (in the correct form):

change   hear   ~~know~~   recognise   say   sleep   speak

1 Scott and Tracy have only met once before. They _hardly know_ each other.
2 You're speaking very quietly. I can _____ you.
3 I'm very tired this morning. I _____ last night.
4 We were so shocked when we heard the news, we could _____ .
5 Kate was very quiet this evening. She _____ a word.
6 You look the same now as you looked 15 years ago. You've _____ .
7 I met Dave a few days ago. I hadn't seen him for a long time and he looks very different now. I _____ him.

101.5 Complete these sentences with **hardly** + any/anybody/anything/anywhere/ever.

1 I'll have to go shopping. There's _hardly anything_ to eat.
2 It was a very warm day and there was _____ wind.
3 'Do you know much about computers?' 'No, _____ .'
4 The hotel was almost empty. There was _____ staying there.
5 I listen to the radio quite often, but I _____ watch television.
6 Our new boss is not very popular. _____ likes her.
7 It was very crowded in the room. There was _____ to sit.
8 We used to be good friends, but we _____ see each other now.
9 It was nice driving this morning. There was _____ traffic.
10 I hate this town. There's _____ to do and _____ to go.

→ Additional exercise 31 (page 320)

A Compare **so** and **such**:

We use **so** + *adjective/adverb*:
 	
so stupid   so quick
so nice   so quickly
 	
☐ I didn't like the book. The story was **so stupid**.
☐ I like Liz and Joe. They are **so nice**.
	We use **such** + *noun*:
	  such a story such people
	We also use **such** + *adjective* + *noun*:
	  such a stupid **story** **such** nice **people**
	☐ I didn't like the book. It was **such a stupid story**. (*not* a so stupid story)
	☐ I like Liz and Joe. They are **such nice people**. (*not* so nice people)
	We say **such a …** (*not* a such):
	  such a big dog (*not* a such big dog)

B **So** and **such** make the meaning of an adjective (or adverb) stronger:

☐ It's a beautiful day, isn't it? It's **so warm**. (= really warm) ☐ It's difficult to understand him because he talks **so quietly**. You can use **so … that**: ☐ The book was **so good that** I couldn't put it down. ☐ I was **so tired that** I fell asleep in the armchair. We usually leave out **that**: ☐ I was **so tired** I fell asleep.	☐ It was a great holiday. We had **such a good time**. (= a really good time) You can use **such … that**: ☐ It was **such a good book that** I couldn't put it down. ☐ It was **such nice weather that** we spent the whole day on the beach. We usually leave out **that**: ☐ It was **such nice weather** we spent …

C We also use **so** and **such** with the meaning 'like this':

☐ Somebody told me the house was built 100 years ago. I didn't realize it was **so old**. (= as old as it is) ☐ I'm tired because I got up at six. I don't usually get up **so early**. ☐ I expected the weather to be cooler. I'm surprised it is **so warm**.	☐ I didn't realise it was **such an old house**. ☐ You know it's not true. How can you say **such a thing**? Note the expression **no such …** : ☐ You won't find the word 'blid' in the dictionary. There's **no such word**. (= this word does not exist)

D Compare:

so long ☐ I haven't seen her for **so long** I've forgotten what she looks like. **so far** ☐ I didn't know it was **so far**. **so much, so many** ☐ I'm sorry I'm late – there was **so much** traffic.	**such a long time** ☐ I haven't seen her for **such a long time**. (*not* so long time) **such a long way** ☐ I didn't know it was **such a long way**. **such a lot (of)** ☐ I'm sorry I'm late – there was **such a lot** of traffic.

Not so … as → Unit 107A   **Such as** → Unit 117B

102.1 Put in **so**, **such** or **such a.**

1 It's difficult to understand him because he speaks ....*so*.... quietly.
2 I like Liz and Joe. They're ...*such*.... nice people.
3 It was a great holiday. We had ....*such a*.... good time.
4 I was surprised that he looked .... well after his recent illness.
5 Everything is .... expensive these days, isn't it?
6 The weather is beautiful, isn't it? I didn't expect it to be .... nice day.
7 I have to go. I didn't realise it was .... late.
8 He always looks good. He wears .... nice clothes.
9 It was .... boring film that I fell asleep while I was watching it.
10 I couldn't believe the news. It was .... shock.
11 I think she works too hard. She looks .... tired all the time.
12 The food at the hotel was .... awful. I've never eaten .... awful food.
13 They've got .... much money they don't know what to do with it.
14 I didn't realise you lived .... long way from the city centre.
15 The party was really great. It was .... pity you couldn't come.

102.2 Make one sentence from two. Use **so** or **such.**

1 ~~She worked hard.~~	You could hear it from miles away.
2 ~~It was a beautiful day.~~	You would think it was her native language.
3 I was tired.	We spent the whole day indoors.
4 We had a good time on holiday.	~~She made herself ill.~~
5 She speaks English well.	I couldn't keep my eyes open.
6 I've got a lot to do.	I didn't eat anything else for the rest of the day.
7 The music was loud.	~~We decided to go to the beach.~~
8 I had a big breakfast.	I didn't know what to say.
9 It was horrible weather.	I don't know where to begin.
10 I was surprised.	We didn't want to come home.

1 *She worked so hard she made herself ill.*
2 *It was such a beautiful day we decided to go to the beach.*
3 I was ....
4 ....
5 ....
6 ....
7 ....
8 ....
9 ....
10 ....

102.3 Use your own ideas to complete these pairs of sentences.

1 a We enjoyed our holiday. It was so ....*relaxing*........................ .
  b We enjoyed our holiday. We had such ....*a good time*.................... .
2 a I like Catherine. She's so ....
  b I like Catherine. She's such ....
3 a I like New York. It's so ....
  b I like New York. It's such ....
4 a I wouldn't like to be a teacher. It's so ....
  b I wouldn't like to be a teacher. It's such ....
5 a It's great to see you again! I haven't seen you for so ....
  b It's great to see you again! I haven't seen you for such ....

A

Enough goes *after* adjectives and adverbs:

- ☐ I can't run very far. I'm **not fit enough**. (*not* enough fit)
- ☐ Let's go. We've waited **long enough**.
- ☐ Is Joe going to apply for the job? Is he **experienced enough**?

I'm not fit enough.

Compare **too ...** and **not ... enough**:

- ☐ You never stop working. You work **too hard**.
  (= more than is necessary)
- ☐ You're lazy. You **don't** work **hard enough**.
  (= less than is necessary)

B

Enough normally goes *before* nouns:

- ☐ I can't run very far. I haven't got **enough energy**. (*not* energy enough)
- ☐ Is Joe going to apply for the job? Does he have **enough experience**?
- ☐ We've got **enough money**. We don't need any more.
- ☐ Some of us had to sit on the floor because there weren't **enough chairs**.

Note that we say:

- ☐ We didn't have **enough time**. (*not* the time wasn't enough)
- ☐ There is **enough money**. (*not* the money is enough)

You can use **enough** alone (without a noun):

- ☐ We don't need any more money. We've got **enough**.

Compare **too much/many** and **enough**:

- ☐ There's **too much furniture** in this room. There's not **enough space**.
- ☐ There were **too many people** and not **enough chairs**.

C

We say **enough/too ... for** somebody/something:

- ☐ We haven't got **enough** money **for a holiday**.
- ☐ Is Joe experienced **enough for the job**?
- ☐ This shirt is **too** big **for me**. I need a smaller size.

But we say **enough/too ... to** do something (*not* for doing). For example:

- ☐ We haven't got **enough money to go** on holiday. (*not* for going)
- ☐ Is Joe **experienced enough to do** the job?
- ☐ They're **too young to get** married. / They're not **old enough to get** married.
- ☐ Let's get a taxi. It's **too far to walk** home from here.
- ☐ The bridge is just **wide enough** for two cars **to pass** each other.

D

We say:

	The food was very hot. We couldn't eat it.
and	The food was so hot that we couldn't eat it.
but	The food was **too hot to eat**. (*without* it)

Some more examples like this:

- ☐ These boxes are **too heavy to carry**.
  (*not* too heavy to carry them)
- ☐ The wallet was **too big to put** in my pocket.
  (*not* too big to put it)
- ☐ This chair isn't **strong enough to stand on**.
  (*not* strong enough to stand on it)

To ... and for ... (purpose) → Unit 64   Adjective + to ... (difficult to understand etc.) → Unit 65

Exercises

103.1 Complete the sentences using **enough** + the following words:

> big   ~~chairs~~   cups   ~~fit~~   milk   money   qualifications   room   time   warm   well

1 I can't run very far. I'm not ...... *fit enough* ....
2 Some of us had to sit on the floor because there weren't ...... *enough chairs* ....
3 I'd like to buy a car, but I haven't got .... at the moment.
4 Have you got .... in your coffee or would you like some more?
5 Are you .... ? Or shall I switch on the heating?
6 It's only a small car. There isn't .... for all of us.
7 Steve didn't feel .... to go to work this morning.
8 I enjoyed my trip to Paris, but there wasn't .... to do everything
  I wanted.
9 Do you think I've got .... to apply for the job?
10 Try this jacket on and see if it's .... for you.
11 There weren't .... for everybody to have coffee at the same time.

103.2 Complete the answers to the questions. Use **too** or **enough** + the word(s) in brackets.

1	Are they going to get married?	(old)	No, they're not ...... *old enough to get married* ....
2	I need to talk to you about something.	(busy)	Well, I'm afraid I'm .... to you now.
3	Let's go to the cinema.	(late)	No, it's .... to the cinema.
4	Why don't we sit outside?	(warm)	It's not .... outside.
5	Would you like to be a politician?	(shy)	No, I'm .... a politician.
6	Would you like to be a teacher?	(patience)	No, I haven't got .... a teacher.
7	Did you hear what he was saying?	(far away)	No, we were .... what he was saying.
8	Can he read a newspaper in English?	(English)	No, he doesn't know .... a newspaper.

103.3 Make one sentence from two. Complete the new sentence using **too** or **enough**.

1 We couldn't carry the boxes. They were too heavy.
  The boxes were too heavy to carry.
2 I can't drink this coffee. It's too hot.
  This coffee is ....
3 Nobody could move the piano. It was too heavy.
  The piano ....
4 Don't eat these apples. They're not ripe enough.
  These apples ....
5 I can't explain the situation. It is too complicated.
  The situation ....
6 We couldn't climb over the wall. It was too high.
  The wall ....
7 Three people can't sit on this sofa. It isn't big enough.
  This sofa ....
8 You can't see some things without a microscope. They are too small.
  Some ....

Quite, pretty, rather and fairly

A

You can use **quite/pretty/rather/fairly** + adjectives or adverbs. So you can say:

    ☐ It's **quite cold**.   It's **pretty cold**.   It's **rather cold**.   It's **fairly cold**.

Quite/pretty/rather/fairly = less than 'very' but more than 'a little'.

B

Quite and **pretty** are very similar in meaning:

    ☐ You'll need a coat when you go out. It's **quite cold / pretty cold**. (= less than 'very cold', but more than 'a little cold')
    ☐ I'm surprised you haven't heard of her. She's **quite famous / pretty famous**.
    ☐ Amanda lives **quite near** me, so we see each other **pretty often**.

Pretty is an informal word and is used mainly in spoken English.

Quite goes before **a/an**:

    ☐ We live in **quite an old house**. (*not* a quite old house)

Compare:

    ☐ Sally has **quite a** good job.
        Sally has **a pretty** good job.

You can also use **quite** (but not **pretty**) in the following ways:

quite a/an + noun (without an adjective):

    ☐ I didn't expect to see them. It was **quite a surprise**. (= quite a big surprise)

quite a lot (of ...):

    ☐ There were **quite a lot of** people at the meeting.

quite + verb, especially **like** and **enjoy**:

    ☐ I **quite like** tennis, but it's not my favourite sport.

C

Rather is similar to **quite** and **pretty**. We often use **rather** for negative ideas:

    ☐ The weather isn't so good. It's **rather cloudy**.
    ☐ Paul is **rather shy**. He doesn't talk very much.

Quite and **pretty** are also possible in these examples.

When we use **rather** for positive ideas (**good/nice** etc.), it means 'unusually' or 'surprisingly':

    ☐ These oranges are **rather good**. Where did you get them?

D

Fairly is weaker than **quite/rather/pretty**. For example, if something is **fairly good**, it is not very good and it could be better:

    ☐ My room is **fairly big**, but I'd prefer a bigger one.
    ☐ We see each other **fairly often**, but not as often as we used to.

E

Quite also means 'completely'. For example:

    ☐ 'Are you sure?' 'Yes, **quite sure**.' (= completely sure)

Quite means 'completely' with a number of adjectives, especially:

sure	right	true	clear	different	incredible	amazing
certain	wrong	safe	obvious	unnecessary	extraordinary	impossible

    ☐ She was **quite different** from what I expected. (= completely different)
    ☐ Everything they said was **quite true**. (= completely true)

We also use **quite** (= completely) with some verbs. For example:

    ☐ I **quite agree** with you. (= I completely agree)

Not quite = not completely:

    ☐ They **haven't quite finished** their dinner yet.
    ☐ I **don't quite understand** what you mean.
    ☐ 'Are you ready yet?' '**Not quite**.' (= not completely)

104.1 Complete the sentences using **quite** + the following:

~~famous~~   good   hungry   late   noisy   often   old   surprised

1 I'm surprised you haven't heard of her. She's ..... *quite famous* ..... .
2 I'm .... Is there anything to eat?
3 'How were the photographs you took?' '.. . Better than usual.'
4 I go to the cinema .... – maybe once a month.
5 We live near a very busy road, so it's often ....
6 I didn't expect Laura to contact me. I was .... when she phoned.
7 I went to bed .... last night, so I'm a bit tired this morning.
8 I don't know exactly when these houses were built, but they're ....

104.2 Complete the sentences using **quite** + the following:

a busy day	a good voice	a nice time	a lot of traffic
~~a nice day~~	a long way	a strong wind	

1 The weather was better than we had expected. It was ..... *quite a nice day* ..... .
2 Tom often sings. He's got ....
3 The bus stop wasn't very near the hotel. We had to walk ....
4 It's warm today, but there's ....
5 The journey took longer than I expected. There was ....
6 I'm tired. I've had ....
7 Our holiday was OK. We had ....

104.3 Use your own ideas to complete these sentences. Use **rather** + adjective.

1 The weather isn't so good. It's ..... *rather cloudy* ..... .
2 I enjoyed the film, but it was ....
3 The hotel we stayed at wasn't very good. I was ....
4 I think it's .... that Chris went away without telling anybody.
5 Lucy doesn't like having to wait. Sometimes she's ....

104.4 What does **quite** mean in these sentences? Tick (✓) the right meaning.

	more than a little, less than very (Section B)	completely (Section E)
1 It's <u>quite cold</u>. You'd better wear your coat.	✓	
2 'Are you sure?' 'Yes, <u>quite sure</u>.'		✓
3 Maria's English is <u>quite good</u>.		
4 I couldn't believe it. It was <u>quite incredible</u>.		
5 My bedroom is <u>quite big</u>.		
6 I'm <u>quite tired</u>. I think I'll go to bed.		
7 I <u>quite agree</u> with you.		

104.5 Complete these sentences using **quite** + the following:

different   impossible   right   safe   sure   ~~true~~   unnecessary

1 I didn't believe her at first, but in fact what she said was ..... *quite true* ..... .
2 You won't fall. The ladder is ....
3 I'm afraid I can't do what you ask. It's ....
4 I couldn't agree with you more. You are ....
5 You can't compare the two things. They are ....
6 You needn't have done that. It was ....
7 I think I saw them go out, but I'm not ....

Comparison 1
(cheaper, more expensive etc.)

A   Study these examples:

> How shall we travel? By car or by train?
>> Let's go by car. It's **cheaper**.
>> Don't go by train. It's **more expensive**.
>
> **Cheaper** and **more expensive** are *comparative* forms.

After comparatives you can use **than** (see Unit 107):
- ☐ It's **cheaper** to go by car **than** by train.
- ☐ Going by train is **more expensive than** going by car.

B   The comparative form is **-er** or **more** … .

<table>
<tr><td>

We use **-er** for short words (one syllable):

cheap → cheaper   **fast** → faster
large → larger   **thin** → thinner

We also use **-er** for two-syllable words that end in **-y** (**-y** → **ier**):

lucky → luckier   early → earlier
easy → easier   pretty → prettier

For spelling, see Appendix 6.

</td><td>

We use **more** … for longer words (two syllables or more):

more serious   more often
more expensive   more comfortable

We also use **more** … for adverbs that end in **-ly**:

more slowly   more seriously
more quietly   more carefully

</td></tr>
</table>

Compare these examples:

<table>
<tr><td>

- ☐ You're **older** than me.
- ☐ The exam was fairly easy – **easier** than I expected.
- ☐ Can you walk a bit **faster**?
- ☐ I'd like to have a **bigger** car.
- ☐ Last night I went to bed **earlier** than usual.

</td><td>

- ☐ You're **more patient** than me.
- ☐ The exam was quite difficult – **more difficult** than I expected.
- ☐ Can you walk a bit **more slowly**?
- ☐ I'd like to have a **more reliable** car.
- ☐ I don't play tennis much these days. I used to play **more often**.

</td></tr>
</table>

You can use **-er** *or* **more** … with some two-syllable adjectives, especially:

   clever   **narrow**   **quiet**   **shallow**   **simple**

- ☐ It's too noisy here. Can we go somewhere **quieter / more quiet**?

C   A few adjectives and adverbs have irregular comparative forms:

good/well → **better**
- ☐ The garden looks **better** since you tidied it up.
- ☐ I know him **well** – probably **better** than anybody else knows him.

bad/badly → **worse**:
- ☐ 'How is your headache? Better?'   'No, it's **worse**.'
- ☐ He did very badly in the exam – **worse** than expected.

far → **further** (*or* **farther**):
- ☐ It's a long walk from here to the park – **further** than I thought. (*or* **farther** than)

Further (*but not* farther) can also mean 'more' or 'additional':
- ☐ Let me know if you hear any **further** news. (= any more news)

Comparison 2–3 → Units 106–107   Superlatives (cheapest / most expensive etc.) → Unit 108

Exercises

105.1 Complete the sentences using a comparative form (**older / more important** etc.).

1 It's too noisy here. Can we go somewhere ____quieter____ ?
2 This coffee is very weak. I like it a bit _____ .
3 The hotel was surprisingly big. I expected it to be _____ .
4 The hotel was surprisingly cheap. I expected it to be _____ .
5 The weather is too cold here. I'd like to live somewhere _____ .
6 My job is a bit boring sometimes. I'd like to do something _____ .
7 It's a pity you live so far away. I wish you lived _____ .
8 I was surprised how easy it was to use the computer. I thought it would be
_____ .
9 Your work isn't very good. I'm sure you can do _____ .
10 Don't worry. The situation isn't so bad. It could be _____ .
11 I was surprised we got here so quickly. I expected the journey to take _____ .
12 You're talking very loudly. Can you speak a bit _____ ?
13 You hardly ever phone me. Why don't you phone me _____ ?
14 You're standing too near the camera. Can you move a bit _____ away?
15 You were a bit depressed yesterday, but you look _____ today.

105.2 Complete the sentences. Each time use the comparative form of one of the words in the box.
Use **than** where necessary.

big	crowded	~~early~~	easily	high	important
interested	peaceful	~~reliable~~	serious	simple	thin

1 I was feeling tired last night, so I went to bed ____earlier than____ usual.
2 I'd like to have a ____more reliable____ car. The one I've got keeps breaking down.
3 Unfortunately her illness was _____ we thought at first.
4 You look _____ . Have you lost weight?
5 I want a _____ flat. We don't have enough space here.
6 He doesn't study very hard. He's _____ in having a good time.
7 Health and happiness are _____ money.
8 The instructions were very complicated. They could have been _____ .
9 There were a lot of people on the bus. It was _____ usual.
10 I like living in the countryside. It's _____ living in a town.
11 You'll find your way around the town _____ if you have a good map.
12 In some parts of the country, prices are _____ in others.

105.3 Read the situations and complete the sentences. Use a comparative form (**-er** or **more ...**).

1 Yesterday the temperature was six degrees. Today it's only three degrees.
   It's ____colder today than it was yesterday.____
2 The journey takes four hours by car and five hours by train.
   It takes _____
3 Dave and I went for a run. I ran ten kilometres. Dave stopped after eight kilometres.
   I ran _____
4 Chris and Joe both did badly in the test. Chris got 30%, but Joe only got 25%.
   Joe did _____
5 I expected my friends to arrive at about 4 o'clock. In fact they arrived at 2.30.
   My friends _____
6 You can go by bus or by train. The buses run every 30 minutes. The trains run every hour.
   The buses _____
7 We were very busy at work today. We're not usually as busy as that.
   We _____

Comparison 2 (much better / any better / better and better / the sooner the better)

A Before comparatives you can use:

much   a lot   far (= a lot)   **a bit   a little   slightly** (= a little)

- □ Let's go by car. It's **much cheaper.** (*or* **a lot cheaper**)
- □ 'How do you feel?'   '**Much better,** thanks.'
- □ Don't go by train. It's **a lot more expensive.** (*or* **much more expensive**)
- □ Could you speak **a bit more slowly**? (*or* **a little more slowly**)
- □ This bag is **slightly heavier** than the other one.
- □ Her illness was **far more serious** than we thought at first. (*or* **much more serious / a lot more serious**)

B You can use **any** and **no** + comparative (**any longer / no bigger** etc.):

- □ I've waited long enough. I'm not waiting **any longer.** (= not even a little longer)
- □ We expected their house to be very big, but it's **no bigger** than ours.   *or*
  … it isn't **any bigger** than ours. (= not even a little bigger)
- □ How do you feel now? Do you feel **any better**?
- □ This hotel is better than the other one, and it's **no more expensive.**

C Better and better / more and more etc.

We repeat comparatives (**better and better** etc.) to say that something changes continuously:

- □ Your English is improving. It's getting **better and better.**
- □ The city is growing fast. It's getting **bigger and bigger.**
- □ Cathy got **more and more bored** in her job. In the end she left.
- □ These days **more and more** people are learning English.

D The … the …

You can say **the** (sooner/bigger/more etc.) **the better**:

- □ 'What time shall we leave?'   '**The sooner the better.**' (= as soon as possible)
- □ A: What sort of box do you want? A big one?
  B: Yes, **the bigger the better.** (= as big as possible)
- □ When you're travelling, **the less luggage** you have **the better.**

We also use **the … the …** to say that one thing depends on another thing:

- □ **The warmer** the weather, **the better** I feel. (= if the weather is warmer, I feel better)
- □ **The sooner** we leave, **the earlier** we will arrive.
- □ **The younger** you are, **the easier** it is to learn.
- □ **The more expensive** the hotel, **the better** the service.
- □ **The more** electricity you use, **the higher** your bill will be.
- □ **The more** I thought about the plan, **the less** I liked it.

E Older and elder

The comparative of **old** is **older**:

- □ David looks **older** than he really is.

You can use **elder** (*or* **older**) when you talk about people in a family. You can say (my/your etc.) **elder sister/brother/daughter/son**:

- □ **My elder sister** is a TV producer. (*or* My **older** sister …)

We say 'my **elder sister**', but we do not say that 'somebody is elder':

- □ My sister is **older** than me. (*not* elder than me)

Any/no → Unit 86   Comparison 1, 3 → Units 105, 107   Eldest → Unit 108D
Even + comparative → Unit 112C

106.1 Use the words in brackets to complete the sentences. Use **much / a bit** etc. + a comparative form. Use **than** where necessary.

1 Her illness was ...much more serious than... we thought at first. (much / serious)
2 This bag is too small. I need something .... (much / big)
3 I'm afraid the problem is .... it seems. (much / complicated)
4 It was very hot yesterday. Today it's .... (a bit / cool)
5 I enjoyed our visit to the museum. It was .... I expected.
   (far / interesting)
6 You're driving too fast. Can you drive .... ? (a bit / slowly)
7 It's .... to learn a foreign language in a country where it is
   spoken. (a lot / easy)
8 I thought she was younger than me, but in fact she's ....
   (slightly / old)

106.2 Complete the sentences using **any/no** + comparative. Use **than** where necessary.

1 I've waited long enough. I'm not waiting ...any longer... .
2 I'm sorry I'm a bit late, but I couldn't get here ....
3 This shop isn't expensive. The prices are .... anywhere else.
4 I need to stop for a rest. I can't walk ....
5 The traffic isn't particularly bad today. It's .... usual.

106.3 Complete the sentences using the structure in Section C (**... and ...**).

1 Cathy got ...more and more bored... in her job. In the end she left. (bored)
2 That hole in your sweater is getting .... (big)
3 My bags seemed to get .... as I carried them. (heavy)
4 As I waited for my interview, I became .... (nervous)
5 As the day went on, the weather got .... (bad)
6 Health care is becoming .... (expensive)
7 Since Anna went to Canada, her English has got .... (good)
8 As the conversation went on, Paul became .... (talkative)

106.4 These sentences are like those in Section D. Use the words in brackets (in the correct form) to complete the sentences.

1 I like warm weather.
   The warmer the weather, ...the better I feel... . (feel)
2 I didn't really like him when we first met.
   But the more I got to know him, ... (like)
3 If you're in business, you want to make a profit.
   The more goods you sell, ... (profit)
4 It's hard to concentrate when you're tired.
   The more tired you are, ... (hard)
5 Kate had to wait a very long time.
   The longer she waited, ... (impatient / become)

106.5 Which is correct, **older** or **elder**? Or both of them?

1 My <u>older / elder</u> sister is a TV producer. (<u>older</u> and <u>elder</u> are both correct)
2 I'm surprised Diane is only 25. I thought she was <u>older / elder</u>.
3 Jane's younger sister is still at school. Her <u>older / elder</u> sister is a nurse.
4 Martin is <u>older / elder</u> than his brother.

A Study this example situation:

Sarah, Joe and David are all very rich. Sarah has £20 million, Joe has £15 million and David has £10 million. So:

Joe is rich.
He is **richer than** David.
But he **isn't as rich as** Sarah.
(= Sarah is **richer than** he is)

SARAH   JOE   DAVID

Some more examples of **not as ... (as)**:

- ☐ Richard **isn't as old as** he looks. (= he looks **older than** he is)
- ☐ The town centre **wasn't as crowded as** usual. (= it is usually **more crowded**)
- ☐ Jenny **didn't** do **as well** in the exam **as** she had hoped. (= she had hoped to do **better**)
- ☐ The weather is better today. It's **not as cold**. (= yesterday was **colder**)
- ☐ I **don't** know **as many** people **as** you do. (= you know **more** people)
- ☐ 'How much did it cost? Fifty pounds?' 'No, **not as much as** that.' (= less than fifty pounds)

You can also say **not so ... (as)**:

- ☐ It's not warm, but it isn't **so cold as** yesterday. (= it isn't **as cold as** ...)

Less ... than is similar to **not as ... as**:

- ☐ I spent **less money than** you. (= I **didn't** spend **as** much money **as** you)
- ☐ The city centre was **less crowded than** usual. (= it **wasn't as** crowded **as** usual)

B We also use **as ... as** (*but not* so ... as) in positive sentences and in questions:

- ☐ I'm sorry I'm late. I got here **as fast as** I could.
- ☐ There's plenty of food. You can have **as much as** you want.
- ☐ Let's walk. It's **just as quick as** taking the bus.
- ☐ Can you send me the money **as soon as possible**, please?

Also **twice as ... as, three times as ... as** etc. :

- ☐ Petrol is **twice as expensive as** it was a few years ago.
- ☐ Their house is about **three times as big as** ours.

C We say **the same as** (*not* the same like):

- ☐ Laura's salary is **the same as** mine. *or* Laura gets **the same** salary **as** me.
- ☐ David is **the same** age **as** James.
- ☐ 'What would you like to drink?' 'I'll have **the same as** you.'

D **Than me / than I am** etc.

You can say:

- ☐ You're taller **than I am**.   *or* You're taller **than me**.
  (*not usually* You're taller than I)
- ☐ He's not as clever **as she is**.   *or* He's not as clever **as her**.
- ☐ They have more money **than we have**. *or* They have more money **than us**.
- ☐ I can't run as fast **as he can**.   *or* I can't run as fast **as him**.

Comparison 1–2 → Units 105–106   **As long as** → Unit 115B   **As and like** → Unit 117

Exercises

107.1 Complete the sentences using **as ... as.**

1 I'm quite tall, but you are taller. I'm not _as tall as you_ .
2 My salary is high, but yours is higher. My salary isn't ....
3 You know a bit about cars, but I know more.
   You don't ....
4 It's still cold, but it was colder yesterday.
   It isn't ....
5 I still feel quite tired, but I felt a lot more tired yesterday.
   I don't ....
6 Our neighbours have lived here for quite a long time, but we've lived here longer.
   Our neighbours haven't ....
7 I was a bit nervous before the interview, but usually I'm a lot more nervous.
   I wasn't ....

107.2 Write a new sentence with the same meaning.

1 Richard is younger than he looks. Richard isn't _as old as he looks_ .
2 I didn't spend as much money as you. You _spent more money than me_ .
3 The station was nearer than I thought. The station wasn't ....
4 The meal didn't cost as much as I expected. The meal cost ....
5 I go out less than I used to. I don't ....
6 Karen's hair isn't as long as it used to be. Karen used to ....
7 I know them better than you do. You don't ....
8 There are fewer people at this meeting than at the last one.
   There aren't ....

107.3 Complete the sentences using **as ... as** + the following:

bad	**comfortable**	~~**fast**~~	**long**	**often**	**quietly**	**soon**	**well**	**well-qualified**

1 I'm sorry I'm late. I got here _as fast as_ I could.
2 It was a difficult question. I answered it .... I could.
3 'How long can I stay with you?' 'You can stay .... you like.'
4 I need the information quickly, so let me know .... possible.
5 I like to keep fit, so I go swimming .... I can.
6 I didn't want to wake anybody, so I came in .... I could.

   In the following sentences use **just as ... as.**

7 I'm going to sleep on the floor. It's .... the bed.
8 Why did he get the job rather than me? I'm .... him.
9 At first I thought he was nice, but really he's .... everybody else.

107.4 Write sentences using **the same as.**

1 David and James are both 22 years old. David _is the same age as James_ .
2 You and I both have dark brown hair. Your hair ....
3 I arrived at 10.25 and so did you. I ....
4 My birthday is 5 April. Tom's birthday is 5 April too. My ....

107.5 Complete the sentences with **than ...** or **as ... .**

1 I can't reach as high as you. You are taller _than me_ .
2 He doesn't know much. I know more ....
3 I don't work particularly hard. Most people work as hard ....
4 We were very surprised. Nobody was more surprised ....
5 She's not a very good player. I'm a better player ....
6 They've been very lucky. I wish we were as lucky ....

A Study these examples:

> What is **the longest** river in the world?
> What was **the most enjoyable** holiday you've ever had?
>
> **Longest** and **most enjoyable** are *superlative* forms.

B The superlative form is **-est** or **most** ... . In general, we use **-est** for short words and **most** ... for longer words. The rules are the same as those for the comparative – see Unit 105.

long → longest	**hot** → hottest	**easy** → easiest	**hard** → hardest
but **most** famous	**most** boring	**most** difficult	**most** expensive

A few adjectives are irregular:

> good → **best**   bad → **worst**   far → **furthest/farthest**

For spelling, see Appendix 6.

C We normally use **the** before a superlative (**the** longest / **the** most famous etc.):

- ☐ Yesterday was **the hottest** day of the year.
- ☐ The film was really boring. It was **the most boring** film I've ever seen.
- ☐ She is a really nice person – one of **the nicest** people I know.
- ☐ Why does he always come to see me at **the worst** possible moment?

Compare superlative and comparative:

- ☐ This hotel is **the cheapest** in town. *(superlative)*
  This hotel is **cheaper** than all the others in town. *(comparative)*
- ☐ He's **the most patient** person I've ever met.
  He's much **more patient** than I am.

D **Oldest** and **eldest**

The superlative of **old** is **oldest**:

- ☐ That church is **the oldest** building in the town. (*not* the eldest)

We use **eldest** (*or* **oldest**) when we are talking about people in a family:

- ☐ **My eldest son** is 13 years old. (*or* My **oldest** son)
- ☐ Are you **the eldest** in your family? (*or* the **oldest**)

E After superlatives we normally use **in** with places:

- ☐ What's the longest river **in the world**? (*not* of the world)
- ☐ We had a nice room. It was one of the best **in the hotel**. (*not* of the hotel)

We also use **in** for organisations and groups of people (a class / a company etc.):

- ☐ Who is the youngest student **in the class**? (*not* of the class)

For a period of time, we normally use **of**:

- ☐ What was the happiest day **of your life**?
- ☐ Yesterday was the hottest day **of the year**.

F We often use the *present perfect* (I have done) after a superlative (see also Unit 8A):

- ☐ What's **the most important** decision **you've ever had** to make?
- ☐ That was **the best** holiday **I've had** for a long time.

108.1 Complete the sentences. Use a superlative (-est or most ...) + a preposition (of or in).

1 It's a very good room. It _is the best room in_ the hotel.
2 It's a very cheap restaurant. It's .... the town.
3 It was a very happy day. It was .... my life.
4 She's a very intelligent student. She .... the class.
5 It's a very valuable painting. It .... the gallery.
6 Spring is a very busy time for me. It .... the year.

In the following sentences use **one of** + a superlative + a preposition.

7 It's a very good room. It _is one of the best rooms in_ the hotel.
8 He's a very rich man. He's one .... the world.
9 It's a very big castle. It .... Britain.
10 She's a very good player. She .... the team.
11 It was a very bad experience. It .... my life.
12 He's a very dangerous criminal. He .... the country.

108.2 Complete the sentences. Use a superlative (-est or most ...) or a comparative (-er or more ...).

1 We stayed at _the cheapest_ hotel in the town. (cheap)
2 Our hotel was _cheaper_ than all the others in the town. (cheap)
3 The United States is very large, but Canada is .... (large)
4 What's .... country in the world? (small)
5 I wasn't feeling well yesterday, but I feel a bit .... today. (good)
6 It was an awful day. It was .... day of my life. (bad)
7 What is .... sport in your country? (popular)
8 Everest is .... mountain in the world. It is ....
    than any other mountain. (high)
9 We had a great holiday. It was one of .... holidays we've ever
    had. (enjoyable)
10 I prefer this chair to the other one. It's .... (comfortable)
11 What's .... way of getting from here to the station? (quick)
12 Sue and Kevin have got three daughters. .... is 14 years old. (old)

108.3 What do you say in these situations? Use a superlative + ever. Use the words in brackets (in the correct form).

1 You've just been to the cinema. The film was extremely boring. You tell your friend:
    (boring / film / see) That's _the most boring film I've ever seen_ .
2 Your friend has just told you a joke, which you think is very funny. You say:
    (funny / joke / hear) That's ....
3 You're drinking coffee with a friend. It's really good coffee. You say:
    (good / coffee / taste) This... .
4 You are talking to a friend about Mary. Mary is very generous. You tell your friend about her:
    (generous / person / meet) She... .
5 You have just run ten kilometres. You've never run further than this. You say to your friend:
    (far / run) That ....
6 You decided to give up your job. Now you think this was a bad mistake. You say to your
    friend:
    (bad / mistake / make) It ....
7 Your friend meets a lot of people, some of them famous. You ask your friend:
    (famous / person / meet?) Who .... ?

Word order 1: verb + object; place and time

A *Verb + object*

The *verb* and the *object* normally go together. We do not usually put other words between them:

	verb +	*object*	
I	like	my job	very much. (*not* I like very much my job)
Did you	see	your friends	yesterday?
Liz often	plays	tennis.	

Study these examples. The verb and the object go together each time:

- □ Do you eat meat every day?
  (*not* Do you eat every day meat?)

- □ Everybody enjoyed the party very much.
  (*not* enjoyed very much the party)

- □ Our guide spoke English fluently.
  (*not* spoke fluently English)

- □ I lost all my money and I also lost my passport .
  (*not* I lost also my passport)

- □ At the end of the street you'll see a supermarket on your left.
  (*not* see on your left a supermarket)

B *Place and time*

Usually the *verb* and the *place* (where?) go together:

  go home   **live in a city**   **walk to work** etc.

If the verb has an *object*, the place comes after the *verb + object*:

  take somebody home   **meet a friend in the street**

Time (when? / how often? / how long?) usually goes after *place*:

	place	+	*time*	
Ben walks	to work		every morning.	(*not* every morning to work)
Sam has been	in Canada		since April.	
We arrived	at the airport		early.	

Study these examples. *Time* goes after *place*:

- □ I'm going to Paris on Monday . (*not* I'm going on Monday to Paris)

- □ They have lived in the same house for a long time .

- □ Don't be late. Make sure you're here by 8 o'clock .

- □ Sarah gave me a lift home after the party .

- □ You really shouldn't go to bed so late .

It is often possible to put *time* at the beginning of the sentence:

- □ **On Monday** I'm going to Paris.
- □ **Every morning** Ben walks to work.

Some time words (for example, **always/never/often**) usually go with the verb in the middle of the sentence. See Unit 110.

Word order in questions → Units 49–50   Adjective order → Unit 99   Word order 2 → Unit 110

Exercises

109.1 Is the word order right or wrong? Correct the sentences where necessary.

1 Everybody enjoyed the party very much.   _OK_
2 Ben walks every morning to work.   _Ben walks to work every morning._
3 Joe doesn't like very much football.   ....
4 I drink three or four cups of coffee every morning.   ....
5 I ate quickly my breakfast and went out.   ....
6 Are you going to invite to the party a lot of people?   ....
7 I phoned Tom immediately after hearing the news.   ....
8 Did you go late to bed last night?   ....
9 Did you learn a lot of things at school today?   ....
10 I met on my way home a friend of mine.   ....

109.2 Put the parts of the sentence in the correct order.

1 (the party / very much / everybody enjoyed)   _Everybody enjoyed the party very much._
2 (we won / easily / the game)   ....
3 (quietly / the door / I closed)   ....
4 (Diane / quite well / speaks / German)   ....
5 (Sam / all the time / TV / watches)   ....
6 (again / please don't ask / that question)

    ....

7 (football / every weekend / does Kevin play?)

    ....

8 (some money / I borrowed / from a friend of mine)

    ....

109.3 Complete the sentences. Put the parts in the correct order.

1 (for a long time / have lived / in the same house)
   They _have lived in the same house for a long time_ .
2 (to the supermarket / every Friday / go)
   I ....
3 (home / did you come / so late)
   Why .... ?
4 (her children / takes / every day / to school)
   Sarah ....
5 (been / recently / to the cinema)
   I haven't ....
6 (at the top of the page / your name / write)
   Please ....
7 (her name / after a few minutes / remembered)
   I ....
8 (around the town / all morning / walked)
   We ....
9 (on Saturday night / didn't see you / at the party)
   I ....
10 (some interesting books / found / in the library)
   We ....
11 (her umbrella / last night / in a restaurant / left)
   Jackie ....
12 (opposite the park / a new hotel / are building)
   They ....

Word order 2: adverbs with the verb

A Some adverbs (for example, **always, also, probably**) go with the verb in the middle of a sentence:
- □ Helen **always drives** to work.
- □ We were feeling very tired and we **were also** hungry.
- □ The concert **will probably be cancelled**.

B Study these rules for the position of adverbs in the middle of a sentence. (They are only general rules, so there are exceptions.)

(1) If the verb is one word (**drives/fell/cooked** etc.), the adverb usually goes *before* the verb:

	adverb	*verb*	
Helen	**always**	**drives**	to work.
I	**almost**	**fell**	as I was going down the stairs.

- □ I cleaned the house and **also cooked** the dinner. (*not* cooked also)
- □ Lucy **hardly ever watches** television and **rarely reads** newspapers.
- □ 'Shall I give you my address?' 'No, I **already have** it.'

Note that these adverbs (**always/often/also** etc.) go before **have to** … :
- □ Joe never phones me. I **always have** to phone him. (*not* I have always to phone)

(2) But adverbs go *after* **am/is/are/was/were**:
- □ We were feeling very tired and we **were also** hungry.
- □ Why are you **always** late? You're **never** on time.
- □ The traffic **isn't usually** as bad as it was this morning.

(3) If the verb is two or more words (for example, **can remember / doesn't eat / will be cancelled**), the adverb usually goes *after the first verb* (**can/doesn't/will** etc.):

	verb 1	*adverb*	*verb 2*	
I	**can**	**never**	**remember**	her name.
Clare	**doesn't**	**often**	**eat**	meat.
	Are you	**definitely**	**going**	away next week?
The concert	**will**	**probably**	**be**	cancelled.

- □ You **have always been** very kind to me.
- □ Jack can't cook. He **can't even boil** an egg.
- □ **Do** you **still work** for the same company?
- □ The house **was only built** a year ago and it's **already falling** down.

Note that **probably** goes before a negative (**isn't/won't** etc.). So we say:
- □ I **probably won't see** you.   *or*   I will **probably not see** you. (*not* I won't probably)

C We also use **all** and **both** in these positions:
- □ We **all felt** ill after the meal. (*not* we felt all ill)
- □ My parents **are both** teachers. (*not* my parents both are teachers)
- □ Sarah and Jane **have both applied** for the job.
- □ We **are all going** out this evening.

D Sometimes we use **is/will/did** etc. instead of repeating part of a sentence (see Unit 51). Note the position of **always/never** etc. in these sentences:
- □ He always says he won't be late, but he **always is**. (= he **is always** late)
- □ I've never done it and I **never will**. (= I **will never** do it)
We normally put **always/never** etc. *before* the verb in sentences like these.

110.1 Are the <u>underlined</u> words in the right position or not? Correct the sentences where necessary.

1 Helen drives <u>always</u> to work.   *Helen always drives to work.*
2 I cleaned the house and <u>also</u> cooked the dinner.   *OK*
3 I have <u>usually</u> a shower in the morning.
4 We <u>soon</u> found the solution to the problem.
5 Steve gets <u>hardly ever</u> angry.
6 I did some shopping and I went <u>also</u> to the bank.
7 Jane has <u>always</u> to hurry in the morning.
8 We <u>all</u> were tired, so we <u>all</u> fell asleep.
9 She <u>always</u> says she'll phone me, but she <u>never</u> does.

110.2 Rewrite the sentences to include the word in brackets.

1 Clare doesn't eat meat. (often)   *Clare doesn't often eat meat.*
2 a We were on holiday in Spain. (all)
  b We were staying at the same hotel. (all)
  c We enjoyed ourselves. (all)
3 Catherine is very generous. (always)
4 I don't have to work on Saturdays. (usually)
5 Do you watch TV in the evenings? (always)
6 Martin is learning French, and he is learning Italian. (also)
  Martin is learning French and he
7 a The new hotel is very expensive. (probably)
  b It costs a lot to stay there. (probably)
8 a I can help you. (probably)
  b I can't help you. (probably)

110.3 Complete the sentences. Use the words in brackets in the correct order.

1 I *can never remember* her name. (remember / never / can)
2 I _____ sugar in coffee. (take / usually)
3 I _____ hungry when I get home from work. (am / usually)
4 A: Where's Joe?
  B: He _____ home early. (gone / has / probably)
5 Mark and Diane _____ in Manchester. (both / were / born)
6 Liz is a good pianist. She _____ very well. (sing / also / can)
7 Our cat _____ under the bed. (often / sleeps)
8 They live in the same street as me, but I _____ to them.
  (never / have / spoken)
9 We _____ a long time for the bus. (have / always / to wait)
10 My eyesight isn't very good. I _____ with glasses.
  (read / can / only)
11 I _____ early tomorrow. (probably / leaving / will / be)
12 I'm afraid I _____ able to come to the party.
  (probably / be / won't)
13 It's difficult to contact Sue. She _____ at home when I phone
  her. (is / hardly ever)
14 We _____ in the same place. We haven't moved.
  (still / are / living)
15 If we hadn't taken the same train, we _____ each other.
  (never / met / would / have)
16 A: Are you tired?
  B: Yes, I _____ at this time of day. (am / always)

Still, yet and already
Any more / any longer / no longer

A Still

We use **still** to say that a situation or action is continuing. It hasn't changed or stopped:
- ☐ It's ten o'clock and Joe is **still** in bed.
- ☐ When I went to bed, Chris was **still** working.
- ☐ Do you **still** want to go away or have you changed your mind?

Still usually goes in the middle of the sentence with the verb (see Unit 110).

B Any more / any longer / no longer

We use **not … any more** or **not … any longer** to say that a situation has changed. **Any more** and **any longer** go at the end of a sentence:
- ☐ Lucy doesn't work here **any more** (*or* **any longer**). She left last month.
  (*not* Lucy doesn't still work here.)
- ☐ We used to be good friends, but we aren't **any more** (*or* **any longer**).

You can also use **no longer**. **No longer** goes in the middle of the sentence:
- ☐ Lucy **no longer** works here.
Note that we do not normally use **no more** in this way:
- ☐ We are **no longer** friends. (*not* We are no more friends.)

Compare **still** and **not … any more**:
- ☐ Sally **still** works here, but Lucy doesn't work here **any more**.

C Yet

Yet = until now. We use **yet** mainly in negative sentences (**He isn't** here **yet**) and questions (**Is he** here **yet?**). **Yet** shows that the speaker is expecting something to happen.
Yet usually goes at the end of a sentence:
- ☐ It's 10 o'clock and Joe **isn't** here **yet**.
- ☐ **Have you met** your new neighbours **yet**?
- ☐ 'Where are you going for your holidays?' 'We **don't** know **yet**.'

We often use **yet** with the *present perfect* (**Have** you **met** … **yet**?'). See Unit 7C.

Compare **yet** and **still**:
- ☐ Mike lost his job six months ago and **is still** unemployed.
  Mike lost his job six months ago and **hasn't found** another job **yet**.
- ☐ **Is** it **still** raining?
  Has it **stopped** raining **yet**?

Still is also possible in *negative* sentences (before the negative):
- ☐ She said she would be here an hour ago and she **still** hasn't come.
This is similar to 'she hasn't come **yet**'. But **still … not** shows a stronger feeling of surprise or impatience. Compare:
- ☐ I wrote to him last week. He **hasn't** replied **yet**. (but I expect he will reply soon)
- ☐ I wrote to him months ago and he **still** hasn't replied. (he should have replied before now)

D Already

We use **already** to say that something happened sooner than expected. **Already** usually goes in the middle of a sentence (see Unit 110):
- ☐ 'What time is Sue leaving?' 'She has **already** left.' (= sooner than you expected)
- ☐ Shall I tell Joe what happened or does he **already** know?
- ☐ I've only just had lunch and I'm **already** hungry.

Present perfect + already/yet → Unit 7C   Word order → Unit 110

Exercises

111.1 Compare what Paul said a few years ago with what he says now. Some things are the same as before and some things have changed. Write sentences with **still** and **any more**.

Paul a few years ago

> I travel a lot.
> I work in a shop.
> I write poems.
> I want to be a teacher.
> I'm interested in politics.
> I'm single.
> I go fishing a lot.

Paul now

> I travel a lot.
> I work in a hospital.
> I gave up writing poems.
> I want to be a teacher.
> I'm not interested in politics.
> I'm single.
> I haven't been fishing for years.

1 (travel)   _He still travels a lot._
2 (shop)   _He doesn't work in a shop any more._
3 (poems)   He ....
4 (teacher) ....

5 (politics) ....
6 (single) ....
7 (fishing) ....
8 (beard) ....

Now write three sentences about Paul using **no longer**.

9   _He no longer works in a shop._
10 ....

11 ....
12 ....

111.2 For each sentence (with **still**) write a sentence with a similar meaning using **not ... yet** + one of the following verbs:

> **decide**   **find**   **finish**   **go**   ~~**stop**~~   **take off**   **wake up**

1 It's still raining.   _It hasn't stopped raining yet._
2 Gary is still here.   He ....
3 They're still repairing the road.   They ....
4 The children are still asleep.   ....
5 Is Ann still looking for a place to live?   ....?
6 I'm still wondering what to do.   ....
7 The plane is still waiting on the runway.   ....

111.3 Put in **still**, **yet**, **already** or **any more** in the underlined sentence (or part of the sentence). Study the examples carefully.

1 Mike lost his job a year ago and <u>he is unemployed</u>.   _he is still unemployed_
2 Shall I tell Joe what happened or <u>does he know</u>?   _does he already know_
3 I'm hungry. <u>Is dinner ready</u>?   _Is dinner ready yet?_
4 I was hungry earlier, but <u>I'm not hungry</u>.   _I'm not hungry any more_
5 Can we wait a few minutes? <u>I don't want to go out</u>. ....
6 Jenny used to work at the airport, but <u>she doesn't work there</u>. ....
7 I used to live in Amsterdam. <u>I have a lot of friends there</u>. ....
8 'Shall I introduce you to Joe?' 'There's no need. <u>We've met</u>.' ....
9 <u>Do you live in the same place</u> or have you moved? ....
10 Would you like to eat with us or <u>have you eaten</u>? ....
11 'Where's John?' '<u>He's not here</u>. He'll be here soon.' ....
12 Tim said he'd be here at 8.30. It's 9 o'clock now and <u>he isn't here</u>. ....
13 Do you want to join the club or <u>are you a member</u>? ....
14 It happened a long time ago, but <u>I can remember it very clearly</u>. ....
15 I've put on weight. <u>These trousers don't fit me</u>. ....
16 'Have you finished with the paper?' 'No, <u>I'm reading it</u>.' ....

....

Unit 112 Even

A Study this example situation:

Tina loves watching television.

She has a TV set in every room of the house – **even** the bathroom.

We use **even** to say that something is unusual or surprising. It is not usual to have a TV set in the bathroom.

Some more examples:
- These photographs are really awful. **Even I** take better photographs than these. (and I'm certainly not a good photographer)
- He always wears a coat – **even in hot weather**.
- Nobody would help her – **not even her best friend**.

or **Not even** her best friend would help her.

B Very often we use **even** with the verb in the middle of a sentence (see Unit 110):
- Sue has travelled all over the world. She has **even** been to the Antarctic. (It's especially unusual to go to the Antarctic, so she must have travelled a lot.)
- They are very rich. They **even** have their own private jet.

Study these examples with **not even**:
- I can't cook. I **can't even** boil an egg. (and boiling an egg is very easy)
- They weren't very friendly to us. They **didn't even** say hello.
- Jenny is very fit. She's just run five miles and she's **not even** out of breath.

C You can use **even** + *comparative* (**cheaper** / **more expensive** etc.):
- I got up very early, but Jack got up **even earlier**.
- I knew I didn't have much money, but I've got **even less** than I thought.
- We were surprised to get a letter from her. We were **even more surprised** when she came to see us a few days later.

D Even though / even when / even if

You can use **even though** / **even when** / **even if** + *subject* + *verb*:
- **Even though she can't** drive, she has bought a car.
  <u>subject + verb</u>
- He never shouts, **even when he's** angry.
- I'll probably see you tomorrow. But **even if I don't see** you tomorrow, we're sure to see each other before the weekend.

You cannot use **even** in this way (+ *subject* + *verb*). We say:
- **Even though she can't** drive, she has bought a car. (*not* Even she can't drive)
- I can't reach the shelf **even if I stand** on a chair. (*not* even I stand)

Compare **even if** and **if**:
- We're going to the beach tomorrow. It doesn't matter what the weather is like. We're going **even if** it's raining.
- We want to go to the beach tomorrow, but we won't go **if** it's raining.

If and when → Unit 25D   **Though / even though** → Unit 113E

112.1 Julie, Sarah and Amanda are three friends who went on holiday together. Use the information given about them to complete the sentences using **even** or **not even**.

Julie 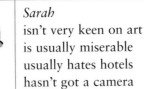	Sarah	Amanda
is usually happy	isn't very keen on art	is almost always late
is usually on time	is usually miserable	is a keen photographer
likes getting up early	usually hates hotels	loves staying in hotels
is very interested in art	hasn't got a camera	isn't very good at getting up

1 They stayed at a hotel. Everybody liked it, _even Sarah_ .
2 They arranged to meet. They all arrived on time, ...
3 They went to an art gallery. Nobody enjoyed it, ...
4 Yesterday they had to get up early. They all managed to do this, ...
5 They were together yesterday. They were all in a good mood, ...
6 None of them took any photographs, ...

112.2 Make sentences with **even**. Use the words in brackets.

1 Sue has been all over the world. (the Antarctic) _She has even been to the Antarctic._
2 We painted the whole room. (the floor) We ....
3 Rachel has met lots of famous people. (the prime minister)
   She ....
4 You could hear the noise from a long way away. (from the next street)
   You ....

In the following sentences you have to use **not ... even**.

5 They didn't say anything to us. (hello) _They didn't even say hello._
6 I can't remember anything about her. (her name) I ....
7 There isn't anything to do in this town. (a cinema) ....
8 He didn't tell anybody where he was going. (his wife)
   ....
9 I don't know anyone in our street. (the people next door)
   ....

112.3 Complete the sentences using **even + comparative**.

1 It was very hot yesterday, but today it's _even hotter_ .
2 The church is 500 years old, but the house next to it is ....
3 That's a very good idea, but I've got an .... one.
4 The first question was very difficult to answer. The second one was ....
5 I did very badly in the exam, but most of my friends did ....
6 Neither of us was hungry. I ate very little and my friend ate ....

112.4 Put in **if, even, even if** or **even though**.

1 _Even though_ she can't drive, she has bought a car.
2 The bus leaves in five minutes, but we can still catch it .... we run.
3 The bus leaves in two minutes. We won't catch it now .... we run.
4 His Spanish isn't very good – .... after three years in Spain.
5 His Spanish isn't very good .... he's lived in Spain for three years.
6 .... with the heating on, it was very cold in the house.
7 I couldn't sleep .... I was very tired.
8 I won't forgive them for what they did, ... they apologise.
9 .... I hadn't eaten anything for 24 hours, I wasn't hungry.

→ Additional exercise 32 **(page 321)**

Although / though / even though
In spite of / despite

A

Study this example situation:

Last year Paul and Joanne had a holiday by the sea. It rained a lot, but they enjoyed themselves.

You can say:
Although it rained a lot, they enjoyed themselves.
(= It rained a lot, *but* they …)
or

In spite of
Despite } the rain, they enjoyed themselves.

B

After **although** we use a *subject + verb*:
- ☐ **Although it rained** a lot, we enjoyed our holiday.
- ☐ I didn't get the job **although I had** the necessary qualifications.

Compare the meaning of **although** and **because**:
- ☐ We went out **although** it was raining.
- ☐ We didn't go out **because** it was raining.

C

After **in spite of** or **despite**, we use a *noun*, a *pronoun* (**this/that/what** etc.) or **-ing**:
- ☐ **In spite of the rain**, we enjoyed our holiday.
- ☐ I didn't get the job **in spite of having** the necessary qualifications.
- ☐ She wasn't well, but **in spite of this** she went to work.
- ☐ **In spite of what** I said yesterday, I still love you.

Despite is the same as **in spite of**. We say **in spite of**, but **despite** (*without* of):
- ☐ She wasn't well, but **despite this** she went to work. (*not* despite of this)

You can say **in spite of the fact (that)** … and **despite the fact (that)** … :
- ☐ I didn't get the job { **in spite of the fact (that)** / **despite the fact (that)** } I had the necessary qualifications.

Compare **in spite of** and **because of**:
- ☐ We went out **in spite of** the rain. (*or* … **despite** the rain.)
- ☐ We didn't go out **because of** the rain.

D

Compare **although** and **in spite of / despite**:
- ☐ **Although the traffic was** bad, / **In spite of the traffic,** } we arrived on time. (*not* In spite of the traffic was bad)

- ☐ I couldn't sleep { **although I was** very tired. / **despite being** very tired. } (*not* despite I was tired)

E

Sometimes we use **though** instead of **although**:
- ☐ I didn't get the job **though** I had the necessary qualifications.

In spoken English we often use **though** at the end of a sentence:
- ☐ The house isn't very nice. I like the garden **though**. (= but I like the garden)
- ☐ I see them every day. I've never spoken to them **though**. (= but I've never spoken to them)

Even though (*but not* 'even' alone) is a stronger form of **although**:
- ☐ **Even though** I was really tired, I couldn't sleep. (*not* Even I was really tired …)

Even → Unit 112

113.1 Complete the sentences. Use **although** + a sentence from the box.

I didn't speak the language	~~he has a very important job~~
I had never seen her before	we don't like them very much
it was quite cold	the heating was on
I'd met her twice before	we've known each other a long time

1 _Although he has a very important job_ , he isn't particularly well-paid.
2 .... , I recognised her from a photograph.
3 She wasn't wearing a coat ....
4 We thought we'd better invite them to the party ....
5 .... , I managed to make myself understood.
6 .... , the room wasn't warm.
7 I didn't recognise her ....
8 We're not very good friends ....

113.2 Complete the sentences with **although / in spite of / because / because of**.

1 _Although_ it rained a lot, we enjoyed our holiday.
2 a .... all our careful plans, a lot of things went wrong.
  b .... we'd planned everything carefully, a lot of things went wrong.
3 a I went home early .... I was feeling unwell.
  b I went to work the next day .... I was still feeling unwell.
4 a She only accepted the job .... the salary, which was very high.
  b She accepted the job .... the salary, which was rather low.
5 a I managed to get to sleep .... there was a lot of noise.
  b I couldn't get to sleep .... the noise.

Use your own ideas to complete the following sentences:

6 a He passed the exam although ....
  b He passed the exam because ....
7 a I didn't eat anything although ....
  b I didn't eat anything in spite of ....

113.3 Make one sentence from two. Use the word(s) in brackets in your sentences.

1 I couldn't sleep. I was very tired. (despite)
  I couldn't sleep despite being very tired.
2 They have very little money. They are happy. (in spite of)
  In spite ....
3 My foot was injured. I managed to walk to the nearest village. (although)
  ....
4 I enjoyed the film. The story was silly. (in spite of)
  ....
5 We live in the same street. We hardly ever see each other. (despite)
  ....
6 I got very wet in the rain. I was only out for five minutes. (even though)
  ....

113.4 Use the words in brackets to make a sentence with **though** at the end.

1 The house isn't very nice. (like / garden) _I like the garden though._
2 It's warm today. (very windy) ....
3 We didn't like the food. (ate) ....
4 Liz is very nice. (don't like / husband) I ....

→ Additional exercise 32 (page 321)

A Study this example situation:

Your car should have a spare wheel because it is possible you will have a puncture.

Your car should have a spare wheel **in case** you have a puncture.

In case you have a puncture = because it is possible you will have a puncture.

Some more examples of **in case**:

- ☐ I'll leave my mobile phone switched on **in case Jane calls**. (= because it is possible she will call)
- ☐ I'll draw a map for you **in case you have difficulty finding our house**. (= because it is possible you will have difficulty)
- ☐ I'll remind them about the meeting **in case they've forgotten**. (= because it is possible they have forgotten)

We use **just in case** for a smaller possibility:

- ☐ I don't think it will rain, but I'll take an umbrella **just in case**. (= **just in case** it rains)

Do not use **will** after **in case**. Use a present tense for the future (see Unit 25):

- ☐ I'll leave my phone switched on **in case** Jane **calls**. (*not* in case Jane will call)

B **In case** is not the same as **if**. We use **in case** to say *why* somebody does (or doesn't do) something. You do something *now* **in case** something happens *later*.

Compare:

in case	if
☐ We'll buy some more food **in case** Tom comes. (= Perhaps Tom will come; we'll buy some more food now, whether he comes or not; then we'll *already* have the food *if* he comes.)	☐ We'll buy some more food **if** Tom comes. (= Perhaps Tom will come; if he comes, we'll buy some more food; if he doesn't come, we won't buy any more food.)
☐ I'll give you my phone number **in case** you need to contact me.	☐ You can phone me at the hotel **if** you need to contact me.
☐ You should insure your bike **in case** it is stolen.	☐ You should inform the police **if** your bike is stolen.

C You can use **in case** + *past* to say why somebody did something:

- ☐ I left my phone switched on **in case Jane called**. (= because it was possible that Jane would call)
- ☐ I drew a map for Sarah **in case she had difficulty finding the house**.
- ☐ We rang the doorbell again **in case they hadn't heard it the first time**.

D **In case of** is not the same as **in case**. **In case of** ... = if there is ... (especially on notices etc.):

- ☐ **In case of fire**, please leave the building as quickly as possible. (= if there is a fire)
- ☐ **In case of emergency**, telephone this number. (= if there is an emergency)

Exercises

114.1 Barbara is going for a long walk in the country. You think she should take:

~~some chocolate~~   **a map**   **an anorak**   **a camera**   **some water**

You think she should take these things because:

it's possible she'll get lost	~~she might get hungry~~
perhaps she'll be thirsty	maybe it will rain
she might want to take some photographs	

What do you say to Barbara? Write sentences with **in case**.

1   _Take some chocolate with you in case you get hungry._
2   Take ....
3   ....
4   ....
5   ....

114.2 What do you say in these situations? Use **in case**.

1   It's possible that Mary will need to contact you, so you give her your phone number.
You say: Here's my phone number _in case you need to contact me_ .
2   A friend of yours is going away for a long time. Maybe you won't see her again before she goes, so you decide to say goodbye now.
You say: I'll say goodbye now ....
3   You are shopping in a supermarket with a friend. You think you have everything you need, but perhaps you've forgotten something. Your friend has the list. You ask her to check it.
You say: Can you .... ?
4   You are giving a friend some advice about using a computer. You think he should back up (= *copy*) his files because the computer might crash (and he would lose all his data).
You say: You should back up ....

114.3 Write sentences with **in case**.

1   There was a possibility that Jane would call. So I left my phone switched on.
I left _my phone switched on in case Jane called_ .
2   Mike thought that he might forget the name of the book. So he wrote it down.
He wrote down ....
3   I thought my parents might be worried about me. So I phoned them.
I phoned ....
4   I sent an email to Liz, but she didn't reply. So I sent another email because perhaps she hadn't received the first one.
I sent ....
5   I met some people when I was on holiday in France. They said they might come to London one day. I live in London, so I gave them my address.
I gave ....

114.4 Put in **in case** or **if**.

1   I'll draw a map for you _in case_ you have difficulty finding our house.
2   You should tell the police _if_ you have any information about the crime.
3   I hope you'll come to London sometime. .... you come, you can stay with us.
4   This letter is for Susan. Can you give it to her .... you see her?
5   Write your name and address on your bag .... you lose it.
6   Go to the lost property office .... you lose your bag.
7   The burglar alarm will ring .... somebody tries to break into the house.
8   You should lock your bike to something .... somebody tries to steal it.
9   I was advised to get insurance .... I needed medical treatment while I was abroad.

→ Additional exercise 32 (page 321)

Unless   As long as   Provided/providing

A   Unless

Study this example situation:

The club is for members only.

You can't go in **unless you are a member**.

This means:

You can't go in *except if* you are a member.   *or*

You can go in *only if* you are a member.

Unless = except if.

Some more examples of **unless**:

- □ I'll see you tomorrow **unless I have to work late**. (= except if I have to work late)
- □ There are no buses to the beach. **Unless you have a car**, it's difficult to get there.
  (= except if you have a car)
- □ 'Shall I tell Liz what happened?' '**Not unless** she asks you.' (= only if she asks you)
- □ Sally hates complaining. She wouldn't complain about something **unless it was really bad**.
  (= except if it was really bad)
- □ We can take a taxi to the restaurant – **unless you'd prefer to walk**. (= except if you'd prefer to walk)

Instead of **unless** it is often possible to say **if ... not**:

- □ **Unless we leave now**, we'll be late. *or* **If we don't leave now**, we'll ...

B   As long as etc.

as long as *or* so long as
provided **(that)** *or* providing **(that)** } All these expressions mean 'if' or 'on condition that'.

For example:

- □ You can borrow my car { **as long as** / **so long as** } you promise not to drive too fast.

  (= you can borrow my car, but you must promise not to drive too fast – this is a condition)

- □ Travelling by car is convenient { **provided (that)** / **providing (that)** } you have somewhere to park.

  (= but only if you have somewhere to park)

- □ **Providing (that)** / **Provided (that)** } the room is clean, I don't mind which hotel we stay at.

  (= the room must be clean – otherwise I don't mind)

C

When you are talking about the future, do *not* use **will** after **unless / as long as / so long as / provided / providing**. Use a *present* tense (see Unit 25):

- □ I'm not going out **unless** it **stops** raining. (*not* unless it will stop)
- □ **Providing** the weather **is** good, we're going to have a picnic. (*not* providing it will be good)

115.1 Write a new sentence with the same meaning. Use **unless** in your sentence.

1 You must try a bit harder or you won't pass the exam.
   You won't pass the exam unless you try a bit harder.

2 Listen carefully or you won't know what to do.
   You won't know what to do ....

3 She must apologise to me or I'll never speak to her again.
   ....

4 You have to speak very slowly or he won't be able to understand you.
   ....

5 Business must improve soon, or the company will have to close.
   ....

115.2 Write sentences with **unless**.

1 The club isn't open to everyone. You are allowed in only if you're a member.
   You aren't allowed in the club unless you're a member.

2 I don't want to go to the party alone. I'm going only if you go too.
   I'm not going ....

3 Don't worry about the dog. It will attack you only if you move suddenly.
   The dog ....

4 Ben isn't very talkative. He'll speak to you only if you ask him something.
   Ben ....

5 Today is a public holiday. The doctor will see you only if it's an emergency.
   The doctor ....

115.3 Choose the correct word or expression for each sentence.

1 You can borrow my car <u>unless / as long as</u> you promise not to drive too fast. (<u>as long as</u> *is correct*)

2 I'm playing tennis tomorrow <u>unless / providing</u> it rains.

3 I'm playing tennis tomorrow <u>unless / providing</u> it doesn't rain.

4 I don't mind if you come home late <u>unless / as long as</u> you come in quietly.

5 I'm going now <u>unless / provided</u> you want me to stay.

6 I don't watch TV <u>unless / as long as</u> I've got nothing else to do.

7 Children are allowed to use the swimming pool <u>unless / provided</u> they are with an adult.

8 <u>Unless /provided</u> they are with an adult, children are not allowed to use the swimming pool.

9 We can sit here in the corner <u>unless / as long as</u> you'd rather sit over there by the window.

10 A: Our holiday cost a lot of money.
   B: Did it? Well, that doesn't matter <u>unless / as long as</u> you enjoyed yourselves.

115.4 Use your own ideas to complete these sentences.

1 We'll be late unless _we get a taxi_ .

2 I like hot weather as long as ....

3 It takes Kate about 20 minutes to drive to work provided ....

4 I don't mind walking home as long as ....

5 I like to walk to work in the morning unless ....

6 We can meet tomorrow unless ....

7 You can borrow the money providing ....

8 You won't achieve anything unless ....

Unit 116

As (As I walked along the street ... / As I was hungry ...)

A

As = at the same time as

You can use **as** when two things happen at the same time:
- □ We all waved goodbye to Liz **as** she drove away.
  (We **waved** and she **drove** away at the same time)
- □ I watched her **as** she opened the letter.
- □ **As** I walked along the street, I looked in the shop windows.
- □ Can you turn off the light **as** you go out, please?

Bye!

LIZ

Or you can say that something happened **as you were doing** something else (in the middle of doing something else):
- □ Kate slipped **as she was getting off** the bus.
- □ We met Paul **as we were leaving** the hotel.

For the *past continuous* (**was getting / were going** etc.), see Unit 6.

You can also use **just as** (= exactly at that moment):
- □ **Just as** I sat down, the phone rang.
- □ I had to leave **just as** the conversation was getting interesting.

We also use **as** when two things happen together in a longer period of time:
- □ **As** the day went on, the weather got worse.
- □ I began to enjoy the job more **as** I got used to it.

the day went on

the weather got worse

Compare **as** and **when**:

We use **as** only if two things happen at the same time. □ **As we walked home**, we talked about what we would have for dinner. (= at the same time)	Use **when** (*not* as) if one thing happens after another. □ **When we got home**, we started cooking the dinner. (*not* As we got home)

B

As = because

As also means 'because':
- □ **As I was hungry**, I decided to find somewhere to eat. (= because I was hungry)
- □ **As it was a public holiday** last Thursday, most of the shops were shut.
  (= because it was a public holiday)
- □ **As we have plenty of time** before our flight, let's go and have a coffee.
- □ Yesterday we watched television all evening **as we didn't have anything better to do.**
- □ **As I don't often watch television any more**, I've decided to give my TV set to a friend of mine.

You can also use **since** in this way:
- □ **Since** we have plenty of time, let's go and have a coffee.

Compare **as** and **when**:

□ I couldn't contact David **as he was away on holiday** and he doesn't have a mobile phone. (= because he was away)	□ David's passport was stolen **when he was away on holiday.** (= during the time he was away)
□ **As they lived near us**, we used to see them quite often. (= because they lived near us)	□ **When they lived near us**, we used to see them quite often. (= at the time they lived near us)

As ... as → Unit 107   **Like and as** → Unit 117   **As if** → Unit 118

116.1 (Section A) Use **as** to join sentences from the boxes.

1 ~~we all waved goodbye to Liz~~
2 we all smiled
3 I burnt myself
4 the crowd cheered
5 a dog ran out in front of the car

we were driving along the road
I was taking a hot dish out of the oven
~~she drove away~~
we posed for the photograph
the two teams ran onto the field

1 We all waved goodbye to Liz as she drove away. ....
2 ....
3 ....
4 ....
5 ....

116.2 (Section B) Join sentences from the boxes. Begin each sentence with **as**.

1 ~~it was a public holiday~~
2 it was a nice day
3 we didn't want to wake anybody up
4 the door was open
5 none of us had a watch

I went in
we came in very quietly
~~most of the shops were shut~~
we didn't know what time it was
we went for a walk by the sea

1 As it was a public holiday, most of the shops were shut. ....
2 ....
3 ....
4 ....
5 ....

116.3 What does **as** mean in these sentences?

	because	at the same time as
1 **As** they live near me, I see them quite often.	✓	
2 Kate slipped **as** she was getting off the bus.		✓
3 **As** I was tired, I went to bed early.		
4 Unfortunately, **as** I was parking the car, I hit the car behind.		
5 **As** we climbed the hill, we got more and more tired.		
6 We decided to go out to eat **as** we had no food at home.		
7 **As** we don't use the car very often, we've decided to sell it.		

116.4 In some of these sentences, you need **when** (not **as**). Correct the sentences where necessary.

1 Julia got married <u>as she was 22</u>.   when she was 22
2 As the day went on, the weather got worse.   OK
3 He dropped the glass as he was taking it out of the cupboard. ....
4 My camera was stolen as I was asleep on the beach. ....
5 As I left school, I went to work in a shop. ....
6 The train slowed down as it approached the station. ....
7 I used to live near the sea as I was a child. ....

116.5 Use your own ideas to complete these sentences.

1 I saw you as ....
2 It started to rain just as ....
3 As I didn't have enough money for a taxi, ...
4 Just as I took the photograph, ...

→ Additional exercise 32 **(page 321)**   **233**

Like and as

A   Like = 'similar to', 'the same as'. You cannot use **as** in this way:

- What a beautiful house! It's **like a palace**. (*not* as a palace)
- 'What does Sandra do?' 'She's a teacher, **like me**.' (*not* as me)
- Be careful! The floor has been polished. It's **like walking on ice**. (*not* as walking)
- It's raining again. I hate weather **like this**. (*not* as this)

In these sentences, **like** is a *preposition*. So it is followed by a *noun* (like **a palace**), a *pronoun* (like **me** / like **this**) or **-ing** (like walk**ing**).

You can also say '… **like** (somebody/something) do**ing** something':

- 'What's that noise?' 'It sounds **like a baby** crying.'

B   Sometimes **like** = for example:

- Some sports, **like motor-racing**, can be dangerous.

You can also use **such as** (= for example):

- Some sports, **such as** motor-racing, can be dangerous.

C   As = in the same way as, or in the same condition as. We use **as** before *subject + verb*:

- I didn't move anything. I left everything **as it was**.
- You should have done it **as I showed you**.

Like is also possible in informal spoken English:

- I left everything **like it was**.

Compare **as** and **like**:

- You should have done it **as I showed you**. (*or* **like I showed you**)
- You should have done it **like this**. (*not* as this)

Note that we say **as usual** / **as always**:

- You're late **as usual**.
- **As always**, Nick was the first to complain.

D   Sometimes **as** (+ *subject + verb*) has other meanings. For example, after **do**:

- You can do **as you like**. (= do what you like)
- They did **as they promised**. (= They did what they promised.)

We also say **as you know** / **as I said** / **as she expected** / **as I thought** etc. :

- **As you know**, it's Emma's birthday next week. (= you know this already)
- Andy failed his driving test, **as he expected**. (= he expected this before)

Like is not usual in these expressions, except with **say** (**like I said**):

- **As I said** yesterday, I'm sure we can solve the problem. *or* **Like I said** yesterday …

E   As can also be a *preposition*, but the meaning is different from **like**. Compare:

□ Sue Casey is the manager of a company. **As the manager**, she has to make many important decisions. (**As the manager** = in her position as the manager.)	□ Mary Stone is the assistant manager. **Like the manager** (Sue Casey), she also has to make important decisions. (**Like the manager** = similar to the manager)

As (*preposition*) = in the position of, in the form of etc. :

- A few years ago I worked **as a taxi driver**. (*not* like a taxi driver)
- We haven't got a car, so we use the garage **as a workshop**.
- Many words, for example 'work' and 'rain', can be used **as verbs or nouns**.
- London is fine **as a place to visit**, but I wouldn't like to live there.
- The news of the tragedy came **as a great shock**.

Exercises

117.1 In some of these sentences, you need **like** (not **as**). Correct the sentences where necessary.

1 It's raining again. I hate weather <u>as this</u>.   <u>weather like this</u>
2 Andy failed his driving test, as he expected.   <u>OK</u>
3 Do you think Caroline looks as her mother?
4 Tim gets on my nerves. I can't stand people as him.
5 Why didn't you do it as I told you to do it?
6 Brian is a student, as most of his friends.
7 You never listen. Talking to you is as talking to the wall.
8 As I said yesterday, I'm thinking of changing my job.
9 Tom's idea seems a good one. Let's do as he suggests.
10 I'll phone you tomorrow as usual, OK?
11 Suddenly there was a terrible noise. It was as a bomb exploding.
12 She's a very good swimmer. She swims as a fish.

117.2 Complete the sentences using **like** or **as** + the following:

a beginner	blocks of ice	~~a palace~~	a birthday present
a child	a church	winter	a tourist guide

1 This house is beautiful. It's _like a palace_ .
2 My feet are really cold. They're _____ .
3 I've been playing tennis for years, but I still play _____ .
4 Marion once had a part-time job _____ .
5 I wonder what that building with the tower is. It looks _____ .
6 My brother gave me this watch _____ a long time ago.
7 It's very cold for the middle of summer. It's _____ .
8 He's 22 years old, but he sometimes behaves _____ .

117.3 Put in **like** or **as**. Sometimes either word is possible.

1 We heard a noise ___like___ a baby crying.
2 Your English is very fluent. I wish I could speak _____ you.
3 Don't take my advice if you don't want to. You can do _____ you like.
4 You waste too much time doing things _____ sitting in cafés all day.
5 I wish I had a car _____ yours.
6 You don't need to change your clothes. You can go out _____ you are.
7 My neighbour's house is full of lots of interesting things. It's _____ a museum.
8 We saw Kevin last night. He was very cheerful, _____ always.
9 Sally has been working _____ a waitress for the last two months.
10 While we were on holiday, we spent most of our time doing energetic things _____ sailing, water skiing and swimming.
11 You're different from the other people I know. I don't know anyone _____ you.
12 We don't need all the bedrooms in the house, so we use one of them _____ a study.
13 The news that Sue and Gary were getting married came _____ a complete surprise to me.
14 _____ her father, Catherine has a very good voice.
15 At the moment I've got a temporary job in a bookshop. It's OK _____ a temporary job, but I wouldn't like to do it permanently.
16 _____ you can imagine, we were very tired after such a long journey.
17 This tea is awful. It tastes _____ water.
18 I think I prefer this room _____ it was, before we decorated it.

As if / as though / like

A
You can use **as if** or **as though** to say how somebody or something **looks/sounds/feels**:
  □ That house **looks as if** it's going to fall down.
  □ Helen **sounded as if** she had a cold, didn't she?
  □ I've just come back from holiday, but I feel very
     tired. I don't **feel as if** I've just had a holiday.

You can use **as though** in all these examples:
  □ I don't feel **as though** I've just had a holiday.

In informal spoken English you can also use **like**:
  □ That house **looks like** it's going to fall down.

Compare:
  □ You look **tired**. (look + *adjective*)
     You look **as if you haven't slept**. (look as if + *subject* + *verb*)

B
You can say **It looks as if …** / **It sounds as if …** :
  □ Sandra is very late, isn't she? **It looks
     as if** she isn't coming.
  □ We took an umbrella because **it looked
     as if** it was going to rain.
  □ Do you hear that music next door? **It
     sounds as if** they are having a party.

> It sounds as if they're having a party next door.

You can also use **as though** or **like**:
  □ **It looks as though** she isn't coming. *or*
     It looks like she isn't coming.

C
You can use **as if** or **as though** with other verbs to say how somebody does something:
  □ He ran **as if he was running for his life**.
  □ After the interruption, the speaker went on talking **as if nothing had happened**.
  □ When I told them my plan, they looked at me **as though I was mad**.

In informal spoken English, you can also use **like** in these examples.

D
After **as if** (or **as though**), we sometimes use the *past* when we are talking about the *present*.
For example:
  □ I don't like Tim. He talks as if he **knew** everything.

The meaning is not past in this sentence. We use the past (as if he **knew**) because the idea is not
real: Tim does *not* know everything. We use the past in the same way in **if** sentences and after
wish (see Unit 39).
Some more examples:
  □ She's always asking me to do things for her – **as if I didn't** have enough to do already.
     (I *do* have enough to do)
  □ Gary's only 40. Why do you talk about him **as if he was** an old man? (he isn't an
     old man)

When you use the past in this way, you can use **were** instead of **was**:
  □ Why do you talk about him **as if he were** (*or* **was**) an old man?
  □ They treat me **as if I were** (*or* **was**) their own son. (I'm not their son)

If I was/were → Unit 39C   **Look/sound** etc. + adjective → Unit 99C   **Like and as** → Unit 117

Exercises

118.1 What do you say in these situations? Use **look/sound/feel + as if** ... . Use the words in brackets to make your sentence.

1 You meet Bill. He has a black eye and some plasters on his face. (be / a fight)
You say to him: <u>You look as if you've been in a fight.</u>
2 Christine comes into the room. She looks absolutely terrified. (see / a ghost)
You say to her: What's the matter? You ....
3 Joe is on holiday. He's talking to you on the phone and sounds very happy. (enjoy / yourself)
You say to him: You ....
4 You have just run one kilometre. You are absolutely exhausted. (run / a marathon)
You say to a friend: I ....

118.2 Make sentences beginning **It looks as if** ... **/ It sounds as if** ... .

| you should see a doctor | there's been an accident | they are having an argument |
| it's going to rain | ~~she isn't coming~~ | we'll have to walk |

1 Sandra said she would be here an hour ago.
You say: <u>It looks as if she isn't coming.</u>
2 The sky is full of black clouds.
You say: It ....
3 You hear two people shouting at each other next door.
You say: ....
4 You see an ambulance, some policemen and two damaged cars at the side of the road.
You say: ....
5 You and a friend have just missed the last bus home.
You say: ....
6 Dave isn't feeling well. He tells you all about it.
You say: ....

118.3 Complete the sentences with **as if**. Choose from the box, putting the verbs in the correct form.

she / enjoy / it	I / go / be sick	he / not / eat / for a week
~~he / need / a good rest~~	she / hurt / her leg	he / mean / what he / say
I / not / exist	she / not / want / come	

1 Mark looks very tired. He looks <u>as if he needs a good rest</u> .
2 I don't think Paul was joking. He looked ....
3 What's the matter with Liz? She's walking ....
4 Peter was extremely hungry and ate his dinner very quickly.
He ate ....
5 Caroline had a bored expression on her face during the concert.
She didn't look ....
6 I've just eaten too many chocolates. Now I don't feel well.
I feel ....
7 I phoned Liz and invited her to the party, but she wasn't very enthusiastic about it.
She sounded ....
8 I went into the office, but nobody spoke to me or looked at me.
Everybody ignored me ....

118.4 These sentences are like the ones in Section D. Complete each sentence using **as if**.

1 Brian is a terrible driver. He drives <u>as if he were</u> the only driver on the road.
2 I'm 20 years old, so please don't talk to me .... I .... a child.
3 Steve has never met Nicola, but he talks about her .... his best friend.
4 It was a long time ago that we first met, but I remember it .... yesterday.

For, during and while

For and **during**

We use **for** + a period of time to say how long something goes on:

    for **two hours**   for a **week**   for **ages**

- ☐ We watched television **for two hours** last night.
- ☐ Diane is going away **for a week** in September.
- ☐ Where have you been? I've been waiting **for ages**.
- ☐ Are you going away **for the weekend?**

We use **during** + *noun* to say when something happens (*not* how long):

    during **the film**   during **our holiday**   during **the night**

- ☐ I fell asleep **during the film**.
- ☐ We met some really nice people **during our holiday**.
- ☐ The ground is wet. It must have rained **during the night**.

With 'time words' (for example: **the morning / the afternoon / the summer**), you can usually say **in** or **during**:

- ☐ It must have rained **in the night**. (*or* **during the night**)
- ☐ I'll phone you sometime **during the afternoon**. (*or* **in the afternoon**)

You cannot use **during** to say how long something goes on:

- ☐ It rained **for** three days without stopping. (*not* during three days)

Compare **during** and **for**:

- ☐ I fell asleep **during the film**. I was asleep **for half an hour**.

During and **while**

Compare:

We use **during** + *noun*:	We use **while** + *subject* + *verb*:

☐ I fell asleep **during the film**.
      └*noun*┘
	☐ I fell asleep **while I was watching TV**.
	        └*subject + verb*┘

☐ We met a lot of interesting people **during our holiday**.	☐ We met a lot of interesting people **while we were on holiday**.
☐ Robert suddenly began to feel ill **during the exam**.	☐ Robert suddenly began to feel ill **while he was doing the exam**.

Some more examples of **while**:

- ☐ We saw Clare **while we were waiting** for the bus.
- ☐ **While you were** out, there was a phone call for you.
- ☐ Chris read a book **while I watched** television.

When you are talking about the future, use the *present* (*not* will) after **while**:

- ☐ I'll be in London next week. I hope to see Tom **while I'm** there. (*not* while I will be there)
- ☐ What are you going to do **while** you **are** waiting? (*not* while you will be waiting)

See also Unit 25.

119.1 Put in **for** or **during**.

1 It rained ....*for*.... three days without stopping.
2 I fell asleep ....*during*.... the film.
3 I went to the theatre last night. I met Sue .... the interval.
4 Martin hasn't lived in Britain all his life. He lived in Brazil .... four years.
5 Production at the factory was seriously affected .... the strike.
6 I felt really ill last week. I could hardly eat anything .... three days.
7 I waited for you .... half an hour and decided that you weren't coming.
8 Sarah was very angry with me. She didn't speak to me .... a week.
9 We usually go out at weekends, but we don't often go out .... the week.
10 Jack started a new job a few weeks ago. Before that he was out of work .... six months.
11 I need a change. I think I'll go away .... a few days.
12 The president gave a long speech. She spoke .... two hours.
13 We were hungry when we arrived. We hadn't had anything to eat .... the journey.
14 We were hungry when we arrived. We hadn't had anything to eat .... eight hours.

119.2 Put in **during** or **while**.

1 We met a lot of interesting people ....*while*.... we were on holiday.
2 We met a lot of interesting people ....*during*.... our holiday.
3 I met Mike .... I was shopping.
4 .... I was on holiday, I didn't read any newspapers or watch TV.
5 .... our stay in Paris, we visited a lot of museums and galleries.
6 The phone rang three times .... we were having dinner.
7 The phone rang three times .... the night.
8 I had been away for many years. .... that time, many things had changed.
9 What did they say about me .... I was out of the room?
10 I went out for dinner last night. Unfortunately I began to feel ill .... the meal and had to go home.
11 Please don't interrupt me .... I'm speaking.
12 There were many interruptions .... the president's speech.
13 Can you lay the table .... I get the dinner ready?
14 We were hungry when we arrived. We hadn't had anything to eat .... we were travelling.

119.3 Use your own ideas to complete these sentences.

1 I fell asleep while ....*I was watching television.*....
2 I fell asleep during ....*the film.*....
3 I hurt my arm while ....
4 Can you wait here while ....
5 Most of the students looked bored during ....
6 I was asked a lot of questions during ....
7 Don't open the car door while ....
8 The lights suddenly went out while ....
9 It started to rain during ....
10 It started to rain while ....

→ Additional exercise 33 (page 321)

A   By (+ a time) = not later than:

- ☐ I sent the letter to them today, so they should receive it **by Monday**. (= on or before Monday, not later than Monday)
- ☐ We'd better hurry. We have to be home **by 5 o'clock**. (= at or before 5 o'clock, not later than 5 o'clock)
- ☐ Where's Sarah? She should be here **by now**. (= now or before now – so she should have already arrived)

This milk has to be used **by 14 August**.

USE BY 14 AUGUST

B   We use **until** (*or* **till**) to say *how long* a situation continues:

- ☐ 'Shall we go now?'   'No, let's **wait until** (*or* **till**) it stops raining.
- ☐ I couldn't get up this morning. { **I stayed in bed until** half past ten. / **I didn't** get up **until** half past ten. }

Compare **until** and **by**:

Something *continues* **until** a time in the future:	Something *happens* **by** a time in the future:
☐ David **will be away until** Monday. (so he'll be back *on* Monday)	☐ David **will be back by** Monday. (= he'll be back not later than Monday)
☐ I'll **be working until** 11.30. (so I'll stop working *at* 11.30)	☐ I'll **have finished my work by** 11.30. (= I'll finish my work not later than 11.30.)

C   You can say '**by the time** something happens'. Study these examples:

- ☐ It's too late to go to the bank now. **By the time we get there**, it will be closed. (= the bank will close between now and the time we get there)
- ☐ *(from a postcard)* Our holiday ends tomorrow. So **by the time you receive this postcard**, I'll be back home. (= I will arrive home between tomorrow and the time you receive this postcard)
- ☐ Hurry up! **By the time we get to the cinema**, the film will already have started.

You can say '**by the time** something happened' (for the past):

- ☐ Karen's car broke down on the way to the party last night. **By the time she arrived**, most of the other guests had left. (= it took her a long time to get to the party and most of the guests left during this time)
- ☐ I had a lot of work to do yesterday evening. I was very tired **by the time I finished**. (= it took me a long time to do the work, and I became more and more tired during this time)
- ☐ We went to the cinema last night. It took us a long time to find somewhere to park the car. **By the time we got to the cinema**, the film had already started.

Also **by then** *or* **by that time**:

- ☐ Karen finally arrived at the party at midnight, but **by then** (*or* **by that time**), most of the guests had left.

Exercises

120.1 Make sentences with **by**.

1 We have to be home not later than 5 o'clock.
    <u>We have to be home by 5 o'clock.</u>
2 I have to be at the airport not later than 8.30.
    I have to be at the airport ....
3 Let me know not later than Saturday whether you can come to the party.
    Let me know ....
4 Please make sure that you're here not later than 2 o'clock.
    Please make sure that ....
5 If we leave now, we should arrive not later than lunchtime.
    If we leave now, ...

120.2 Put in **by** or **until**.

1 Steve has gone away. He'll be away ......<u>until</u>...... Monday.
2 Sorry, but I must go. I have to be home .... 5 o'clock.
3 I've been offered a job. I haven't decided yet whether to accept it or not. I have to decide
    .... Friday.
4 I think I'll wait .... Thursday before making a decision.
5 It's too late to go shopping. The shops are open only .... 5.30. They'll be closed
    .... now.
6 I'd better pay the phone bill. It has to be paid .... tomorrow.
7 Don't pay the bill today. Wait .... tomorrow.
8 A: Have you finished redecorating your house?
    B: Not yet. We hope to finish .... the end of the week.
9 A: I'm going out now. I'll be back at about 10.30. Will you still be here?
    B: I don't think so. I'll probably have gone out .... then.
10 I'm moving into my new flat next week. I'm staying with a friend .... then.
11 I've got a lot of work to do. .... the time I finish, it will be time to go to bed.
12 If you want to take part in the competition, you have to apply .... 3 April.

120.3 Use your own ideas to complete these sentences. Use **by** or **until**.

1 David is away at the moment. He'll be away <u>until Monday</u> .
2 David is away at the moment. He'll be back <u>by Monday</u> .
3 I'm just going out. I won't be very long. Wait here ....
4 I'm going out to buy a few things. It's 4.30 now. I won't be long. I'll be back ....
5 If you want to apply for the job, your application must be received ....
6 Last night I watched TV ....

120.4 Read the situations and complete the sentences using **By the time** ... .

1 I was invited to a party, but I got there much later than I intended.
    <u>By the time I got to the party</u> , most of the other guests had left.
2 I intended to catch a train, but it took me longer than expected to get to the station.
    .... , my train had already left.
3 I wanted to go shopping after finishing my work. But I finished much later than expected.
    .... , it was too late to go shopping.
4 I saw two men who looked as if they were trying to steal a car. I called the police, but it was
    some time before they arrived.
    .... , the two men had disappeared.
5 We climbed a mountain and it took us a very long time to get to the top. There wasn't
    much time to enjoy the view.
    .... , we had to come down again.

→ Additional exercise 33 (page 321)

A Compare **at**, **on** and **in**:

  □ They arrived **at 5 o'clock**.
  □ They arrived **on Friday**.
  □ They arrived **in October**. / They arrived **in 1968**.

We use:

at for the time of day
at five o'clock   **at** 11.45   **at** midnight   **at** lunchtime   **at** sunset etc.

on for days and dates
on Friday / **on** Fridays   **on** 16 May 1999   **on** Christmas Day   **on** my birthday

in for longer periods (for example: months/years/seasons)
in October   **in** 1988   **in** the 18th century   **in** the past
in (the) winter   **in** the 1990s   **in** the Middle Ages   **in** (the) future

B We use **at** in these expressions:

at night	□ I don't like going out **at night**.
at the weekend / **at weekends**	□ Will you be here **at the weekend**?
at Christmas	□ Do you give each other presents **at Christmas**?
at the moment / **at present**	□ Mr Benn is busy **at the moment** / **at present**.
at the same time	□ Emily and I arrived **at the same time**.

C We say:

in the morning(s)	*but*	**on Friday morning(s)**
in the afternoon(s)		**on Sunday afternoon(s)**
in the evening(s)		**on Monday evening(s)** etc.

  □ I'll see you **in the morning**.   □ I'll see you **on Friday morning**.
  □ Do you work **in the evenings**?   □ Do you work **on Saturday evenings**?

D We do not use **at/on/in** before **last/next/this/every**:

  □ I'll see you **next Friday**. (*not* on next Friday)
  □ They got married **last March**.

In spoken English we often leave out **on** before days (**Sunday/Monday** etc.). So you can say:

  □ I'll see you **on Friday**. *or* I'll see you **Friday**.
  □ I don't go out **on Monday mornings**. *or* I don't go out **Monday mornings**.

E **In a few minutes** / **in six months** etc.

  □ The train will be leaving **in a few minutes**. (= a few minutes from now)
  □ Andy has gone away. He'll be back **in a week**. (= a week from now)
  □ She'll be here **in a moment**. (= a moment from now)

You can also say 'in six months' **time**', 'in a week's **time**' etc. :

  □ They're getting married **in six months' time**. *or* … **in six months**.

We also use **in** … to say how long it takes to do something:

  □ I learnt to drive **in four weeks**. (= it took me four weeks to learn)

On/in time, at/in the end → Unit 122   **In/at/on (position)** → Units 123–125
In/at/on (other uses) → Unit 127   American English → Appendix 7

242

121.1 Complete the sentences. Use **at**, **on** or **in** + the following:

the evening	about 20 minutes	~~1492~~	the same time
the moment	21 July 1969	the 1920s	night
Saturdays	the Middle Ages	11 seconds	

1   Columbus made his first voyage from Europe to America __in 1492_____ .
2   If the sky is clear, you can see the stars _____ .
3   After working hard during the day, I like to relax _____ .
4   Neil Armstrong was the first man to walk on the moon _____ .
5   It's difficult to listen if everyone is speaking _____ .
6   Jazz became popular in the United States _____ .
7   I'm just going out to the shop. I'll be back _____ ,
8   *(on the phone)* 'Can I speak to Dan?'   'I'm afraid he's not here _____ .'
9   Many of Europe's great cathedrals were built _____ .
10 Ben is a very fast runner. He can run 100 metres _____ .
11 Liz works from Monday to Friday. Sometimes she also works _____ .

121.2 Put in **at**, **on** or **in**.

1   Mozart was born in Salzburg __in__ 1756.
2   I haven't seen Kate for a few days. I last saw her _____ Tuesday.
3   The price of electricity is going up _____ October.
4   _____ weekends, we often go for long walks in the country.
5   I've been invited to a wedding _____ 14 February.
6   Jonathan is 63. He'll be retiring from his job _____ two years' time.
7   I'm busy just now, but I'll be with you _____ a moment.
8   Jenny's brother is an engineer, but he doesn't have a job _____ the moment.
9   There are usually a lot of parties _____ New Year's Eve.
10 I don't like driving _____ night.
11 My car is being repaired at the garage. It will be ready _____ two hours.
12 The telephone and the doorbell rang _____ the same time.
13 Mary and David always go out for dinner _____ their wedding anniversary.
14 It was a short book and easy to read. I read it _____ a day.
15 _____ Saturday night I went to bed _____ midnight.
16 We travelled overnight to Paris and arrived _____ 5 o'clock _____ the morning.
17 The course begins _____ 7 January and ends sometime _____ April.
18 I might not be at home _____ Tuesday morning, but I'll be there _____ the afternoon.

121.3 Which is correct: a, b, or both of them?

1 a I'll see you on Friday.	b I'll see you Friday.	__both__
2 a I'll see you on next Friday.	b I'll see you next Friday.	__b__
3 a Paul got married in April.	b Paul got married April.	_____
4 a They never go out on Sunday evenings.	b They never go out Sunday evenings.	_____
5 a We often have a short holiday on Christmas.	b We often have a short holiday at Christmas.	_____
6 a What are you doing the weekend?	b What are you doing at the weekend?	_____
7 a Will you be here on Tuesday?	b Will you be here Tuesday?	_____
8 a We were ill at the same time.	b We were ill in the same time.	_____
9 a Sue got married at 18 May 1996.	b Sue got married on 18 May 1996.	_____
10 a He left school last June.	b He left school in last June.	_____

→ Additional exercise 33 **(page 321)**   **243**

On time and in time
At the end and in the end

A On time and in time

On time = punctual, not late. If something happens **on time**, it happens at the time which was planned:

- ☐ The 11.45 train left **on time**. (= it left at 11.45)
- ☐ 'I'll meet you at 7.30.' 'OK, but please be **on time**.' (= don't be late, be there at 7.30)
- ☐ The conference was well-organised. Everything began and finished **on time**.

The opposite of **on time** is **late**:

- ☐ Be **on time**. Don't be **late**.

In time (for something / to do something) = soon enough:

- ☐ Will you be home **in time** for dinner? (= soon enough for dinner)
- ☐ I've sent Emma a birthday present. I hope it arrives **in time** (for her birthday). (= on or before her birthday)
- ☐ I'm in a hurry. I want to be home **in time to see** the game on television. (= soon enough to see the game)

The opposite of **in time** is **too late**:

- ☐ I got home **too late** to see the game on television.

You can say **just in time** (= almost too late):

- ☐ We got to the station **just in time** for our train.
- ☐ A child ran into the road in front of the car – I managed to stop **just in time**.

B At the end and in the end

At the end (of something) = at the time when something ends. For example:

at the end of the month	at the end of January	at the end of the game
at the end of the film	at the end of the course	at the end of the concert

- ☐ I'm going away **at the end of January** / **at the end of the month**.
- ☐ **At the end of the concert**, there was great applause.
- ☐ The players shook hands **at the end of the game**.

You cannot say '**in the end of** …'. So you cannot say 'in the end of January' or 'in the end of the concert'.

The opposite of **at the end** (of …) is **at the beginning** (of …):

- ☐ I'm going away **at the beginning of January**. (*not* in the beginning)

In the end = finally.

We use **in the end** when we say what the final result of a situation was:

- ☐ We had a lot of problems with our car. We sold it **in the end**. (= finally we sold it)
- ☐ He got more and more angry. **In the end** he just walked out of the room.
- ☐ Alan couldn't decide where to go for his holidays. He didn't go anywhere **in the end**. (*not* at the end)

The opposite of **in the end** is usually **at first**:

- ☐ **At first** we didn't get on very well, but **in the end** we became good friends.

At/on/in (time) → Unit 121

122.1 Complete the sentences with **on time** or **in time**.

1 The bus was late this morning, but it's usually ....*on time*..... .
2 The film was supposed to start at 8.30, but it didn't begin ....
3 I like to get up .... to have a big breakfast before going to work.
4 We want to start the meeting .... , so please don't be late.
5 I've just washed this shirt. I want to wear it this evening, so I hope it will be dry

   ....

6 The train service isn't very good. The trains are rarely ....
7 I nearly missed my flight this morning. I got to the airport just ....
8 I nearly forgot that it was Joe's birthday. Fortunately I remembered ....
9 Why are you never .... ? You always keep everybody waiting.

122.2 Read the situations and make sentences using **just in time**.

1 A child ran into the road in front of your car. You saw the child at the last moment.
   (manage / stop) ....*I managed to stop just in time.*....
2 You were walking home. Just after you got home, it started to rain very heavily.
   (get / home) I ....
3 Tim was going to sit on the chair you had just painted. You said, 'Don't sit on that chair!',
   so he didn't. (stop / him) I ....
4 You and a friend went to the cinema. You were late and you thought you would miss the
   beginning of the film. But the film began just as you sat down in the cinema.
   (get / cinema / beginning of the film)
   We ....

122.3 Complete the sentences using **at the end** + the following:

the course	~~the game~~	the interview	the month	the race

1 The players shook hands ....*at the end of the game*.... .
2 I usually get paid ....
3 The students had a party ....
4 Two of the runners collapsed ....
5 To my surprise, I was offered the job ....

122.4 Write sentences with **In the end**. Use the verb in brackets.

1 We had a lot of problems with our car. (sell) ....*In the end we sold it.*....
2 Judy got more and more fed up with her job.
   (resign) ....
3 I tried to learn German, but I found it too difficult.
   (give up) ....
4 We couldn't decide whether to go to the party or not.
   (not / go) ....

122.5 Put in **at** or **in**.

1 I'm going away ....*at*.... the end of the month.
2 It took me a long time to find a job. .... the end I got a job in a hotel.
3 Are you going away .... the beginning of August or .... the end?
4 I couldn't decide what to buy Laura for her birthday. I didn't buy her anything ....
   the end.
5 We waited ages for a taxi. We gave up .... the end and walked home.
6 I'll be moving to a new address .... the end of September.
7 We had a few problems at first, but .... the end everything was OK.
8 I'm going away .... the end of this week.
9 A: I didn't know what to do.
   B: Yes, you were in a difficult position. What did you do .... the end?

A **In**

in a room
in a building
in a box

in a garden
in a town/country
in the city centre

in a pool
in the sea
in a river

- ☐ There's no-one **in the room** / **in the building** / **in the garden**.
- ☐ What have you got **in your hand** / **in your mouth**?
- ☐ When we were **in Italy**, we spent a few days **in Venice**.
- ☐ I have a friend who lives **in a small village in the mountains**.
- ☐ There were some people swimming **in the pool** / **in the sea** / **in the river**.

B **At**

at the bus stop
at the door
at the window

at the roundabout

at reception

- ☐ Do you know that man standing **at the door** / **at the window**?
- ☐ Turn left **at the traffic lights** / **at the church** / **at the roundabout**.
- ☐ We have to get off the bus **at the next stop**.
- ☐ When you leave the hotel, please leave your key **at reception**. (= at the reception desk)

C **On**

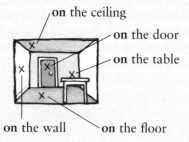

on the ceiling
on the door
on the table
on the wall
on the floor

on her nose

on a page

on an island

- ☐ I sat **on the floor** / **on the ground** / **on the grass** / **on the beach** / **on a chair**.
- ☐ There's a dirty mark **on the wall** / **on the ceiling** / **on your nose** / **on your shirt**.
- ☐ Have you seen the notice **on the notice board** / **on the door**?
- ☐ You'll find details of TV programmes **on page seven** (of the newspaper).
- ☐ The hotel is **on a small island** in the middle of the lake.

D Compare **in** and **at**:

- ☐ There were a lot of people **in the shop**. It was very crowded.
  Go along this road, then turn left **at the shop**.
- ☐ I'll meet you **in the hotel lobby**.
  I'll meet you **at the entrance to the hotel**.

Compare **in** and **on**:

- ☐ There is some water **in the bottle**.
  There is a label **on the bottle**.

Compare **at** and **on**:

- ☐ There is somebody **at the door**. Shall I go and see who it is?
  There is a notice **on the door**. It says 'Do not disturb'.

in the bottle

on the bottle

123.1 Answer the questions about the pictures. Use **in**, **at** or **on** with the words below the pictures.

1 (bottle)	2 (arm)	3 (traffic lights)	4 (door)
5 (wall)	6 (Paris)	7 (gate)	8 (beach)

1 Where's the label? ___On the bottle.___
2 Where's the fly? _____
3 Where is the car waiting? _____
4 a Where's the notice? _____
    b Where's the key? _____
5 Where are the shelves? _____
6 Where's the Eiffel Tower? _____
7 a Where's the man standing? _____
    b Where's the bird? _____
8 Where are the children playing? _____

123.2 Complete the sentences. Use **in**, **at** or **on** + the following:

the window	your coffee	the mountains	that tree
my guitar	~~the river~~	the island	the next garage

1 Look at those people swimming ___in the river___ .
2 One of the strings _____ is broken.
3 There's something wrong with the car. We'd better stop _____ .
4 Would you like sugar _____ ?
5 The leaves _____ are a beautiful colour.
6 Last year we had a wonderful skiing holiday _____ .
7 There's nobody living _____ . It's uninhabited.
8 He spends most of the day sitting _____ and looking outside.

123.3 Complete the sentences with **in**, **at** or **on**.

1 There was a long queue of people ___at___ the bus stop.
2 Nicola was wearing a silver ring _____ her little finger.
3 There was an accident _____ the crossroads this morning.
4 I wasn't sure whether I had come to the right office. There was no name _____ the door.
5 There are some beautiful trees _____ the park.
6 You'll find the sports results _____ the back page of the newspaper.
7 I wouldn't like an office job. I couldn't spend the whole day sitting _____ a desk.
8 My brother lives _____ a small village _____ the south-west of England.
9 The man the police are looking for has a scar _____ his right cheek.
10 The headquarters of the company are _____ Milan.
11 I like that picture hanging _____ the wall _____ the kitchen.
12 If you come here by bus, get off _____ the stop after the traffic lights.

→ Additional exercise 34 (page 322)   **247**

In/at/on (position) 2

A

We say that somebody/something is:

in a line / in a row / in a queue	in bed
in the sky / in the world	in the country / in the countryside
in an office / in a department	in a photograph / in a picture
in a book / in a (news)paper / in a magazine / in a letter	

- □ When I go to the cinema, I like to sit **in the front row**.
- □ James isn't up yet. He's still **in bed**.
- □ It was a lovely day. There wasn't a cloud **in the sky**.
- □ I've just started working **in the sales department**.
- □ Who is the woman **in that photograph**?
- □ Have you seen this picture **in today's paper**?

in a row

B

on the left / on the right   on the left-hand side / right-hand side
on the ground floor / on the first floor / on the second floor etc.
on a map / on a menu / on a list
on a farm

- □ In Britain we drive **on the left**. (*or* ... **on the left-hand side**.)
- □ Our flat is **on the second floor** of the building.
- □ Here's a shopping list. Don't buy anything that's not **on the list**.
- □ Have you ever worked **on a farm**?

We say that a place is **on a river / on a road / on the coast**:
- □ Budapest is **on the (river) Danube**.
- □ Portsmouth is **on the south coast** of England.

BUDAPEST

DANUBE

Also **on the way**:
- □ We stopped at a small village **on the way** to London.

C

at the top (of) / **at the bottom** (of) / **at the end** (of)
- □ Write your name **at the top of the page**.
- □ Jane's house is **at the other end of the street**.

at the top (of the page)

at the bottom (of the page)

D

in the front / **in the back** of a car
- □ I was sitting **in the back** (of the car) when we crashed.

at the front / **at the back** of a building / theatre / group of people etc.
- □ The garden is **at the back of the house**.
- □ Let's sit **at the front** (of the cinema).
- □ We were **at the back**, so we couldn't see very well.

on the front / **on the back** of a letter / piece of paper etc.
- □ I wrote the date **on the back of the photograph**.

at the back

at the front

E

in the corner of a room
- □ The television is **in the corner** of the room.

at the corner *or* **on the corner** of a street
- □ There is a post box **at/on the corner** of the street.

in the corner

at/on the corner

In the world → Unit 108E   **In/at/on (position)** → Units 123, 125   **American English** → Appendix 7

124.1 Answer the questions about the pictures. Use **in**, **at** or **on** with the words below the pictures.

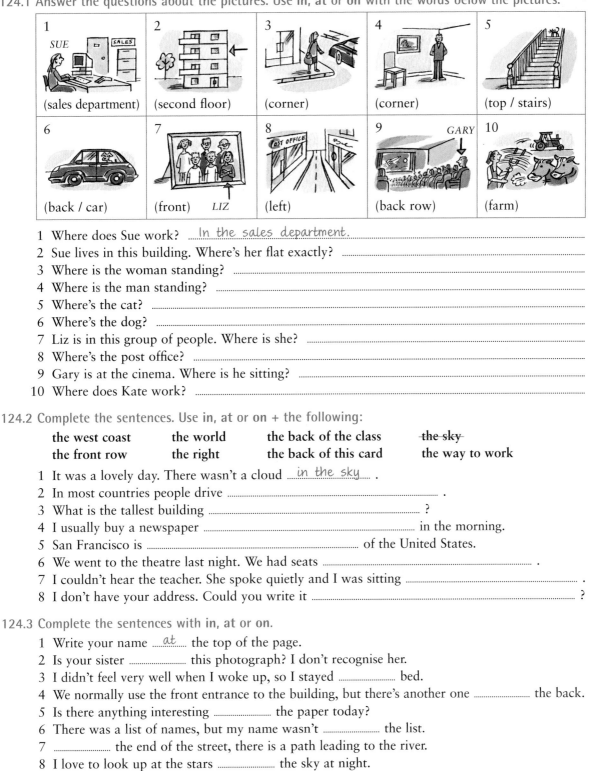

| 1 SUE (sales department) | 2 (second floor) | 3 (corner) | 4 (corner) | 5 (top / stairs) |
| 6 (back / car) | 7 (front) LIZ | 8 (left) | 9 GARY (back row) | 10 (farm) |

1 Where does Sue work?   <u>In the sales department.</u>
2 Sue lives in this building. Where's her flat exactly? ....
3 Where is the woman standing? ....
4 Where is the man standing? ....
5 Where's the cat? ....
6 Where's the dog? ....
7 Liz is in this group of people. Where is she? ....
8 Where's the post office? ....
9 Gary is at the cinema. Where is he sitting? ....
10 Where does Kate work? ....

124.2 Complete the sentences. Use **in**, **at** or **on** + the following:

| the west coast | the world | the back of the class | ~~the sky~~ |
| the front row | the right | the back of this card | the way to work |

1 It was a lovely day. There wasn't a cloud .... <u>in the sky</u> .... .
2 In most countries people drive ....
3 What is the tallest building .... ?
4 I usually buy a newspaper .... in the morning.
5 San Francisco is .... of the United States.
6 We went to the theatre last night. We had seats ....
7 I couldn't hear the teacher. She spoke quietly and I was sitting ....
8 I don't have your address. Could you write it .... ?

124.3 Complete the sentences with **in**, **at** or **on**.

1 Write your name .... <u>at</u> .... the top of the page.
2 Is your sister .... this photograph? I don't recognise her.
3 I didn't feel very well when I woke up, so I stayed .... bed.
4 We normally use the front entrance to the building, but there's another one .... the back.
5 Is there anything interesting .... the paper today?
6 There was a list of names, but my name wasn't .... the list.
7 .... the end of the street, there is a path leading to the river.
8 I love to look up at the stars .... the sky at night.
9 When I'm a passenger in a car, I prefer to sit .... the front.
10 It's a very small village. You probably won't find it .... your map.
11 Joe works .... the furniture department of a large store.
12 Paris is .... the river Seine.
13 I don't like cities. I'd much prefer to live .... the country.
14 My office in .... the top floor. It's .... the left as you come out of the lift.

→ Additional exercise 34 (page 322)

In/at/on (position) 3

A

In hospital / at home etc.

We say that somebody is **in hospital / in prison / in jail**:
- ☐ Ann's mother is **in hospital**.

We say that somebody is **at home / at work / at school / at university / at college**:
- ☐ I'll be **at work** until 5.30, but I'll be **at home** all evening.
- ☐ Julia is studying chemistry **at university**.

Also **at sea** (= on a voyage). Compare **at sea** and **in the sea**:
- ☐ It was a long voyage. We were **at sea** for 30 days.
- ☐ I love swimming **in the sea**.

B

At a party / at a concert etc.

We say that somebody is **at an event** (**at a party / at a conference** etc.):
- ☐ Were there many people **at the party / at the meeting / at the wedding**?
- ☐ I saw Steve **at a football match / at a concert** on Saturday.

C

In and at for buildings

You can often use **in** or **at** with buildings. For example, you can eat **in a restaurant** or **at a restaurant**; you can buy something **in a supermarket** or **at a supermarket**. We usually say **at** when we say where an event takes place (for example: a concert, a film, a party, a meeting):
- ☐ We went to a concert **at the Royal Festival Hall**.
- ☐ The meeting took place **at the company's head office** in Frankfurt.

We say **at the station / at the airport**:
- ☐ Don't meet me **at the station**. I can get a taxi.

We say **at somebody's house**:
- ☐ I was **at Sue's house** last night. *or* I was **at Sue's** last night.

Also **at the doctor's, at the hairdresser's** etc.

We use **in** when we are thinking about the building itself. Compare:
- ☐ We had dinner **at the hotel**.
  All the rooms **in the hotel** have air conditioning. (*not* at the hotel)
- ☐ I was **at Sue's** (house) last night.
  It's always cold **in Sue's house**. The heating doesn't work very well. (*not* at Sue's house)

D

In and at for towns etc.

We normally use **in** with cities, towns and villages:
- ☐ Sam's parents live **in Nottingham**. (*not* at Nottingham)
- ☐ The Louvre is a famous art museum **in Paris**. (*not* at Paris)

But you can use **at** *or* **in** when you think of the place as *a point or station on a journey*:
- ☐ Does this train stop **at** (*or* **in**) **Nottingham**? (= at Nottingham station)
- ☐ We stopped **at** (*or* **in**) a small **village** on the way to London.

E

On a bus / in a car etc.

We usually say **on a bus / on a train / on a plane / on a ship** *but* **in a car / in a taxi**:
- ☐ **The bus** was very full. There were too many people **on it**.
- ☐ Mary arrived **in a taxi**.

We say **on a bike** (= bicycle) / **on a motorbike / on a horse**:
- ☐ Jane passed me **on her bike**.

At school / in hospital etc. → Unit 74   **In/at/on (position)** → Units 123–24   **To/at/in/into** → Unit 126
By car / by bike etc. → Unit 128B

125.1 Complete the sentences about the pictures. Use **in**, **at** or **on** with the words below the pictures.

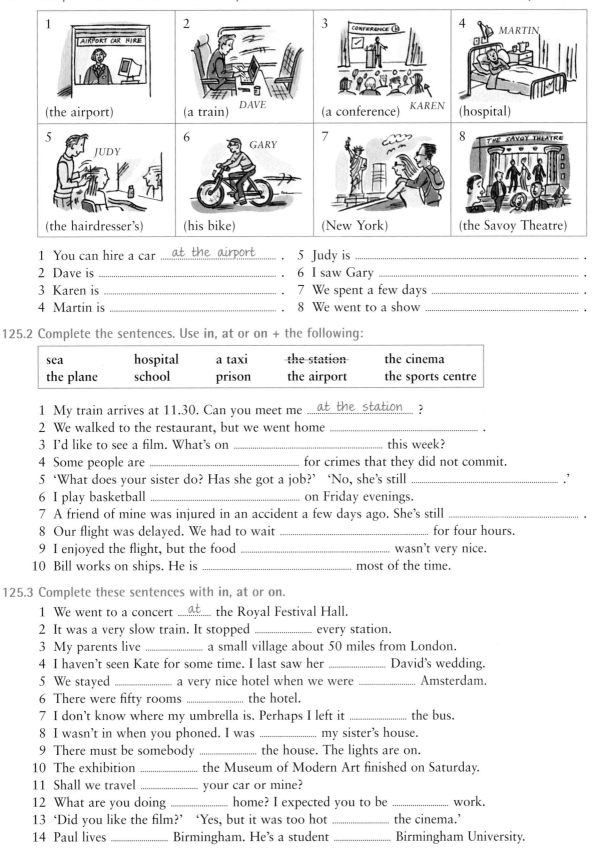

| 1 (the airport) | 2 DAVE (a train) | 3 KAREN (a conference) | 4 MARTIN (hospital) |
| 5 JUDY (the hairdresser's) | 6 GARY (his bike) | 7 (New York) | 8 (the Savoy Theatre) |

1 You can hire a car ..... *at the airport* ..... .   5 Judy is ....
2 Dave is ....   6 I saw Gary ....
3 Karen is ....   7 We spent a few days ....
4 Martin is ....   8 We went to a show ....

125.2 Complete the sentences. Use **in**, **at** or **on** + the following:

sea	hospital	a taxi	~~the station~~	the cinema
the plane	school	prison	the airport	the sports centre

1 My train arrives at 11.30. Can you meet me ..... *at the station* ..... ?
2 We walked to the restaurant, but we went home ....
3 I'd like to see a film. What's on .... this week?
4 Some people are .... for crimes that they did not commit.
5 'What does your sister do? Has she got a job?' 'No, she's still ....'
6 I play basketball .... on Friday evenings.
7 A friend of mine was injured in an accident a few days ago. She's still ....
8 Our flight was delayed. We had to wait .... for four hours.
9 I enjoyed the flight, but the food .... wasn't very nice.
10 Bill works on ships. He is .... most of the time.

125.3 Complete these sentences with **in**, **at** or **on**.

1 We went to a concert ..... *at* ..... the Royal Festival Hall.
2 It was a very slow train. It stopped .... every station.
3 My parents live .... a small village about 50 miles from London.
4 I haven't seen Kate for some time. I last saw her .... David's wedding.
5 We stayed .... a very nice hotel when we were .... Amsterdam.
6 There were fifty rooms .... the hotel.
7 I don't know where my umbrella is. Perhaps I left it .... the bus.
8 I wasn't in when you phoned. I was .... my sister's house.
9 There must be somebody .... the house. The lights are on.
10 The exhibition .... the Museum of Modern Art finished on Saturday.
11 Shall we travel .... your car or mine?
12 What are you doing .... home? I expected you to be .... work.
13 'Did you like the film?' 'Yes, but it was too hot .... the cinema.'
14 Paul lives .... Birmingham. He's a student .... Birmingham University.

→ Additional exercise 34 (page 322)

A

We say **go/come/travel** (etc.) **to** a place or event. For example:

go to China	**go to** bed	**come to** my house
go back to Italy	**go to** the bank	**be taken to** hospital
return to London	**go to** a concert	**be sent to** prison
welcome (somebody) **to** (a place)		**drive to** the airport

TO → ☐

- □ When are your friends **going back to** Italy? (*not* going back in Italy)
- □ Three people were injured in the accident and **taken to** hospital.
- □ **Welcome to** our country! (*not* Welcome in)

In the same way we say 'a **journey to** / a **trip to** / a **visit to** / on **my way to** ...' etc. :

- □ Did you enjoy **your trip to** Paris / **your visit to** the zoo?

Compare **to** (for *movement*) and **in/at** (for *position*):

- □ They are **going to** France.   *but*   They **live in** France.
- □ Can you **come to** the party?   *but*   I'll **see you at** the party.

B Been to

We say '**been to** (a place)':

- □ I've **been to** Italy four times, but I've never **been to Rome**.
- □ Amanda has never **been to a football match** in her life.

C Get and arrive

We say **get to** (a place):

- □ What time did they **get to London** / **to work** / **to the party?**

But we say **arrive in** ... or **arrive at** ... (*not* arrive to).
We say **arrive in** a town or country:

- □ They **arrived in London** / **in Spain** a week ago.

For other places (buildings etc.) or events, we say **arrive at**:

- □ When did they **arrive at the hotel** / **at the airport** / **at the party?**

D Home

We say: **go home** / **come home** / **get home** / **arrive home** / **on the way home** etc. (no preposition).
We do not say 'to home':

- □ I'm tired. Let's **go home** now. (*not* go to home)
- □ I met Linda **on my way home**. (*not* my way to home)

E Into

Go into, get into ... etc. = enter (a room / a building / a car etc.):

- □ I opened the door, **went into** the room and sat down.
- □ A bird **flew into** the kitchen through the window.

INTO → ☐

With some verbs (especially **go/get/put**) we often use **in** (instead of **into**):

- □ She **got in** the car and drove away. (*or* She **got into** the car ...)
- □ I read the letter and **put it** back **in the envelope**.

The opposite of **into** is **out of**:

- □ She **got out of** the car and **went into** a shop.

We usually say '**get on/off** a bus / a train / a plane' (*not usually* get into/out of):

- □ She **got on the bus** and I never saw her again.

126.1 Put in **to/at/in/into** where necessary. If no preposition is necessary, leave the space empty.

1 Three people were taken ....*to*.... hospital after the accident.
2 I met Kate on my way ...*-*.... home. *(no preposition)*
3 We left our luggage .... the station and went to find something to eat.
4 Shall we take a taxi .... the station or shall we walk?
5 I have to go .... the bank today to change some money.
6 The river Rhine flows .... the North Sea.
7 'Have you got your camera?' 'No, I left it .... home.'
8 Have you ever been .... China?
9 I had lost my key, but I managed to climb .... the house through a window.
10 We got stuck in a traffic jam on our way .... the airport.
11 We had lunch .... the airport while we were waiting for our plane.
12 Welcome .... the hotel. We hope you enjoy your stay here.
13 We drove along the main road for about a kilometre and then turned .... a narrow side street.
14 Did you enjoy your visit .... the zoo?
15 I'm tired. As soon as I get .... home, I'm going .... bed.
16 Marcel is French. He has just returned .... France after two years .... Brazil.
17 Carl was born .... Chicago, but his family moved .... New York when he was three. He still lives .... New York.

126.2 Have you been to these places? If so, how many times? Choose three of the places and write a sentence using **been to**.

Athens   Australia   Ireland   Paris   Rome   Sweden   Tokyo   the United States

1 *(example answers)*   I've never been to Australia. / I've been to Ireland once.
2 ....
3 ....
4 ....

126.3 Put in **to/at/in** where necessary. If no preposition is necessary, leave the space empty.

1 What time does this train get ....*to*.... London?
2 What time does this train arrive .... London?
3 What time did you get .... home last night?
4 What time do you usually arrive .... work in the morning?
5 When we got .... the cinema, there was a long queue outside.
6 I arrived .... home feeling very tired.

126.4 Write sentences using **got + into / out of / on / off**.

1 You were walking home. A friend passed you in her car. She saw you, stopped and offered you a lift. She opened the door. What did you do?   I got into the car.
2 You were waiting for the bus. At last your bus came. The doors opened. What did you do then? I ....
3 You drove home in your car. You stopped outside your house and parked the car. What did you do then? ....
4 You were travelling by train to Manchester. When the train got to Manchester, what did you do? ....
5 You needed a taxi. After a few minutes a taxi stopped for you. You opened the door. What did you do then? ....
6 You were travelling by air. At the end of your flight, your plane landed at the airport and stopped. The doors were opened, you took your bag and stood up. What did you do then? ....

→ Additional exercise 34 (page 322)

In/at/on (other uses)

A Expressions with **in**

in the rain / in the sun (= sunshine) **/ in the shade / in the dark / in bad weather** etc.

☐ We sat **in the shade**. It was too hot to sit **in the sun**.

☐ Don't go out **in the rain**. Wait until it stops.

(write) **in ink / in biro / in pencil**

☐ When you do the exam, you're not allowed to write **in pencil**.

Also (write) **in words / in figures / in BLOCK CAPITALS** etc.

☐ Please write your name **in block capitals**.

☐ Write the story **in your own words**. (= don't copy somebody else)

(be/fall) **in love** (**with** somebody)

☐ Have you ever been **in love with** anybody?

in (my) **opinion**

☐ **In my opinion**, the film wasn't very good.

B At the age of … etc.

We say 'at the age of 16 / at 120 miles an hour / at 100 degrees etc.':

☐ Tracy left school **at 16**. *or* … **at the age of 16**.

☐ The train was travelling **at 120 miles an hour**.

☐ Water boils **at 100 degrees Celsius**.

> We are now flying **at a speed** of 800 kilometres an hour and **at an altitude** of 9,000 metres.

C On holiday / on a tour etc.

We say: (be/go) **on holiday / on business / on a trip / on a tour / on a cruise** etc.

☐ I'm going **on holiday** next week.

☐ Emma's away **on business** at the moment.

☐ One day I'd like to go **on a world tour**.

You can also say 'go to a place **for a** holiday **/ for my** holiday(s)':

☐ Steve has gone to France **for a holiday**.

D Other expressions with **on**

on television / on the radio

☐ I didn't watch the news **on television**, but I heard it **on the radio**.

on the phone/telephone

☐ I've never met her, but I've spoken to her **on the phone** a few times.

(be/go) **on strike**

☐ There are no trains today. The drivers are **on strike**.

(be/go) **on a diet**

☐ I've put on a lot of weight. I'll have to go **on a diet**.

(be) **on fire**

☐ Look! That car is **on fire**.

on the whole (= in general)

☐ Sometimes I have problems at work, but **on the whole** I enjoy my job.

on purpose (= intentionally)

☐ I'm sorry. I didn't mean to annoy you. I didn't do it **on purpose**.

In/at/on (time) → Unit 121   In/at/on (position) → Units 123–125

127.1 Complete the sentences using **in** + the following:

block capitals	cold weather	love	my opinion
pencil	~~the rain~~	the shade	

1 Don't go out _in the rain_ . Wait until it stops.
2 Matt likes to keep warm, so he doesn't go out much ....
3 If you write .... and make a mistake, you can rub it out and correct it.
4 They fell .... almost immediately and were married in a few weeks.
5 Please write your address clearly, preferably ....
6 It's too hot in the sun. I'm going to sit ....
7 Amanda thought the restaurant was OK, but .... it wasn't very good.

127.2 Complete the sentences using **on** + the following:

business	a diet	~~fire~~	holiday	the phone
purpose	strike	television	a tour	the whole

1 Look! That car is _on fire_ ! Somebody call the fire brigade.
2 Workers at the factory have gone .... for better pay and conditions.
3 Soon after we arrived, we were taken .... of the city.
4 I feel lazy this evening. Is there anything worth watching .... ?
5 I'm sorry. It was an accident. I didn't do it ....
6 Richard has put on a lot of weight recently. I think he should go ....
7 Jane's job involves a lot of travelling. She often has to go away ....
8 A: I'm going .... next week.
   B: Where are you going? Somewhere nice?
9 A: Is Sarah here?
   B: Yes, but she's .... at the moment. She won't be long.
10 A: How was your exam?
    B: Well, there were some difficult questions, but .... it was OK.

127.3 Complete the sentences with **on, in, at** or **for**.

1 Water boils _at_ 100 degrees Celsius.
2 When I was 14, I went .... a trip to France organised by my school.
3 There was panic when people realised that the building was .... fire.
4 Julia's grandmother died recently .... the age of 79.
5 Can you turn the light on, please? I don't want to sit .... the dark.
6 We didn't go .... holiday last year. We stayed at home.
7 I'm going to Switzerland .... a short holiday next month.
8 I won't be here next week. I'll be .... holiday.
9 Technology has developed .... great speed.
10 Alan got married .... 17, which is rather young to get married.
11 I heard an interesting programme .... the radio this morning.
12 .... my opinion, violent films should not be shown .... television.
13 I wouldn't like to go .... a cruise. I think I'd get bored.
14 I mustn't eat too much. I'm supposed to be .... a diet.
15 I wouldn't like his job. He spends most of his time talking .... the phone.
16 The earth travels round the sun .... 107,000 kilometres an hour.
17 'Did you enjoy your holiday?' 'Not every minute, but .... the whole, yes.'
18 When you write a cheque, you have to write the amount .... words and figures.

→ Additional exercise 34 (page 322)

A

We use **by** in many expressions to say how we do something. For example, you can:

send something **by post**   contact somebody **by phone / by email / by fax**
do something **by hand**   pay **by cheque / by credit card**

☐ Can I pay **by credit card**?
☐ You can contact me **by phone**, **by fax** or **by email**.

But we say **pay cash** or **pay in cash** (*not* by cash).

We also say **by mistake / by accident / by chance**:

☐ We hadn't arranged to meet. We met **by chance**.

But we say 'do something **on purpose**' (= you mean to do it):

☐ I didn't do it **on purpose**. It was an accident.

Note that we say **by chance, by cheque** etc. (*not* by the chance / by a cheque). In these expressions we use **by** + *noun* without **the** or **a**.

B

In the same way we use **by** ... to say how somebody travels:

by car / by train / by plane / by boat / by ship / by bus / by bike etc.
by road / by rail / by air / by sea / by underground

☐ Joanne usually goes to work **by bus**.
☐ Do you prefer to travel **by air** or **by train**?

But we say **on foot**:

☐ Did you come here **by car** or **on foot**?

You cannot use **by** if you say **my car / the train / a taxi** etc. We use **by** + *noun* without 'a/the/my' etc. We say:

by car   *but*   **in my** car (*not* by my car)
by train   *but*   **on the** train (*not* by the train)

We use **in** for cars and taxis:

☐ They didn't come **in their car**. They came **in a taxi**.

We use **on** for bicycles and public transport (buses, trains etc.):

☐ We travelled **on the 6.45 train**.

C

We say that 'something is done **by** somebody/something' (*passive*):

☐ Have you ever been bitten **by a dog**?
☐ The programme was watched **by millions of people**.

Compare **by** and **with**:

☐ The door must have been opened **with a key**. (*not* by a key)
    (= somebody used a key to open it)
☐ The door must have been opened **by somebody** with a key.

We say 'a play **by Shakespeare**' / 'a painting **by Rembrandt**' / 'a novel **by Tolstoy**' etc. :

☐ Have you read anything **by Ernest Hemingway**?

D

By also means 'beside':

☐ Come and sit **by me**. (= beside me)
☐ 'Where's the light switch?' '**By the door**.'

switch

E

Note the following use of **by**:

☐ Clare's salary has just gone up **from** £2,000 a month **to** £2,200. So it has increased **by £200 / by ten per cent**.
☐ Carl and Mike had a race over 200 metres. Carl won **by about three metres**.

new salary ——— £2,200
increased **by £200**
old salary ——— £2,000

Passive + by → Unit 42B   By + -ing → Unit 60B   By myself → Unit 83C   By (time) → Unit 120

128.1 Complete the sentences using **by** + the following:

~~chance~~   credit card   hand   mistake   satellite

1 We hadn't arranged to meet. We met _____by chance_____ .
2 I didn't intend to take your umbrella. I took it _____ .
3 Don't put the sweater in the washing machine. It has to be washed _____ .
4 I don't need cash. I can pay the bill _____ .
5 The two cities were connected _____ for a television programme.

128.2 Put in **by**, **in** or **on**.

1 Joanne usually goes to work _____by_____ bus.
2 I saw Jane this morning. She was _____ the bus.
3 How did you get here? Did you come _____ train?
4 I decided not to go _____ car. I went _____ my bike instead.
5 I didn't feel like walking home, so I came home _____ a taxi.
6 Sorry we're late. We missed the bus, so we had to come _____ foot.
7 How long does it take to cross the Atlantic _____ ship?

128.3 Write three sentences like the examples. Write about a song, a painting, a film, a book etc.

1 _War and Peace is a book by Tolstoy._
2 _Romeo and Juliet is a play by Shakespeare._
3 _____
4 _____
5 _____

128.4 Put in **by**, **in**, **on** or **with**.

1 Have you ever been bitten _____by_____ a dog?
2 The plane was badly damaged _____ lightning.
3 We managed to put the fire out _____ a fire extinguisher.
4 Who is that man standing _____ the window?
5 These photographs were taken _____ a friend of mine.
6 I don't mind going _____ car, but I don't want to go _____ your car.
7 There was a small table _____ the bed _____ a lamp and a clock _____ it.

128.5 All these sentences have a mistake. Correct them.

1 Did you come here by Kate's car or yours?   _in Kate's car_
2 I don't like travelling on bus.   _____
3 These photographs were taken by a very good camera.   _____
4 I know this music is from Beethoven, but I can't
   remember what it's called.   _____
5 I couldn't pay by cash – I didn't have any money on me.   _____
6 We lost the game only because of a mistake of one of
   our players.   _____

128.6 Complete the sentences using **by**.

1 Clare's salary was £2,000 a month. Now it is £2,200.
   Her salary _has increased by £200 a month._
2 My daily newspaper used to cost 60 pence. From today it costs 70 pence.
   The price has gone up _____
3 There was an election. Helen won. She got 25 votes and Norman got 23.
   Helen won _____
4 I went to Kate's house to see her, but she had gone out five minutes before I arrived.
   I missed _____

→ Additional exercise 34 (page 322)

A   Noun + for ...

a cheque FOR (a sum of money)
- □ They sent me a **cheque for** £150.

a demand / a need FOR ...
- □ The company closed down because there wasn't enough **demand for** its product.
- □ There's no excuse for behaviour like that. There's no **need for** it.

a reason FOR ...
- □ The train was late, but nobody knew the **reason for** the delay. (*not* reason of)

B   Noun + of ...

an advantage / a disadvantage OF ...
- □ The **advantage of living alone** is that you can do what you like.
but there is an advantage in (*or* to) doing something
- □ **There are** many advantages **in** living alone. (*or* ... **to** living alone)

a cause OF ...
- □ The **cause of** the explosion is unknown.

a photograph / a picture / a map / a plan / a drawing (etc.) OF ...
- □ Rachel showed me some **photographs of** her family.
- □ I had a **map of** the town, so I was able to find my way around.

C   Noun + in ...

an increase / a decrease / a rise / a fall IN (prices etc.)
- □ There has been an **increase in** the number of road accidents recently.
- □ Last year was a bad one for the company. There was a big **fall in** sales.

D   Noun + to ...

damage TO ...
- □ The accident was my fault, so I had to pay for the **damage to** the other car.

an invitation TO ... (a party / a wedding etc.)
- □ Did you get an **invitation to** the party?

a solution TO (a problem) / a key TO (a door) / an answer TO (a question) / a reply TO (a letter) / a reaction TO ...
- □ I hope we'll find a **solution to** the problem. (*not* a solution of the problem)
- □ I was surprised at her **reaction to** my suggestion.

an attitude TO ... (*or* TOWARDS ...)
- □ His **attitude to** his job is very negative.   *or*   His **attitude towards** his job ...

E   Noun + with ... / between ...

a relationship / a connection / contact WITH ...
- □ Do you have a good **relationship with** your parents?
- □ The police want to question a man in **connection with** the robbery.

but a relationship / a connection / contact / a difference BETWEEN two things or people
- □ The police believe that there is no **connection between** the two crimes.
- □ There are some **differences between** British and American English.

Exercises

129.1 Complete the second sentence so that it has the same meaning as the first.

1 What caused the explosion? What was the cause <u>of the explosion</u> ?
2 We're trying to solve the problem. We're trying to find a solution ....
3 Sue gets on well with her brother. Sue has a good relationship ....
4 The cost of living has gone up a lot.
   There has been a big increase ....
5 I don't know how to answer your question.
   I can't think of an answer ....
6 I don't think that a new road is necessary.
   I don't think there is any need ....
7 I think that working at home has many advantages.
   I think that there are many advantages ....
8 The number of people without jobs fell last month.
   Last month there was a fall ....
9 Nobody wants to buy shoes like these any more.
   There is no demand ....
10 In what way is your job different from mine?
   What is the difference .... ?

129.2 Complete the sentences using the following nouns + the correct preposition:

cause	connection	contact	damage	invitation
key	~~map~~	pictures	reason	reply

1 On the wall there were some pictures and a <u>map of</u> the world.
2 Thank you for the .... your party next week.
3 Since she left home two years ago, Sophie has had little .... her family.
4 I can't open this door. Have you got a .... the other door?
5 The .... the fire at the hotel last night is still unknown.
6 I emailed Jim last week, but I still haven't received a .... my message.
7 The two companies are completely independent. There is no .... them.
8 Jane showed me some old .... the city as it looked 100 years ago.
9 Carol has decided to give up her job. I don't know her .... doing this.
10 It wasn't a bad accident. The .... the car wasn't serious.

129.3 Complete the sentences with the correct preposition.

1 There are some differences <u>between</u> British and American English.
2 Money isn't the solution .... every problem.
3 There has been an increase .... the amount of traffic using this road.
4 When I opened the envelope, I was delighted to find a cheque .... £500.
5 The advantage .... having a car is that you don't have to rely on public transport.
6 There are many advantages .... being able to speak a foreign language.
7 Everything can be explained. There's a reason .... everything.
8 When Paul left home, his attitude .... his parents seemed to change.
9 Ben and I used to be good friends, but I don't have much contact .... him now.
10 There has been a sharp rise .... property prices in the past few years.
11 What was Emma's reaction .... the news?
12 If I give you the camera, can you take a photograph .... me?
13 The company has rejected the workers' demands .... a rise .... pay.
14 What was the answer .... question 3 in the test?
15 The fact that Jane was offered a job has no connection .... the fact that she is a friend of the managing director.

→ Additional exercise 35 (page 322)

Adjective + preposition 1

A It was **nice of** you to …

nice / kind / good / generous / polite / stupid / silly etc. **OF** somebody (to do something)
- ☐ Thank you. It was very **kind of you** to help me.
- ☐ It is **stupid of me** to go out without a coat in such cold weather.

but (be) **nice / kind / good / generous / polite / rude / friendly / cruel** etc. **TO** somebody
- ☐ They have always been very **nice to** me. (*not* with me)
- ☐ Why were you so **unfriendly to** Lucy?

B *Adjective +* **about / with**

angry / annoyed / furious { **ABOUT** something
{ **WITH** somebody **FOR** doing something
- ☐ It's stupid to get **angry about** things that don't matter.
- ☐ Are you **annoyed with** me **for** being late?

excited / worried / upset / nervous / happy etc. **ABOUT** a situation
- ☐ Are you **excited about** going away next week?
- ☐ Lisa is **upset about** not being invited to the party.

delighted / pleased / satisfied / happy / disappointed WITH something you receive, or the result of something
- ☐ I was **delighted with** the present you gave me.
- ☐ Were you **happy with** your exam results?

C *Adjective +* **at / by / with**

surprised / shocked / amazed / astonished AT / BY something
- ☐ Everybody was **surprised AT** (*or* **BY**) the news.
- ☐ I hope you weren't **shocked BY** (*or* **AT**) what I said.

impressed WITH / BY somebody/something
- ☐ I'm very **impressed with** (*or* by) her English. It's very good.

fed up / bored WITH something
- ☐ I don't enjoy my job any more. I'm **fed up with** it. / I'm **bored with** it.

D Sorry **about / for**

sorry ABOUT a situation or something that happened
- ☐ I'm **sorry about** the mess. I'll clear it up later.
- ☐ We're all **sorry about** Julie losing her job.

sorry FOR / ABOUT something you did
- ☐ Alex is very **sorry for** what he said. (*or* **sorry about** what he said)
- ☐ I'm **sorry for** shouting at you yesterday. (*or* **sorry about** shouting)

You can also say 'I'm sorry I (did something)':
- ☐ I'm **sorry I shouted** at you yesterday.

feel / be sorry FOR somebody who is in a bad situation
- ☐ I **feel sorry for** Matt. He's had a lot of bad luck. (*not* I feel sorry about Matt)

Preposition + –ing → Unit 60   Adjective + to … → Unit 65   Sorry to … / sorry for … → Unit 66C
Adjective + preposition 2 → Unit 131

260

130.1 Write sentences using **nice of ...** , **kind of ...** etc.

1	I went out in the cold without a coat.	(silly) _That was silly of you._
2	Sue offered to drive me to the airport.	(nice) That was .... her.
3	I needed money and Tom gave me some.	(generous) That ....
4	They didn't invite us to their party.	(not very nice) That ....
5	Can I help you with your luggage?	(very kind) .... you.
6	Kevin didn't thank me for the present.	(not very polite) ....
7	They've had an argument and now they refuse to speak to each other.	(a bit childish) ....

130.2 Complete the sentences using the following adjectives + the correct preposition:

   annoyed   annoyed   astonished   bored   ~~excited~~   impressed   kind   sorry

1 Are you ....._excited about_..... going away next week?
2 Thank you for all your help. You've been very .... me.
3 I wouldn't like to be in her position. I feel .... her.
4 What have I done wrong? Why are you .... me?
5 Why do you always get so .... things that don't matter?
6 I wasn't very .... the service in the restaurant. We had to wait ages before our food arrived.
7 Ben isn't very happy at college. He says he's .... the course he's doing.
8 I had never seen so many people before. I was .... the crowds.

130.3 Put in the correct preposition.

1 I was delighted .....with..... the present you gave me.
2 It was very nice .... you to do my shopping for me. Thank you very much.
3 Why are you always so rude .... your parents? Can't you be nice .... them?
4 It was careless .... you to leave the door unlocked when you went out.
5 They didn't reply to our letter, which wasn't very polite .... them.
6 We always have the same food every day. I'm fed up .... it.
7 I can't understand people who are cruel .... animals.
8 We enjoyed our holiday, but we were a bit disappointed .... the hotel.
9 I was surprised .... the way he behaved. It was completely out of character.
10 I've been trying to learn Spanish, but I'm not very satisfied .... my progress.
11 Linda doesn't look very well. I'm worried .... her.
12 Are you angry .... what happened?
13 I'm sorry .... what I did. I hope you're not angry .... me.
14 The people next door are furious .... us .... making so much noise last night.
15 Jill starts her new job next week. She's quite excited .... it.
16 I'm sorry .... the smell of paint in this room. I've just decorated it.
17 I was shocked .... what I saw. I'd never seen anything like it before.
18 The man we interviewed for the job was intelligent, but we weren't very impressed .... his appearance.
19 Are you still upset .... what I said to you yesterday?
20 He said he was sorry .... the situation, but there was nothing he could do.
21 I felt sorry .... the children when we went on holiday. It rained every day and they had to spend most of the time indoors.

→ Additional exercise 35 (page 322)

Adjective + preposition 2

A   *Adjective +* of (1)

afraid / frightened / terrified / scared OF ...
- □ 'Are you **afraid of** spiders?'   'Yes, I'm **terrified of** them.'

fond / proud / ashamed / jealous / envious OF ...
- □ Why are you always so **jealous of** other people?

suspicious / critical / tolerant OF ...
- □ He didn't trust me. He was **suspicious of** my intentions.

B   *Adjective +* of (2)

aware / conscious OF ...
- □ 'Did you know he was married?'   'No, I wasn't **aware of** that.'

capable / incapable OF ...
- □ I'm sure you are **capable of** passing the examination.

full / short OF ...
- □ The letter I wrote was **full of** mistakes. (*not* full with)
- □ I'm a bit **short of** money. Can you lend me some?

typical OF ...
- □ He's late again. It's **typical of** him to keep everybody waiting.

tired / sick OF ...
- □ Come on, let's go! I'm **tired of** waiting. (= I've had enough of waiting.)

certain / sure OF *or* **ABOUT ...**
- □ I think she's arriving this evening, but I'm not **sure of** that. *or* ... **sure about** that.

C   *Adjective +* at / to / from / in / on / with / for

good / bad / brilliant / better / hopeless etc. **AT ...**
- □ I'm not very **good at** repairing things. (*not* good in repairing things)

married / engaged TO ...
- □ Linda is **married to** an American. (*not* married with)
- *but*   Linda is married **with three children.** (= she is married and has three children)

similar TO ...
- □ Your writing is **similar to** mine.

different FROM *or* **different TO ...**
- □ The film was **different from** what I'd expected. (*or* **different to** what I'd expected.)

interested IN ...
- □ Are you **interested in** art?

keen ON ...
- □ We stayed at home because Chris wasn't very **keen on** going out.

dependent ON ... (*but* **independent OF ...**)
- □ I don't want to be **dependent on** anybody.

crowded WITH (people etc.)
- □ The streets were **crowded with** tourists. (*but* **full of** tourists)

famous FOR ...
- □ The Italian city of Florence is **famous for** its art treasures.

responsible FOR ...
- □ Who was **responsible for** all that noise last night?

Preposition + –ing → Unit 60   **Afraid of/to ...** → Unit 66A   Adjective + preposition 1 → Unit 130
American English → Appendix 7

131.1 Complete the second sentence so that it has the same meaning as the first.

1 There were lots of tourists in the streets.   The streets were crowded _with tourists_ .
2 There was a lot of furniture in the room.   The room was full _____ .
3 I don't like sport very much.   I'm not very keen _____ .
4 We don't have enough time.   We're a bit short _____ .
5 I'm not a very good tennis player.   I'm not very good _____ .
6 Catherine's husband is Russian.   Catherine is married _____ .
7 I don't trust Robert.   I'm suspicious _____ .
8 My problem is not the same as yours.   My problem is different _____ .

131.2 Complete the sentences using the following adjectives + the correct preposition:

     afraid   different   interested   proud   responsible   similar   ~~sure~~

1 I think she's arriving this evening, but I'm not _sure of_ that.
2 Your camera is _____ mine, but it isn't exactly the same.
3 Don't worry. I'll look after you. There's nothing to be _____ .
4 I never watch the news on television. I'm not _____ the news.
5 The editor is the person who is _____ what appears in a newspaper.
6 Sarah is a keen gardener. She's very _____ her garden and loves showing it to visitors.
7 I was surprised when I met Lisa for the first time. She was _____ what I expected.

131.3 Put in the correct preposition.

1 The letter I wrote was full _of_ mistakes.
2 My home town is not an especially interesting place. It's not famous _____ anything.
3 Kate is very fond _____ her younger brother.
4 I don't like going up ladders. I'm scared _____ heights.
5 You look bored. You don't seem interested _____ what I'm saying.
6 Did you know that Liz is engaged _____ a friend of mine?
7 I'm not ashamed _____ what I did. In fact I'm quite proud _____ it.
8 I suggested that we should all go out for a meal, but nobody else was keen _____ the idea.
9 These days everybody is aware _____ the dangers of smoking.
10 The station platform was crowded _____ people waiting for the train.
11 Sue is much more successful than I am. Sometimes I feel a bit jealous _____ her.
12 I'm tired _____ doing the same thing every day. I need a change.
13 Do you know anyone who might be interested _____ buying an old car?
14 We've got plenty to eat. The fridge is full _____ food.
15 She is a very honest person. I don't think she is capable _____ telling a lie.
16 Helen works hard and she's extremely good _____ her job.
17 I'm not surprised he changed his mind at the last moment. That's typical _____ him.
18 Mark has no money of his own. He's totally dependent _____ his parents.
19 We're short _____ staff in our office at the moment. We need more people to do the work.

131.4 Write sentences about yourself. Are you good at these things or not? Use the following:

     good   quite good   not very good   hopeless

1 (repairing things) _I'm not very good at repairing things._
2 (telling jokes) _____
3 (mathematics) _____
4 (remembering names) _____

→ Additional exercise 35 **(page 322)**

A Verb + **to**

talk / **speak TO** somebody (**with** is also possible but less usual)
- ☐ Who was that man you were **talking to**?

listen TO ...
- ☐ We spent the evening **listening to** music. (*not* listening music)

write (a letter) **TO** ...
- ☐ I **wrote to** the hotel complaining about the poor service we had received.

apologise TO somebody (for ...)
- ☐ They **apologised to me** for what happened. (*not* They apologised me)

explain something **TO** somebody
- ☐ Can you **explain** this word **to me**? (*not* explain me this word)

explain / **describe** (to somebody) what/how/why ...
- ☐ I **explained to them** why I was worried. (*not* I explained them)
- ☐ Let me **describe to you** what I saw. (*not* Let me describe you)

B We do not use **to** with these verbs:

phone / **telephone** / **call** somebody
- ☐ Did you **phone your father** yesterday? (*not* phone to your father)

answer somebody/something
- ☐ He refused to **answer my question**. (*not* answer to my question)

ask somebody
- ☐ Can I **ask you** a question? (*not* ask to you)

thank somebody (for something)
- ☐ He **thanked me** for helping him. (*not* He thanked to me)

C Verb + **at**

look / **stare** / **glance AT** ... , **have a look** / **take a look AT** ...
- ☐ Why are you **looking at** me like that?

laugh AT ...
- ☐ I look stupid with this haircut. Everybody will **laugh at** me.

aim / **point** (something) **AT** ... , **shoot** / **fire** (a gun) **AT** ...
- ☐ Don't **point** that knife **at** me. It's dangerous.
- ☐ We saw someone with a gun **shooting at** birds, but he didn't hit any.

D Some verbs can be followed by **at** or **to**, with a difference of meaning. For example:

shout AT somebody (when you are angry)
- ☐ He got very angry and started **shouting at** me.

shout TO somebody (so that they can hear you)
- ☐ He **shouted to** me from the other side of the street.

throw something **AT** somebody/something (in order to hit them)
- ☐ Somebody **threw** an egg **at** the minister.

throw something **TO** somebody (for somebody to catch)
- ☐ Lisa shouted 'Catch!' and **threw** the keys **to** me from the window.

Verb + preposition 2–4 → Units 133–136   Ask for → Unit 133C   Apologise for / thank somebody for
→ Unit 135B   Other verbs + to → Unit 136D   American English → Appendix 7

132.1 You ask somebody to explain things that you don't understand. Write questions beginning **Can you explain ... ?**

1 (I don't understand this word.)
   <u>Can you explain this word to me?</u>

2 (I don't understand what you mean.)
   <u>Can you explain to me what you mean?</u>

3 (I don't understand this question.)
   Can you explain ....

4 (I don't understand the problem.)
   Can ....

5 (I don't understand how this machine works.)

   ....

6 (I don't understand what I have to do.)

   ....

132.2 Put in **to** where necessary. If the sentence is already complete, leave the space empty.

1 I know who she is, but I've never spoken ...<u>to</u>... her.
2 Why didn't you answer ....<u>–</u>.... my letter?
3 I like to listen .... the radio while I'm having breakfast.
4 We'd better phone .... the restaurant to reserve a table.
5 'Did Mike apologise .... you?' 'Yes, he said he was very sorry.'
6 I explained .... everybody the reasons for my decision.
7 I thanked .... everybody for all the help they had given me.
8 Ask me what you like, and I'll try and answer .... your questions.
9 Mike described .... me exactly what happened.
10 Karen won't be able to help you, so there's no point in asking .... her.

132.3 Complete the sentences. Use the following verbs (in the correct form) + the correct preposition:

~~explain~~   glance   ~~laugh~~   listen   point   speak   throw   throw

1 I look stupid with this haircut. Everybody will ...<u>laugh at</u>... me.
2 I don't understand this. Can you ...<u>explain</u>... it ...<u>to</u>... me?
3 Sue and Kevin had an argument and now they're not .... one another.
4 Be careful with those scissors! Don't .... them .... me!
5 I .... my watch to see what the time was.
6 Please .... me! I've got something important to tell you.
7 Don't .... stones .... the birds! It's cruel.
8 If you don't want that sandwich, ... it .... the birds. They'll eat it.

132.4 Put in **to** or **at**.

1 I wrote ...<u>to</u>... the hotel complaining about the poor service we had received.
2 Look .... these flowers. Aren't they pretty?
3 Please don't shout .... me! Try to calm down.
4 I saw Sue as I was cycling along the road. I shouted .... her, but she didn't hear me.
5 Don't listen .... what he says. He doesn't know what he's talking about.
6 What's so funny? What are you laughing .... ?
7 Do you think I could have a look .... your magazine, please?
8 I'm a bit lonely. I need somebody to talk ....
9 She was so angry she threw a book .... the wall.
10 The woman sitting opposite me on the train kept staring .... me.
11 Can I speak .... you a moment? There's something I want to ask you.

→ Additional exercise 36 (page 323)

A   Verb + about

talk / read / know ABOUT ... , **tell** somebody **ABOUT ...**
- We **talked about** a lot of things at the meeting.

have a discussion ABOUT something, *but* **discuss** something (no preposition)
- We had **a discussion about** what we should do.
- We **discussed** a lot of things at the meeting. (*not* discussed about)

do something **ABOUT** something = *do something to improve a bad situation*
- If you're worried about the problem, you should **do** something **about** it.

B   Care about, care for and take care of

care ABOUT somebody/something = *think that somebody/something is important*
- He's very selfish. He doesn't **care about** other people.

We say '**care what/where/how ...**' etc. (*without* about)
- You can do what you like. I don't **care what** you do.

care FOR somebody/something
(1) = *like something* (usually in questions and negative sentences)
- Would you **care for** a cup of coffee? (= Would you like ... ?)
- I don't **care for** very hot weather. (= I don't like ...)
(2) = *look after somebody*
- Alan is 85 and lives alone. He needs somebody to **care for** him.

take care OF ... = *look after*
- Have a nice holiday. **Take care of** yourself! (= look after yourself)

C   Verb + for

ask (somebody) **FOR ...**
- I wrote to the company **asking** them **for** more information about the job.
but 'I **asked** him **the way** to ...', 'She **asked** me **my name**' (no preposition)

apply (**TO** a person, a company etc.) **FOR** a job etc.
- I think you'd be good at this job. Why don't you **apply for** it?

wait FOR ...
- Don't **wait for** me. I'll join you later.
- I'm not going out yet. I'm **waiting for** the rain to stop.

search (a person / a place / a bag etc.) **FOR ...**
- I've **searched** the house **for** my keys, but I still can't find them.

leave (a place) **FOR** another place
- I haven't seen her since she **left** (home) **for** the office this morning.
  (*not* left to the office)

D   Look for and look after

look FOR ... = *search for, try to find*
- I've lost my keys. Can you help me to **look for** them?

look AFTER ... = *take care of*
- Alan is 85 and lives alone. He needs somebody to **look after** him. (*not* look for)
- You can borrow this book, but you must promise to **look after** it.

133.1 Put in the correct preposition. If no preposition is necessary, leave the space empty.

1 I'm not going out yet. I'm waiting ....for.... the rain to stop.
2 I couldn't find the street I was looking for, so I stopped someone to ask .... directions.
3 I've applied .... a job at the factory. I don't know if I'll get it.
4 I've applied .... three colleges. I hope one of them accepts me.
5 I've searched everywhere .... John, but I haven't been able to find him.
6 I don't want to talk .... what happened last night. Let's forget it.
7 I don't want to discuss .... what happened last night. Let's forget it.
8 We had an interesting discussion .... the problem, but we didn't reach a decision.
9 We discussed .... the problem, but we didn't reach a decision.
10 I don't want to go out yet. I'm waiting .... the post to arrive.
11 Ken and Sonia are touring Italy. They're in Rome at the moment, but tomorrow they leave
.... Venice.
12 The roof of the house is in very bad condition. I think we ought to do something .... it.
13 We waited .... Steve for half an hour, but he never came.
14 Tomorrow morning I have to catch a plane. I'm leaving my house .... the airport at
7.30.

133.2 Complete the sentences with the following verbs (in the correct form) + preposition:

apply   ask   do   leave   look   search   talk   wait

1 Police are ....searching for.... the man who escaped from prison.
2 We're still .... a reply to our letter. We haven't heard anything yet.
3 I think Ben likes his job, but he doesn't .... it much.
4 When I'd finished my meal, I .... the waiter .... the bill.
5 Cathy is unemployed. She has .... several jobs, but she hasn't had any
luck.
6 If something is wrong, why don't you .... something .... it?
7 Linda's car is very old, but it's in excellent condition. She .... it very
well.
8 Diane is from Boston, but now she lives in Paris. She .... Boston .... Paris
when she was 19.

133.3 Put in the correct preposition after **care**. If no preposition is necessary, leave the space empty.

1 He's very selfish. He doesn't care ....about.... other people.
2 Are you hungry? Would you care .... something to eat?
3 She doesn't care .... the exam. She doesn't care whether she passes or fails.
4 Please let me borrow your camera. I promise I'll take good care .... it.
5 'Do you like this coat?' 'Not really. I don't care .... the colour.'
6 Don't worry about the shopping. I'll take care .... that.
7 I want to have a good holiday. I don't care .... the cost.
8 I want to have a good holiday. I don't care .... how much it costs.

133.4 Complete the sentences with **look for** or **look after**. Use the correct form of **look (looks/looked/looking)**.

1 I ....looked for.... my keys, but I couldn't find them anywhere.
2 Kate is .... a job. I hope she finds one soon.
3 Who .... you when you were ill?
4 I'm .... Elizabeth. Have you seen her?
5 The car park was full, so we had to .... somewhere else to park.
6 A babysitter is somebody who .... other people's children.

→ Additional exercise 36 **(page 323)**

Verb + preposition 3   about and of

A

dream ABOUT … (when you are asleep)
- □ I **dreamt about** you last night.

dream OF/ABOUT being something / doing something = *imagine*
- □ Do you **dream of/about** being rich and famous?

(I) **wouldn't dream OF** doing something = *I would never do it*
- □ 'Don't tell anyone what I said.'   'No, I **wouldn't dream of** it.' (= I would never do it)

B

hear ABOUT … = *be told about something*
- □ Did you **hear about** what happened at the club on Saturday night?

hear OF … = *know that somebody/something exists*
- □ 'Who is Tom Hart?'   'I have no idea. I've never **heard of** him'. (*not* heard from him)

hear FROM … = *receive a letter, phone call or message from somebody*
- □ 'Have you **heard from** Jane recently?'   'Yes, she phoned a few days ago.'

C

think ABOUT … and **think OF …**

When you **think ABOUT** something, you consider it, you concentrate your mind on it:
- □ I've **thought about** what you said and I've decided to take your advice.
- □ 'Will you lend me the money?'   'I'll **think about** it.'

When you **think OF** something, the idea comes to your mind:
- □ He told me his name, but I can't **think of** it now. (*not* think about it)
- □ That's a good idea. Why didn't I **think of** that? (*not* think about that)

We also use **think of** when we ask or give an opinion:
- □ 'What did you **think of** the film?'   'I didn't **think** much **of** it.' (= I didn't like it much)

The difference is sometimes very small and you can use **of** or **about**:
- □ When I'm alone, I often **think of** (*or* about) you.

You can say **think of** *or* **think about** doing something (for possible future actions):
- □ My sister is **thinking of** (*or* about) going to Canada. (= she is considering it)

D

remind somebody **ABOUT …** = *tell somebody not to forget*
- □ I'm glad you **reminded** me **about** the meeting. I'd completely forgotten about it.

remind somebody **OF …** = *cause somebody to remember*
- □ This house **reminds** me **of** the one I lived in when I was a child.
- □ Look at this photograph of Richard. Who does he **remind** you **of**?

E

complain (TO somebody) **ABOUT …** = *say that you are not satisfied*
- □ We **complained to** the manager of the restaurant **about** the food.

complain OF a pain, an illness etc. = *say that you have a pain etc.*
- □ We called the doctor because George was **complaining of** a pain in his stomach.

F

warn somebody **ABOUT** a person or thing which is bad, dangerous, unusual etc.
- □ I knew he was a strange person. I had been **warned about** him. (*not* warned of him)
- □ Vicky **warned me about** the traffic. She said it would be bad.

warn somebody **ABOUT/OF** a danger, something bad which might happen later
- □ Scientists have **warned us about/of** the effects of global warming.

Remind/warn somebody to … → Unit 55B

134.1 Put in the correct preposition.

1 Did you hear ..._about_... what happened at the party on Saturday?
2 'I had a strange dream last night.' 'Did you? What did you dream .... ?'
3 Our neighbours complained .... us .... the noise we made last night.
4 Kevin was complaining .... pains in his chest, so he went to the doctor.
5 I love this music. It reminds me .... a warm day in spring.
6 He loves his job. He thinks .... his job all the time, he dreams .... it, he talks
   .... it and I'm fed up with hearing .... it.
7 I tried to remember the name of the book, but I couldn't think .... it.
8 Jackie warned me .... the water. She said it wasn't safe to drink.
9 We warned our children .... the dangers of playing in the street.

134.2 Complete the sentences using the following verbs (in the correct form) + the correct preposition:

complain   **dream**   **hear**   **remind**   **remind**   ~~think~~   **think**   **warn**

1 That's a good idea. Why didn't I ..._think of_.... that?
2 Bill is never satisfied. He is always .... something.
3 I can't make a decision yet. I need time to .... your proposal.
4 Before you go into the house, I must .... you .... the dog. He is very
   aggressive sometimes, so be careful.
5 She's not a well-known singer. Not many people have .... her.
6 A: You wouldn't go away without telling me, would you?
   B: Of course not. I wouldn't .... it.
7 I would have forgotten my appointment if Jane hadn't .... me .... it.
8 Do you see that man over there? Does he .... you .... anybody you know?

134.3 Complete the sentences using **hear** or **heard** + the correct preposition (**about/of/from**).

1 I've never ..._heard of_.... Tom Hart. Who is he?
2 'Did you .... the accident last night?' 'Yes, Vicky told me.'
3 Jill used to phone quite often, but I haven't .... her for a long time now.
4 A: Have you .... a writer called William Hudson?
   B: No, I don't think so. What sort of writer is he?
5 Thank you for your letter. It was good to ....you again.
6 'Do you want to .... our holiday?' 'Not now. Tell me later.'
7 I live in a small town in the north of England. You've probably never .... it.

134.4 Complete the sentences using **think about** or **think of**. Sometimes both **about** and **of** are possible. Use the correct form of **think** (**think/thinking/thought**).

1 You look serious. What are you ..._thinking about_.... ?
2 I like to have time to make decisions. I like to .... things carefully.
3 I don't know what to get Sarah for her birthday. Can you .... anything?
4 A: I've finished reading the book you lent me.
   B: Have you? What did you .... it? Did you like it?
5 We're .... going out for a meal this evening. Would you like to come?
6 I don't really want to go out with Tom tonight. I'll have to .... an
   excuse.
7 When I was offered the job, I didn't accept immediately. I went away and
   .... it for a while. In the end I decided to take the job.
8 I don't .... much .... this coffee. It's like water.
9 Carol is very homesick. She's always .... her family back home.

→ Additional exercise 36 (page 323)

A | Verb + of

accuse / suspect somebody **OF** …
- ☐ Sue **accused** me **of** being selfish.
- ☐ Some students were **suspected of** cheating in the exam.

approve / disapprove OF …
- ☐ His parents don't **approve of** what he does, but they can't stop him.

die OF (*or* **FROM**) an illness etc.
- ☐ 'What did he **die of**?' 'A heart attack.'

consist OF …
- ☐ We had an enormous meal. It **consisted of** seven courses.

B | Verb + for

pay (somebody) **FOR** …
- ☐ I didn't have enough money to **pay for** the meal. (*not* pay the meal)

but   **pay** a bill / a fine / tax / rent / a sum of money etc. (no preposition)
- ☐ I didn't have enough money to **pay the rent**.

thank / forgive somebody **FOR** …
- ☐ I'll never **forgive** them **for** what they did.

apologise (to somebody) **FOR** …
- ☐ When I realised I was wrong, I **apologised** (to them) **for** my mistake.

blame somebody/something **FOR** … , somebody is **to blame FOR** …
- ☐ Everybody **blamed** me **for** the accident.
- ☐ Everybody said that I was **to blame for** the accident.

blame (a problem etc.) **ON** …
- ☐ Everybody **blamed** the accident **on** me.

C | Verb + from

suffer FROM an illness etc.
- ☐ The number of people **suffering from** heart disease has increased.

protect somebody/something **FROM** (*or* **AGAINST**) …
- ☐ Sun block **protects** the skin **from** the sun. (*or* … **against** the sun.)

D | Verb + on

depend / rely ON …
- ☐ 'What time will you be home?' 'I don't know. It **depends on** the traffic.
- ☐ You can **rely on** Jill. She always keeps her promises.

You can use **depend** + when/where/how etc. with or without **on**:
- ☐ 'Are you going to buy it?' 'It **depends how much** it is.' (*or* It depends **on** how much)

live ON money/food
- ☐ Michael's salary is very low. It isn't enough to **live on**.

congratulate / compliment somebody **ON** …
- ☐ I **congratulated** her **ON** her success in the exam.

Exercises

135.1 Complete the second sentence so that it means the same as the first.

1 Sue said I was selfish. Sue accused me __of being selfish__ .

2 The misunderstanding was my fault, so I apologised.
   I apologised _____ .

3 Jane won the tournament, so I congratulated her.
   I congratulated Jane _____ .

4 He has enemies, but he has a bodyguard to protect him.
   He has a bodyguard to protect him _____ .

5 There are eleven players in a football team.
   A football team consists _____ .

6 Sandra eats only bread and eggs. She lives _____ .

135.2 Complete the second sentence using **for** or **on**. These sentences all have **blame**.

1 Liz said that what happened was Joe's fault. Liz blamed Joe __for what happened__ .

2 You always say everything is my fault.
   You always blame me _____ .

3 Do you think the economic crisis is the fault of the government?
   Do you blame the government _____ ?

4 I think the increase in violent crime is the fault of television.
   I blame the increase in violent crime _____ .

Now rewrite sentences 3 and 4 using **to blame for**.

5 (3) Do you think the government _____ ?

6 (4) I think that _____ .

135.3 Complete the sentences using the following verbs (in the correct form) + the correct preposition:

    accuse   **apologise**   ~~approve~~   **congratulate**   **depend**   **live**   **pay**

1 His parents don't __approve of__ what he does, but they can't stop him.

2 When you went to the theatre with Paul, who _____ the tickets?

3 It's not very pleasant when you are _____ something you didn't do.

4 A: Are you going to the beach tomorrow?
   B: I hope so. It _____ the weather.

5 Things are very cheap there. You can _____ very little money.

6 When I saw David, I _____ him _____ passing his driving test.

7 You were very rude to Liz. Don't you think you should _____ her?

135.4 Put in the correct preposition. If no preposition is necessary, leave the space empty.

1 Some students were suspected __of__ cheating in the exam.

2 Sally is often not well. She suffers _____ very bad headaches.

3 You know that you can rely _____ me if you ever need any help.

4 It is terrible that some people are dying _____ hunger while others eat too much.

5 Are you going to apologise _____ what you did?

6 The accident was my fault, so I had to pay _____ the repairs.

7 I didn't have enough money to pay _____ the bill.

8 I complimented her _____ her English. She spoke very fluently and her pronunciation was excellent.

9 She hasn't got a job. She depends _____ her parents for money.

10 I don't know whether I'll go out tonight. It depends _____ how I feel.

11 They wore warm clothes to protect themselves _____ the cold.

12 The apartment consists _____ three rooms, a kitchen and bathroom.

→ Additional exercise 36 (page 323)

Verb + preposition 5   in/into/with/to/on

A   Verb + in

believe IN …
- Do you **believe in** God? (= Do you believe that God exists?)
- I **believe in** saying what I think. (= I believe it is right to say what I think)

but 'believe something' (= believe it is true), 'believe somebody' (= believe they are telling the truth)
- The story can't be true. I don't **believe it**. (*not* believe in it)

specialise IN …
- Helen is a lawyer. She **specialises in** company law.

succeed IN …
- I hope you **succeed in** finding the job you want.

B   Verb + into

break INTO …
- Our house was **broken into** a few days ago, but nothing was stolen.

crash / drive / bump / run INTO …
- He lost control of the car and **crashed into** a wall.

divide / cut / split something **INTO** two or more parts
- The book is **divided into** three parts.

translate a book etc. **FROM** one language **INTO** another
- Ernest Hemingway's books have been **translated into** many languages.

C   Verb + with

collide WITH …
- There was an accident this morning. A bus **collided with** a car.

fill something **WITH …** (*but* full of … – see Unit 131B)
- Take this saucepan and **fill it with** water.

provide / supply somebody **WITH …**
- The school **provides** all its students **with** books.

D   Verb + to

happen TO …
- What **happened to** that gold watch you used to have? (= where is it now?)

invite somebody **TO** a party / a wedding etc.
- They only **invited** a few people **to** their wedding.

prefer one thing/person **TO** another
- I **prefer** tea **to** coffee

E   Verb + on

concentrate ON …
- Don't look out of the window. **Concentrate on** your work.

insist ON …
- I wanted to go alone, but some friends of mine **insisted on** coming with me.

spend (money) **ON …**
- How much do you **spend on** food each week?

Verb + preposition + **–ing** → Unit 62   Other verbs + to → Unit 132   Other verbs + on → Unit 135D

136.1 Complete the second sentence so that it means the same as the first.

1 There was a collision between a bus and a car.
A bus collided __with a car__ .

2 I don't mind big cities, but I prefer small towns.
I prefer _____ .

3 I got all the information I needed from Jane.
Jane provided me _____ .

4 This morning I bought a pair of shoes, which cost £70.
This morning I spent _____ .

136.2 Complete the sentences using the following verbs (in the correct form) + the correct preposition:

believe   concentrate   divide   drive   fill   happen   ~~insist~~   invite   succeed

1 I wanted to go alone, but Sue __insisted on__ coming with me.
2 I haven't seen Mike for ages. I wonder what has _____ him.
3 We've been _____ the party, but unfortunately we can't go.
4 It's a very large house. It's _____ four flats.
5 I don't _____ ghosts. I think people only imagine that they see them.
6 Steve gave me an empty bucket and told me to _____ it _____ water.
7 I was driving along when the car in front of me stopped suddenly. Unfortunately I couldn't stop in time and _____ the back of it.
8 Don't try and do two things together. _____ one thing at a time.
9 It wasn't easy, but in the end we _____ finding a solution to the problem.

136.3 Put in the correct preposition. If the sentence is already complete, leave the space empty.

1 The school provides all its students __with__ books.
2 A strange thing happened _____ me a few days ago.
3 Mark decided to give up sport so that he could concentrate _____ his studies.
4 I don't believe _____ working very hard. It's not worth it.
5 My present job isn't wonderful, but I prefer it _____ what I did before.
6 I hope you succeed _____ getting what you want.
7 As I was coming out of the room, I collided _____ somebody who was coming in.
8 There was an awful noise as the car crashed _____ a tree.
9 Patrick is a photographer. He specialises _____ sports photography.
10 Do you spend much money _____ clothes?
11 The country is divided _____ six regions.
12 I prefer travelling by train _____ driving. It's much more pleasant.
13 I was amazed when Joe walked into the room. I couldn't believe _____ it.
14 Somebody broke _____ my car and stole the radio.
15 I was quite cold, but Tom insisted _____ having the window open.
16 Some words are difficult to translate _____ one language _____ another.
17 What happened _____ the money I lent you? What did you spend it _____ ?
18 The teacher decided to split the class _____ four groups.
19 I filled the tank, but unfortunately I filled it _____ the wrong kind of petrol.

136.4 Use your own ideas to complete these sentences. Use a preposition.

1 I wanted to go out alone, but my friend insisted __on coming with me__ .
2 I spend a lot of money _____ .
3 I saw the accident. The car crashed _____ .
4 Chris prefers basketball _____ .
5 Shakespeare's plays have been translated _____ .

→ Additional exercise 36 (page 323)

A

We often use verbs with the following words:

in	on	up	away	round	about	over	by
out	off	down	back	through	along	forward	

So you can say **look out / get on / take off / run away** etc. These are *phrasal verbs*.

We often use **on/off/out** etc. with verbs of movement. For example:

get on	☐ The bus was full. We couldn't **get on**.
drive off	☐ A woman got into the car and **drove off**.
come back	☐ Sally is leaving tomorrow and **coming back** on Saturday.
turn round	☐ When I touched him on the shoulder, he **turned round**.

But often the second word (**on/off/out** etc.) gives a special meaning to the verb. For example:

break down	☐ Sorry I'm late. The car **broke down**. (= the engine stopped working)
look out	☐ **Look out!** There's a car coming. (= be careful)
take off	☐ It was my first flight. I was nervous as the plane **took off**. (= went into the air)
get on	☐ How was the exam? How did you **get on**? (= How did you do?)
get by	☐ My French isn't very good, but it's enough to **get by**. (= manage)

For more phrasal verbs, see Units 138–145.

B

Sometimes a phrasal verb is followed by a *preposition*. For example:

phrasal verb	*preposition*	
run away	**from**	☐ Why did you **run away from** me?
keep up	**with**	☐ You're walking too fast. I can't **keep up with** you.
look up	**at**	☐ We **looked up at** the plane as it flew above us.
look forward	**to**	☐ Are you **looking forward to** your holiday?

C

Sometimes a phrasal verb has an *object*. Usually there are two possible positions for the object. So you can say:

I **turned on** the light.   *or*   I **turned** the light **on**.
        object   *object*

If the object is a *pronoun* (**it/them/me/him** etc.), only one position is possible:

I **turned it on**. (*not* I turned on it)

Some more examples:

☐ Could you { **fill in** this form? / **fill** this form **in**? }

but   They gave me a form and told me to **fill it in**. (*not* fill in it)

☐ Don't { **throw away** this postcard. / **throw** this postcard **away**. }

but   I want to keep this postcard, so don't **throw it away**. (*not* throw away it)

☐ I'm going to { **take off** my shoes. / **take** my shoes **off**. }

but   These shoes are uncomfortable. I'm going to **take them off**. (*not* take off them)

☐ Don't { **wake up** the baby. / **wake** the baby **up**. }

but   The baby is asleep. Don't **wake her up**. (*not* wake up her)

137.1 Complete each sentence using a verb from A (in the correct form) + a word from B. You can use a word more than once.

A | fly   get   go   look   sit   speak |
B | away   by   down   on   out   round   up |

1 The bus was full. We couldn't ....*get on*.... .
2 I've been standing for the last two hours. I'm going to .... for a bit.
3 A cat tried to catch the bird, but it .... just in time.
4 We were trapped in the building. We couldn't ....
5 I can't hear you very well. Can you .... a little?
6 'Do you speak German?' 'Not very well, but I can ....'
7 House prices are very high. They've .... a lot in the last few years.
8 I thought there was somebody behind me, but when I .... , there was nobody there.

137.2 Complete the sentences using a word from A and a word from B. You can use a word more than once.

A | away   back   forward   in   up |
B | at   through   to   with |

1 You're walking too fast. I can't keep ....*up with*.... you.
2 My holidays are nearly over. Next week I'll be .... work.
3 We went .... the top floor of the building to admire the view.
4 Are you looking .... the party next week?
5 There was a bank robbery last week. The robbers got .... £50,000.
6 I love to look .... the stars in the sky at night.
7 I was sitting in the kitchen when suddenly a bird flew .... the open window.

137.3 Complete the sentences using the following verbs + **it/them/me**:

~~fill in~~   get out   give back   switch on   take off   wake up

1 They gave me a form and told me to ....*fill it in*.... .
2 I'm going to bed now. Can you .... at 6.30?
3 I've got something in my eye and I can't ....
4 I don't like it when people borrow things and don't ....
5 I want to use the kettle. How do I .... ?
6 My shoes are dirty. I'd better .... before going into the house.

137.4 Use your own ideas to complete the sentences. Use a noun (**this newspaper** etc.) or a pronoun (**it/them** etc.) + the word in brackets (**away/up** etc.).

1 Don't throw ....*away this newspaper*.... . I want to keep it. (away)
2 'Do you want this postcard?' 'No, you can throw ....*it away*.... .' (away)
3 I borrowed these books from the library. I have to take .... tomorrow. (back)
4 We can turn .... Nobody is watching it. (off)
5 A: How did the vase get broken?
   B: I'm afraid I knocked .... while I was cleaning. (over)
6 Shh! My mother is asleep. I don't want to wake .... (up)
7 It's quite cold. You should put .... if you're going out. (on)
8 It was only a small fire. I was able to put .... quite easily. (out)
9 A: Is this hotel more expensive than when we stayed here last year?
   B: Yes, they've put .... (up)
10 It's a bit dark in this room. Shall I turn .... ? (on)

→ Additional exercises 37–41 (pages 323–25)

Phrasal verbs 2   in/out

A   Compare **in** and **out**:

in = into a room, a building, a car etc.
- ☐ How did the thieves **get in**?
- ☐ Here's a key, so you can **let yourself in**.
- ☐ Sally walked up to the edge of the pool and **dived in**. (= into the water)
- ☐ I've got a new flat. I'm **moving in** on Friday.
- ☐ As soon as I got to the airport, I **checked in**.

In the same way you can say **go in**, **come in**, **walk in**, **break in** etc.

Compare **in** and **into**:
- ☐ I'm moving **in** next week.
- ☐ I'm moving **into my new flat** on Friday.

out = out of a room, building, a car etc.
- ☐ He just stood up and **walked out**.
- ☐ I had no key, so I was **locked out**.
- ☐ She swam up and down the pool, and then **climbed out**.
- ☐ Tim opened the window and **looked out**.
- ☐ (at a hotel) What time do we have to **check out**?

In the same way you can say **go out**, **get out**, **move out**, **let** somebody **out** etc.

Compare **out** and **out of**:
- ☐ He walked **out**.
- ☐ He walked **out of the room**.

B   Other verbs + **in**

drop in / call in = *visit somebody for a short time without arranging to do this*
- ☐ I **dropped in** to see Chris on my way home.

join in = *take part in an activity that is already going on*
- ☐ We're playing a game. Why don't you **join in**?

plug in an electrical machine = *connect it to the electricity supply*
- ☐ The fridge isn't working because you haven't **plugged** it **in**.

plug in

fill in a form, a questionnaire etc. = *write the necessary information on a form*
- ☐ Please **fill in** the application form and send it to us by 28 February.

You can also say **fill out** a form.

take somebody **in** = *deceive somebody*
- ☐ The man said he was a policeman and I believed him. I was completely **taken in**.

C   Other verbs + **out**

eat out = *eat at a restaurant, not at home*
- ☐ There wasn't anything to eat at home, so we decided to **eat out**.

drop out of college / university / a course / a race = *stop before you have completely finished a course/race etc.*
- ☐ Gary went to university but **dropped out** after a year.

get out of something that you arranged to do = *avoid doing it*
- ☐ I promised I'd go to the wedding. I don't want to go, but I can't **get out** of it now.

cut something **out** (of a newspaper etc.)
- ☐ There was a beautiful picture in the magazine, so I **cut** it **out** and kept it.

leave something **out** = *omit it, not include it*
- ☐ In the sentence 'She said that she was ill', you can **leave out** the word 'that'.

cross something **out** / **rub** something **out**
- ☐ Some of the names on the list had been **crossed out**.   ~~Sarah~~   *cross out*

Exercises

138.1 Complete each sentence using a verb in the correct form.

1 Here's a key so that you can ......*let*...... yourself in.
2 Liz doesn't like cooking, so she .... out a lot.
3 Eve isn't living in this flat any more. She .... out a few weeks ago.
4 If you're in our part of town, you must .... in and see us.
5 When I .... in at the airport, I was told my flight would be delayed.
6 There were some advertisements in the paper that I wanted to keep, so I ....
   them out.
7 I wanted to iron some clothes, but there was nowhere to .... the iron in.
8 I hate .... in questionnaires.
9 Steve was upset because he'd been .... out of the team.
10 Be careful! The water's not very deep here, so don't .... in.
11 If you write in pencil and you make a mistake, you can .... it out.
12 Paul started doing a Spanish course, but he .... out after a few weeks.

138.2 Complete the sentences with **in**, **into**, **out** or **out of**.

1 I've got a new flat. I'm moving ......*in*...... on Friday.
2 We checked .... the hotel as soon as we arrived.
3 As soon as we arrived at the hotel, we checked ....
4 The car stopped and the driver got ....
5 Thieves broke .... the house while we were away.
6 Why did Sarah drop .... college? Did she fail her exams?

138.3 Complete each sentence using a verb + **in** or **out (of)**.

1 Sally walked to the edge of the pool, ...*dived in*...... and swam to the other end.
2 Not all the runners finished the race. Three of them ....
3 I went to see Joe and Sue in their new house. They .... last week.
4 I've told you everything you need to know. I don't think I've ....
   anything.
5 Some people in the crowd started singing. Then a few more people ....
   and soon everybody was singing.
6 We go to restaurants a lot. We like ....
7 Don't be .... by him. If I were you, I wouldn't believe anything he says.
8 I .... to see Laura a few days ago. She was fine.
9 A: Can we meet tomorrow morning at ten?
   B: Probably. I'm supposed to go to another meeting, but I think I can
   .... it.

138.4 Complete the sentences. Use the word in brackets in the correct form.

1 A: The fridge isn't working.
   B: That's because you haven't ......*plugged it in*...... . (plug)
2 A: What do I have to do with these forms?
   B: .... and send them to this address. (fill)
3 A: I've made a mistake on this form.
   B: That's all right. Just .... and correct it. (cross)
4 A: Did you believe the story they told you?
   B: Yes, I'm afraid they completely .... (take)
5 A: Have you been to that new club in Bridge Street?
   B: We wanted to go there a few nights ago, but the doorman wouldn't ....
   because we weren't members. (let)

→ Additional exercises 37–41 **(pages 323–25)**

A

out = not burning, not shining

go out	☐ Suddenly all the lights in the building **went out**.
put out a fire / a cigarette / a light	☐ We managed to **put** the fire **out**.
turn out a light	☐ I **turned** the lights **out** before leaving.
blow out a candle	☐ We don't need the candle. You can **blow** it **out**.

B   work out

work out = *do physical exercises*
  ☐ Rachel **works out** at the gym three times a week.

work out = *develop, progress*
  ☐ Good luck for the future. I hope everything **works out** well for you.
  ☐ A: Why did James leave the company?
     B: Things didn't **work out**. (= things didn't work out well)

work out (for mathematical calculations)
  ☐ The total bill for three people is £84.60. That **works out** at £28.20 each.

work something **out** = *calculate, think about a problem and find the answer*
  ☐ 345 × 76? I need to do this on paper. I can't **work** it **out** in my head.

C   Other verbs + **out**

carry out an order / an experiment / a survey / an investigation / a plan etc.
  ☐ Soldiers are expected to **carry out** orders.
  ☐ An investigation into the accident will be **carried out** as soon as possible.

fall out (**with** somebody) = *stop being friends*
  ☐ They used to be very good friends. I'm surprised to hear that they have **fallen out**.
  ☐ David **fell out with** his father and left home.

find out that/what/when … etc., **find out about** something = *get information*
  ☐ The police never **found out** who committed the murder.
  ☐ I've just **found out** that it's Helen's birthday today.
  ☐ I called the tourist office to **find out** about hotels in the town.

give/hand things **out** = *give to each person*
  ☐ At the end of the lecture, the speaker **gave out** information sheets to the audience.

point something **out** (**to** somebody) = *draw attention to something*
  ☐ As we drove through the city, our guide **pointed out** all the sights.
  ☐ I didn't realise I'd made a mistake until somebody **pointed** it **out to** me.

run out (**of** something)
  ☐ We **ran out of** petrol on the motorway. (= we used all our petrol)

sort something **out** = *find a solution to, put in order*
  ☐ There are a few problems we need to **sort out**.
  ☐ All these papers are mixed up. I'll have to **sort** them **out**.

turn out to be … / **turn out** good/nice etc. / **turn out** that …
  ☐ Nobody believed Paul at first, but he **turned out** to be right. (= it became clear in the end that he was right)
  ☐ The weather wasn't so good in the morning, but it **turned out** nice later.
  ☐ I thought they knew each other, but it **turned out** that they'd never met.

try out a machine, a system, a new idea etc. = *test it to see if it is OK*
  ☐ The company is **trying out** a new computer system at the moment.

139.1 Which words can go together? Choose from the box.

| a candle | a cigarette | a light | a mess | a mistake | a new product | an order |

1 turn out _a light_
2 point out ....
3 blow out ....
4 carry out ....
5 put out ....
6 try out ....
7 sort out ....

139.2 Complete each sentence using a verb + out.

1 The company is ...._trying out_.... a new computer system at the moment.
2 Steve is very fit. He does a lot of sport and .... regularly.
3 The road will be closed for two days next week while building work is ....
4 We didn't manage to discuss everything at the meeting. We .... of time.
5 You have to .... the problem yourself. I can't do it for you.
6 I phoned the station to .... what time the train arrived.
7 The new drug will be .... on a small group of patients.
8 I thought the two books were the same until a friend of mine .... the difference.
9 They got married a few years ago but it didn't .... , and they separated.
10 There was a power cut and all the lights ....
11 We thought she was American at first, but she .... to be Swedish.
12 Sometimes it .... cheaper to eat in a restaurant than to cook at home.
13 I haven't applied for the job yet. I want to .... more about the company first.
14 It took the fire brigade two hours to .... the fire.

139.3 For each picture, complete the sentence using a verb + out.

1	2	3 _earlier_ _now_
They've _run out of petrol_ .	The man with the beard is .... leaflets.	The weather has ....
4	5	6 _LISA_
They've	One of Joe's jobs in the office is	Lisa is trying to .... how ....

139.4 Complete the sentences. Each time use a verb + out.

1 A: Shall I leave the light on?
  B: No, you can _turn it out_ .
2 A: This recipe looks interesting.
  B: Yes, let's ....
3 A: How much money do I owe you exactly?
  B: Just a moment. I'll have to ....
4 A: What happened about your problem with your bank?
  B: It's OK now. I went to see them and we ....

Phrasal verbs 4   on/off (1)

A   On and off for lights, machines etc.

We say: the light **is on** / **put** the light **on** / **leave** the light **on** etc.
            turn the light **on/off**   *or*   **switch** the light **on/off**

- ☐ Shall I **leave** the lights **on** or **turn** them **off**?
- ☐ 'Is the heating **on**?'   'No, I **switched** it **off**.'
- ☐ We need some boiling water, so I'll **put** the kettle **on**.

Also **put on** some music / a CD / a video etc.

- ☐ I haven't listened to this CD yet. Shall I **put** it **on**?

B   On and off for events etc.

go on = *happen*
- ☐ What's all that noise? What's **going on**? (= what's happening)

call something **off** = *cancel it*
- ☐ The open air concert had to be **called off** because of the weather.

put something **off**, **put off** doing something = *delay it*
- ☐ The wedding has been **put off** until January.
- ☐ We can't **put off** making a decision. We have to decide now.

C   On and off for clothes etc.

put on clothes, glasses, make-up, a seat belt etc.
- ☐ My hands were cold, so I **put** my gloves **on**.

Also **put on** weight = *get heavier*
- ☐ I've **put on** two kilograms in the last month.

try on clothes (to see if they fit)
- ☐ I **tried on** a jacket in the shop, but it didn't fit me very well.

take off clothes, glasses etc.
- ☐ It was warm, so I **took off** my jacket.

D   Off = away from a person or place

be off (to a place)
- ☐ Tomorrow I'**m off** to Paris / I'**m off** on holiday.
    (= I'm going to Paris / I'm going on holiday)

walk off / **run off** / **drive off** / **ride off** / **go off** (similar to **walk away** / **run away** etc.)
- ☐ Diane got on her bike and **rode off**.
- ☐ Mark left home at the age of eighteen and **went off** to Canada.

set off = *start a journey*
- ☐ We **set off** very early to avoid the traffic. (= We left early)

take off = *leave the ground (for planes)*
- ☐ After a long delay the plane finally **took off**.

see somebody off = *go with them to the airport/station to say goodbye*
- ☐ Helen was going away. We went to the station with her to **see her off**.

Exercises

140.1 Complete the sentences using **put on** + the following:

> a CD   the heating   the kettle   ~~the light~~   the oven

1 It was getting dark, so I ___put the light on___ .
2 It was getting cold, so I _____ .
3 I wanted to bake a cake, so I _____ .
4 I wanted to make some tea, so I _____ .
5 I wanted to listen to some music, so I _____ .

140.2 Complete the sentences. Each time use a verb + **on** or **off**.

1 It was warm, so I ___took off___ my jacket.
2 What are all these people doing? What's _____ ?
3 The weather was too bad for the plane to _____ , so the flight was delayed.
4 I didn't want to be disturbed, so I _____ my mobile phone.
5 Rachel got into her car and _____ at high speed.
6 Tim has _____ weight since I last saw him. He used to be quite thin.
7 A: What time are you leaving tomorrow?
    B: I'm not sure yet, but I'd like to _____ as early as possible.
8 Don't _____ until tomorrow what you can do today.
9 There was going to be a strike by bus drivers, but now they have been offered more money and the strike has been _____ .
10 Are you cold? Shall I get you a sweater to _____ ?
11 When I go away, I prefer to be alone at the station or airport. I don't like it when people come to _____ me _____ .

140.3 Look at the pictures and complete the sentences.

1 Her hands were cold, so she ___put her gloves on___ .

2 The plane _____ at 10.55.

3 *MARIA*   Maria _____ , but it was too big for her.

4 The match _____ because of the weather.

5 *MARK*   Bye!   Mark's parents went to the airport to _____ .

6 He took his sunglasses out of his pocket and _____ .

→ Additional exercises 37–41 **(pages 323–25)**

A   *Verb + on* = continue doing something

drive on / walk on / play on = *continue walking/driving/playing etc.*
- Shall we stop at this petrol station or shall we **drive on** to the next one?

go on = *continue*
- The party **went on** until 4 o'clock in the morning.

go on / carry on (doing something) = *continue (doing something)*
- We can't **go on** spending money like this. We'll have nothing left soon.
- I don't want to **carry on** working here. I'm going to look for another job.

Also **go on with / carry on with** something
- Don't let me disturb you. Please **carry on with** what you're doing.

keep on doing something = *do it continuously or repeatedly*
- He **keeps on** criticising me. I'm fed up with it!

B   Get on

get on = *progress*
- How are you **getting on** in your new job? (= How is it going?)

get on (**with** somebody) = *have a good relationship*
- Joanne and Karen don't **get on**. They're always arguing.
- Richard **gets on** well **with** his neighbours. They're all very friendly.

get on with something = *continue doing something you have to do, usually after an interruption*
- I must **get on with** my work. I have a lot to do.

C   *Verb + off*

doze off / drop off / nod off = *fall asleep*
- The lecture wasn't very interesting. In fact I **dropped off** in the middle of it.

finish something **off** = *do the last part of something*
- A: Have you finished painting the kitchen?
  B: Nearly. I'll **finish** it **off** tomorrow.

go off = *explode*
- A bomb **went off** in the city centre, but fortunately nobody was hurt.

Also an alarm can **go off** = *ring*
- Did you hear the alarm **go off**?

put somebody **off** (doing something) = *cause somebody not to want something or to do something*
- We wanted to go to the exhibition, but we were **put off** by the long queue.
- What **put** you **off** applying for the job? Was the salary too low?

rip somebody **off** = *cheat somebody (informal)*
- Did you really pay £1,000 for that painting? I think you were **ripped off**.
  (= you paid too much)

show off = *try to impress people with your ability, your knowledge etc.*
- Look at that boy on the bike riding with no hands. He's just **showing off**.

tell somebody **off** = *speak angrily to somebody because they did something wrong*
- Clare's mother **told** her **off** for wearing dirty shoes in the house.

Go on / carry on → Unit 53B   Phrasal verbs 1 (Introduction) → Unit 137
More verbs + on/off → Unit 140

141.1 Change the <u>underlined</u> words. Keep the same meaning, but use a verb + **on** or **off**.

1 Did you hear the bomb <u>explode</u>?
Did you hear the bomb ....*go off*.... ?
2 The meeting <u>continued</u> longer than I expected.
The meeting .... longer than I expected.
3 We didn't stop to rest. We <u>continued walking</u>.
We didn't stop to rest. We ....
4 I <u>fell asleep</u> while I was watching TV.
I .... while I was watching TV.
5 Gary doesn't want to retire. He wants to <u>continue</u> working.
Gary doesn't want to retire. He wants to .... working.
6 The fire alarm <u>rang</u> in the middle of the night.
The fire alarm .... in the middle of the night.
7 Martin <u>phones me continuously</u>. It's very annoying.
Martin .... It's very annoying.

141.2 Complete each sentence using a verb + **on** or **off**.

1 We can't ....*go on*.... spending money like this. We'll have nothing left soon.
2 I was standing by the car when suddenly the alarm ....
3 I'm not ready to go home yet. I have a few things to ....
4 'Shall I stop the car here?' 'No, ...'
5 Bill paid too much for the car he bought. I think he was ....
6 'Is Emma enjoying her course at university?' 'Yes, she's .... very well.'
7 I was very tired at work today. I nearly .... at my desk a couple of times.
8 Ben was .... by his boss for being late for work repeatedly.
9 I really like working with my colleagues. We all .... really well together.
10 There was a very loud noise. It sounded like a bomb ....
11 I .... making the same mistake. It's very frustrating.
12 I've just had a coffee break, and now I must .... with my work.
13 Peter is always trying to impress people. He's always ....
14 We decided not to go into the museum. We were .... by the cost of tickets.

141.3 Complete the sentences. Use the following verbs (in the correct form) + **on** or **off**. Sometimes you will need other words as well:

carry   finish   ~~get~~   get   get   go   rip   tell

1 A: How ....*are you getting on*.... in your new job?
B: Fine, thanks. It's going very well.
2 A: Have you written the letter you had to write?
B: I've started it. I'll .... in the morning.
3 A: We took a taxi to the airport. It cost £40.
B: £40! Normally it costs about £20. You ....
4 A: Why were you late for work this morning?
B: I overslept. My alarm clock didn't ....
5 A: How .... in your interview? Do you think you'll get the job?
B: I hope so. The interview was OK.
6 A: Did you stop playing tennis when it started to rain?
B: No, we .... The rain wasn't very heavy.
7 A: Some children at the next table in the restaurant were behaving very badly.
B: Why didn't their parents .... ?
8 A: Why does Paul want to leave his job?
B: He .... his boss.

→ Additional exercises 37–41 **(pages 323–25)**

Phrasal verbs 6   up/down

A

Compare **up** and **down**:

put something **up** (on a wall etc.)
- □ I **put** some pictures **up** on the wall.

pick something **up**
- □ There was a letter on the floor. I **picked** it **up** and looked at it.

stand up
- □ Alan **stood up** and walked out.

turn something **up**
- □ I can't hear the TV. Can you **turn** it **up** a bit?

take something **down** (from a wall etc.)
- □ I didn't like the picture, so I **took** it **down**.

put something **down**
- □ I stopped writing and **put down** my pen.

sit down / bend down / lie down
- □ I **bent down** to tie my shoelace.

turn something **down**
- □ The oven is too hot. **Turn** it **down** to 150 degrees.

B

Knock down etc.

knock down a building / **blow** something **down** / **cut** something **down** etc.
- □ Some old houses were **knocked down** to make way for the new shopping centre.
- □ Why did you **cut down** the tree in your garden?

Also be **knocked down** (by a car etc.)
- □ A man was **knocked down** by a car and taken to hospital.

C

Down = getting less

slow down = *go more slowly*
- □ You're driving too fast. **Slow down**.

calm (somebody) **down** = *become calmer, make somebody calmer*
- □ **Calm down**. There's no point in getting angry.

cut down (**on** something) = *eat, drink or do something less often*
- □ I'm trying to **cut down on** coffee. I drink far too much of it.

D

Other verbs + **down**

break down = *stop working (for machines, cars, relationships etc.)*
- □ The car **broke down** and I had to phone for help.
- □ Their marriage **broke down** after only a few months.

close down / shut down = *stop doing business*
- □ There used to be a shop at the end of the street; it **closed down** a few years ago.

let somebody **down** = *disappoint somebody because you didn't do what they hoped*
- □ You can always rely on Pete. He'll never **let** you **down**.

turn somebody/something **down** = *refuse an application, an offer etc.*
- □ I applied for several jobs, but I was **turned down** for each one.
- □ Rachel was offered the job, but she decided to **turn** it **down**.

write something **down** = *write something on paper because you may need the information later*
- □ I can't remember Tim's address. I **wrote** it **down**, but I can't find it.

142.1 Complete the sentences. Use the following verbs (in the correct form) + **up** or **down**:

calm   let   put   ~~take~~   turn   turn

1 I don't like this picture on the wall. I'm going to ___take it down___ .
2 The music is too loud. Can you _____ ?
3 David was very angry. I tried to _____ .
4 I've bought some new curtains. Can you help me _____ ?
5 I promised I would help Anna. I don't want to _____ .
6 I was offered the job, but I decided I didn't want it. So I _____ .

142.2 For each picture, complete the sentences using a verb + **up** or **down**. In most sentences you will need other words as well.

1 There used to be a tree next to the house, but we ___cut it down___ .
2 There used to be some shelves on the wall, but I _____ .
3 The ceiling was so low, he couldn't _____ straight.
4 She couldn't hear the radio very well, so she _____ .
5 While they were waiting for the bus, they _____ on the ground.
6 A few trees _____ in the storm last week.
7 Sarah gave me her phone number. I _____ on a piece of paper.
8 Liz dropped her keys, so she _____ and _____ .

142.3 Complete each sentence using a verb (in the correct form) + **down**.

1 I stopped writing and ___put down___ my pen.
2 I was really angry. It took me a long time to _____ .
3 The train _____ as it approached the station.
4 Sarah applied to study medicine at university, but she _____ .
5 Our car is very reliable. It has never _____ .
6 I need to spend less money. I'm going to _____ on things I don't really need.
7 I didn't play very well. I felt that I had _____ the other players in the team.
8 The shop _____ because it was losing money.
9 This is a very ugly building. Many people would like it to _____ .
10 I can't understand why you _____ the chance of working abroad for a year. It would have been a great experience for you.
11 A: Did you see the accident? What happened exactly?
   B: A man _____ by a car as he was crossing the road.
12 Peter got married when he was 20, but unfortunately the marriage _____ a few years later.

→ Additional exercises 37–41 (pages 323–25)

A

go up / **come up** / **walk up** (to ...) = *approach*
- □ A man **came up to** me in the street and asked me for money.

catch up (**with** somebody), **catch** somebody **up** = *move faster than somebody in front of you so that you reach them*
- □ I'm not ready to go yet. You go on and I'll **catch up with** you / I'll **catch** you **up**.

keep up (**with** somebody) = *continue at the same speed or level*
- □ You're walking too fast. I can't **keep up** (**with** you).
- □ You're doing well. **Keep** it **up**!

B

set up an organisation, a company, a business, a system, a website etc. = *start it*
- □ The government has **set up** a committee to investigate the problem.

take up a hobby, a sport, an activity etc. = *start doing it*
- □ Laura **took up** photography a few years ago. She takes really good pictures.

fix up a meeting etc. = *arrange it*
- □ We've **fixed up** a meeting for next Monday.

C

grow up = *become an adult*
- □ Sarah was born in Ireland but **grew up** in England.

bring up a child = *raise, look after a child*
- □ Her parents died when she was a child and she was **brought up** by her grandparents.

D

clean up / **clear up** / **tidy up** something = *make it clean, tidy etc.*
- □ Look at this mess! Who's going to **tidy up**? (*or* **tidy** it **up**)

wash up = *wash the plates, dishes etc. after a meal*
- □ I hate **washing up**. (*or* I hate **doing the washing-up**.)

E

end up somewhere, **end up** doing something etc.
- □ There was a fight in the street and three men **ended up** in hospital. (= that's what happened to these men in the end)
- □ I couldn't find a hotel and **ended up** sleeping on a bench at the station. (= that's what happened to me in the end)

give up = *stop trying*, **give** something **up** = *stop doing it*
- □ Don't **give up**. Keep trying!
- □ Sue got bored with her job and decided to **give** it **up**. (= stop doing it)

make up something / be **made up of** something
- □ Children under 16 **make up** half the population of the city. (= half the population are children under 16)
- □ Air is **made up** mainly **of** nitrogen and oxygen. (= Air consists of ...)

take up space or time = *use space or time*
- □ Most of the space in the room was **taken up** by a large table.

turn up / **show up** = *arrive, appear*
- □ We arranged to meet Dave last night, but he didn't **turn up**.

use something **up** = *use all of it so that nothing is left*
- □ I'm going to take a few more photographs. I want to **use up** the rest of the film.

Phrasal verbs 1 (Introduction) → Unit 137   More verbs + up → Units 142, 144

143.1 Look at the pictures and complete the sentences. Use <u>three</u> words each time, including a verb from Section A.

A man ....<u>came up to</u>........ me in the street and asked me the way to the station.

Sue .... the front door of the house and rang the doorbell.

Tom was a long way behind the other runners, but he managed to .... them.

Tanya was running too fast for Paul. He couldn't .... her.

143.2 Complete the sentences. Use the following verbs (in the correct form) + **up**:

~~end~~   end   give   give   grow   make   take   take   turn   use   wash

1 I couldn't find a hotel and ....<u>ended up</u>.... sleeping on a bench at the station.
2 I'm feeling very tired now. I've .... all my energy.
3 After dinner I .... and put the dishes away.
4 People often ask children what they want to be when they ....
5 We invited Tim to the party, but he didn't ....
6 Two years ago Mark .... his studies to be a professional footballer.
7 A: Do you do any sports?
   B: Not at the moment, but I'm thinking of .... tennis.
8 You don't have enough determination. You .... too easily.
9 Karen travelled a lot for a few years and .... in Canada, where she still lives.
10 I do a lot of gardening. It .... most of my free time.
11 There are two universities in the city, and students .... 20 per cent of the population.

143.3 Complete the sentences. Use the following verbs + **up** (with any other necessary words):

bring   ~~catch~~   **fix**   ~~give~~   **go**   **keep**   **keep**   **make**   **set**   **tidy**

1 Sue got bored with her job and decided to ....<u>give it up</u>.... .
2 I'm not ready yet. You go on and I'll ....<u>catch up with</u>.... you.
3 The room is in a mess. I'd better ....
4 We expect to go away on holiday sometime in July, but we haven't .... yet.
5 Stephen is having problems at school. He can't .... the rest of the class.
6 Although I .... in the country, I have always preferred cities.
7 Our team started the game well, but we couldn't .... , and in the end we lost.
8 I saw Mike at the party, so I .... him and said hello.
9 When I was on holiday, I joined a tour group. The group .... two Americans, three Germans, five Italians and myself.
10 Helen has her own internet website. A friend of hers helped her to ....

A

bring up a topic etc. = *introduce it in a conversation*
- ☐ I don't want to hear any more about this matter. Please don't **bring** it **up** again.

come up = *be introduced in a conversation*
- ☐ Some interesting matters **came up** in our discussion yesterday.

come up with an idea, a suggestion etc. = *produce an idea*
- ☐ Sarah is very creative. She's always **coming up with** new ideas.

make something **up** = *invent something that is not true*
- ☐ What Kevin told you about himself wasn't true. He **made** it all **up**.

B

cheer up = *be happier*, **cheer** somebody **up** = *make somebody feel happier*
- ☐ You look so sad! **Cheer up!**
- ☐ Helen is depressed at the moment. What can we do to **cheer her up**?

save up for something / to do something = *save money to buy something*
- ☐ Dan is **saving up** for a trip round the world.

clear up = *become bright (for weather)*
- ☐ It was raining when I got up, but it **cleared up** during the morning.

C

blow up = *explode*, **blow** something **up** = *destroy it with a bomb etc.*
- ☐ The engine caught fire and **blew up**.
- ☐ The bridge was **blown up** during the war.

tear something **up** = *tear it into pieces*
- ☐ I didn't read the letter. I just **tore** it **up** and threw it away.

beat somebody **up** = *hit someone repeatedly so that they are badly hurt*
- ☐ A friend of mine was attacked and **beaten up** a few days ago. He was badly hurt and had to go to hospital.

D

break up / split up (with somebody) = *separate*
- ☐ I'm surprised to hear that Sue and Paul have **split up**. They seemed very happy together when I last saw them.

do up a coat, a shoelace, buttons etc. = *fasten, tie etc.*
- ☐ It's quite cold. **Do up** your coat before you go out.

do up a building, a room etc. = *repair and improve it*
- ☐ The kitchen looks great now that it has been **done up**.

look something **up** in a dictionary/encyclopaedia etc.
- ☐ If you don't know the meaning of a word, you can **look** it **up** in a dictionary.

put up with something = *tolerate it*
- ☐ We live on a busy road, so we have to **put up with** a lot of noise from the traffic.

hold up a person, a plan etc. = *delay*
- ☐ Don't wait for me. I don't want to **hold** you **up**.
- ☐ Plans to build a new factory have been **held up** because of the company's financial problems.

mix up people/things, **get** people/things **mixed up** = *you think one is the other*
- ☐ The two brothers look very similar. Many people **mix** them **up**. (*or* … **get** them **mixed up**)

Phrasal verbs 1 (Introduction) → Unit 137   More verbs + up → Units 142–143

144.1 Which goes with which?

1 I'm going to tear up	A a new camera	1 ___F___
2 Jane came up with	B a lot of bad weather	2 ....
3 Paul is always making up	C your jacket	3 ....
4 I think you should do up	D an interesting suggestion	4 ....
5 I don't think you should bring up	E excuses	5 ....
6 I'm saving up for	F ~~the letter~~	6 ....
7 We had to put up with	G that subject	7 ....

144.2 Look at the pictures and complete the sentences. You will need two or three words each time.

1 *this morning* / *now*
The weather was horrible this morning, but it's ....*cleared up*.... now.

2 LINDA   Sorry I'm late.
Linda was late because she was .... in the traffic.

3
They bought an old house and ....
.... It's really nice now.

4 PETE   Come out for a meal with us!
Pete was really depressed. We took him out for a meal to ....

144.3 Complete the sentences. Each time use a verb (in the correct form) + **up**. Sometimes you will need other words as well.

1 Some interesting matters ....*came up*.... in our discussion yesterday.
2 The ship .... and sank. The cause of the explosion was never discovered.
3 Two men have been arrested after a man was .... outside a restaurant last night. The injured man was taken to hospital.
4 'Is Robert still going out with Tina?' 'No, they've ....'
5 I put my shoes on and .... the shoelaces.
6 The weather is horrible this morning, isn't it? I hope it .... later.
7 I wanted to phone Chris, but I dialled Laura's number by mistake. I got their phone numbers ....

144.4 Complete the sentences. Each time use a verb + **up**. Sometimes you will need other words as well.

1 Don't wait for me. I don't want to ....*hold you up*.... .
2 I don't know what this word means. I'll have to ....
3 There's nothing we can do about the problem. We'll just have to .... it.
4 'Was that story true?' 'No, I ....'
5 I think we should follow Tom's suggestion. Nobody has .... a better plan.
6 I hate this photograph. I'm going to ....
7 I'm trying to spend less money at the moment. I'm .... a trip to Australia.

A   Compare **away** and **back**:

away = away from home ☐ We're **going away** on holiday today. **away** = away from a place, a person etc. ☐ The woman got into her car and **drove away**. ☐ I tried to take a picture of the bird, but it **flew away**. ☐ I dropped the ticket and it **blew away** in the wind. ☐ The police searched the house and **took away** a computer. In the same way you can say: **walk away, run away, look away** etc.	**back** = back home ☐ We'll **be back** in three weeks. **back** = back to a place, a person etc. ☐ A: I'm going out now. B: What time will you **be back**? ☐ After eating at a restaurant, we **walked back** to our hotel. ☐ I've still got Jane's keys. I forgot to **give** them **back** to her. ☐ When you've finished with that book, can you **put** it **back** on the shelf? In the same way you can say: **go back, come back, get back, take** something **back** etc.

B   Other verbs + **away**

get away = *escape, leave with difficulty*
☐ We tried to catch the thief, but he managed to **get away**.

get away with something = *do something wrong without being caught*
☐ I parked in a no-parking zone, but I **got away with** it.

keep away (**from** …) = *don't go near*
☐ **Keep away from** the edge of the pool. You might fall in.

give something **away** = *give it to somebody else because you don't want it any more*
☐ 'Did you sell your old computer?'   'No, I **gave** it **away**.'

put something **away** = *put it in the place where it is kept, usually out of sight*
☐ When the children had finished playing with their toys, they **put** them **away**.

throw something **away** = *put it in the rubbish*
☐ I kept the letter, but I **threw away** the envelope.

C   Other verbs + **back**

wave back / smile back / shout back / write back / hit somebody **back**
☐ I waved to her and she **waved back**.

call/phone/ring (somebody) **back** = *return a phone call*
☐ I can't talk to you now. I'll **call** you **back** in ten minutes.

get back to somebody = *reply to them by phone etc.*
☐ I sent him an email, but he never **got back to** me.

look back (**on** something) = *think about what happened in the past*
☐ My first job was in a travel agency. I didn't like it very much at the time but, **looking back on** it, I learnt a lot and it was a very useful experience.

pay back money, **pay** somebody **back**
☐ If you borrow money, you have to **pay** it **back**.
☐ Thanks for lending me the money. I'll **pay** you **back** next week.

Phrasal verbs 1 (Introduction) → Unit 137

Exercises

145.1 Complete each sentence using a verb in the correct form.

1 The woman got into her car and __drove__ away.
2 Here's the money you need. _____ me back when you can.
3 Don't _____ that box away. It could be useful.
4 Jane doesn't do anything at work. I don't know how she _____ away with it.
5 I'm going out now. I'll _____ back at about 10.30.
6 You should think more about the future; don't _____ back all the time.
7 Gary is very generous. He won some money in the lottery and _____ it all away.
8 I'll _____ back to you as soon as I have the information you need.

145.2 Complete the sentences. Each time use a verb + away or back.

1 I was away all day yesterday. I __got back__ very late.
2 I haven't seen our neighbours for a while. I think they must _____ .
3 'I'm going out now.' 'OK. What time will you _____ ?'
4 A man was trying to break into a car. When he saw me, he _____ .
5 I smiled at him, but he didn't _____ .
6 If you cheat in the exam, you might _____ with it. But you might get caught.
7 Be careful! That's an electric fence. _____ from it.

145.3 Look at the pictures and complete the sentences.

1	2	3
She waved to him and he __waved back__ .	It was windy. I dropped a twenty-pound note and it _____ .	*SUE* Sue opened the letter, read it and _____ in the envelope.
4	5 *ELLIE* *BEN*	6
He tried to talk to her, but she just _____ .	Ellie threw the ball to Ben and he _____ .	His shoes were worn out, so he _____ .

145.4 Complete the sentences. Use the verb in brackets + away or back.

1 A: Do you still have my keys?
   B: No. Don't you remember? I __gave them back__ to you yesterday? (give)
2 A: Do you want this magazine?
   B: No, I've finished with it. You can _____ . (throw)
3 A: How are your new jeans? Do they fit you OK?
   B: No, I'm going to _____ to the shop. (take)
4 A: Here's the money you asked me to lend you.
   B: Thanks. I'll _____ as soon as I can. (pay)
5 A: What happened to all the books you used to have?
   B: I didn't want them any more, so I _____ . (give)
6 A: Did you phone Sarah?
   B: She wasn't there. I left a message asking her to _____ . (call)

→ Additional exercises 37–41 (pages 323–25)

Appendix 1
Regular and irregular verbs

1.1   *Regular verbs*

If a verb is regular, the past simple and past participle end in **-ed**. For example:

infinitive	clean	finish	use	paint	stop	carry
past simple *past participle* }	cleaned	finished	used	painted	stopped	carried

For spelling rules, see Appendix 6.

For the *past simple* (**I cleaned** / they **finished** / she **carried** etc.), see Unit 5.

We use the *past participle* to make the perfect tenses and all the passive forms.
Perfect tenses (**have/has/had** cleaned):
- □ I **have cleaned** the windows. (*present perfect* – see Units 7–8)
- □ They were still working. They **had**n't **finished**. (*past perfect* – see Unit 15)

Passive (**is** cleaned / **was** cleaned etc.):
- □ He **was carried** out of the room. (*past simple passive*) } see Units 42–44
- □ This gate has just **been painted**. (*present perfect passive*) }

1.2   *Irregular verbs*

When the past simple and past participle do *not* end in **-ed** (for example, **I saw** / **I have seen**), the verb is *irregular*.

With some irregular verbs, all three forms (*infinitive*, *past simple* and *past participle*) are the same. For example, **hit**:
- □ Don't **hit** me. (*infinitive*)
- □ Somebody **hit** me as I came into the room. (*past simple*)
- □ I've never **hit** anybody in my life. (*past participle – present perfect*)
- □ George was **hit** on the head by a stone. (*past participle – passive*)

With other irregular verbs, the past simple is the same as the past participle (but different from the infinitive). For example, **tell → told**:
- □ Can you **tell** me what to do? (*infinitive*)
- □ She **told** me to come back the next day. (*past simple*)
- □ Have you **told** anybody about your new job? (*past participle – present perfect*)
- □ I was **told** to come back the next day. (*past participle – passive*)

With other irregular verbs, all three forms are different. For example, **wake → woke/woken**:
- □ I'll **wake** you up. (*infinitive*)
- □ I **woke** up in the middle of the night. (*past simple*)
- □ The baby has **woken** up. (*past participle – present perfect*)
- □ I was **woken** up by a loud noise. (*past participle – passive*)

1.3   The following verbs can be regular or irregular:

burn	→ burned	*or*	burnt		**smell**	→ smelled	*or*	smelt
dream	→ dreamed	*or*	dreamt [dremt]*		**spell**	→ spelled	*or*	spelt
lean	→ leaned	*or*	leant [lent]*		**spill**	→ spilled	*or*	spilt
learn	→ learned	*or*	learnt		**spoil**	→ spoiled	*or*	spoilt

* pronunciation

So you can say:
- □ I **leant** out of the window.   *or*   I **leaned** out of the window.
- □ The dinner has been **spoiled**.   *or*   The dinner has been **spoilt**.

In British English the irregular form (**burnt/learnt** etc.) is more usual. For American English, see Appendix 7.

1.4   List of irregular verbs

infinitive	past simple	past participle
be	was/were	been
beat	beat	beaten
become	became	become
begin	began	begun
bend	bent	bent
bet	bet	bet
bite	bit	bitten
blow	blew	blown
break	broke	broken
bring	brought	brought
broadcast	broadcast	broadcast
build	built	built
burst	burst	burst
buy	bought	bought
catch	caught	caught
choose	chose	chosen
come	came	come
cost	cost	cost
creep	crept	crept
cut	cut	cut
deal	dealt	dealt
dig	dug	dug
do	did	done
draw	drew	drawn
drink	drank	drunk
drive	drove	driven
eat	ate	eaten
fall	fell	fallen
feed	fed	fed
feel	felt	felt
fight	fought	fought
find	found	found
flee	fled	fled
fly	flew	flown
forbid	forbade	forbidden
forget	forgot	forgotten
forgive	forgave	forgiven
freeze	froze	frozen
get	got	got
give	gave	given
go	went	gone
grow	grew	grown
hang	hung	hung
have	had	had
hear	heard	heard
hide	hid	hidden
hit	hit	hit
hold	held	held
hurt	hurt	hurt
keep	kept	kept
kneel	knelt	knelt
know	knew	known
lay	laid	laid
lead	led	led
leave	left	left
lend	lent	lent
let	let	let
lie	lay	lain

infinitive	past simple	past participle
light	lit	lit
lose	lost	lost
make	made	made
mean	meant	meant
meet	met	met
pay	paid	paid
put	put	put
read	read [red]*	read [red]*
ride	rode	ridden
ring	rang	rung
rise	rose	risen
run	ran	run
say	said	said
see	saw	seen
seek	sought	sought
sell	sold	sold
send	sent	sent
set	set	set
sew	sewed	sewn/sewed
shake	shook	shaken
shine	shone	shone
shoot	shot	shot
show	showed	shown/showed
shrink	shrank	shrunk
shut	shut	shut
sing	sang	sung
sink	sank	sunk
sit	sat	sat
sleep	slept	slept
slide	slid	slid
speak	spoke	spoken
spend	spent	spent
spit	spat	spat
split	split	split
spread	spread	spread
spring	sprang	sprung
stand	stood	stood
steal	stole	stolen
stick	stuck	stuck
sting	stung	stung
stink	stank	stunk
strike	struck	struck
swear	swore	sworn
sweep	swept	swept
swim	swam	swum
swing	swung	swung
take	took	taken
teach	taught	taught
tear	tore	torn
tell	told	told
think	thought	thought
throw	threw	thrown
understand	understood	understood
wake	woke	woken
wear	wore	worn
weep	wept	wept
win	won	won
write	wrote	written

* *pronunciation*

Appendix 2
Present and past tenses

	simple	*continuous*
present	**I do** *present simple* (→ Units 2–4) ☐ Ann often **plays** tennis. ☐ I **work** in a bank, but I **don't enjoy** it much. ☐ **Do** you **like** parties? ☐ It **doesn't rain** so much in summer.	**I am doing** *present continuous* (→ Units 1, 3–4) ☐ 'Where's Ann?' 'She's **playing** tennis.' ☐ Please don't disturb me now. **I'm working.** ☐ Hello. **Are** you **enjoying** the party? ☐ It **isn't raining** at the moment.
present perfect	**I have done** *present perfect simple* (→ Units 7–8, 10–14) ☐ Ann **has played** tennis many times. ☐ I've **lost** my key. **Have** you **seen** it anywhere? ☐ How long **have** you and Chris **known** each other? ☐ A: Is it still raining? B: No, it **has stopped.** ☐ The house is dirty. I **haven't cleaned** it for weeks.	**I have been doing** *present perfect continuous* (→ Units 9–11) ☐ Ann is tired. She **has been playing** tennis. ☐ You're out of breath. **Have** you **been running?** ☐ How long **have** you **been learning** English? ☐ It's still raining. It **has been raining** all day. ☐ I **haven't been feeling** well recently. Perhaps I should go to the doctor.
past	**I did** *past simple* (→ Units 5–6, 13–14) ☐ Ann **played** tennis yesterday afternoon. ☐ I **lost** my key a few days ago. ☐ There was a film on TV last night, but we **didn't watch** it. ☐ What **did** you **do** when you finished work yesterday?	**I was doing** *past continuous* (→ Unit 6) ☐ I saw Ann at the sports centre yesterday. She **was playing** tennis. ☐ I dropped my key when I **was trying** to open the door. ☐ The television was on, but we **weren't watching** it. ☐ What **were** you **doing** at this time yesterday?
past perfect	**I had done** *past perfect* (→ Unit 15) ☐ It wasn't her first game of tennis. She **had played** many times before. ☐ They couldn't get into the house because they **had lost** the key. ☐ The house was dirty because I **hadn't cleaned** it for weeks.	**I had been doing** *past perfect continuous* (→ Unit 16) ☐ Ann was tired yesterday evening because she **had been playing** tennis in the afternoon. ☐ George decided to go to the doctor because he **hadn't been feeling** well.

For the passive, see Units 42–44.

Appendix 3
The future

3.1 *List of future forms:*

☐ I'm **leaving** tomorrow.	*present continuous*	(→ Unit 19A)
☐ My train **leaves** at 9.30.	*present simple*	(→ Unit 19B)
☐ I'm **going to leave** tomorrow.	(be) **going to**	(→ Units 20, 23)
☐ I'll **leave** tomorrow.	**will**	(→ Units 21–23)
☐ I'll **be leaving** tomorrow.	*future continuous*	(→ Unit 24)
☐ I'll **have left** by this time tomorrow.	*future perfect*	(→ Unit 24)
☐ I hope to see you before I **leave** tomorrow.	*present simple*	(→ Unit 25)

3.2 *Future actions*

We use the present continuous (**I'm doing**) for arrangements:
- ☐ I'm **leaving** tomorrow. I've got my plane ticket. (already planned and arranged)
- ☐ 'When **are** they **getting** married?' 'On 24 July.'

We use the present simple (**I leave** / it **leaves** etc.) for timetables, programmes etc. :
- ☐ My train **leaves** at 11.30. (according to the timetable)
- ☐ What time **does** the film **begin**?

We use (**be**) **going to** … to say what somebody has already decided to do:
- ☐ I've decided not to stay here any longer. I'm **going to leave** tomorrow. (*or* I'm **leaving** tomorrow.)
- ☐ 'Your shoes are dirty.' 'Yes, I know. I'm **going to clean** them.'

We use **will** (**'ll**) when we decide or agree to do something at the time of speaking:
- ☐ A: I don't want you to stay here any longer.
     B: OK. I'll **leave** tomorrow. (B decides this at the time of speaking)
- ☐ That bag looks heavy. I'll **help** you with it.
- ☐ I **won't tell** anybody what happened. I promise. (**won't** = **will not**)

3.3 *Future happenings and situations*

Most often we use **will** to talk about future happenings ('something **will happen**') or situations ('something **will be**'):
- ☐ I don't think John is happy at work. I think he**'ll leave** soon.
- ☐ This time next year I**'ll be** in Japan. Where **will** you **be**?

We use (**be**) **going to** when the situation *now* shows what **is going to happen** *in the future*:
- ☐ Look at those black clouds. It**'s going to rain**. (you can see the clouds *now*)

3.4 *Future continuous and future perfect*

Will be (**do**)**ing** = will be in the middle of (doing something):
- ☐ This time next week I'll be on holiday. I**'ll be lying** on a beach or **swimming** in the sea.

We also use **will be -ing** for future actions (see Unit 24C):
- ☐ What time **will** you **be leaving** tomorrow?

We use **will have** (**done**) to say that something will already be complete before a time in the future:
- ☐ I won't be here this time tomorrow. I'll **have** already **left**.

3.5 We use the *present* (*not* will) after **when/if/while/before** etc. (see Unit 25):
- ☐ I hope to see you **before** I **leave** tomorrow. (*not* before I will leave)
- ☐ **When** you **are** in London again, come and see us. (*not* When you will be)
- ☐ **If** we **don't hurry**, we'll be late.

Appendix 4
Modal verbs (can/could/will/would etc.)

This appendix is a summary of modal verbs. For more information, see Units 21–41.

4.1 Compare **can/could** etc. for actions:

can	□ I **can go** out tonight. (= there is nothing to stop me)
	□ I **can't go** out tonight.
could	□ I **could go** out tonight, but I'm not very keen.
	□ I **couldn't go** out last night. (= I wasn't able)
can *or* may	□ **Can / May** I **go** out tonight? (= do you allow me)
will/won't	□ I think I**'ll go** out tonight.
	□ I promise I **won't go** out.
would	□ I **would go** out tonight, but I have too much to do.
	□ I promised I **wouldn't go** out.
shall	□ **Shall** I **go** out tonight? (do you think it is a good idea?)
should *or* ought to	□ I **should / ought to go** out tonight. (= it would be a good thing to do)
must	□ I **must go** out tonight. (= it is necessary)
	□ I **mustn't go** out tonight. (= it is necessary that I do *not* go out)
needn't	□ I **needn't go** out tonight. (= it is not necessary)

Compare **could have … / would have …** etc. :

could	□ I **could have gone** out last night, but I decided to stay at home.
would	□ I **would have gone** out last night, but I had too much to do.
should *or* ought to	□ I **should / ought to have gone** out last night. I'm sorry I didn't.
needn't	□ I **needn't have gone** out last night. (= I went out, but it was not necessary)

4.2 We use **will/would/may** etc. to say whether something is possible, impossible, probable, certain etc. Compare:

will	□ 'What time **will** she **be** here?' 'She**'ll be** here soon.'
would	□ She **would be** here now, but she's been delayed.
should *or* ought to	□ She **should / ought to be** here soon. (= I expect she will be here soon)
may *or* might *or* could	□ She **may / might / could be** here now. I'm not sure. (= it's possible that she is here)
must	□ She **must be** here. I saw her come in.
can't	□ She **can't** possibly **be** here. I know for certain that she's away on holiday.

Compare **would have … / should have …** etc. :

will	□ She **will have arrived** by now. (= before now)
would	□ She **would have arrived** earlier, but she was delayed.
should *or* ought to	□ I wonder where she is. She **should / ought to have arrived** by now.
may *or* might *or* could	□ She **may / might / could have arrived**. I'm not sure. (= it's possible that she has arrived)
must	□ She **must have arrived** by now. (= I'm sure – there is no other possibility)
can't	□ She **can't** possibly **have arrived** yet. It's much too early. (= it's impossible)

Appendix 5
Short forms (I'm / you've / didn't etc.)

5.1 In spoken English we usually say **I'm / you've / didn't** etc. (*short forms* or *contractions*) rather than **I am / you have / did not** etc. We also use these short forms in informal writing (for example, a letter or message to a friend).

When we write short forms, we use an *apostrophe* (') for the missing letter(s):

  I'm = I <u>a</u>m   you've = you h<u>a</u>ve   didn't = did n<u>o</u>t

5.2 List of short forms:

'm = am	I'm						
's = is *or* has		he's	she's	it's			
're = are					you're	we're	they're
've = have	I've				you've	we've	they've
'll = will	I'll	he'll	she'll		you'll	we'll	they'll
'd = would *or* had	I'd	he'd	she'd		you'd	we'd	they'd

's can be is or has:
  □ She's ill. (= She **is** ill.)
  □ She's gone away. (= She **has** gone)
but **let's = let us:**
  □ Let's go now. (= Let **us** go)

'd can be would or had:
  □ I'd see a doctor if I were you. (= I **would** see)
  □ I'd never seen her before. (= I **had** never seen)

We use some of these short forms (especially **'s**) after question words (**who/what** etc.) and after **that/there/here:**

  who's   what's   where's   how's   that's   there's   here's   who'll   there'll   who'd
  □ **Who's** that woman over there? (= who **is**)
  □ **What's** happened? (= what **has**)
  □ Do you think **there'll** be many people at the party? (= there **will**)

We also use short forms (especially **'s**) after a noun:
  □ **Catherine's** going out tonight. (= Catherine **is**)
  □ **My best friend's** just got married. (= My best friend **has**)

You cannot use **'m / 's / 're / 've / 'll / 'd** at the end of a sentence (because the verb is stressed in this position):
  □ 'Are you tired?' 'Yes, I **am**.' (*not* Yes, I'm.)
  □ Do you know where she **is**? (*not* Do you know where she's?)

5.3 Negative short forms

isn't	(= is not)	**don't**	(= do not)	**haven't**	(= have not)
aren't	(= are not)	**doesn't**	(= does not)	**hasn't**	(= has not)
wasn't	(= was not)	**didn't**	(= did not)	**hadn't**	(= had not)
weren't	(= were not)				
can't	(= cannot)	**couldn't**	(= could not)	**mustn't**	(= must not)
won't	(= will not)	**wouldn't**	(= would not)	**needn't**	(= need not)
shan't	(= shall not)	**shouldn't**	(= should not)	**daren't**	(= dare not)

Negative short forms for **is** and **are** can be:
  he **isn't** / she **isn't** / it **isn't**   *or*   he's **not** / she's **not** / it's **not**
  you **aren't** / we **aren't** / they **aren't**   *or*   you're **not** / we're **not** / they're **not**

Appendix 6
Spelling

6.1 Nouns, verbs and adjectives can have the following endings:

noun + -s/-es *(plural)*	books	ideas	matches
verb + -s/-es (after **he/she/it**)	works	enjoys	washes
verb + -ing	working	enjoying	washing
verb + -ed	worked	enjoyed	washed
adjective + -er *(comparative)*	cheaper	quicker	brighter
adjective + -est *(superlative)*	cheapest	quickest	brightest
adjective + -ly *(adverb)*	cheaply	quickly	brightly

When we use these endings, there are sometimes changes in spelling. These changes are listed below.

6.2 Nouns and verbs + -s/-es

The ending is -es when the word ends in **-s/-ss/-sh/-ch/-x**:

bus/buses	miss/misses	wash/washes
match/matches	search/searches	box/boxes

Note also:

potato/potatoes	tomato/tomatoes
do/does	go/goes

6.3 Words ending in -y (baby, carry, easy etc.)

> If a word ends in a *consonant** + **y** (**-by/-ry/-sy/-vy** etc.)
>
> **y** changes to **ie** before the ending **-s**:
>
> | | | | |
> |---|---|---|---|
> | baby/babies | story/stories | country/countries | secretary/secretaries |
> | hurry/hurries | study/studies | apply/applies | try/tries |
>
> **y** changes to **i** before the ending **-ed**:
>
> | | | | |
> |---|---|---|---|
> | hurry/hurried | study/studied | apply/applied | try/tried |
>
> **y** changes to **i** before the endings **-er** and **-est**:
>
> | | | |
> |---|---|---|
> | easy/easier/easiest | heavy/heavier/heaviest | lucky/luckier/luckiest |
>
> **y** changes to **i** before the ending **-ly**:
>
> | | | |
> |---|---|---|
> | easy/easily | heavy/heavily | temporary/temporarily |

y does *not* change before **-ing**:

hurrying	studying	applying	trying

y does *not* change if the word ends in a *vowel** + **y** (**-ay/-ey/-oy/-uy**):

play/plays/played	monkey/monkeys	enjoy/enjoys/enjoyed	buy/buys

An exception is: **day/daily**

Note also: **pay/paid**   **lay/laid**   **say/said**

6.4 Verbs ending in -ie (die, lie, tie)

If a verb ends in **-ie**, **ie** changes to **y** before the ending **-ing**:

die/dying	lie/lying	tie/tying

---

* **a e i o u** are *vowel* letters.
The other letters (**b c d f g** etc.) are *consonant* letters.

6.5 Words ending in -e (hope, dance, wide etc.)

Verbs

If a verb ends in -e, we leave out e before the ending -**ing**:
   hope/hop**ing**   smile/smil**ing**   dance/danc**ing**   confuse/confus**ing**

Exceptions are **be/being**
and verbs ending in -ee: see/see**ing**   agree/agree**ing**

If a verb ends in -e, we add -**d** for the past (of regular verbs):
   hope/hope**d**   smile/smile**d**   dance/dance**d**   confuse/confuse**d**

Adjectives and adverbs

If an adjective ends in -e, we add -**r** and -**st** for the comparative and superlative:
   wide/wide**r**/wide**st**   late/late**r**/late**st**   large/large**r**/large**st**

If an adjective ends in -e, we *keep* e before -**ly** in the adverb:
   polite/polite**ly**   extreme/extreme**ly**   absolute/absolute**ly**

If an adjective ends in -le (simple, terrible etc.), the adverb ending is -**ply**, -**bly** etc. :
   simple/sim**ply**   terrible/terri**bly**   reasonable/reasona**bly**

6.6 Doubling consonants (**stop/stopping/stopped, wet/wetter/wettest** etc.)

Sometimes a word ends in *vowel + consonant*. For example:
   stop   plan   **rub**   big   wet   thin   prefer   regret

Before the endings -**ing**/-**ed**/-**er**/-**est**, we double the consonant at the end. So **p → pp**,
n → nn etc. For example:

stop	p → **pp**	stopping	stopped
plan	n → **nn**	planning	planned
rub	b → **bb**	rubbing	rubbed
big	g → **gg**	bigger	biggest
wet	t → **tt**	wetter	wettest
thin	n → **nn**	thinner	thinnest

If the word has more than one syllable (**prefer, begin** etc.), we double the consonant at the end
only if the final syllable is stressed:
   preFER / preferring / preferred   perMIT / permitting / permitted
   reGRET / regretting / regretted   beGIN / beginning

If the final syllable is not stressed, we do *not* double the final consonant:
   VISit / visiting / visited   deVELop / developing / developed
   HAPpen / happening / happened   reMEMber / remembering / remembered

In British English, verbs ending in -l have -ll- before -ing and -ed whether the final syllable is
stressed or not:
   travel / travelling / travelled   cancel / cancelling / cancelled

For American spelling, see Appendix 7.

Note that
we do *not* double the final consonant if the word ends in *two* consonants (-rt, -lp, -ng etc.):
   start / starting / started   help / helping / helped   long / longer / longest

we do *not* double the final consonant if there are *two* vowel letters before it (-oil, -eed etc.):
   boil / boiling / boiled   need / needing / needed   explain / explaining / explained
   cheap / cheaper / cheapest   loud / louder / loudest   quiet / quieter / quietest

we do *not* double y or w at the end of words. (At the end of words y and w are not
consonants.)
   stay / staying / stayed   grow / growing   new / newer / newest

Appendix 7
American English

There are a few grammatical differences between British English and American English:

Unit	BRITISH	AMERICAN
7A–B and 13A	The *present perfect* is used for an action in the past with a result now: ☐ I've lost my key. **Have** you **seen** it? ☐ Sally isn't here. She's **gone** out. The *present perfect* is used with **just**, **already** and **yet**: ☐ I'm not hungry. I've **just had** lunch. ☐ A: What time is Mark leaving? B: He **has already left**. ☐ **Have** you **finished** your work **yet**?	The *present perfect* OR *past simple* can be used: ☐ I've lost my key. **Have** you **seen** it? *or* I lost my key. **Did** you **see** it? ☐ Sally isn't here. { She's **gone** out. { She **went** out. The *present perfect* OR *past simple* can be used: ☐ I'm not hungry. { I've **just had** lunch. { I **just had** lunch. ☐ A: What time is Mark leaving? B: { He **has already left**. { He **already left**. ☐ **Have** you **finished** your work **yet**? *or* **Did** you **finish** your work **yet**?
17C	British speakers usually say: **have** a bath **have** a shower **have** a break **have** a holiday	American speakers say: **take** a bath **take** a shower **take** a break **take** a vacation
21D and 22D	**Will** or **shall** can be used with **I/we**: ☐ I **will/shall** be late this evening. **Shall I ... ?** and **shall we ... ?** are used to ask for advice etc. : ☐ Which way **shall we** go?	**Shall** is unusual: ☐ I **will** be late this evening. **Should I ... ?** and **should we ... ?** are more usual to ask for advice etc. : ☐ Which way **should we** go?
28	British speakers use **can't** to say they believe something is not probable: ☐ Sue hasn't contacted me. She **can't** have got my message.	American speakers use **must not** in this situation: ☐ Sue hasn't contacted me. She **must not** have gotten my message.
32	You can use **needn't** or **don't need to**: ☐ We **needn't** hurry. *or* We **don't need to** hurry.	**Needn't** is unusual. The usual form is **don't need to**: ☐ We **don't need to** hurry.
34A–B	After **demand**, **insist** etc. you can use **should**: ☐ I demanded that he **should apologise**. ☐ We insisted that something **should be done** about the problem.	The *subjunctive* is normally used. **Should** is unusual after **demand**, **insist** etc. : ☐ I demanded that he **apologize**.* ☐ We insisted that something **be done** about the problem.
51B	British speakers generally use **Have you?** / **Isn't she?** etc. ☐ A: Liz isn't feeling well. B: **Isn't she?** What's wrong with her?	American speakers generally use **You have?** / **She isn't?** etc. : ☐ A: Liz isn't feeling well. B: **She isn't?** What's wrong with her?
70B	**Accommodation** is usually uncountable: ☐ There isn't enough **accommodation**.	**Accommodation** can be countable: ☐ There aren't enough **accommodations**.

* Many verbs ending in **-ise** in British English (apolog**ise**/organ**ise**/special**ise** etc.) are spelt with **-ize** (apolog**ize**/organ**ize**/special**ize** etc.) in American English.

Unit	BRITISH	AMERICAN
74B	to/in hospital (without **the**): ☐ Three people were injured and taken to **hospital**.	to/in **the** hospital: ☐ Three people were injured and taken to **the hospital**.
79C	Nouns like **government/team/family** etc. can have a singular or plural verb: ☐ The team **is/are** playing well.	These nouns normally take a singular verb in American English: ☐ The team **is** playing well.
121B	**at the weekend / at weekends**: ☐ Will you be here **at the weekend**?	**on the weekend / on weekends**: ☐ Will you be here **on the weekend**?
124D	**at the front / at the back** (of a group etc.): ☐ Let's sit **at the front** (of the cinema).	**in the front / in the back** (of a group etc.): ☐ Let's sit **in the front** (of the movie theater).
131C	**different from** or **different to**: ☐ It was **different from/to** what I'd expected.	**different from** or **different than**: ☐ It was **different from/than** what I'd expected.
132A	**write to** somebody: ☐ Please **write to** me soon.	**write (to)** somebody (with or without **to**): ☐ Please **write** (to) me soon.
137A	British speakers use both **round** and **around**: ☐ He turned **round**. *or* He turned **around**.	American speakers use **around** (not usually 'round') ☐ He turned **around**.
137C	British speakers use both **fill in** and **fill out**: ☐ Can you **fill in** this form? *or* Can you **fill out** this form?	American speakers use **fill out**: ☐ Can you **fill out** this form?
141B	**get on** = *progress* ☐ How are you **getting on** in your new job? **get on** (with somebody): ☐ Richard **gets on** well with his new neighbours.	American speakers do not use **get on** in this way. **get along** (with somebody): ☐ Richard **gets along** well with his new neighbors.
144D	**do up** a room etc. : ☐ The kitchen looks great now that it has been **done up**.	**do over** a room etc. : ☐ The kitchen looks great now that it has been **done over**.

Appendix	BRITISH	AMERICAN
1.3	The verbs in this section (**burn, spell** etc.) can be regular or irregular (**burned** *or* **burnt**, **spelled** *or* **spelt** etc.). The past participle of **get** is **got**: ☐ Your English has **got** much better. (= has become much better) **Have got** is also an alternative to **have**: ☐ I've **got** two brothers. (= I have two brothers.)	The verbs in this section are normally regular (**burned, spelled** etc.). The past participle of **get** is **gotten**: ☐ Your English has **gotten** much better. **Have got** = have (as in British English): ☐ I've **got** two brothers.
6.6	British spelling: travel → travelling / travelled cancel → cancelling / cancelled	American spelling: travel → traveling / traveled cancel → canceling / canceled

Additional exercises

These exercises are divided into the following sections:

Present and past
Units 1–6, Appendix 2

1   Put the verb into the correct form: present simple (**I do**), present continuous (**I am doing**), past simple (**I did**) or past continuous (**I was doing**).

1 We can go out now. It ___isn't raining___ (not / rain) any more.
2 Catherine ___was waiting___ (wait) for me when I ___arrived___ (arrive).
3 I _____ (get) hungry. Let's go and have something to eat.
4 What _____ (you / do) in your spare time? Do you have any hobbies?
5 The weather was horrible when we _____ (arrive). It was cold and it _____ (rain) hard.
6 Louise usually _____ (phone) me on Fridays, but she _____ (not / phone) last Friday.
7 A: When I last saw you, you _____ (think) of moving to a new flat.
   B: That's right, but in the end I _____ (decide) to stay where I was.
8 Why _____ (you / look) at me like that? What's the matter?
9 It's usually dry here at this time of the year. It _____ (not / rain) much.
10 The phone _____ (ring) three times while we _____ (have) dinner last night.
11 Linda was busy when we _____ (go) to see her yesterday. She had an exam today and she _____ (prepare) for it. We _____ (not / want) to disturb her, so we _____ (not / stay) very long.
12 When I first _____ (tell) Tom the news, he _____ (not / believe) me. He _____ (think) that I _____ (joke).

Present and past

2   Which is correct?

1   Everything is going well. We ~~didn't have~~ / haven't had any problems so far.
   (haven't had *is correct*)
2   Lisa didn't go / hasn't gone to work yesterday. She wasn't feeling well.
3   Look! That man over there wears / is wearing the same sweater as you.
4   Your son is much taller than when I last saw him. He grew / has grown a lot.
5   I still don't know what to do. I didn't decide / haven't decided yet.
6   I wonder why Jim is / is being so nice to me today. He isn't usually like that.
7   Jane had a book open in front of her, but she didn't read / wasn't reading it.
8   I wasn't very busy. I didn't have / wasn't having much to do.
9   It begins / It's beginning to get dark. Shall I turn on the light?
10 After leaving school, Tim got / has got a job in a factory.
11 When Sue heard the news, she wasn't / hasn't been very pleased.
12 This is a nice restaurant, isn't it? Is this the first time you are / you've been here?
13 I need a new job. I'm doing / I've been doing the same job for too long.
14 'Anna has gone out.'   'Oh, has she? What time did she go / has she gone?'
15 'You look tired.'   'Yes, I've played / I've been playing basketball.'
16 Where are you coming / do you come from? Are you American?
17 I'd like to see Tina again. It's a long time since I saw her / that I didn't see her.
18 Robert and Maria have been married since 20 years / for 20 years.

3   Complete each question using a suitable verb.

1   A: I'm looking for Paul. *Have you seen* him?
    B: Yes, he was here a moment ago.
2   A: Why *did you go* to bed so early last night?
    B: I was feeling very tired.
3   A: Where .... ?
    B: Just to the post box. I want to post these letters. I'll be back in a few minutes.
4   A: .... television every evening?
    B: No, only if there's something special on.
5   A: Your house is very beautiful. How long .... here?
    B: Nearly ten years.
6   A: How was your holiday? .... a nice time?
    B: Yes, thanks. It was great.
7   A: .... Julie recently?
    B: Yes, I met her a few days ago.
8   A: Can you describe the woman you saw? What .... ?
    B: A red sweater and black jeans.
9   A: I'm sorry to keep you waiting. .... long?
    B: No, only about ten minutes.
10 A: How long .... you to get to work in the morning?
    B: Usually about 45 minutes. It depends on the traffic.
11 A: .... with that magazine yet?
    B: No, I'm still reading it. I won't be long.
12 A: .... to the United States?
    B: No, never, but I went to Canada a few years ago.

4   Use your own ideas to complete B's sentences.

1 A: What's the new restaurant like? Is it good?
   B: I've no idea. __I've never been__ .... there.
2 A: How well do you know Bill?
   B: Very well. We .... since we were children.
3 A: Did you enjoy your holiday?
   B: Yes, it was really good. It's the best holiday ....
4 A: Is David still here?
   B: No, I'm afraid he isn't. .... about ten minutes ago.
5 A: I like your suit. I haven't seen it before.
   B: It's new. It's the first time ....
6 A: How did you cut your knee?
   B: I slipped and fell when .... tennis.
7 A: Do you ever go swimming?
   B: Not these days. I haven't .... a long time.
8 A: How often do you go to the cinema?
   B: Very rarely. It's nearly a year .... to the cinema.
9 A: I've bought some new shoes. Do you like them?
   B: Yes, they're very nice. Where .... them?

Present and past   Units 1–17, 110, Appendix 2

5   Put the verb into the correct form: past simple (**I did**), past continuous (**I was doing**), past
     perfect (**I had done**) or past perfect continuous (**I had been doing**).

Yesterday afternoon Sarah ....__went__.... (go) to the station to meet Paul. When she
.... (get) there, Paul .... (already / wait)
for her. His train .... (arrive) early.

When I got home, Bill .... (lie) on the sofa. The television was on,
but he .... (not / watch) it. He .... (fall)
asleep and .... (snore) loudly. I .... (turn) the
television off and just then he .... (wake) up.

3

Last night I .... (just / go) to bed and .... (read)
a book when suddenly I .... (hear) a noise. I ....
(get) up to see what it was, but I .... (not / see) anything, so I
.... (go) back to bed.

4

Lisa had to go to New York last week, but she almost .... (miss) the
plane. She .... (stand) in the queue at the check-in desk when she
suddenly .... (realise) that she .... (leave) her
passport at home. Fortunately she lives near the airport, so she .... (have)
time to take a taxi home to get it. She .... (get) back to the airport
just in time for her flight.

5

I .... (meet) Peter and Lucy yesterday as I ....
(walk) through the park. They .... (be) to the Sports Centre where
they .... (play) tennis. They .... (go) to a café
and .... (invite) me to join them, but I ....
(arrange) to meet another friend and .... (not / have) time.

6   Make sentences from the words in brackets. Put the verb into the correct form: present perfect
     (I have done), present perfect continuous (I have been doing), past perfect (I had done) or
     past perfect continuous (I had been doing).

1 Amanda is sitting on the ground. She's out of breath.
   (she / run)   *She has been running.*
2 Where's my bag? I left it under this chair.
   (somebody / take / it) ....
3 We were all surprised when Jenny and Andy got married last year.
   (they / only / know / each other / a few weeks)
   ....
4 It's still raining. I wish it would stop.
   (it / rain / all day) ....
5 Suddenly I woke up. I was confused and didn't know where I was.
   (I / dream) ....

6 I wasn't hungry at lunchtime, so I didn't have anything to eat.
(I / have / a big breakfast) ....

7 Every year Robert and Tina spend a few days at the same hotel by the sea.
(they / go / there for years) ....

8 I've got a headache.
(I / have / it / since I got up) ....

9 Next week Gary is going to run in a marathon.
(he / train / very hard for it) ....

7 Put the verb into the correct form.

Julia and Kevin are old friends. They meet by chance at a rail station.

JULIA: Hello, Kevin. (1) .... (I / not / see)
you for ages. How are you?

KEVIN: I'm fine. How about you?
(2) .... (you / look) well.

JULIA: Yes, I'm very well thanks.
So, (3) .... (you / go) somewhere or
(4) .... (you / meet) somebody off a train?

KEVIN: (5) .... (I / go) to London for a business meeting.

JULIA: Oh. (6) .... (you / often / go) away on business?

KEVIN: Quite often, yes. And you? Where (7) .... (you / go)?

JULIA: Nowhere. (8) .... (I / meet) a friend. Unfortunately
her train (9) .... (be) delayed –
(10) .... (I / wait) here for nearly an hour.

KEVIN: How are your children?

JULIA: They're all fine, thanks. The youngest (11) .... (just / start)
school.

KEVIN: How (12) .... (she / get) on?
(13) .... (she / like) it?

JULIA: Yes, (14) .... (she / think) it's great.

KEVIN: (15) .... (you / work) at the moment? When I last
(16) .... (speak) to you, (17) ....
(you / work) in a travel agency.

JULIA: That's right. Unfortunately the company (18) .... (go) out
of business a couple of months after (19) .... (I / start)
work there, so (20) .... (I / lose) my job.

KEVIN: And (21) .... (you / not / have) a job since then?

JULIA: Not a permanent job. (22) .... (I / have) a few temporary
jobs. By the way, (23) .... (you / see) Joe recently?

KEVIN: Joe? He's in Canada.

JULIA: Really? How long (24) .... (he / be) in Canada?

KEVIN: About a year now. (25) .... (I / see) him a few days before
(26) .... (he / go). (27) .... (he / be)
unemployed for months, so (28) .... (he / decide) to try his
luck somewhere else. (29) .... (he / really / look forward)
to going.

JULIA: So, what (30) .... (he / do) there?

KEVIN: I've no idea. (31) .... (I / not / hear) from him since
(32) .... (he / leave). Anyway, I must go and catch my
train. It was really nice to see you again.

JULIA: You too. Bye. Have a good trip.

KEVIN: Thanks. Bye.

8   Put the verb into the most suitable form.

1 Who .... (invent) the bicycle?
2 'Do you still have a headache?' 'No, ... (it / go). I'm all right now.'
3 I was the last to leave the office yesterday evening. Everybody else .... (go) home when I .... (leave).
4 What .... (you / do) last weekend? .... (you / go) away?
5 I like your car. How long .... (you / have) it?
6 It's a pity the trip was cancelled. I .... (look) forward to it.
7 Jane is an experienced teacher. .... (she / teach) for 15 years.
8 .... (I / buy) a new jacket last week, but .... (I / not / wear) it yet.
9 A few days ago .... (I / see) a man at a party whose face .... (be) very familiar. At first I couldn't think where .... (I / see) him before. Then suddenly .... (I / remember) who .... (it / be).
10 .... (you / hear) of Agatha Christie? .... (she / be) a writer who .... (die) in 1976. .... (she / write) more than 70 detective novels. .... (you / read) any of them?
11 A: What .... (this word / mean)?
    B: I've no idea. .... (I / never / see) it before. Look it up in the dictionary.
12 A: .... (you / get) to the theatre in time for the play last night?
    B: No, we were late. By the time we got there, ... (it / already / begin).
13 I went to Sarah's room and .... (knock) on the door, but there .... (be) no answer. Either .... (she / go) out or .... (she / not / want) to see anyone.
14 Patrick asked me how to use the photocopier. .... (he / never / use) it before, so .... (he / not / know) what to do.
15 Liz .... (go) for a swim after work yesterday. .... (she / need) some exercise because .... (she / sit) in an office all day in front of a computer.

Past continuous and used to   Units 6, 18

9   Complete the sentences using the past continuous (was/were –ing) or used to ... . Use the verb in brackets.

1 I haven't been to the cinema for ages now. We ___used to go___ a lot. (go)
2 Ann didn't see me wave to her. She ___was looking___ in the other direction. (look)
3 I .... a lot but, I don't use my car very much these days. (drive)
4 I asked the taxi driver to slow down. She .... too fast. (drive)
5 Rosemary and Jonathan met for the first time when they .... in the same bank. (work)
6 When I was a child, I .... a lot of bad dreams. (have)
7 I wonder what Joe is doing these days. He .... in Spain when I last heard from him. (live)
8 'Where were you yesterday afternoon?' 'I .... volleyball.' (play)
9 'Do you do any sports?' 'Not these days, but I .... volleyball.' (play)
10 George looked very nice at the party. He .... a very smart suit. (wear)

The future

10   What do you say to your friend in these situations? Use the words given in brackets. Use the present continuous (I am doing), going to or will (I'll).

1   You have made all your holiday arrangements. Your destination is Jamaica.
    FRIEND: Have you decided where to go for your holiday yet?
    YOU: _I'm going to Jamaica._   (I / go)

2   You have made an appointment with the dentist for Friday morning.
    FRIEND: Shall we meet on Friday morning?
    YOU: I can't on Friday. .... (I / go)

3   You and some friends are planning a holiday in Britain. You have decided to hire a car, but you haven't arranged this yet.
    FRIEND: How do you plan to travel round Britain? By train?
    YOU: No, ... (we / hire)

4   Your friend has two young children. She wants to go out tomorrow evening. You offer to look after the children.
    FRIEND: I want to go out tomorrow evening, but I haven't got a babysitter.
    YOU: That's no problem. .... (I / look after)

5   You have already arranged to have lunch with Sue tomorrow.
    FRIEND: Are you free at lunchtime tomorrow?
    YOU: No, ... (have lunch)

6   You are in a restaurant. You and your friend are looking at the menu. Maybe your friend has decided what to have. You ask her/him.
    YOU: What ....? (you / have)
    FRIEND: I don't know. I can't make up my mind.

7   You and a friend are reading. It's getting a bit dark and your friend is having trouble reading. You decide to turn on the light.
    FRIEND: It's getting a bit dark, isn't it? It's difficult to read.
    YOU: Yes. .... (I / turn on)

8   You and a friend are reading. It's getting a bit dark and you decide to turn on the light. You stand up and walk towards the light switch.
    FRIEND: What are you doing?
    YOU: .... (I / turn on)

11   Put the verb into the most suitable form. Use a present tense (simple or continuous), will (I'll) or shall.

Conversation 1 (*in the morning*)

JENNY: (1) _Are you doing_ (you / do) anything tomorrow evening, Helen?
HELEN: No, why?
JENNY: Well, do you fancy going to the cinema? *Strangers on a Plane* is on. I want to see it, but I don't want to go alone.
HELEN: OK, (2) .... (I / come) with you. What time
        (3) .... (we / meet)?
JENNY: Well, the film (4) .... (begin) at 8.45, so
        (5) .... (I / meet) you at about 8.30 outside the cinema, OK?
HELEN: Fine. (6) .... (I / see) Tina later this evening.
        (7) .... (I / ask) her if she wants to come too?
JENNY: Yes, do that. (8) .... (I / see) you tomorrow then. Bye.

Conversation 2 (*later the same day*)

HELEN: Jenny and I (9) .... (go) to the cinema tomorrow
       night to see *Strangers on a Plane*. Why don't you come too?

TINA: I'd love to come. What time (10) .... (the film / begin)?

HELEN: 8.45.

TINA: (11) .... (you / meet) outside the cinema?

HELEN: Yes, at 8.30. Is that OK for you?

TINA: Yes, (12) .... (I / be) there at 8.30.

12   Put the verb into the most suitable form. Sometimes there is more than one possibility.

    1 *A has decided to learn a language.*

       A: I've decided to try and learn a foreign language.

       B: Have you? Which language (1) ..*are you going to learn*.. (you / learn)?

       A: Spanish.

       B: (2) .... (you / do) a course?

       A: Yes, (3) .... (it / start) next week.

       B: That's great. I'm sure (4) .... (you / enjoy) it.

       A: I hope so. But I think (5) .... (it / be) quite difficult.

    2 *A wants to know about B's holiday plans.*

       A: I hear (1) .... (you / go) on holiday soon.

       B: That's right. (2) .... (we / go) to Finland.

       A: I hope (3) .... (you / have) a nice time.

       B: Thanks. (4) .... (I / send) you a postcard and (5) ....
          (I / get) in touch with you when (6) .... (I / get) back.

    3 *A invites B to a party.*

       A: (1) .... (I / have) a party next Saturday. Can you come?

       B: On Saturday? I'm not sure. Some friends of mine (2) .... (come) to
          stay with me next week, but I think (3) .... (they / go) by
          Saturday. But if (4) .... (they / be) still here,
          (5) .... (I / not / be) able to come to the party.

       A: OK. Well, tell me as soon as (6) .... (you / know).

       B: Right. (7) .... (I / phone) you during the week.

    4 *A and B are two secret agents arranging a meeting. They are talking on the phone.*

       A: Well, what time (1) ....
          (we / meet)?

       B: Come to the café by the station at 4 o'clock.
          (2) .... (I / wait) for you
          when (3) .... (you / arrive).
          (4) .... (I / sit) by the window
          and (5) .... (I / wear) a bright green sweater.

       A: OK? (6) .... (Agent 307 / come) too?

       B: No, she can't be there.

       A: Oh. (7) .... (I / bring) the documents?

       B: Yes. (8) .... (I / explain) everything when
          (9) .... (I / see) you. And don't be late.

       A: OK. (10) .... (I / try) to be on time.

13 Put the verb into the correct form. Choose from the following:

present continuous (**I am doing**)	**will ('ll) / won't**
present simple (**I do**)	**will be doing**
going to (**I'm going to do**)	**shall**

1 I feel a bit hungry. I think .... (I / have) something to eat.
2 Why are you putting on your coat? .... (you / go) somewhere?
3 What time .... (I / phone) you this evening? About 7.30?
4 Look! That plane is flying towards the airport. .... (it / land).
5 We must do something soon, before .... (it / be) too late.
6 I'm sorry you've decided to leave the company. ....
   (I / miss) you when .... (you / go).
7 .... (I / give) you my address? If ....
   (I / give) you my address, ... (you / send) me a postcard?
8 Are you still watching that programme? What time .... (it / end)?
9 .... (I / go) to London next weekend for a wedding.
   My sister .... (get) married.
10 I'm not ready yet. .... (I / tell) you when ....
   (I / be) ready. I promise .... (I / not / be) very long.
11 A: Where are you going?
   B: To the hairdresser's. .... (I / have) my hair cut.
12 She was very rude to me. I refuse to speak to her again until ....
   (she / apologise).
13 I wonder where .... (we / live) ten years from now?
14 What do you plan to do when .... (you / finish) your course at
   college?

Past, present and future   Units 1–25

14 Use your own ideas to complete B's sentences.

1 A: How did the accident happen?
   B: I ...*was going*... too fast and couldn't stop in time.
2 A: Is that a new camera?
   B: No, I .... it a long time.
3 A: Is that a new computer?
   B: Yes, I .... it a few weeks ago.
4 A: I can't talk to you right now. You can see I'm very busy.
   B: OK. I .... back in about half an hour.
5 A: This is a nice restaurant. Do you come here often?
   B: No, it's the first time I .... here.
6 A: Do you do any sport?
   B: No, I .... football, but I gave it up.
7 A: I'm sorry I'm late.
   B: That's OK. I .... long.
8 A: When you went to the US last year, was it your first visit?
   B: No, I .... there twice before.
9 A: Do you have any plans for the weekend?
   B: Yes, I .... to a party on Saturday night.
10 A: Do you know what Steve's doing these days?
   B: No, I .... him for ages.
11 A: Will you still be here by the time I get back?
   B: No, I .... by then.

15 Robert is travelling in North America. He sends an email to a friend in Winnipeg (Canada). Put the verb into the most suitable form.

CANADA

Winnipeg — USA — Minneapolis
— Kansas City

To: Chris

Subject: American travels

Default Font ▾ Text Size ▾ **B** *I* <u>U</u> T ≡ ≡ ≡ ≣ ≣

Hi

(1) _I've just arrived_ (I / just / arrive) in Minneapolis. (2) .... (I / travel) for more than a month now, and (3) .... (I / begin) to think about coming home. Everything (4) .... (I / see) so far (5) .... (be) really interesting, and (6) .... (I / meet) some really kind people.

(7) .... (I / leave) Kansas City a week ago. (8) .... (I / stay) there with Emily, the aunt of a friend from college. She was really helpful and hospitable and although (9) .... (I / plan) to stay only a couple of days, (10) .... (I / end up) staying more than a week.

(11) .... (I / enjoy) the journey from Kansas City to here. (12) .... (I / take) the Greyhound bus and (13) .... (meet) some really interesting people – everybody was really friendly.

So now I'm here, and (14) .... (I / stay) here for a few days before (15) .... (I / continue) up to Canada. I'm not sure exactly when (16) .... (I / get) to Winnipeg – it depends what happens while (17) .... (I / be) here. But (18) .... (I / let) you know as soon as (19) .... (I / know) myself.

(20) .... (I / stay) with a family here – they're friends of some people I know at home. Tomorrow (21) .... (we / visit) some people they know who (22) .... (build) a house in the mountains. It isn't finished yet, but (23) .... (it / be) interesting to see what it's like.

Anyway, that's all for now. (24) .... (I / be) in touch again soon.

Robert

Modal verbs (can/must/would etc.)

Units 26–36, Appendix 4

16 Which alternatives are correct? Sometimes only one alternative is correct, and sometimes two of the alternatives are possible.

1 'What time will you be home tonight?' 'I'm not sure. I __A or B__ late.'
   A may be   B might be   C can be   *(both A and B are correct)*

2 I can't find the theatre tickets. They .... out of my pocket.
   A must have fallen   B should have fallen   C had to fall

3 Somebody ran in front of the car as I was driving. Fortunately I .... just in time.
   A could stop   B could have stopped   C managed to stop

4 We've got plenty of time. We .... yet.
   A mustn't leave   B needn't leave   C don't need to leave

5 I .... out but I didn't feel like it, so I stayed at home.
   A could go   B could have gone   C must have gone

6 I'm sorry I .... come to your party last week.
   A couldn't come   B couldn't have come   C wasn't able to come

7 'What do you think of my theory?' 'I'm not sure. You .... right.'
   A could be   B must be   C might be

8 I couldn't wait for you any longer. I .... , and so I went.
   A must go   B must have gone   C had to go

9 'Do you know where Liz is?' 'No. I suppose she .... shopping.'
   A should have gone   B may have gone   C could have gone

10 At first they didn't believe me when I told them what had happened, but in the end
   I .... them that I was telling the truth.
   A was able to convince   B managed to convince   C could convince

11 I promised I'd phone Gary this evening. I ....
   A mustn't forget   B needn't forget   C don't have to forget

12 Why did you leave without me? You .... for me.
   A must have waited   B had to wait   C should have waited

13 Lisa phoned me and suggested .... lunch together.
   A we have   B we should have   C to have

14 You look nice in that jacket, but you hardly ever wear it. .... it more often.
   A You'd better wear   B You should wear   C You ought to wear

15 Shall I buy a car? What's your advice? What .... ?
   A will you do   B would you do   C shall you do

17   Make sentences from the words in brackets.

1 Don't phone them now. (they might / have / lunch)
   They might be having lunch.

2 I ate too much. Now I feel sick. (I shouldn't / eat / so much)
   I shouldn't have eaten so much.

3 I wonder why Tom didn't phone me. (he must / forget)
   ....

4 Why did you go home so early? (you needn't / go / home so early)
   ....

5 You've signed the contract. (it / can't / change / now)
   ....

6 'What's Linda doing?' 'I'm not sure.' (she may / watch / television)
   ....

7 Laura was standing outside the cinema. (she must / wait / for somebody)
   ....

8 He was in prison at the time that the crime was committed. (he couldn't / do / it)
   ....

9 Why weren't you here earlier? (you ought / be / here earlier)
   ....

10 Why didn't you ask me to help you? (I would / help / you)
   ....

11 I'm surprised you weren't told that the road was dangerous. (you should / warn / about it)
   ....

12 Gary was in a strange mood yesterday. (he might not / feel / very well)
   ....

18   Complete B's sentences using **can/could/might/must/should/would** + the verb in brackets. In
       some sentences you need to use **have: must have ... / should have ...** etc. In some sentences
       you need the negative (**can't/couldn't** etc.).

1 A: I'm hungry.
   B: But you've just had lunch. You .....*can't be*..... hungry already. (be)
2 A: I haven't seen our neighbours for ages.
   B: No. They .....*must have gone*..... away. (go)
3 A: What's the weather like? Is it raining?
   B: Not at the moment, but it .... later. (rain)
4 A: Where has Julia gone?
   B: I'm not sure. She .... to the bank. (go)
5 A: I didn't see you at Michael's party last week.
   B: No, I had to work that night, so I .... (go)
6 A: I saw you at Michael's party last week.
   B: No, you .... me. I didn't go to Michael's party. (see)
7 A: What time will we get to Sue's house?
   B: Well, it takes about one and a half hours, so if we leave at 3 o'clock, we
       .... there by 4.30. (get)
8 A: When was the last time you saw Bill?
   B: Years ago. I .... him if I saw him now. (recognise)
9 A: Did you hear the explosion?
   B: What explosion?
   A: There was a loud explosion about an hour ago. You .... it. (hear)
10 A: We weren't sure which way to go. In the end we turned right.
   B: You went the wrong way. You .... left. (turn)

---

if (conditional)   Units 25, 38–40

19   Put the verb into the correct form.

1 If you .....*found*..... a wallet in the street, what would you do with it? (find)
2 I must hurry. My friend will be annoyed if I .....*'m not*..... on time. (not / be)
3 I didn't realise that Gary was in hospital. If I .....*had known*..... he was in hospital, I would
   have gone to visit him. (know)
4 If the phone .... , can you answer it? (ring)
5 I can't decide what to do. What would you do if you .... in my
   position? (be)
6 A: What shall we do tomorrow?
   B: Well, if it .... a nice day, we can go to the beach. (be)
7 A: Let's go to the beach.
   B: No, it's too cold. If it .... warmer, I wouldn't mind going. (be)
8 A: Did you go to the beach yesterday?
   B: No, it was too cold. If it .... warmer, we might have gone. (be)
9 If you .... enough money to go anywhere in the world, where would you
   go? (have)
10 I'm glad we had a map. I'm sure we would have got lost if we .... one.
   (not / have)
11 The accident was your fault. If you .... more carefully, it wouldn't have
   happened. (drive)
12 A: Why do you read newspapers?
   B: Well, if I .... newspapers, I wouldn't know what was happening in the
       world. (not / read)

20 Complete the sentences.

1 Liz is tired all the time. She shouldn't go to bed so late.
If *Liz didn't go to bed so late, she wouldn't be tired all the time.*

2 It's rather late. I don't think Sarah will come to see us now.
I'd be surprised if Sarah ....

3 I'm sorry I disturbed you. I didn't know you were busy.
If I'd known you were busy, I ....

4 I don't want them to be upset, so I've decided not to tell them what happened.
They'd .... if ....

5 The dog attacked you, but only because you frightened it.
If ....

6 Unfortunately I didn't have an umbrella and so I got very wet in the rain.
I ....

7 Martin failed his driving test last week. He was very nervous and that's why he failed.
If he ....

21 Use your own ideas to complete the sentences.

1 I'd go out this evening if ....

2 I'd have gone out last night if ....

3 If you hadn't reminded me, ...

4 We wouldn't have been late if ....

5 If I'd been able to get tickets, ...

6 Who would you phone if .... ?

7 Cities would be nicer places if ....

8 If there was no television, ...

Passive

22 Put the verb into the most suitable passive form.

1 There's somebody behind us. I think we *are being followed* (follow).

2 A mystery is something that *can't be explained* (can't / explain).

3 We didn't play football yesterday. The match .... (cancel).

4 The television .... (repair). It's working again now.

5 In the middle of the village there is a church which .... (restore) at the moment. The work is almost finished.

6 The tower is the oldest part of the church. It .... (believe) to be over 600 years old.

7 If I didn't do my job properly, I .... (would / sack).

8 A: I left a newspaper on the desk last night and it isn't there now.
B: It .... (might / throw) away.

9 I learnt to swim when I was very young. I .... (teach) by my mother.

10 After .... (arrest), I was taken to the police station.

11 '... (you / ever / arrest)?' 'No, never.'

12 Two people .... (report) to .... (injure) in an explosion at a factory in Birmingham early this morning.

23 Put the verb into the correct form, active or passive.

1 This house is quite old. It ....._was built_.... (build) over 100 years ago.
2 My grandfather was a builder. He ....._built_.... (build) this house many years ago.
3 'Is your car still for sale?' 'No, I .... (sell) it.'
4 A: Is the house at the end of the street still for sale?
  B: No, it .... (sell).
5 Sometimes mistakes .... (make). It's inevitable.
6 I wouldn't leave your car unlocked. It .... (might / steal).
7 My bag has disappeared. It .... (must / steal).
8 I can't find my hat. Somebody .... (must / take) it by mistake.
9 It's a serious problem. I don't know how it .... (can / solve).
10 We didn't leave early enough. We .... (should / leave) earlier.
11 Nearly every time I travel by plane, my flight .... (delay).
12 A new bridge .... (build) across the river. Work started last year
  and the bridge .... (expect) to open next year.

24 Read these newspaper reports and put the verbs into the most suitable form.

1 Castle Fire

Winton Castle (1) ...._was damaged_....... (damage) in a fire last night. The fire, which (2) .... (discover) at about 9 o'clock, spread very quickly. Nobody (3) .... (injure), but two people had to (4) .... (rescue) from an upstairs room. A number of paintings (5) .... (believe / destroy). It (6) .... (not / know) how the fire started.

2 SHOP ROBBERY

In Paxham yesterday a shop assistant (1) .... (force) to hand over £500 after (2) .... (threaten) by a man with a knife. The man escaped in a car which (3) .... (steal) earlier in the day. The car (4) .... (later / find) in a car park where it (5) .... (abandon) by the thief. A man (6) .... (arrest) in connection with the robbery and (7) .... (still / question) by the police.

3 ROAD DELAYS

Repair work started yesterday on the Paxham–Longworth road. The road (1) .... (resurface) and there will be long delays. Drivers (2) .... (ask) to use an alternative route if possible. The work (3) .... (expect) to last two weeks. Next Sunday the road (4) .... (close), and traffic (5) .... (divert).

4 Accident

A woman (1) .... (take) to hospital after her car collided with a lorry near Norstock yesterday. She (2) .... (allow) home later after treatment. The road (3) .... (block) for an hour after the accident, and traffic had to (4) .... (divert). A police inspector said afterwards: 'The woman was lucky. She could (5) .... (kill).'

Reported speech

25 Complete the sentences using reported speech.

1

Can I speak to Paul, please?

I'll try again later.

Paul has gone out. I don't know when he'll be back.
Do you want to leave a message?

YOU

A woman phoned at lunchtime yesterday and asked _if she could speak to Paul_ . I told
.... and ....
.... I asked ....
.... , but she said .... later. But she never did.

2

We have no record of any reservation in your name.

We're sorry, but the hotel is full.

RECEPTION

Do you have any rooms free anyway?

I went to London recently, but my visit didn't begin well. I had reserved a hotel room, but
when I got to the hotel they told ....
.... When I asked .... ,
they said .... , but ....
There was nothing I could do. I just had to look for somewhere else to stay.

3

Why are you visiting the country?

How long do you intend to stay?

Where will you be staying during your visit?

We're on holiday.

After getting off the plane, we had to queue for an hour to get through immigration. Finally
it was our turn. The immigration official asked us ....
.... , and we told ....
Then he wanted to know .... and
....
He seemed satisfied with our answers, checked our passports and wished us a pleasant stay.

4

I'll phone you from the airport when I arrive.

Don't come to the airport. I'll take the bus.

SUE

A: What time is Sue arriving this afternoon?
B: About three. She said ....
....

A: Aren't you going to meet her?
B: No, she said .... She said
....

5

A few days ago a man phoned from a marketing company and started asking me questions. He wanted to know .... and asked .... I don't like people phoning and asking questions like that, so I told .... and I put the phone down.

6   *now*   *earlier*

Louise and Sarah are in a restaurant waiting for Paul.

LOUISE: I wonder where Paul is. He said ....
SARAH: Maybe he's got lost.
LOUISE: I don't think so. He said ....
         And I told ....

7

JOE: Is there anything to eat?
JANE: You just said ....
JOE: Well, I am now. I'd love a banana.
JANE: A banana? But you said ....
       You told ....

-ing and infinitive   **Units 53–66**

26   Put the verb into the correct form.

1 How old were you when you learnt __to drive__ ? (drive)
2 I don't mind __walking__ home, but I'd rather __get__ a taxi. (walk, get)
3 I can't make a decision. I keep .... my mind. (change)
4 He had made his decision and refused .... his mind. (change)
5 Why did you change your decision? What made you .... your mind? (change)
6 It was a really good holiday. I really enjoyed .... by the sea again. (be)
7 Did I really tell you I was unhappy? I don't remember .... that. (say)
8 'Remember .... Tom tomorrow.' 'OK. I won't forget.' (phone)
9 The water here is not very good. I'd avoid .... it if I were you. (drink)

10 I pretended .... interested in the conversation, but really it was very boring. (be)

11 I got up and looked out of the window .... what the weather was like. (see)

12 I have a friend who claims .... able to speak five languages. (be)

13 I like .... carefully about things before .... a decision. (think, make)

14 I had a flat in the centre of town but I didn't like .... there, so I decided .... (live, move)

15 Steve used .... a footballer. He had to stop .... because of an injury. (be, play)

16 After .... by the police, the man admitted .... the car but denied .... at 100 miles an hour. (stop, steal, drive)

17 A: How do you make this machine .... ? (work)
   A: I'm not sure. Try .... that button and see what happens. (press)

27 Make sentences from the words in brackets.

1 I can't find the tickets. (I / seem / lose / them)
  I seem to have lost them.

2 I haven't got far to go. (it / not / worth / take / a taxi)
  It's not worth taking a taxi.

3 I'm feeling a bit tired. (I / not / fancy / go / out)
  ....

4 Tim isn't very reliable. (he / tend / forget / things)
  ....

5 I've got a lot of luggage. (you / mind / help / me?)
  ....

6 There's nobody at home. (everybody / seem / go out)
  ....

7 We don't like our flat. (we / think / move)
  ....

8 The vase was very valuable. (I / afraid / touch / it)
  ....

9 Bill never carries money with him. (he / afraid / robbed)
  ....

10 I wouldn't go to see the film. (it / not / worth / see)
  ....

11 I'm very tired after that long walk. (I / not / used / walk / so far)
  ....

12 Sue is on holiday. I received a postcard from her yesterday. (she / seem / enjoy / herself)
  ....

13 Dave had lots of photographs he'd taken while on holiday. (he / insist / show / them to me)
  ....

14 I don't want to do the shopping. (I'd rather / somebody else / do / it)
  ....

28 Complete the second sentence so that the meaning is similar to the first.

1 I was surprised I passed the exam.
I didn't expect _to pass the exam_ .

2 Did you manage to solve the problem?
Did you succeed _in solving the problem_ ?

3 I don't read newspapers any more.
I've given up ....

4 I'd prefer not to go out tonight.
I'd rather ....

5 He can't walk very well.
He has difficulty ....

6 Shall I phone you this evening?
Do you want .... ?

7 Nobody saw me come in.
I came in without ....

8 They said I was a cheat.
I was accused ....

9 It will be good to see them again.
I'm looking forward ....

10 What do you think I should do?
What do you advise me .... ?

11 It's a pity I couldn't go out with you.
I'd like ....

12 I'm sorry that I didn't take your advice.
I regret ....

---

a/an and the

Units 69–78

29 Put in a/an or the where necessary. Leave the space empty if the sentence is already complete.

1 I don't usually like staying at ___ hotels, but last summer we spent a few days at _a_ very nice hotel by _the_ sea.

2 .... tennis is my favourite sport. I play once or twice .... week if I can, but I'm not .... very good player.

3 I won't be home for .... dinner this evening. I'm meeting some friends after .... work and we're going to .... cinema.

4 .... unemployment is increasing at the moment and it's getting difficult for .... people to find .... work.

5 There was .... accident as I was going .... home last night. Two people were taken to .... hospital. I think .... most accidents are caused by .... people driving too fast.

6 Carol is .... economist. She used to work in .... investment department of .... Lloyds Bank. Now she works for .... American bank in .... United States.

7 A: What's .... name of .... hotel where you're staying?
B: .... Imperial. It's in .... Queen Street in .... city centre. It's near .... station.

8 I have two brothers. .... older one is training to be .... pilot with .... British Airways. .... younger one is still at .... school. When he leaves .... school, he wants to go to .... university to study .... law.

Pronouns and determiners   **Units 82–91**

30   Which alternatives are correct? Sometimes only one alternative is correct, and sometimes two alternatives are possible.

1   I don't remember ....A.... about the accident.   (A *is correct*)
    A anything   B something   C nothing
2   Chris and I have known .... for quite a long time.
    A us   B each other   C ourselves
3   'How often do the buses run?'   '.. twenty minutes.'
    A All   B Each   C Every
4   I shouted for help, but .... came.
    A nobody   B no-one   C anybody
5   Last night we went out with some friends of ....
    A us   B our   C ours
6   It didn't take us a long time to get here. .... traffic.
    A It wasn't much   B There wasn't much   C It wasn't a lot
7   Can I have .... milk in my coffee, please?
    A a little   B any   C some
8   Sometimes I find it difficult to ....
    A concentrate   B concentrate me   C concentrate myself
9   There's .... on at the cinema that I want to see, so there's no point in going.
    A something   B anything   C nothing
10 I drink .... water every day.
    A much   B a lot of   C lots of
11 .... in the city centre are open on Sunday.
    A Most of shops   B Most of the shops   C The most of the shops
12 There were about twenty people in the photo. I didn't recognise .... of them.
    A any   B none   C either
13 I've been waiting .... for Sarah to phone.
    A all morning   B the whole morning   C all the morning
14 I can't afford to buy anything in this shop. .... so expensive.
    A All is   B Everything is   C All are

Adjectives and adverbs   **Units 98–108**

31   There are mistakes in some of these sentences. Correct the sentences where necessary. Write 'OK' if the sentence is already correct.

1   The building was total destroyed in the fire.   _totally destroyed_
2   I didn't like the book. It was such a stupid story.   _OK_
3   The city is very polluted. It's the more polluted place
    I've ever been to.   ....
4   I was disappointing that I didn't get the job. I was well-
    qualified and the interview went well.   ....
5   It's warm today, but there's quite a strong wind.   ....
6   Joe works hardly, but he doesn't get paid very much. ....
7   The company's offices are in a modern large building. ....
8   Dan is a very fast runner. I wish I could run as fast as him. ....
9   I missed the three last days of the course because I was ill. ....
10 You don't look happy. What's the matter?   ....

320

11 The weather has been unusual cold for the time of the year. ....

12 The water in the pool was too dirty to swim in it. ....

13 I got impatient because we had to wait so long time. ....

14 Is this box big enough or do you need a bigger one? ....

15 This morning I got up more early than usual. ....

Conjunctions   Units 25, 38, 112–118

32 Which is correct?

1 I'll try to be on time, but don't worry <u>if</u> / ~~when~~ I'm late. (<u>if</u> is *correct*)

2 Don't throw that bag away. <u>If / When</u> you don't want it, I'll have it.

3 Please report to reception <u>if / when</u> you arrive at the hotel.

4 We've arranged to play tennis tomorrow, but we won't play <u>if / when</u> it's raining.

5 Jennifer is in her final year at school. She still doesn't know what she's going to do <u>if / when</u> she leaves.

6 What would you do <u>if / when</u> you lost your keys?

7 I hope I'll be able to come to the party, but I'll let you know <u>if / unless</u> I can't.

8 I don't want to be disturbed, so don't phone me <u>if / unless</u> it's something important.

9 Please sign the contract <u>if / unless</u> you're happy with the conditions.

10 I like travelling by ship <u>as long as / unless</u> the sea is not rough.

11 You might not remember the name of the hotel, so write it down <u>if / in case</u> you forget it.

12 It's not cold now, but take your coat with you <u>if / in case</u> it gets cold later.

13 Take your coat with you and then you can put it on <u>if / in case</u> it gets cold later.

14 They always have the television on, <u>even if / if</u> nobody is watching it.

15 <u>Even / Although</u> we played very well, we lost the match.

16 <u>Despite / Although</u> we've known each other a long time, we're not particularly close friends.

17 'When did you leave school?' '<u>As / When</u> I was 17.'

18 I think Ann will be very pleased <u>as / when</u> she hears the news.

Prepositions (time)   Units 12, 119–122

33 Put in one of the following: **at   on   in   during   for   since   by   until**

1 Jack has gone away. He'll be back ....*in*.... a week.

2 We're having a party .... Saturday. Can you come?

3 I've got an interview next week. It's .... 9.30 .... Tuesday morning.

4 Sue isn't usually here .... weekends. She goes away.

5 The train service is very good. The trains are nearly always .... time.

6 It was a confusing situation. Many things were happening .... the same time.

7 I couldn't decide whether or not to buy the sweater. .... the end I decided to leave it.

8 The road is busy all the time, even .... night.

9 I met a lot of nice people .... my stay in New York.

10 I saw Helen .... Friday, but I haven't seen her .... then.

11 Brian has been doing the same job .... five years.

12 Lisa's birthday is .... the end of March. I'm not sure exactly which day it is.

13 We have some friends staying with us .... the moment. They're staying .... Friday.

14 If you're interested in applying for the job, your application must be received .... Friday.

15 I'm just going out. I won't be long – I'll be back .... ten minutes.

Prepositions (position and other uses)

Units 123–128

34 Put in the missing preposition.

1 I'd love to be able to visit every country .... the world.
2 Jessica White is my favourite author. Have you read anything .... her?
3 'Is there a bank near here?' 'Yes, there's one .... the end of this road.'
4 Tim is away at the moment. He's .... holiday.
5 We live .... the country, a long way from the nearest town.
6 I've got a stain .... my jacket. I'll have to have it cleaned.
7 We went .... a party .... Linda's house on Saturday.
8 Boston is .... the east coast of the United States.
9 Look at the leaves .... that tree. They're a beautiful colour.
10 'Have you ever been .... Tokyo?' 'No, I've never been .... Japan.'
11 Mozart died .... Vienna in 1791 .... the age of 35.
12 'Are you .... this photograph?' 'Yes, that's me, ... the left.'
13 We went .... the theatre last night. We had seats .... the front row.
14 'Where's the light switch?' 'It's .... the wall .... the door.'
15 It was late when we arrived .... the hotel.
16 I couldn't decide what to eat. There was nothing .... the menu that I liked.
17 We live .... a tower block. Our flat is .... the fifteenth floor.
18 A: What did you think of the film?
   B: Some parts were a bit stupid, but .... the whole I enjoyed it.
19 'When you paid the hotel bill, did you pay cash?' 'No, I paid .... credit card.'
20 'How did you get here? .... the bus?' 'No, ... car.'
21 A: I wonder what's .... television this evening. Have you got a newspaper?
   B: Yes, the TV programmes are .... the back page.
22 Helen works for a telecommunications company. She works .... the customer services department.
23 Anna spent two years working .... London before returning .... Italy.
24 'Did you enjoy your trip .... the beach?' 'Yes, it was great.'
25 Next summer we're going .... a trip to Canada.

Noun/adjective + preposition

Units 129–131

35 Put in the missing preposition.

1 The plan has been changed, but nobody seems to know the reason .... this.
2 Don't ask me to decide. I'm not very good .... making decisions.
3 Some people say that Sue is unfriendly, but she's always very nice .... me.
4 What do you think is the best solution .... the problem?
5 There has been a big increase .... the price of land recently.
6 He lives a rather lonely life. He doesn't have much contact .... other people.
7 Paul is a keen photographer. He likes taking pictures .... people.
8 Michael got married .... a woman he met when he was studying at college.
9 He's very brave. He's not afraid .... anything.
10 I'm surprised .... the amount of traffic today. I didn't think it would be so busy.
11 Thank you for lending me the guidebook. It was full .... useful information.
12 Please come in and sit down. I'm sorry .... the mess.

Verb + preposition

Units 132–136

36 Complete each sentence with a preposition where necessary. If no preposition is necessary, leave the space empty.

1 She works quite hard. You can't accuse her _____ being lazy.
2 Who's going to look _____ your children while you're at work?
3 The problem is becoming serious. We have to discuss _____ it.
4 The problem is becoming serious. We have to do something _____ it.
5 I prefer this chair _____ the other one. It's more comfortable.
6 I must phone _____ the office to tell them I won't be at work today.
7 The river divides the city _____ two parts.
8 'What do you think _____ your new boss?' 'She's all right, I suppose.'
9 Can somebody please explain _____ me what I have to do?
10 I said hello to her, but she didn't answer _____ me.
11 'Do you like staying at hotels?' 'It depends _____ the hotel.'
12 'Have you ever been to Borla?' 'No, I've never heard _____ it. Where is it?'
13 You remind me _____ somebody I knew a long time ago. You look just like her.
14 This is wonderful news! I can't believe _____ it.
15 George is not an idealist – he believes _____ being practical.
16 What's funny? What are you laughing _____ ?
17 What have you done with all the money you had? What did you spend it _____ ?
18 If Kevin asks _____ you _____ money, don't give him any.
19 I apologised _____ Sarah _____ keeping her waiting so long.
20 Lisa was very helpful. I thanked _____ her _____ everything she'd done.

Phrasal verbs

Units 137–145

37 A says something and B replies. Which goes with which?

A	B	
1 ~~I've made a mistake on this form.~~	a Don't worry. I'll tidy it up.	1 _d_
2 I'm too warm with my coat on.	b No problem. I can fix it up.	2 _____
3 This jacket looks nice.	c Kate pointed it out.	3 _____
4 My phone number is 576920.	d ~~That's OK. Just cross it out and correct it.~~	4 _____
5 This room is in a mess.		5 _____
6 What's 45 euros in dollars?	e Yes, why don't you try it on?	6 _____
7 How did you find the mistake?	f OK, I won't bring it up.	7 _____
8 I'm not sure whether to accept their offer or not.	g Just a moment. I'll write it down.	8 _____
9 I need a place to stay when I'm in London.	h Why don't you take it off then?	9 _____
10 It's a subject he doesn't like to talk about.	i You can look it up.	10 _____
11 I don't know what this word means.	j I think you should turn it down.	11 _____
	k Give me a moment to work it out.	

38 Only one alternative is correct. Which is it?

1 Nobody believed Paul at first but he ....B.... to be right.   (B *is correct*)
   A came out   B turned out   C worked out   D carried out

2 Here's some good news. It will ....
   A turn you up   B put you up   C blow you up   D cheer you up

3 I was annoyed with the way the children were behaving, so I ....
   A told them up   B told them off   C told them out   D told them over

4 The club committee is .... of the president, the secretary and seven other members.
   A set up   B made up   C set out   D made out

5 You were going to apply for the job, and then you decided not to. So what .... ?
   A put you off   B put you out   C turned you off   D turned you away

6 I had no idea that he was lying to me. I was completely ....
   A taken in   B taken down   C taken off   D taken over

7 Barbara started a course at college, but she .... after six months.
   A went out   B fell out   C turned out   D dropped out

8 You can't predict everything. Often things don't .... as you expect.
   A make out   B break out   C work out   D get out

9 Why are all these people here? What's .... ?
   A going off   B getting off   C going on   D getting on

10 It's a very busy airport. There are planes .... or landing every few minutes.
   A going up   B taking off   C getting up   D driving off

11 The traffic was moving slowly because a bus had .... and was blocking the road.
   A broken down   B fallen down   C fallen over   D broken up

12 How are you .... in your new job? Are you enjoying it?
   A keeping on   B going on   C carrying on   D getting on

39 Complete the sentences. Use two words each time.

1 Keep ....*away from*.... the edge of the pool. You might fall in.
2 I didn't notice that the two pictures were different until Liz pointed it .... me.
3 I asked Dan if he had any suggestions about what we should do, but he didn't come .... anything.
4 I'm glad Sarah is coming to the party. I'm really looking .... seeing her again.
5 Things are changing all the time. It's difficult to keep .... all these changes.
6 Unfortunately I ran .... film, so I couldn't take any more photographs.
7 Don't let me interrupt you. Carry .... your work.
8 Steve was very happy in his job until he fell .... his boss. After that, it was impossible for them to work together, and Steve decided to leave.
9 I've had enough of being treated like this. I'm not going to put .... it any more.
10 I didn't enjoy the trip very much at the time, but when I look .... it now, I realise it was a good experience and I'm glad I went on it.
11 The wedding was supposed to be a secret, so how did you find .... it? Did Jenny tell you?
12 There is a very nice atmosphere in the office where I work. Everybody gets .... everybody else.

40   Complete each sentence using a phrasal verb that means the same as the words in brackets.

1 The football match had to be ___called off___ because of the weather. (cancelled)
2 The story Kate told wasn't true. She ___made it up___ . (invented it)
3 A bomb _____ near the station, but no-one was injured. (exploded)
4 George finally _____ nearly an hour late. (arrived)
5 Here's an application form. Can you _____ and sign it, please? (complete it)
6 A number of buildings are going to be _____ to make way for the new road. (demolished)
7 I'm having a few problems with my computer which need to be _____ as soon as possible. (put right)
8 Be positive! You must never _____ ! (stop trying)
9 I was very tired and _____ in front of the television. (fell asleep)
10 After eight years together, they've decided to _____ . (separate)
11 The noise is terrible. I can't _____ any longer. (tolerate it)
12 We don't have a lot of money, but we have enough to _____ . (manage)
13 I'm sorry I'm late. The meeting _____ later than I expected. (continued)
14 We need to make a decision today at the latest. We can't _____ any longer. (delay it)

41   Complete the sentences. Use one word each time.

1 You're driving too fast. Please ___slow___ down.
2 It was only a small fire and I managed to _____ it out with a bucket of water.
3 The house is empty at the moment, but I think the new tenants are _____ in next week.
4 I've _____ on weight. My clothes don't fit any more.
5 Their house is really nice now. They've _____ it up really well.
6 I was talking to the woman sitting next to me on the plane, and it _____ out that she works for the same company as my brother.
7 'Do you know what happened?' 'Not yet, but I'm going to _____ out.'
8 There's no need to get angry. _____ down!
9 If you're going on a long walk, plan your route carefully before you _____ off.
10 Sarah has just phoned to say that she'll be late. She's been _____ up.
11 You've written my name wrong. It's Martin, not Marin – you _____ out the T.
12 Three days at £45 a day – that _____ out at £135.
13 We had a really interesting discussion, but Jane didn't _____ in. She just listened.
14 Jonathan is pretty fit. He _____ out in the gym every day.
15 Come and see us more often. You must _____ in any time you like.
16 We are still discussing the contract. There are still a couple of things to _____ out.
17 My alarm clock _____ off in the middle of the night and _____ me up.

Index